W9-APZ-506

From Obstruction
to Moderation

From Obstruction to Moderation

The Transformation of Senate Conservatism, 1938–1952

John W. Malsberger

SUP

Selinsgrove: Susquehanna University Press
London: Associated University Presses

Associated University Presses
440 Forsgate Drive
Cranbury, NJ 08512

Associated University Presses
16 Barter Street
London WC1A 2AH, England

Associated University Presses
P.O. Box 338, Port Credit
Mississauga, Ontario
Canada L5G 4L8

The paper used in this publication meets the requirements of the American National Standard for Permanence of Paper for Printed Library Materials Z39.48-1984.

Library of Congress Cataloging-in-Publication Data

Malsberger, John W. (John William)
     From obstruction to moderation : the transformation of Senate
conservatism, 1938–1952 / John W. Malsberger.
          p.   cm.
     Includes bibliographical references and index.
     ISBN 1-57591-026-8 (alk. paper)
     1. United States. Congress. Senate—Voting.   2. Conservatism—
United States.   3. United States—Politics and
government—1933–1953.   I. Title.
JK1161.M34   2000
328.73'0775—dc21   99-40422
                                                                CIP

*For my mother
and
For the memory of my father*

Contents

Acknowledgments

IN THE MANY YEARS THAT IT HAS TAKEN TO BRING THIS WORK TO completion, I have profited immeasurably from the help of many individuals and institutions. Without their assistance this book could never have been finished.

Professor James W. Hilty of Temple University taught me much about the study of modern American politics, assisted generously with the roll call analysis, and patiently read several early versions of this work. The careful attention that Professors Herbert J. Bass and Joseph G. Rayback of Temple University gave to this work in its formative stages helped me to sharpen the analysis.

Muhlenberg College generously supported my work through both summer travel grants that made possible much of my archival research and a timely sabbatical that provided me with uninterrupted time to write. My friend and colleague in the Muhlenberg History Department, Daniel J. Wilson, offered many useful suggestions and was instrumental in helping me find a publisher.

I am also deeply grateful to the staffs of the many institutions, listed in the bibliography, where senators' papers are located. The staffs of these libraries were unfailingly kind and enormously generous in assisting my work with their often massive collections. The staffs of four institutions, Seeley G. Mudd Manuscript Library at Princeton University, Bailey-Howell Memorial Library at the University of Vermont, William R. Perkins Library at Duke University, and the Richard B. Russell Library for Political Research and Studies at the University of Georgia were especially helpful in calling my attention to important parts of their collections that I would otherwise have overlooked.

Last, but surely not least, my efforts would not have been possible without the unflagging encouragement, support, and love of my family. Words alone cannot convey their contribution to this work.

I am grateful to the following institutions for permission to quote from their holdings: the Division of Rare and Manuscript Collections, Cornell University Library, for the Irving Ives Papers; the Rare Book, Manuscript, and Special Collections Library, Duke

University, for the Josiah William Bailey Papers and the Clyde Roark Hoey Papers; the South Carolina Library, University of South Carolina, for the Olin D. Johnston Papers; the Department of Special Collections, University of Florida Libraries, for the Spessard L. Holland Papers; the Special Collections Department, Robert Scott Small Library, College of Charleston, for the Burnet R. Maybank Papers; Syracuse University Library, Department of Special Collections, for the Ralph Flanders Papers; Dartmouth College Library, Special Collections: Archives, Manuscripts, Rare Books, for the Charles Tobey Papers; the Massachusetts Historical Society, for the Henry Cabot Lodge, Jr. Papers and the Leverett Saltonstall Papers; the Richard B. Russell Library for Political Research and Studies; University of Georgia, for the Richard B. Russell, Jr. Papers; Special Collections, University of Vermont, for the George D. Aiken Papers and the Warren Austin Papers; the Maryland Historical Society, for the George L. Radcliffe Papers; and Seeley G. Mudd Manuscript Library, Princeton University, for the H. Alexander Smith Papers.

Introduction

THIS STUDY BEGAN AS AN ATTEMPT TO DETERMINE WHAT HAPPENED to the classic conservative coalition of southern Democrats and Republicans in the Senate after 1938. Most longitudinal studies of the coalition, beginning with V. O. Key's *Southern Politics in State and Nation,* suggested that after 1938 the conservative coalition grew in both size and success to become a formidable force in postwar American politics. This conclusion was buttressed by many of the historical surveys of postwar American politics that invariably spoke of a conservative resurgence in the 1940s directly threatening the reforms of Franklin Roosevelt's New Deal. Indeed, a staple argument made about postwar American politics has been that the reforms made by the New Deal were not truly secure until Dwight Eisenhower, a moderate Republican, was elected president in 1952.[1]

A careful reading of Senate politics between 1938 and 1952, however, raises a number of questions about the traditional accounts of the era. First of all, if there was a conservative resurgence in the 1940s, why was no major part of the New Deal agenda repealed? Those programs eliminated during World War II either were rendered superfluous by the economic mobilization, such as WPA work relief, or as in the case of the NRPB, were ended with FDR's approval. Second, why were some substantial advances beyond FDR's legacy of reform made in the policy agenda during the 1940s? In 1949 the Senate adopted a housing bill whose principal goal of constructing low-cost public housing was in marked contrast to the 1937 Wagner Housing Act's objective of stimulating the economy. Similarly, in the late 1940s the upper house approved several bills extending federal aid to education, an issue that received scant attention during the Roosevelt years. Finally, strong and repeated Senate endorsement of an internationalist foreign policy throughout the decade also underscored the important changes that occurred in the policy agenda in the 1940s. These questions suggested, therefore, that the traditional analysis that portrays a resurgent conservatism battling against New Deal liberalism after 1938 draws too simple a portrait of postwar Senate politics.

11

This study contends that if there was a conservative resurgence after 1938, it was often led by a different breed of conservative than that which challenged FDR's agenda throughout the early years of the New Deal. Indeed, this study argues that after 1938 Senate conservatives did not form a monolithic bloc of naysayers, hardened in their dedication to rugged individualism and an unfettered free enterprise system, as they are often portrayed. Rather, after 1938 Senate conservatism became increasingly fragmented into two factions, the Old Guard obstructionists and the more moderate "new" conservatives.

The obstructionist conservatives were those Democrats and Republicans such as Burton Wheeler, Bennett Clark, Josiah Bailey, W. Lee "Pappy" O'Daniel, Kenneth Wherry, Robert Taft, James Kem, Hugh Butler, and John Bricker who generally opposed all that Franklin Roosevelt and the New Deal represented. Heirs to a philosophy that had arisen in the rural, agrarian past, the obstructionist conservatives were drawn disproportionately from interior states which, because of their geographic location, had remained relatively insulated from the industrial and international upheavals of the twentieth century. Consequently, they continued, for the most part, to view the expanding positive state in the 1940s, as well as the unfolding internationalistic foreign policy, as antithetical to the American tradition of individual liberty secured by limited government. The obstructionists' continued opposition to the policies of the Roosevelt and Truman Adminstrations, this study contends, was a product of the geographical location of the states they represented, together with the ever present partisanship, electoral vulnerablilty, and political ambition with which American politicians contend.

The "new" conservatives, on the other hand, came gradually to embrace a different ideology after 1938. Disproportionately representing coastal states, which had often borne the full brunt of the industrial revolution, such new conservatives as Irving Ives, H. Alexander Smith, George Aiken, Ralph Flanders, Leverett Saltonstall, Clyde Hoey, Burnet Maybank, and Spessard Holland learned through the Depression and World War II that individuals in modern America were increasingly interdependent. In similar fashion, their states' coastal location helped the new conservatives to understand that the economic and strategic interests of industrial America were inextricably intertwined with those of the world community. Because of their different experiences resulting from their states' location, as well as their own reading of partisan and electoral factors, the new conservatives gradually adjusted their ideology after

1938 to accept both an enlarged role for the state and an internationalist foreign policy. The new conservatives, for the most part, never believed that they were abandoning their conservative principles. Rather, their efforts were aimed mainly at adapting or modernizing American conservatism to account for the tremendous changes in American life that became apparent in the twentieth century.[2]

THE IDEOLOGICAL ROOTS OF THE TWO CONSERVATISMS

The ideology of obstructionist conservatives in the 1930s and 1940s, this study contends, was rooted in the nineteenth century, pre-industrial world of ideas. Prior to the rise of industrial capitalism in the late nineteenth century, most Americans lived in what the historian Robert Weibe has called "island communities." Largely isolated from one another, each town and village had to rely chiefly on itself for survival. This manner of existence, in turn, played an important role in how they defined their existence. Most pre-industrial Americans regarded the individual as sovereign, one who rose or fell in direct proportion to his or her abilities. In addition, because American political thought since Colonial times had posited an inverse relationship between individual liberty and government power, most pre-industrial Americans maintained a healthy skepticism of government power. Faced with a choice between more or less government involvement, most pre-industrial Americans would have opted for limited government.[3]

Another important value to pre-industrial Americans was thrift. Before the advent of mass production, America was a land of economic scarcity. Pre-industrial Americans, therefore, naturally saw their survival linked directly to their ability to save and live within their means. Ben Franklin's oft-quoted maxim that "a penny saved is a penny earned," or the biblical encomium, "waste not, want not" were ideological hallmarks that helped pre-industrial Americans order their existence.[4]

The emergence of big business and mass production techniques in the late nineteenth century forced Americans to redefine in many ways the basis of their existence. As individuals were transformed from shopkeepers and independent artisans into small cogs in a vast industrial labor force, traditional American notions of individual autonomy were gradually undermined. When practically all aspects of their work life, including the hours toiled, the wages earned, and the tasks performed, were determined by unseen managers, factory workers in the late nineteenth century found it increasingly difficult to hold onto the traditional American concept that the individual was master of his own fate. Similarly, when confronted by a wide range of problems that were created by or at least exacerbated by industrial capitalism, including poverty, unemployment, urban slums, and crime, it became increasingly difficult for many Americans in the late nineteenth century to continue to subscribe to the Jeffersonian notion that limited government was the surest way to promote individual liberty and equality. Gradually, therefore, Americans began to sense that industrialization was spawning a new order, one no longer centered on the individual, but on the mass of individuals, and that new values and institutions were required to make sense of this new order of existence.[5]

Many students of politics today contend that out of this "search for order" unleashed by industrialization, a new consensus emerged by the end of the Progressive era. This new consensus, or "corporate liberalism," embraced the positive state as the solution to the many problems associated with large-scale corporations. By providing for constant government regulation of big business, corporate liberalism was designed, in part, to check many of the unsocial or rapacious tendencies of corporate capitalism. At the same time, however, proponents of corporate liberalism understood that by halting the worst abuses of big business, expanded government regulation also insulated the emerging corporate capitalistic system from the radical demands of the Populists, the Socialists, and others to break up big business in order to restore the competitive conditions of the past. Thus, historians of corporate liberalism have maintained that the philosophy was not a modification of classical liberalism, but rather a perversion or rejection of it. Corporate liberalism, they maintain, was a political philosophy developed largely by economic and intellectual elites to protect and promote the corporate capitalistic system that emerged in the late nineteenth and early twentieth centuries. Where classical liberalism had been devoted to protecting the individual from government oppression and establishing conditions under which all individuals had equal opportunity, corporate liberalism used the power of the state to protect a society that was organized, hierarchical, and thus, inherently antidemocratic.[6]

This study's findings suggest that Senate conservatives entered the Great Depression with an ideology that was still rooted primarily in nineteenth century, pre-industrial values and continued into the late 1930s to offer united opposition to the statist assumptions inherent in corporate liberalism. In foreign affairs, for example, their aversion to entangling foreign alliances and their support for high protective tariffs, such as the 1931 Hawley-Smoot Tariff, reflected the insular values that had guided the nation throughout the nineteenth century. Similarly, conservatives in the early 1930s continued generally to perceive individuals as masters of their own destiny and, therefore, continued to define government's proper role in terms of Jeffersonian limits. Business and economic affairs, they maintained, were best regulated through the free and unfettered competition of the marketplace. In economic matters, government was to be an impartial umpire, acting to prevent abuses that prevented individuals or corporations from freely pursuing their self interest, but never taking sides by favoring one interest over another.

Conservative opposition to the New Deal in the 1930s was often founded in the belief that FDR's initiatives violated fundamental American values. The centralization of power in Washington and especially in the Executive branch, of course, was anathema to their belief in limited government and individual autonomy. Conservatives in the 1930s were similarly repulsed by the growing amount of government interference with the free enterprise system that the New Deal encouraged. By guaranteeing workers' rights to unionize, for example, or by regulating wages, hours, and working conditions, conservatives in the 1930s sensed that the New Deal was overturning their long-held belief that government should be an impartial umpire. Their goal, as James T. Patterson reminds us, was "to 'conserve' an America which they believed to have existed before 1933."[7]

The ability of the New Deal to restore the public's optimism, and at least a measure of prosperity, forced Senate conservatives to be on the defensive throughout most of the 1930s. Even though they were able to thwart FDR's Court Packing plan in 1937 and subsequently slow the pace of reform, conservatives' efforts to roll back the New Deal were largely unsuccessful. American entry into World War II added to conservatives' woes. Fighting the war against the Axis powers required an even greater expansion of government's role and thereby afforded the American public with another potent lesson about the benevolent capabilities of modern government. The cumulative effect of the Depression and World War II served, this study maintains, to transform Senate conservatism. While the obstructionists continued throughout the 1940s to struggle to restore the constitutional and economic systems of pre-industrial America, the new conservatives gradually accommodated their political philosophy to the positive state, the corporate capitalistic economy, and American internationalism.

THE NEW CONSERVATISM

The more moderate philosophy of the new conservatives arose primarily from two factors. One factor was clearly partisan politics. Some senators, especially Republicans and/or those who harbored presidential ambitions, seemed to conclude by the early 1940s that continued blanket opposition to the New Deal was political suicide. Republican Arthur Vandenberg of Michigan, for example, a perennial contender for the GOP presidential nomination, appeared to retreat from his persistent criticism of the New Deal agenda in January 1940. Writing in the *American Mecury,* the Michigan Republican argued "that eight years of the New Deal have launched certain social concepts which, in their objectives, cannot and should not be revised." The views of Vandenberg and other Republican candidates were likely bolstered by the findings of two opinion pollsters employed by the GOP Program Committee. Taking advantage of the then relatively new techniques of public opinion surveys, the GOP Program Committee in early 1940 concluded a two-year analysis of registered Republicans' attitudes on current social and economic problems. Its report in May 1940 argued that, while the party still included some "diehards" who rejected the New Deal in its entirety, "the great majority of Republicans are convinced that the country has been irrevocably committed to the essentials of the social program of the New Deal . . ." But if partisan political considerations influenced the thinking of some conservatives, clearly many elected after 1938 embraced a more moderate political philosophy, which had been tempered by the Great Depression and World War II.[8]

The other, and perhaps more important factor that accounted for the transformation of Senate conservatism was a new understanding of individualism in a mass industrial society. The new conservatives, in dealing with the twin cataclysms of depression and world war, gradually realized that the existence of the individual in twentieth century America was markedly different than it had been in the nineteenth century rural, agrarian nation. "We can see clearly," Republican Irving Ives of New York observed in 1950, "that during the first half of the Twentieth Century there has occurred such a world-wide upheaval of Ninteenth Century institutions and traditions as to amount to no less than a gigantic social, economic and political revolution." One of the most important changes, he understood, was that America had become an industrial nation in which the individual's welfare was largely dependent on the decisions and actions taken by other individuals. Ives's Republican colleague,

Ralph Flanders of Vermont, viewed modern America similarly. "We are tied together in a thousand ways," he observed in 1946, "merchants, railroad people, industrial wage earners, farmers, bankers, and professional men. No one class can cease its proper function without harming and embittering the whole."[9]

The increasing interdependence of individuals in modern society, in turn, forced the new conservatives to recognize that the persistence of such social problems as unemployment or inadequate housing posed a serious threat to the survival of freedom and capitalism in America. As a result, they generally acknowledged the need for an expanded role of government as vital for the protection and advancement of individual welfare. At the same time, however, the new Senate conservatives tended to be more wary than liberals about the beneficence of the positive state, fearful that if unchecked, the growth of government power would crush, rather than protect, liberty and private enterprise. Their goal, then, was to strike a balance between the legitimate needs of a modern industrial society and the traditional American emphasis on individual liberty and initiative.

The new conservatives' views of foreign affairs were also deeply affected by the events of the 1930s and 1940s. The Depression and World War II brought home to them with dramatic force the extent to which the nation's prosperity and security were tied to the well-being of the international community. Thus, they generally endorsed American participation in mutual defense organizations and international economic cooperation, believing that such a course was vital to industrial America. Such attitudes distinguished them from the obstructionists of the era, who usually voted to severely limit American participation in international organizations and to reject economic cooperation with the world community. On the other hand, in contrast to the liberals' postwar internationalism, the foreign policy of the new conservatives tended to place more emphasis on maintaining American sovereignty in all international cooperative organizations, preserving the Senate's constitutional role in foreign policy, and on holding down the cost of the nation's overseas commitments.

Thus, on both foreign and domestic issues, the new conservatives in the Senate during the 1940s occupied a unique position on the American political spectrum. While their philosophy shared the obstructionists' desire to preserve both the maximum degree of individual liberty at home as well as the greatest amount of American sovereignty in foreign affairs, it recognized at the same time that the tremendous changes that had occurred in American life in the first half of the twentieth century frequently demanded governmental activism as advocated by the liberals.

RESEARCH DESIGN

Two means have been employed in this study to identify the two groups of Senate conservatives and their respective political philosophies. The principal method was to read carefully a wide variety of contemporary sources to determine how the senators of this era viewed the issues of their day, how they viewed each other, and how they were viewed by political analysts. This method included a reading of leading daily newspapers from different ideological persuasions, such as the *New York Times,* the *Washington Post,* the *Chicago Tribune,* the *New York Herald Tribune,* and the *St. Louis Post-Dispatch* for the periods that Congress was in session. A reading of the leading news magazines for the years 1938–1952, such as *Newsweek, Time,* and *U.S. News and World Report*; of journals of opinion, such as *The Nation* and *The New Republic*; and of select articles in contemporary academic journals added clarity to the contours of the political landscape. These efforts were supplemented, of course, by close attention to the published and unpublished primary and secondary works dealing with the U.S. Senate and American politics in this era, a list that is expanding rapidly. Finally, I examined a wide range of senators' papers from different regions and parties of this era to gain clearer insight into how individual legislators regarded the major political issues of their day. All of these sources helped to reconstruct the world of Senate politics between 1938 and 1952 and made abundantly clear the ideological differences that increasingly divided conservatives in the upper house, as well as the reasons for the philosophical transformation among members of the right wing.

In addition, I used several statistical methods to reveal and analyze patterns in the roll call votes taken for every session between 1938 and 1952. A dimensional analysis was first made of the roll call votes, to identify the new conservatives and to determine if this statistical evidence supported or contradicted the evidence on the transformation of Senate conservatism garnered from the traditional sources. A guiding assumption of the dimensional analysis in this study is that individual legislators, in making policy decisions, follow what the political scientist Aage Clausen calls "the policy dimension theory." This theory argues that, because the number of bills confronting a legislator is so huge, he or she first sorts the bills according to their content into one of several broad "policy dimensions," for which the legislator has a predetermined position. Clausen posits that once a legislator has assigned a bill to a general policy dimension, he or she compares it to his or her position on that dimension (e.g., strongly supportive, moderately supportive, mildly supportive, and so on). The theory predicts that a legislator will usually reject a bill that exceeds his or her position on the general policy dimension, and will accept a bill that is equal to or less than his or her policy position, "*providing* that the only perceived alternative is weaker or no legislation at all." The theory also predicts that a legislator's position in a given dimension will remain fairly stable over time.[10]

Based on this assumption, Guttman scales were constructed for up to fourteen broad policy dimensions in each of the Senate sessions between 1938 and 1952. The fourteen dimensions were Reciprocal Trade, National Defense, Foreign Policy, Civil Rights-Civil Liberties, Labor, Agriculture, Social Welfare, Fiscal Policy, Business Regulation, Extension of Executive Power, Extension of Federal Authority, Economy in Government Spending, Displaced Persons, and Public Power. Roll call votes for each of the Senate sessions (excluding those on which less than 10% of the votes were in opposition) were sorted, based on their substantive policy content into one of the fourteen policy dimensions. Because the biases and judgments of the researcher are invariably involved in this initial sorting process, another method, known as cluster analysis, was used to sort statistically, by means of pair-wise association, all of the roll calls assigned to each of the fourteen policy dimensions. The value of *phi,* a statistic used to measure the strength of association between two different variables, was then determined for every possible pair of votes in each of the policy dimensions, and only those pairs attaining a *phi* value of at least +0.65 were considered statistically significant. Clusters of statistically significant votes were selected from each of the policy dimensions and the votes of individual senators in these clusters were then arranged, beginning with those most supportive of the policy dimension and ending with those least supportive. In this fashion the senators were divided into groups forming a simple scale, each group more supportive of the policy dimension than the group below it but less supportive than the group above it.[11] Because the new conservatives were generally assumed to have a more positive voting record (i.e., were more supportive) on most issues than obstructionists, but a less positive record than liberals, the scales were divided into three broad categories of high support, medium support, and low support. It was assumed that these divisions were equivalent on all scales (except for Economy in Government Spending, where the positions were reversed) to liberals, new conservatives, and obstructionists, respectively.

Although the ideal situation would have been for each scale to break down into three equal categories, the first priority was to allow the "natural" divisions, (i.e., where the senators themselves made the greatest distinction) to serve as the dividing line between each level of support. No new conservative, however, was perfectly consistent and scored in the middle position on all dimensions. Some voted occasionally with liberals on social welfare issues or foreign aid, while others sometimes joined forces with obstructionists on such issues as labor or economy in government spending. Thus, to minimize the researcher's bias in the identification of new conservatives, a third statistical method was employed. A master list of each senator's scale position for every scalable policy dimension in each Congress was prepared. The policy dimensions in each master list were arranged from those that produced the fewest senators in the high support category to those that produced the largest number. A composite scale score was then calculated for each senator in every Congress by summing his or her position on each dimension (high support = 1, medium support = 2, and low support = 3) and dividing this total by the number of policy dimensions on which he or she scaled. Any senator who failed to scale on at least half of the scalable policy dimensions in a given Congress was excluded. The composite scale scores ranged from +1.0 for senators who scored in the "high support" category on every scalable dimension (strong liberals), to +3.0 for senators who scored in the low support category on every scalable dimension (strong obstructionists). Based on these composite scores, senators were then assigned to one of three roughly equal categories in a fashion similar to that employed with the individual Guttman scales. That is, a senator deemed to have voted as a liberal in a given Congress was one whose composite scale score ranged from +1.0 to +1.67; one deemed to have a new conservative voting record had a score ranging from +1.68 to +2.33; and one who voted as an obstructionist was one whose score fell between +2.34 to +3.0. As was true for the method used in preparing individual Guttman scales, however, in assigning senators to a category in the composite scales every effort was made to allow the "natural" divisions to prevail.

While the results of the statistical analysis will be discussed more thoroughly in the individual chapters, it should be noted here that they largely confirm the patterns evident in the traditional sources.

That is, most of the senators who, from the perspective of the traditional sources, appeared to be grappling to define a new, more modern conservatism in the 1940s turned up in the second, medium support position as anticipated. Of course, rarely did any of the new conservatives appear consistently in the medium support position for every Congress in which they served. Rather, such pressures as the increased partisanship of election years, the desire, especially among Democrats, to support their presidents in this period, constituent demands, and other factors occasionally pushed or pulled senators in this tumultuous period into either the high support or low support categories.

CONCLUSION

The chapters that follow examine the transformation of Senate conservatism in chronological fashion. I will analyze the factors that contributed to the transformation of conservatism, identify those senators who comprised the two groups to the right of New Deal liberals, and assess the significance of the transformation of conservatism for modern American politics. This study is ultimately concerned with how the controversy, which in the late 1930s surrounded both the positive state as defined by the New Deal and American internationalism, was altered into a broad consensus that by 1952 united substantial elements of both the political left and right. It makes clear that if, as historians of corporate liberalism have argued, liberals gravitated toward the center of the political spectrum in the industrial era, American conservatism was also nudged closed to the center.

From Obstruction
to Moderation

1

The Origins of the New Conservatism

Most students of new deal politics have argued that by the late 1930s a conservative resurgence was well under way in the U.S. Senate and was increasingly forcing Franklin Roosevelt's New Deal on the defensive. Indeed, the evidence for a conservative revival seems substantial. Following their convincing victory in thwarting FDR's 1937 Court-Packing Plan, Congressional conservatives assembled an impressive array of successes or near-successes in 1938 and 1939, which further hobbled both the domestic and foreign agenda of the Roosevelt Administration. In 1938, for example, FDR narrowly avoided defeat on an Executive Reorganization bill and was forced by conservatives to accept a substantially watered-down version of the undistributed profits tax, long regarded as an essential ingredient of the New Deal's fiscal policies. Conservatives appeared to score even more impressive victories the following year when they unexpectedly slashed $150 million from a bill to continue WPA relief efforts and initially blocked FDR's efforts to have the Neutrality Acts repealed. These and other actions suggested to both contemporary observers and more recent students of American politics that throughout 1938 and 1939 Congressional conservatives steadily gained momentum and appeared poised, prior to the outbreak of world war in September 1939, to begin their long-sought goal of dismantling the New Deal.[1]

A closer reading of Senate politics in 1938 and 1939 reveals, however, that beneath the victories won by New Deal opponents, there were some important signs of a transformation underway in Senate conservatism. The results of the 1938 elections, as well as the regional division of votes on such measures as the 1938 Spend-Lend bill and repeal of the Neutrality Act, suggested that especially within the Republican party, obstructionist conservatism, with its emphasis on rugged individualism, limited government, and an isolationist foreign policy, was beginning to give way to a new, more modern brand of conservatism that reflected the needs of the twentieth century urban, industrial society.

25

I

By the time the second session of the 75th Congress convened in January 1938, most political observers expected that Congressional conservatives would continue the assault on Franklin Roosevelt's New Deal that had begun with the 1937 Court Reorganization bill. The *New York Times* argued on 3 January, for example, that a sizable number of Democrats believed it was necessary to alter some of the more extreme New Deal programs and to eliminate what many regarded as its antibusiness orientation. Some of these Democrats, such as James Byrnes of South Carolina, Pat Harrison of Mississippi, George Radcliffe of Maryland, and Joseph O'Mahoney of Wisconsin, had been such strong proponents of the early New Deal that observers had often regarded them as "rubber stamps." But by the late 1930s many of them reverted to a more conservative political philosophy. James Byrnes of South Carolina, for example, who was sometimes referred to as the "White House Messenger Boy" during Roosevelt's first term, had become so disenchanted with the antibusiness course of the later New Deal that journalists described him as "independent of the President, working for acceptance, broad modification or even rejection of the President's proposals, as he thinks best." Similarly, George Radcliffe admitted that he had viewed the early New Deal largely as an emergency expedient to see the nation through its worst economic crisis. "In my support of various [New Deal] measures," he recalled near the end of his political career, "I emphasized the fact . . . that many of these . . . should be temporary in nature and that we should return to a free and more independent economy as soon as possible."[2]

The influence that resurgent conservatism was able to exert over the political agenda was apparent in three important issues the Senate considered in 1938: an Executive Reorganization Bill, extension of the excess profits tax, and a $3.5 billion Spend-Lend Recovery bill. The first measure, the Executive Reorganization bill, which was introduced in March, sought to expand still further the powers of the President, which most conservatives believed had grown at an alarming rate since 1933. The bill proposed that the President be given broad powers to reorganize the Executive branch by consolidating or abolishing any executive agency. In addition, he was authorized to replace the three-man Civil Service Commission with a single administrator, to replace the controller general with an auditor general, to create a Department of Public Welfare, to hire six new administrative assistants for the White House, and to make permanent the National Resources Committee. Any actions taken by the President under the authority of the act were, furthermore, to become effective automatically unless specifically prohibited by Congress within sixty days. To conservatives who had witnessed a steady increase in Executive power since 1933, the 1938 Reorganization bill appeared to be yet another effort by the Roosevelt Administration to reduce the role of the Legislature, thereby undermining the Constitutional system of checks and balances.[3]

The conservatives' concerns were readily apparent in the debate over the bill's proposed replacement of the controller general. Deliberately established in 1921 to give Congress "a double check on money it appropriated," the controller general audited government accounts to make certain that all funds were spent by government agencies for the purpose intended by Congress. Although the President was ultimately responsible for the expenditure of public funds, he could not act until the controller general signed warrants to release the funds. In this manner, the controller general was widely regarded as the "watchdog of the Treasury." Under the 1938 Reorganization Act, however, the controller general was to be replaced by an auditor general who was to audit federal accounts only after appropriated funds had been spent and to follow procedures established by the director of the budget, a presidential appointee. In the mind of Republican Warren Austin of Vermont, this section of the Reorganization bill gave to the Executive branch the power to levy taxes and to spend money, and thus posed a serious threat to America's ancient republican tradition. "This [bill]," he wrote in the midst of the debate, "is advancing backward three or four centuries, and returning to the days of the Stuart kings. Not since that time have the people who live under the British constitutional system and the American constitutional system submitted the property of the people, . . . wholly . . . to the opinion and the decision of the spenders."[4]

Conservative opponents of reorganization coalesced around Wheeler, the independent Democrat from Montana, who only months earlier had helped assemble the coalition of Democrats and Republicans that had defeated the Court-Packing bill. In an effort to preserve the separation of government powers, Wheeler offered an amendment to the Reorganization bill, requiring a joint Congressional resolution of approval before any of the President's reorganization plans became effective. Wheeler's amendment was narrowly defeated on 18 March, however, when a number of Democrats who had previously opposed the Administration on key issues, including "Cotton Ed" Smith, Robert Reynolds, George Radcliffe, James Byrnes, Pat Harrison, and Joseph O'Mahoney, voted to preserve the

President's power. Six days later the same group of Democrats provided the Administration with another important victory by voting to defeat an amendment offered by conservative Democrat Harry F. Byrd to strike that section of the bill abolishing the controller general. In the end, the incipient conservative rebellion appeared to fail when the Senate, by a margin of only seven votes, in late March gave FDR the reorganization powers he sought.[5]

Yet it was apparent that the Administration's victory in the Reorganization bill was made possible only through intensive lobbying in an election year. Wavering Democrats were alternately threatened and cajoled by FDR, James Farley, and other Administration leaders. During the debate the political commentator Dorothy Thompson reported that the White House was exerting constant pressure on senators in the form of promises of patronage and vows to withhold endorsements in upcoming elections. Josiah W. Bailey of North Carolina and William King of Utah provided another glimpse into the Administration's tactics when they charged, during floor debate of the bill, that the White House maintained a "patronage blacklist" against its opponents. King quoted a a government official who told him that "you are on a blacklist. You voted against the bill which created this department, and other senators who voted against the bill are also on the blacklist." Josiah Bailey similarly noted during debate that the rejection of one of his nominees to a government agency had been accompanied by an outburst from the head of the agency, who bluntly informed the conservative Democrat that he should not expect any favors whatsoever from the Administration. As the evidence provided by Thompson, King, and Bailey suggests, FDR, despite his victory in the Senate on Reorganization, had had to exert tremendous pressure on many legislators to overcome an apparently resurgent conservatism.[6]

Resurgent conservatism also forced the Roosevelt Administration to adopt extraordinary tactics in the spring to prevent the repeal of one of the New Deal's main fiscal reforms, the undistributed profits tax on business. The tax, long regarded by most observers as a symbol of the New Deal's commitment to producing a more equitable distribution of wealth, was under sharp attack from conservatives throughout the country by early 1938. As the nation grappled with the lingering effects of the "Roosevelt Recession," many critics complained that the undistributed profits tax was one of the chief reasons for the economic downturn. By preventing the accumulation of surplus capital, they charged, the tax left business in time of depression with no recourse but to slash wages and jobs. But in a broader sense, many Senate conservatives objected to the tax because it stood as an overt symbol of the New Deal's continuing effort to manage the economy, instead of allowing the free enterprise system to solve its own problems. Democrat Peter Gerry of Rhode Island complained, for example, that the profits tax, by interfering with business's capital accumulation, had actually made it more difficult for new businesses to compete against older, more well-established firms. The *New York Herald Tribune,* a voice for the more moderate wing of the GOP, similarly condemned the undistributed profits tax in an editorial on 2 March. In tones that most Senate conservatives in 1938 would have embraced, the newspaper charged that until the President halted his unreasonable attack on the free enterprise system, the economy would continue to founder.[7]

The final version of the Revenue bill adopted by the House retained the profits tax, but applied it only to those corporations whose net income exceeded $25,000. In the Senate, however, the bill was thoroughly rewritten by the Finance Committee, led by Mississippi Democrat Pat Harrison. Chairman since 1933, Harrison had helped guide through to passage many of the important reforms of the "100 Days," despite harboring private reservations about many of them. By 1938, however, the Mississippi Democrat had broken with the New Deal over the Court-Packing bill and FDR's intervention on behalf of Alben Barkley in his 1937 contest with Harrison for the position of Senate Majority leader.[8] During the Finance Committee's consideration of the revenue bill, Harrison argued for complete elimination of the undistributed profits tax, claiming that it hampered economic recovery. If the huge spending of the New Deal was to continue, the Mississippi Democrat insisted that revenue had to be raised by broadening the income tax on individuals. Spurred by Harrison's leadership and the desire to aid business, in early April the Senate approved a revenue bill that eliminated the House's modified version of the excess profits tax in favor of a flat 18% tax on corporate net income exceeding $25,000.[9]

During the Conference Committee's deliberations on the Revenue bill, FDR sent an "extraordinary letter" to the chairmen of the joint committee, Harrison and Robert Doughton of North Carolina, condemning the Senate bill for deleting the undistributed profits tax and urging the conferees to continue the existing tax system. The President's letter surprised many in Congress because Administration supporters had made no attempt during Senate debate to reinstate the profits tax. Many legislators also resented the President's bald attempt to interfere with Conference Committee action. In a Congress where concern over the separation of power was already quite strong, Roosevelt's latest action was too much. "He [FDR] again shows a desire," charged House conferee Allen Treadway of Massachusetts, "to exert his authority and influence over the legislative branch and even to a conference between the two houses. . . . Never before have I known the Executive to force his view upon a conference." The President's intervention, however much anger it created, apparently helped preserve a symbol of New Deal fiscal policy, albeit in significantly diminished form. The agreement reached by the Conference Committee in late April continued the undistributed profits tax for two years, but sharply modified it by fixing the maximum rate at only 2.5% and making it applicable only to corporations with net incomes in excess of $25,000.[10]

By the end of April 1938, FDR had a mixed record in the second session of the 75th Congress. Many Senate conservatives had struggled against both the reorganization bill and extension of the excess profits tax, hoping to restore the balance of governmental powers and the unfettered free enterprise system that they believed had prevailed in America prior to 1933. But through intensive lobbying and a mixture of threats and cajolery, Roosevelt used the psychology of an election year to win an important victory in the Senate on reorganization and to avoid total defeat on the profits tax. Similar trends were in evidence in late April when the Senate turned to a new pump-priming measure proposed by the Administration.

Throughout early 1938, the steadily worsening recession intensified demands on Roosevelt to take action to alleviate the stagnant economic conditions. In a "fireside chat" on 14 April, the President finally acceded to these demands by requesting an emergency appropriation of $5 billion to increase the government's spending and lending powers. Because the Spend-Lend bill, as it was quickly dubbed, again employed the deficit financing plans the New Deal had relied upon since 1933, many conservatives whose fiscal ideas embraced balanced budgets were immediately critical. Predicting that the bill would produce the biggest peacetime deficit in the nation's history, Harry F. Byrd of Virginia dismissed the President's proposal outright. Arthur Vandenberg was equally forthright in rejecting what he believed were the very fiscal policies that were responsible for the renewed recession.[11]

Conservatives in the House were first to attack FDR's Spend-Lend bill. In May, three GOP congressmen released a minority report that made clear that some conservatives opposed not merely the pending bill, but the entire philosophy of government, which they believed the bill represented. The report, prepared by Robert L. Bacon and John Taber of New York, and by Richard Wigglesworth of Massachusetts, proposed to restore health to the economy by repealing the undistributed profits tax, reducing social security taxes, eliminating the WPA, prohibiting PWA pump-priming loans, and revising the Wagner Act. While the GOP report was undoubtedly influenced by election-year politics, the sweeping changes it proposed suggests that many Congressional conservatives in 1938 still viewed the nation as one composed of autonomous individuals competing in a free market economy. In the end, however, the large Democratic majority in the lower house, together with representatives' desire to wind up business in Washington quickly to begin their 1938 election campaigns, overcame conservative objections. By the middle of May, the House had approved a bill giving FDR a free hand to spend the appropriated funds as he saw fit.[12]

In the Senate, where only one-third of the members faced the voters in the fall, memories of the recent battles over Executive reorganization and the excess profits tax were not as easily overcome, and many were reluctant to grant the President such broad power. As early as 24 April, Burton Wheeler proposed the idea of earmarking funds in the bill for specific work projects in order to limit the power granted to the Executive. Wheeler's concerns were reinforced by the attempted purge of dissident Democrats, which began in late May. When Harry Hopkins, the head of the WPA, acting apparently with the President's blessing, publicly endorsed liberal Democrat Otha D. Wearin in his bid to unseat incumbent Democrat Guy M. Gillette in the Iowa primary, fears that relief funds in the Spend-Lend bill might be used for political purposes seemed more credible.[13]

To counteract these concerns, Roosevelt dispatched a letter on 31 May to the bill's floor manager, Alva Adams of Colorado, which sought to direct the Senate's attention away from the political ramifications of the Spend-Lend bill. Noting that unemployment had increased since the bill's introduction, the President argued that no restrictions should be placed on the appropriations, so that they could be used immediately to create jobs.[14] FDR's letter was a political masterstroke. By focusing public attention on the human impact of the Spend-Lend bill, he increased the pressure, particularly on those senators facing re-election, to support the Administration's effort to put people back to work. The President's letter, together with the recent purge attempts, seemed to convince wavering Democrats to back the Administration, lest their objections to this bill make them unpopular with the White House or with the voters. When Senate voting began on 2 June, Administration forces, swelled by the addition of conservative Democrats facing re-election, beat back all crippling amendments before voting 60–10 on 5 June to approve the Spend-Lend bill.[15]

Taken as a whole, then, Senate politics in 1938 suggested that the bark of the conservative coalition could be worse than its bite. Although on many issues an increasing number of Democrats, especially from the South, had talked about the need to resist further expansions of presidential power as well as continued government efforts to manage the free enterprise system, few in the end were willing to vote consistently against a popular president in an election year.

The powerful influence of election-year politics is fully evident in the statistical analysis of roll call votes in the 75th Congress. As table 1–1 indicates, the senators who scaled in the high support and medium support categories are almost all Democrats. Many of the Democrats who scaled in the medium support category, moreover, including Bennett Clark, Frederick Van Nuys, Robert Reynolds, George Radcliffe, Ellison D. "Cotton Ed" Smith, Pat Harrison, Peter Gerry, Richard Russell, and Walter George were senators with increasingly strong anti-Administration credentials by the late 1930s. The presence of such Democrats in the medium support category suggests that FDR's "purge" and the considerable popular support he continued to command led some conservatives to moderate their voting behavior in 1938 for partisan reasons. Indeed, Clark, Van Nuys, Reynolds, Smith, and George faced re-election in November.

Other senators in the medium support group, such as Democrats Edwin Johnson and Alva Adams of Colorado, Burton Wheeler of Montana, and Key Pittman of Nevada, as well as Republicans Arthur Capper of Kansas, Lynn Frazier and Gerald P. Nye of North Dakota, and Independent Ernest Lundeen of Minnesota represented states in the far West or Midwest that had been strongly influenced by the reform spirit of the Populist and Progressive eras. Their medium support for FDR's New Deal in the 75th Congress was likely the extension of the reform ideology that had led their forebears to accept a limited expansion of government power to protect individuals from the monopolistic tendencies of industrial capitalism.

Without consistent votes from Democrats, the small bipartisan group who scaled in the low support category in table 1–1 was largely powerless in 1938 to shape the political agenda as they had in the previous session. Thus, despite the high hopes that the victory in the Court-Packing bill had raised among conservatives, the Senate in 1938 largely preserved the essential outlines of the New Deal and in some ways actually expanded it. In addition to the Ad-

TABLE 1-1

75TH CONGRESS

Name	Policy Dimensions	Score
	1 2 3 4 5 6 7 8 9 10 11 12	

HIGH SUPPORT

Name	Policy Dimensions	Score
Black, D-AL	0 1 1 0 0 0 1 0 1 1 0 1	1.00
Guffey, D-PA	1 1 2 1 1 1 1 1 1 1 1 1	1.08
Minton, D-IN	1 0 1 1 1 2 1 1 1 1 1 1	1.09
Hughes, D-DE	2 1 0 0 0 1 1 0 1 1 1 1	1.13
Barkley, D-KY	1 1 3 1 1 1 1 1 1 1 1 1	1.17
Neely, D-WV	0 1 1 0 1 2 1 1 1 1 1 1	1.17
Thomas, D-UT	1 1 1 1 2 0 1 2 1 1 1 1	1.18
Brown, D-NH	1 1 0 1 1 2 1 1 1 2 1 1	1.18
Hitchcock, D-SD	2 1 1 0 1 0 1 1 2 1 1 1	1.20
Duffy, D-WI	2 0 0 1 2 1 0 1 1 1 1 1	1.22
Sheppard, D-TX	0 1 0 3 1 1 1 1 0 1 1 1	1.22
Schwartz, D-WY	1 1 2 1 2 2 1 1 1 1 1 1	1.25
Logan, D-KY	2 0 3 1 1 1 1 1 1 1 1 1	1.27
Thomas, D-OK	0 2 1 1 2 1 1 0 2 1 1 1	1.30
Bone, D-WA	1 1 2 1 1 2 1 1 1 2 2 1	1.33
Ellender, D-LA	2 1 1 3 1 1 1 1 2 1 1 1	1.34
Brown, D-MI	2 1 2 1 1 1 1 1 1 2 2 1	1.34
Schwellenbach, D-WA	2 1 3 1 1 2 1 1 1 1 1 1	1.34
Hatch, D-NM	2 2 1 1 1 2 2 1 1 1 1 1	1.34
Murray, D-MT	3 1 0 1 2 1 1 1 2 1 1 1	1.36
Norris, I-NE	0 0 0 2 1 0 2 1 2 1 1 1	1.38
Green, D-RI	1 0 2 0 1 1 1 2 1 3 1 1	1.40
Herring, D-IA	2 3 2 0 1 0 2 0 1 1 1 1	1.40
LaFollette, I-WI	0 1 1 0 1 3 1 1 2 2 1 1	1.40
Truman, D-MO	1 1 2 1 1 2 2 1 1 3 1 1	1.42
Lee, D-OK	2 2 1 0 2 0 1 0 2 1 1 1	1.44
Walsh, D-MA	0 1 0 1 3 1 1 0 1 2 2 1	1.44
Wagner, D-NY	0 2 0 1 3 2 1 1 0 1 1 1	1.44
Hayden, D-AZ	0 0 3 2 1 1 2 0 1 1 1 1	1.44
Bilbo, D-MS	2 1 0 3 2 1 1 1 2 1 1 1	1.45

Name	Policy Dimensions	Score
	1 2 3 4 5 6 7 8 9 10 11 12	

HIGH SUPPORT continued

Name	Policy Dimensions	Score
Overton, D-LA	0 2 1 3 1 1 2 1 2 1 1 1	1.45
Pope, D-ID	2 2 1 2 1 3 1 1 2 1 1 1	1.50
Bulkley, D-OH	0 2 1 1 3 0 1 0 0 1 2 1	1.50
Dietrich, D-IL	1 2 3 1 2 0 1 1 1 3 1 1	1.55
Lewis, D-IL	2 2 2 2 2 0 1 2 1 1 1 1	1.55
Pepper, D-FL	1 3 2 0 1 0 1 0 3 1 1 1	1.56
Gillette, D-IA	2 2 2 2 1 0 1 0 2 1 0 1	1.56
O'Mahoney, D-WY	3 1 1 2 2 0 0 0 2 1 1 1	1.56
Shipstead, I-MN	0 2 1 0 2 0 2 1 0 0 2 1	1.57
McGill, D-KS	2 2 2 1 1 3 1 1 2 1 2 1	1.58
McKellar, D-KY	2 3 3 3 1 1 1 1 1 1 1 1	1.58
Moore, D-NJ	1 2 3 0 3 0 1 0 1 1 0 1	1.63
McAdoo, D-CA	0 3 3 0 2 0 1 1 0 1 1 1	1.63
Bankhead, D-AL	0 0 3 0 1 1 2 2 0 1 1 2	1.63
Lonergan, D-CT	1 2 3 1 2 1 2 0 1 1 2 2	1.64

MEDIUM SUPPORT

Name	Policy Dimensions	Score
Caraway, D-AR	2 0 2 0 1 2 2 2 1 1 2 2	1.70
Ashurst, D-AZ	0 3 2 2 2 1 2 0 1 2 1 1	1.70
Lundeen, I-MN	0 2 2 2 1 3 2 1 3 1 2 1	1.82
Wheeler, D-MT	0 2 0 0 2 2 2 1 2 0 3 1	1.88
Harrison, D-MS	2 3 3 0 2 0 2 0 1 1 1 2	1.89
Reynolds, D-NC	2 3 0 3 2 0 2 1 1 0 1 2	1.89
Russell, D-GA	2 0 1 3 2 0 2 0 1 3 1 2	1.89
Pittman, D-NV	0 3 2 2 0 1 2 2 1 2 2 2	1.90
Byrnes, D-SC	1 3 3 3 2 1 2 2 1 2 1 2	1.92
Radcliffe, D-MD	1 3 3 2 3 1 2 2 1 3 1 2	2.00
Frazier, R-ND	3 2 1 2 2 3 2 1 3 2 2 1	2.00
Nye, R-ND	3 2 1 2 2 3 2 2 3 1 2 1	2.00
Bulow, D-SD	0 2 3 2 1 0 2 2 1 3 2 2	2.00
Chavez, D-NM	0 2 3 0 0 0 2 0 3 1 1 2	2.00
George, D-GA	0 3 0 0 2 0 2 1 1 3 2 2	2.00
Adams, D-CO	3 2 3 1 2 1 2 2 3 2 2 2	2.08

Name	Policy Dimensions	Score
	1 2 3 4 5 6 7 8 9 10 11 12	

MEDIUM SUPPORT continued

Name	Policy Dimensions	Score
Van Nuys, D-IN	2 3 0 1 2 0 2 3 1 2 3 2	2.10
Connally, D-TX	0 3 3 3 2 1 2 1 0 2 2 2	2.10
Clark, D-MO	2 3 2 1 0 2 3 0 1 0 3 2	2.11
Capper, R-KS	3 2 1 1 2 3 3 1 3 2 2 3	2.17
Johnson, D-CO	3 3 2 1 2 3 2 2 3 1 2 2	2.17
McCarran, D-NV	3 2 0 1 2 0 3 2 3 1 2 3	2.20
Davis, R-PA	3 2 2 1 3 3 2 0 3 1 3 3	2.27
Smith, D-SC	0 3 3 3 2 0 2 0 0 0 1 2	2.29
Andrews, D-FL	2 3 2 3 2 0 2 0 3 3 2 1	2.30
Gerry, D-RI	3 1 1 0 3 1 3 3 0 2 3 3	2.30
Maloney, D-CT	3 2 0 1 3 1 2 0 3 3 0 3	2.33

LOW SUPPORT

Name	Policy Dimensions	Score
Byrd, D-VA	2 3 1 0 3 2 3 3 1 0 3 3	2.40
Vandenberg, R-MI	3 2 1 2 3 0 3 3 3 3 3 3	2.42
King, D-UT	2 3 0 2 3 1 3 3 1 3 3 3	2.45
Borah, R-ID	3 2 1 0 2 0 3 3 3 3 3 2	2.50
McNary, R-OR	0 2 2 2 3 1 3 0 3 3 3 3	2.50
Tydings, D-MD	0 2 0 0 3 0 3 0 0 2 2 3	2.50
Burke, D-NE	0 3 1 0 3 1 3 3 0 0 3 3	2.50
Copeland, D-NY	3 3 3 1 3 1 3 3 3 2 3 3	2.58
Steweir, R-OR	3 2 3 0 3 0 2 0 3 2 0 3	2.63
Hale, R-ME	3 3 1 0 3 1 3 3 3 3 3 3	2.64
Austin, R-VT	3 2 3 2 3 1 3 3 3 3 3 3	2.67
Lodge, R-MA	3 2 3 2 3 1 3 3 3 3 3 3	2.67
White, R-ME	3 3 1 0 3 0 3 0 3 2 3 3	2.67
Gibson, R-VT	0 0 0 2 3 1 3 3 3 3 3 3	2.67
Holt, D-WV	3 0 1 0 3 0 3 3 3 3 3 3	2.78
Glass, D-VA	0 3 2 0 3 0 3 0 0 0 3 3	2.83
Townsend, R-DE	3 3 0 2 3 0 3 3 3 3 3 3	2.90
Bridges, R-NH	3 3 0 0 3 2 3 3 3 3 3 3	2.90
Bailey, D-NC	3 3 3 3 3 0 3 3 2 3 3 3	2.91
Johnson, R-CA	3 0 3 0 3 0 3 0 3 0 3 3	3.00

Policy Dimension Key:

      0   denotes that a senator did not scale on the dimension
      1. Foreign Aid
      2. Labor
      3. Fiscal Policy
      4. Civil Rights/Civil Liberties
      5. Agriculture
      6. National Defense
      7. Social Welfare
      8. Public Power
      9. Reciprocal Trade
      10. Business Regulation
      11. Extension of Executive Power
      12. Extension of Federal Authority

75TH CONGRESS (N=92)

HIGH SUPPORT (N=45 or 49%)   MEDIUM SUPPORT (N=27 or 29%)

    Democrats = 42 (93%)   Democrats = 22 (81%)
    GOP   = 0 (0%)   GOP   = 4 (15%)
    Independent = 3 (7%)   Independent = 1 (4%)

LOW SUPPORT (N= 20 or 22%)

    Democrats = 8 (40%)
    GOP   = 12 (60%)
    Independent = 0 (0%)

TABLE 1-2

Regional Divisions in Medium and Low Support Groups

MEDIUM SUPPORT (N=27)

Coastal (N=10 or 37%)

Reynolds, D-NC	Davis, R-PA	George, D-GA
Russell, D-GA	Smith, D-SC	Maloney, D-CT
Byrnes, D-SC	Andrews, D-FL	
Radcliffe, D-MD	Gerry, D-RI	

Interior (N=17 or 63%)

Caraway, D-AR	Chavez, D-NM	Nye, R-ND
Ashurst, D-AZ	Adams, D-CO	Bulow, D-SD
Lundeen, I-MN	Van Nuys, D-IN	Johnson, D-CO
Wheeler, D-MT	Connally, D-TX	Frazier, R-ND
Harrison, D-MS	Clark, D- MO	McCarran, D-NV
Pittman, D-NV	Capper, R-KS	

LOW SUPPORT (N=20)

Coastal (N=15 or 75%)

Byrd, D-VA	Gibson, R-VT	Austin, R-VT
McNary, R-OR	Holt, D-WV	Lodge, R-MA
Tydings, D-MD	Glass, D-VA	White, R-ME
Copeland, D-NY	Townsend, R-DE	Bailey, D-NC
Hale, R-ME	Bridges, R-NH	Johnson, R-CA

Interior (N=5 or 25%)

Vandenberg, R-MI
King, D-UT
Borah, R-ID
Burke, D-NE
Steweir, R-OR

ministration victories in reorganization, extension of the excess profits tax and the Spend-Lend bill, the Senate in 1938 established a federal minimimum wage with the Fair Labor Standards Act, approved the 2nd Agricultural Adjustment Act with its reformist "ever-normal granary" provision, and ratified a new public housing measure, the Wagner Housing Act. Indeed, to the liberal *New Republic,* the achievements of the 1938 session of Congress in the face of widespread predictions of a resurgence in conservatism were little short of remarkable. "The wonder is, not that Congress kicked up its heels," it chortled, "but that legislation made as much progress as it did."[16]

If the Democratic party was artifically unified by election-year politics, fractures were appearing in the GOP that point to a transformation beginning in Senate conservatism. Although the Republican party had been solid in its opposition to the domestic policies of the New Deal throughout the 1930s, the winning majority of the 1938 Spend-Lend bill included five of the Senate's fifteen Republicans. Three of the five, Gerald P. Nye and Lynn Frazier of North Dakota and Arthur Capper of Kansas were representatives of the GOP's agrarian progressive wing of the early twentieth century, the "sons of the wild jackass." The other two Republican votes, however, came from Henry Cabot Lodge Jr. of Massachusetts and James J. Davis of Pennsylvania, both of whom represented urban, industrial states that throughout the early twentieth century had been the heartland of GOP "rugged individualism." Their votes for the Spend-Lend bill, as well as the medium support Davis gave to the New Deal in 1938 (Table 1–3), indicate that some conservatives were beginning to modernize their political principles, recognizing that in a mass, industrial society the intervention of the state was sometimes necessary for the promotion of individual rights and liberties.[17]

The results of the November elections provided further evidence of a transformation underway in Senate conservatism. Only two years after suffering one of the worst defeats in electoral history, the GOP showed surprising strength, gaining eighty-one seats in the House and eight in the Senate. More importantly, most observers attributed the GOP resurgence to the fact that many Republican candidates seemingly rejected their party's philosophy of rugged individualism in favor of a more moderate approach to the New Deal's social agenda. Among the newly elected Senate Republicans were Charles Tobey of New Hampshire, Joseph Ball of Minnesota, and Alexander Wiley of Wisconsin, all of whom accepted some or all of the ends endorsed by the New Deal and generally criticized only its means.

In a broad sense, the crop of new Republican senators, as well as the votes of Lodge and Davis on the Spend-Lend bill, are evidence that by 1938 conservatives, especially in the GOP, were beginning to adapt their ideology to the new contours of the American political landscape. To be sure, some of the shift was motivated by pragmatic political decisions made by the minority party to win elections. But conservatives were also beginning to acknowledge that the lesson taught by the Great Depression and the New Deal was that the urban, industrial society of the late 1930s demanded new methods to safeguard individual liberty and the private enterprise system.

TABLE 1-3

75th CONGRESS - DOMESTIC POLICY DIMENSIONS

HIGH SUPPORT

Black, D-AL	1.00	Lee, D-OK	1.29
Minton, D-IN	1.00	O'Mahoney, D-WY	1.29
Hughes, D-DE	1.00	Bone, D-WA	1.33
Neely, D-WV	1.00	McGill, D-KS	1.33
Hitchcock, D-SD	1.00	Wagner, D-NY	1.38
Guffey, D-PA	1.11	Bilbo, D-MS	1.38
Brown, D-NH	1.13	Pope, D-ID	1.38
Murray, D-MT	1.13	Gillette, D-IA	1.43
LaFollette, I-WI	1.13	Overton, D-LA	1.44
Duffy, D-WI	1.17	Truman, D-MO	1.44
Barkley, D-KY	1.22	Bulkley, D-OH	1.50
Thomas, D-UT	1.22	Lewis, D-IL	1.56
Schwartz, D-WY	1.22	Lundeen, I-MN	1.56
Ellender, D-LA	1.22	Green, D-RI	1.57
Brown, D-MI	1.22	Herring, D-IA	1.57
Schwellenbach, D-WA	1.22	Walsh, D-MA	1.57
Hatch, D-NM	1.22	Hayden, D-AZ	1.57
Sheppard, D-TX	1.25	Shipstead, I-MN	1.57
Logan, D-KY	1.25	McAdoo, D-CA	1.63
Thomas, D-OK	1.25		
Pepper, D-FL	1.25		
Norris, I-NE	1.29		

N = 41; D = 37; R = 0; I = 4

TABLE 1-3

75th CONGRESS-DOMESTIC POLICY DIMENSIONS

MEDIUM SUPPORT

Dietrich, D-IL	1.67	McCarran, D-NV	2.00
McKellar, D-TN	1.67	Adams, D-CO	2.00
Frazier, R-ND	1.67	Bulow, D-SD	2.11
Nye, R-ND	1.67	Davis, R-PA	2.13
Bankhead, D-AL	1.71	Pittman, D-NV	2.13
Caraway, D-AR	1.71	George, D-GA	2.14
Moore, D-NJ	1.83	Connally, D-TX	2.22
Wheeler, D-MT	1.83	Byrnes, D-SC	2.22
Chavez, D-NM	1.83	Andrews, D-FL	2.25
Lonergan, D-CT	1.83	VanNuys, D-IN	2.25
Ashurst, D-AZ	1.88	Smith, D-SC	2.29
Capper, R-KS	1.89	Radcliffe, D-MD	2.33
Johnson, D-CO	1.89	Clark, D-MO	2.33
Harrison, D-MS	2.00	Maloney, D-CT	2.33
Reynolds, D-NC	2.00	Gerry, D-RI	2.38
Russell, D-GA	2.00	Borah, R-ID	2.38

N = 32; D = 27; R = 5
Coastal = 12 (37%); Interior = 20 (63%)

LOW SUPPORT

Tydings, D-MD	2.50	Austin, R-VT	2.78
Steweir, R-OR	2.50	Lodge, R-MA	2.78
Vandenberg, R-MI	2.56	Glass, D-VA	2.83
White, R-ME	2.57	Gibson, R-VT	2.86
McNary, R-OR	2.63	King, D-UT	2.88
Copeland, D-NY	2.67	Townsend, R-DE	2.88
Holt, D-WV	2.71	Bridges, R-NH	3.00
Byrd, D-VA	2.71	Bailey, D-NC	3.00
Burke, D-NE	2.71	Johnson, R-CA	3.00
Hale, R-ME	2.75		

N = 19; D = 8; R = 11
Coastal = 16 (84%); Interior = 3 (16%)

TABLE 1-4

75th CONGRESS - FOREIGN POLICY DIMENSIONS

HIGH SUPPORT

Black, D-AL	1.00	Brown, D-NH	1.33
Guffey, D-PA	1.00	Duffy, D-WI	1.33
Barkley, D-KY	1.00	Schwartz, D-WY	1.33
Thomas, D-UT	1.00	Logan, D-KY	1.33
Sheppard, D-TX	1.00	Bone, D-WA	1.33
Green, D-RI	1.00	Brown, D-MI	1.33
Walsh, D-MA	1.00	Truman, D-MO	1.33
Hayden, D-AZ	1.00	McKellar, D-TN	1.33
Dietrich, D-IL	1.00	King, D-UT	1.33
Moore, D-NJ	1.00	Neely, D-WV	1.33
Bankhead, D-AL	1.00	Thomas, D-OK	1.50
Lonergan, D-CT	1.00	Herring, D-IA	1.50
Ashurst, D-AZ	1.00	Overton, D-LA	1.50
Pittman, D-NV	1.00	Lewis, D-IL	1.50
Byrnes, D-SC	1.00	Harrison, D-MS	1.50
Radcliffe, D-MD	1.00	Reynolds, D-NC	1.50
Minton, D-IN	1.33	Russell, D-GA	1.50
Hughes, D-DE	1.33	VanNuys, D-IN	1.50

N = 36; D = 36; R = 0

MEDIUM SUPPORT

Ellender, D-LA	1.67	Norris, I-NE	2.00
Schwellenbach, D-WA	1.67	Lee, D-OK	2.00
Hatch, D-NM	1.67	Pepper, D-FL	2.00
Bilbo, D-MS	1.67	Gillette, D-IA	2.00
Caraway, D-AR	1.67	Wheeler, D-MT	2.00
Clark, D-MO	1.67	Gerry, D-RI	2.00
Byrd, D-VA	1.67	McNary, R-OR	2.00
Hitchcock, D-SD	2.00	Gibson, R-VT.	2.00
Murray, D-MT	2.00		

N = 17; D = 14; R = 2; I = 1
Coastal = 6 (35%); Interior = 11 (65%)

TABLE 1-4

75th CONGRESS - FOREIGN POLICY DIMENSIONS

LOW SUPPORT

Adams, D-CO	2.33	Frazier, R-ND	3.00
Maloney, D-CT	2.33	Nye, R-ND	3.00
Copeland, D-NY	2.33	Capper, R-KS	3.00
Hale, R-ME	2.33	Johnson, D-CO	3.00
Austin, R-VT	2.33	McCarran, D-NV	3.00
Lodge, R-MA	2.33	Davis, R-PA	3.00
Pope, D-ID	2.34	Vandenberg, R-MI	3.00
McGill, D-KS	2.34	Borah, R-ID	3.00
LaFollette, I-WI	2.50	Steweir, R-OR	3.00
O'Mahoney, D-WY	2.50	White, R-ME	3.00
Andrews, D-FL	2.50	Holt, D-WV	3.00
Bailey, D-NC	2.50	Townsend, R-DE	3.00
Bridges, R-NH	2.67	Johnson, R-CA	3.00
Lundeen, I-MN	3.00		

N = 27; D = 11; R = 14; I = 2
Coastal = 14 (52%); Interior = 13 (48%)

II

The first session of the 76th Congress proved, up until the start of war in Europe in September, to be more openly defiant of Administration requests than any legislature since 1933. Most of the change in the Senate's demeanor was attributable to the growing independence of Democrats. Freed from the pressures generated by mid-term elections in November 1938, many Senate Democrats who had grown disenchanted with the pace and the direction of the New Deal found it easier in 1939 to vote against the Administration. Perhaps more importantly, FDR's much publicized "purge" of conservative Democrats in 1938 failed, as all but a few of the dissidents were re-elected, and the failure of the purge convinced many Democrats that they could vote against the New Deal with impunity. As William Leuchtenberg has argued, "since he [FDR] was not expected to run again in 1940, congressmen no longer had anything to fear, nor, since they could not ride on his coattails next time, and since he had less patronage left to dispense, did they have much to hope."[18]

That Franklin Roosevelt would have to deal with an intractable Congress in 1939 became apparent in early January when senators from both parties, citing the partisan use of the WPA in the attempted purge of conservative Democrats, demanded its immediate liquidation. Asserting that the WPA had never attained its goal of offering employment to all able-bodied individuals, Republican Warren Barbour of New Jersey, re-elected to the Senate in 1938 after a two-year hiatus, vowed on 3 January to introduce a bill returning control of relief entirely to the states. Several days later, Democrat William King of Utah put Barbour's vow into form when he introduced a bill to dissolve the WPA within 90 days.[19]

Oblivious to his legislative opposition, FDR took the offensive on the relief issue by requesting in his annual message a sum of $875 million to keep the WPA solvent for the remainder of the fiscal year. Any lesser amount, he warned, would force the dismissal from the relief rolls of thousands of needy individuals. The President also promised to fight any effort to return even partial control of relief to the states. Two days after his annual message, Roosevelt further challenged his opponents when, at a Jackson Day dinner he encouraged anti-Administration Democrats to join the GOP. The President's truculent position on relief funding surprised and dismayed many on Capitol Hill, not only because most congressmen thought the size of his request was too high, but also because of his continuing refusal, in the wake of the failed purge, to acknowledge any problems in the administration of the WPA.[20]

House Democrats were not intimidated by the President's threats. By the lopsided margin of 397–16, the lower chamber voted in mid-January to provide only $725 million to supplement WPA funds through 30 June, rebuking the Roosevelt Administration in the first legislative skirmish of 1939. Before action on the bill shifted to the Senate, however, the President used a press conference to increase pressure on wavering Democrats in the upper house. FDR asserted to reporters that he could not accept the House bill because it was his job to think of the thousands of men, women, and children who would be removed from WPA rolls in the depth of winter if the full $875 million was not appropriated. In the end, Roosevelt's tactics seemed to backfire. To the veteran political analyst Mark Sullivan, the President's remarks were spiteful because they implied that only he had compassion for human suffering.[21]

The verity of Sullivan's observations was confirmed when conservative Democrats in the upper house, emboldened by the failed purge and stung by the Jackson Day warning, moved quickly to uphold the House's decision to slash $150 million from WPA appropriations. Meeting on 20 January in the midst of a snowstorm, which heightened concern for the needy, an Appropriations sub-committee approved two amendments designed to cushion the impact of the funding cut, but refused on an 8–3 vote to restore the full $875 million requested by the Administration. Added to the bill were amendments prohibiting the dismissal before 1 April of more than 5% of the total number on WPA rolls and authorizing the President to request additional funds if those appropriated seemed insufficient. The following day the full Appropriations Committee rejected 17–7 a motion from Kenneth McKellar of Tennessee to restore the $150 million in relief funds and then sent the amended bill to the Senate floor for final action. On both committee votes, the winning majority included such independent Democrats as James Byrnes, Alva Adams, Richard Russell, and John Bankhead, who in the previous session had often sided with the Administration on crucial issues.[22]

Senate floor debate on the relief bill, which opened on 24 January, underscored the growing importance of Democratic independence to the conservatives' fortunes. Among those speaking against the Administration in the Senate were two Democrats who in 1938 had led White House forces in crucial legislative battles. James Byrnes of South Carolina, floor manager for the 1938 Reorganization bill, charged during debate that the White House had exaggerated the size of the appropriations cut. The South Carolinian insisted that when current WPA expenditures and various ongoing pump-priming activities were added to the $725 million in new funds contained in the Senate's bill, the federal government would actually spend more to help the needy in fiscal 1939 than in any previous year. Similarly, Alva Adams of Colorado, who in 1938 had successfully guided the Spend-Lend bill through the upper house, rekindled charges that the relief agency meddled in state and local politics. In an angry speech on the Senate floor, the Colorado Democrat showed his colleagues a notice that had recently been taken from a bulletin board in WPA's Washington headquarters. It read:

Spend 25 cents
Send a telegram to Your Senator Today
Protest WPA Appropriation Cuts
Protest Civil Service Ban on WPA Employees
Protect your Job[23]

This notice, in *Newsweek*'s judgment alienated many senators who previously had been undecided, and, when added to the charges raised by Byrnes and the strong residue of resentment many in the Senate felt toward FDR's pressure, doomed whatever chance remained for the Administration to prevail. The key vote came on 27 January when the upper house defeated a McKellar amendment 47–46 restoring the full $875 million to the relief bill. The loss, which surprised Administration supporters, was reportedly engineered by Byrnes, Adams, Pat Harrison, and Vice President Garner, who were able to convince a sufficient number of Democrats, interested in reducing the budget deficit and slowing the pace of reform, to join with Republicans in approving the reduced WPA appropriation. Deserters from the Administration position included such Democrats as Adams, Byrnes, Harrison, Guy Gillette, George Radcliffe, Walter George, Richard Russell, and Harry Truman, who in previous years had usually voted to uphold New Deal reform. In early 1939, however, with FDR's reputation for political invincibility tarnished by the 1937 Court fight, the "Roosevelt Recession," and the failed 1938 purge, White House lobbying and the pull of party loyalty no longer exerted as strong an influence over Senate Democrats. The new found independence of Senate Democrats was not lost on Hiram Johnson. After the McKellar amendment had been defeated, the California Republican observed pithily to his son that the vote "taught a lot of week-kneed Senators that they can stand up and vote as their consciences dictate without falling dead."[24]

In the aftermath of their victory on relief spending, Senate conservatives displayed a surprising rebelliousness on other issues in 1939. In June, a coalition of conservative Democrats and Republicans launched a filibuster to prevent passage of a conference report which, among other things, continued the President's unilateral power to modify the dollar's value by adjusting its gold content. The following month, Senate conservatives succeeded in slashing nearly 50% of the funds from a new pump-priming bill requested by the Administration to promote recovery in fiscal 1940. An even clearer measure of Congressional antipathy to the Administration came in early August when the Senate adopted the Logan-Walter bill empowering federal courts to overrule decisions made by such quasi-judicial Executive agencies as the NLRB and the SEC. Although the Logan-Walter bill was recommitted shortly before the first session of the 76th Congress adjourned, it signaled clearly the growing opposition, fueled largely by conservatives with which the Roosevelt Administration had to contend in the first eight months of 1939.[25]

That the growing power of Senate conservatives was not restricted to domestic issues was clearly demonstrated when the upper house considered revision of the nation's neutrality legislation in mid-1939. Alarmed by the deteriorating situation in Europe, FDR requested in the spring that Congress repeal those sections of the 1937 Neutrality Act establishing an impartial arms embargo and placing all American trade with belligerents on a "cash and carry" basis. Roosevelt had long criticized the arms embargo because it did not distinguish between aggressor and victim, and although he ultimately succeeded in repealing it, he was again forced to settle for "half a loaf," in part because of the continuing suspicions of Senate conservatives.

Two proposals for neutrality revision were considered by the Senate in early July. The House's Bloom Resolution preserved the embargo on the sale of arms and ammunition, allowing traffic only in "implements of war," and also retained the cash and carry provision on all trade with belligerents.[26] The other proposal, embracing the Administration's position, was a resolution sponsored by the Foreign Relations Committee chairman, Key Pittman of Nevada, that repealed the arms embargo completely and placed all trade with belligerents on a cash and carry basis. Despite the differences between the two resolutions, critics of neutrality revision argued that because both proposed to change the arms embargo, they impaired American neutrality and increased the threat of war. Both resolutions, critics also charged, vested more discretionary power in the President. Indeed, opposition to both measures was so intense that most political observers refused to predict the outcome of the Senate committee's action.[27]

Although the Administration had placed a high priority on neutrality revision, Senate opponents were well prepared. On 7 July, two days before the Foreign Relations Committee began its deliberations, a group estimated to number thirty-four, equally representing both parties, met in the office of California Republican, Hiram Johnson, to lay their plans.[28] In choosing to coalesce around Johnson, opponents of neutrality revision picked a formidable leader. Seventy-two years old in 1939 and a senator since 1917, Johnson had a long record of faithful service to American isolationism. One of the architects of the Senate's rejection of U.S. participation in the League of Nations in 1919, the California Republican had been equally resolute in his opposition to American membership in the World Court during the 1920s. Yet as Senate consideration of neutrality revision began in July 1939, Johnson's politics were increasingly anachronistic in the emerging urban, industrial society. The California Republican represented a vanishing breed of western Republican Progressive that stood for the values of small-town, rural, agrarian America. Fiercely isolationist in foreign affairs, old Progressives like Johnson had mostly become by the late 1930s bitter opponents of FDR's domestic reform, seeing in its increasing reliance on government power and collectivist solutions, a threat to the individualism they valued so strongly. Thus, although they had begun their political career as liberals, by the late 1930s western Republican Progressives were often regarded as conservatives because their views had remained constant in the face of the political upheaval of the 1930s. To Johnson and other Progressives, therefore, FDR's goal of repealing the arms embargo represented a double-barreled threat because it promised both to entangle America in international affairs and to expand presidential power.[29]

On 11 July, four days after the meeting in Hiram Johnson's office, critics of neutrality revision on the Foreign Relations Committee seized the initiative. Immediately after the Committee convened, Bennett Clark moved to postpone any revision until 1940 and, to the great surprise of Administration supporters, the Clark motion was approved, 12–11. Voting to postpone were the five Republicans on the committee (Hiram Johnson, Arthur Vandenberg, Wallace White, William Borah, and Arthur Capper), along with five conservative Democrats (Bennett Clark, Walter George, Robert Reynolds, Guy Gillette, and Frederick Van Nuys), Farmer-Laborite Henrik Shipstead, and Progressive Robert LaFollette. That concern with the nation's foreign policy was not the only issue explaining the Administration's defeat was apparent to Josiah Bailey. Writing in February before the issue had even been broached, the North Carolina Democrat observed that "there is a considerable group here who wish to get this country involved in a war on the theory that once we get into a war, dictatorship will be inevitable. Those of us who are so strong for peace are thinking not only of the dreadfulness of war, but about the consequences in the Republic. We believe that the existence of war would be made the pretext for the abandonment of the constitution once and forever and the taking over of all rights, human and property." Regardless of the motives behind the committee's action, however, the failure of neutrality revision was another clear sign of the growing influence Senate conservatives exerted over the legislative agenda in 1939, thanks largely to the independent voting by Democrats.[30]

In a broader sense the Senate's action on neutrality revision emphasized the degree to which opposition to FDR's foreign policy in 1939 was rooted in the same rural, agrarian values that had fed conservative resistance to the domestic New Deal throughout the

1930s. Senate opponents of neutrality revision were concerned not only with entanglement in foreign affairs, but also with the increase in presidential power that repeal of the impartial arms embargo would produce. As the historian Justus Doenecke has argued, while not all isolationists were conservatives, the two groups were motivated by the same desire to preserve the values of rural, agrarian America. "Intervention, such conservatives believed, would hasten the most destructive trends of Roosevelt's domestic program, with war thrusting powerful and despotic labor unions and a federal 'octopus' upon the country. The independent businessman would lose his autonomy, and the days of the open shop, low taxes, and 'free enterprise' would be gone forever. Fiscal solvency, clean and limited government, rural and small-town values, economic individualism, a self-determined foreign policy—all appeared interconnected and all appeared beyond recall."[31]

If conservative opponents of the New Deal seemed to be gaining the upper hand throughout the summer of 1939, the German invasion of Poland on 1 September quickly altered political alignments in the Senate. The naked German aggression thrust foreign policy to the forefront and much of the debate centered on the continuation of the arms embargo. Throughout the fall internationalists argued that repeal of the embargo was essential to defeat Hitler, whereas isolationists countered that with war now declared, relaxation of the neutrality act would surely lead to American involvement. While the foreign policy crisis hardened the position maintained by the internationalists and the isolationists, it also seemed to convince many conservative Democrats to abandon their independent voting habits and rally around their President. And with many Democratic conservatives at least temporarily back in the Administration fold, the incipient Senate rebellion against the White House rapidly dissipated.

Two weeks after German armies marched into Poland, a somber Franklin Roosevelt called a special session of Congress for 21 September to consider immediate repeal of the arms embargo. This action, the President contended, by returning American trade to the rule of international law, would best preserve neutrality. Senate isolationists were not persuaded. Meeting in Hiram Johnson's office following the President's address, twenty-four senators vowed to fight against any and all revisions to the neutrality act. Although the isolationists' statement raised Administration concern that the forces that had defeated neutrality revision in July were again mobilizing for action, noticeably absent from the opposition's ranks were four conservative members of the Foreign Relations Committee, Walter George, Guy Gillette, Robert Reynolds, and Wallace White, all of whom had voted against revision in the summer.[32]

The change in political alignments produced by the foreign policy crisis was more apparent in action taken by the Foreign Relations Committee. On 24 September the committee began debate on a bill, drafted by Chairman Key Pittman and fourteen committee Democrats, that repealed the arms embargo, authorized the President to extend ninety-day credits to foreign purchasers of U.S. goods, and created "war zones" in hostile waters from which all American ships and citizens were banned. Because isolationists on the committee decided to husband their energies to fight neutrality revision on the Senate floor, the Pittman bill was easily approved four days later by the margin of 16 to 7. Importantly, the vote revealed that the victorious coalition was composed of Administration stalwarts such as Elbert Thomas, Robert Wagner, and Claude Pepper who had long supported neutrality revision, and four conservatives, Walter George, Guy Gillette, Frederick Van Nuys, and Wallace White, who had voted in July to postpone neutrality revision.[33]

Senate floor debate on the Pittman bill proved to be far more intense and bitter. Although the three-week-long debate centered on technical questions of international law and neutrality that were raised by the proposed changes, most analysts agreed that the underlying issue continued to be the President's discretionary power.[34] To defuse the issue of Executive power, the Administration signaled its willingness on 16 October to compromise on every provision of the Pittman bill save repeal of the arms embargo. Eight days later the Senate approved by voice vote two amendments sponsored by Key Pittman and Tom Connally of Texas, removing the ninety-day credit provision and the absolute ban on U.S. shipping in belligerent waters.[35] The speedy acceptance of the amendments ensured that repeal of the arms embargo would succeed. Thereafter, all limiting amendments proposed were easily defeated by a coalition of Administration stalwarts and conservatives who had been convinced that deteriorating international conditions warranted modification of American foreign policy. Rejected on 24 October, for instance, was a Taft amendment establishing a three-hundred-mile combat zone around Europe from which U.S. ships would be prohibited, as well as a Danaher amendment barring the export of American aircraft until the Army and the Navy Air Corps had received three thousand new planes. On both votes, such conservatives as Walter George, Guy Gillette, James Byrnes, Richard Russell, Frederick Van Nuys, Edwin Johnson, and Wallace White, who earlier in the year had regularly spurned White House initiatives, voted consistently with the Administration against the core of Senate isolationists. Following the Administration victories on all limiting amendments, the final approval of the Pittman bill was a foregone conclusion. After summarily turning back a last-minute effort by isolationist Bennett Clark to reinstitute a mandatory arms embargo, on 27 October the Senate approved the Pittman bill by a 63–30 margin.[36]

Taken as a whole, Senate action in 1939 underscored the crucial role Democrats played in the conservative opposition to the New Deal in the late 1930s. When conservative Democrats broke free from the ties of party loyalty or White House intimidation, the Roosevelt Administration suffered some important setbacks. Indeed, in the first seven months of 1939, conservative votes helped slash WPA relief funds, reduce appropriations in the Spend-Lend bill, temporarily eliminate the President's monetary devaluation powers, and spurn the White House's request for Neutrality revision.

The growing independence felt by many Senate Democrats throughout most of 1939 is also apparent in table 1–5. While most of those senators who scaled in the medium support group in the 76th Congress occupied the same position in the previous Congress, the middle-scale position was strengthened in part by the addition of six senators who had given high support to the Administration in the 75th Congress. Importantly, five of these six additions were Democrats: David I. Walsh of Massachusetts, John Overton of Louisiana, Prentiss Brown of Michigan, and Guy Gillette and Clyde Herring of Iowa. Particularly in the cases of Gillette, a survivior of the ill-conceived 1938 "purge," and of Herring, his Iowa colleague who had openly supported him, appeals from the White House for support appear to have been less successful. (The sixth senator was Independent Henrik Shipstead, an avowed isolationist, whose reduced support for the Administration was, as tables 1–6 and 1–7 indicate, a response to the preparedness measures of late 1939 and 1940.)

Table 1–5 also reveals that membership replacement added two more Democrats to the medium support category. In the 76th Congress, Scott Lucas of Illinois and D. Worth Clark of Idaho replaced William H. Dietrich and James P. Pope, respectively, both of whom had given the Administration high support in the 75th Congress.

If the pull of party loyalty was somewhat weaker among Senate Democrats throughout much of 1939, tables 1–6 and 1–7 also reveal that the outbreak of world war in September exerted a different sort of pressure that pushed some party members into stronger sup-

TABLE 1-5

76th CONGRESS

Name	Policy Dimensions	Score
	1 2 3 4 5 6 7 8 9 10 11 12	

HIGH SUPPORT

Name	Policy Dimensions	Score
Schwartz, D-WY	1 1 2 1 1 1 1 1 2 1 1 1	1.17
Neely, D-WV	2 2 1 1 1 1 1 1 1 1 1 1	1.17
Lee, D-OK	2 1 1 0 0 1 1 1 2 1 1 1	1.20
Wagner, D-NY	1 1 1 1 1 1 1 1 3 2 1 1	1.25
Thomas, D-UT	2 1 1 1 1 1 1 1 3 1 1 1	1.25
Sheppard, D-TX	2 1 1 2 1 2 1 1 1 1 1 1	1.25
Mead, D-NY	2 2 1 1 1 1 1 1 2 1 1 1	1.25
Caraway, D-AR	2 2 1 0 0 0 1 0 1 1 1 1	1.25
Minton, D-IN	3 1 1 2 1 1 1 1 1 1 1 1	1.25
Green, D-RI	2 1 1 0 1 1 1 3 1 1 1 1	1.27
Thomas, D-OK	3 1 1 1 0 1 1 0 2 1 1 1	1.30
Smathers, D-NJ	3 1 1 0 0 1 1 2 1 1 1 1	1.30
Slattery, D-IL	3 0 0 2 1 1 0 1 1 1 1 1	1.33
Pepper, D-FL	3 1 1 2 1 1 1 1 1 2 1 1	1.34
Hill, D-AL	3 1 1 2 1 1 1 2 1 1 1 1	1.34
Truman, D-MO	2 0 1 2 2 2 1 1 1 1 1 1	1.36
Bilbo, D-MS	3 1 1 2 1 1 1 2 1 1 0 1	1.36
Norris, I-NE	1 1 2 1 3 1 1 2 1 1 2 1	1.42
Barkley, D-KY	2 1 1 2 2 2 1 1 2 1 1 1	1.42
Murray, D-MT	3 1 1 1 1 1 1 1 1 3 2 1	1.42
Schwellenbach, D-WA	3 1 2 1 1 1 1 1 2 1 2 1	1.42
O'Mahoney, D-WY	1 0 2 1 1 1 1 1 3 3 1 1	1.45
Andrews, D-FL	2 1 1 3 2 1 1 1 1 0 2 1	1.45
Ellender, D-LA	3 2 1 2 1 1 0 2 1 1 1 1	1.45
Russell, D-GA	2 1 1 2 2 2 2 2 1 1 1 1	1.50
Hatch, D-NM	2 1 2 2 1 2 1 2 2 1 1 1	1.50
Guffey, D-PA	3 2 1 2 1 1 1 1 3 1 1 1	1.50
Bone, D-WA	0 0 2 0 2 1 1 1 1 2 2 0	1.50
Downey, D-CA	1 0 2 1 1 1 1 1 1 3 2 3	1.55
Pittman, D-NV	2 1 2 1 1 1 2 0 1 3 2 1	1.55
Hayden, D-AZ	3 1 1 2 1 2 1 2 1 1 1 1	1.55

Name	Policy Dimensions	Score
	1 2 3 4 5 6 7 8 9 10 11 12	

HIGH SUPPORT continued

Stewart, D-TN	3 1 1 2 2 2 0 2 1 1 1 1	1.55
Chavez, D-NM	3 1 2 1 1 1 1 1 2 2 1 3	1.58
Hughes, D-DE	3 2 1 2 1 1 1 3 1 1 1 1	1.58

MEDIUM SUPPORT

Wheeler, D-MT	2 2 2 1 2 1 2 1 1 0 2 2	1.64
Connally, D-TX	3 2 1 2 0 2 2 2 1 1 1 1	1.64
Bankhead, D-AL	3 2 1 3 1 2 1 2 1 1 0 1	1.64
Byrnes, D-SC	3 0 2 2 1 2 1 2 2 1 1 1	1.64
LaFollette, I-WI	1 1 2 1 1 1 1 1 2 3 3 3	1.67
Overton, D-LA	2 2 1 3 0 0 2 1 1 1 1 2	1.67
McKellar, D-TN	3 1 1 2 2 2 2 3 1 1 1 1	1.67
Reynolds, D-NC	2 1 2 2 0 2 2 2 1 1 2 2	1.73
Maloney, D-CT	3 1 2 1 0 1 1 2 3 2 2 1	1.73
Clark, D-ID	2 1 2 2 1 1 1 2 1 2 3 3	1.75
Shipstead, I-MN	2 2 3 1 1 2 2 1 1 3 3 3	1.75
Gillette, D-IA	2 0 1 2 1 3 3 2 2 1 2 1	1.82
Brown, D-MI	3 1 2 1 1 2 0 3 3 1 2 1	1.82
Lucas, D-IL	3 0 2 2 1 2 2 3 2 1 1 1	1.82
McCarran, D-NV	1 2 2 1 2 2 2 1 1 3 2 3	1.83
Ashurst, D-AZ	2 0 2 1 0 2 0 1 2 3 2 2	1.89
Nye, R-ND	1 0 2 1 0 2 1 1 2 3 3 3	1.90
Frazier, R-ND	2 2 0 1 2 1 1 1 2 3 3 3	1.91
Harrison, D-MS	2 3 1 3 0 2 3 2 2 1 1 1	1.91
Lundeen, I-MN	0 2 3 1 2 1 1 1 1 3 3 3	1.91
Miller, D-AR	3 2 2 3 2 2 2 2 1 1 1 2	1.92
Johnson, D-CO	2 1 2 3 2 1 2 2 1 3 3 2	2.00
George, D-GA	2 0 2 3 2 3 3 2 1 1 2 1	2.00
Smith, D-SC	2 0 2 3 2 3 3 0 1 1 2 1	2.00
Donahey, D-OH	3 2 2 0 0 1 0 0 2 1 2 3	2.00
Herring, D-IA	3 0 2 3 1 3 2 2 2 1 2 1	2.00
Capper, R-KS	1 2 3 1 3 2 3 1 1 2 3 3	2.08
VanNuys, D-IN	2 0 2 2 2 3 3 1 3 2 2 1	2.09
Radcliffe, D-MD	0 0 2 3 3 2 3 3 2 1 1 1	2.10
Bailey, D-NC	3 0 2 3 3 3 0 0 0 1 1 1	2.13

Name	Policy Dimensions	Score
	1 2 3 4 5 6 7 8 9 10 11 12	

MEDIUM SUPPORT continued

Name	Policy Dimensions	Score
Davis, R-PA	1 3 3 1 3 2 0 1 3 3 2 2	2.18
Adams, D-CO	3 0 2 1 2 3 2 3 3 2 2 1	2.18
Walsh, D-MA	2 2 2 1 3 2 3 2 3 2 2 3	2.25
Bulow, D-SD	3 3 2 3 2 3 2 1 1 2 2 3	2.25
Clark, D-MO	2 0 2 2 2 2 3 2 3 1 3 3	2.27

LOW SUPPORT

Name	Policy Dimensions	Score
Burke, D-NE	1 0 3 3 2 3 3 2 3 0 1 1	2.30
Austin, R-VT	1 3 3 2 3 2 3 1 3 3 2 0	2.36
Wiley, R-WI	1 0 3 0 0 0 3 2 1 3 3 3	2.38
Holman, R-OR	1 2 3 3 3 3 3 1 3 3 1 3	2.42
Hale, R-ME	1 2 3 3 3 3 3 3 2 1 2	2.42
Gerry, D-RI	2 3 3 1 3 3 3 3 3 2 1 2	2.42
White, R-ME	1 3 3 3 3 0 3 3 3 2 1 2	2.45
Tydings, D-MD	2 3 3 3 3 3 3 0 3 1 1 2	2.45
Barbour, R-NJ	2 3 3 0 3 2 2 2 3 3 2 2	2.45
Glass, D-VA	3 2 2 3 0 3 3 3 3 2 1 2	2.45
McNary, R-OR	1 2 3 0 0 3 3 2 2 3 3 3	2.50
Holt, D-WV	2 2 3 1 3 3 3 2 3 3 2 3	2.50
Gibson, R-VT	0 3 3 2 2 3 3 1 3 3 0 2	2.50
Reed, R-KS	1 3 3 3 3 3 3 1 2 3 3 0	2.55
Bridges, R-NH	1 0 3 3 3 3 3 3 3 3 1 2	2.55
Johnson, R-CA	1 2 3 2 0 3 0 0 3 3 3 3	2.56
King, D-UT	3 3 3 0 3 3 2 0 0 3 2 1	2.56
Danaher, R-CT	1 3 3 1 3 3 3 3 3 2 3 3	2.58
Gurney, R-SD	1 3 3 3 3 3 3 3 3 3 1 2	2.58
Byrd, D-VA	3 3 3 3 3 3 3 3 3 1 1 2	2.58
Townsend, R-DE	1 3 3 3 3 3 3 3 3 2 0 2	2.64
Lodge, R-MA	1 3 3 0 3 3 3 3 3 3 1 3	2.64
Taft, R-OH	1 3 3 2 3 3 3 3 3 3 3 2	2.67
Vandenberg, R-MI	2 3 3 1 3 3 3 3 3 3 3 3	2.75
Tobey, R-NH	2 3 3 3 3 3 3 3 3 3 2 3	2.83

Policy Dimension Key:

    0   denotes that a senator did not scale on the dimension

    1.   Extension of Federal Authority

    2.   Public Power

    3.   Extension of Executive Power

    4.   Labor

    5.   Business Regulation

    6.   Social Welfare

    7.   Economy in Government Spending

    8.   Fiscal Policy

    9.   Agriculture

    10.   Reciprocal Trade

    11.   National Defense

    12.   Foreign Aid

76TH CONGRESS (N=94)

HIGH SUPPORT (N=34 or 36%)

Democrats	= 33 (97%)
GOP	= 0 (0%)
Independents =	1 (3%)

MEDIUM SUPPORT (N=35 or 37%)

Democrats	= 28 (80%)
GOP	= 4 (11%)
Independents =	3 (9%)

LOW SUPPORT (N=25 or 27%)

Democrats	= 7 (28%)
GOP	= 18 (72%)
Independents =	0 (0%)

port of the Administration. The international crisis propelled Josiah Bailey of North Carolina and Edward Burke of Nebraska into the high support group on foreign policy, as well as Francis Maloney of Connecticut into the medium support group. All three Democrats had been staunch opponents of the New Deal in the 75th Congress. Similarly, foreign policy considerations led Democrats Richard Russell, Tom Connally, Hattie Caraway, and Charles Andrews, all of whom had offered only medium support in the 75th Congress, into the high support group in the 76th. Thus, the statistical evidence underscores the conclusions suggested by the repeal of the arms embargo in October. The independence of many Senate Democrats was tenuous and when faced with the surge of patriotism unleashed by the start of World War II, many found it difficult to vote against the Administration's foreign policy.

TABLE 1-6

76th CONGRESS - FOREIGN POLICY DIMENSIONS

HIGH SUPPORT

Schwartz, D-WY	1.00	Connally, D-TX	1.00
Neely, D-WV	1.00	Bankhead, D-AL	1.00
Lee, D-OK	1.00	Byrnes, D-SC	1.00
Thomas, D-UT	1.00	McKellar, D-TN	1.00
Sheppard, D-TX	1.00	Lucas, D-IL	1.00
Mead, D-NY	1.00	Harrison, D-MS	1.00
Caraway, D-AR	1.00	Radcliffe, D-MD	1.00
Minton, D-IN	1.00	Bailey, D-NC	1.00
Green, D-RI	1.00	Burke, D-NE	1.00
Thomas, D-OK	1.00	Wagner, D-NY	1.33
Smathers, D-NJ	1.00	Pepper, D-FL	1.33
Slattery, D-IL	1.00	Norris, I-NE	1.33
Hill, D-AL	1.00	Schwellenbach, D-WA	1.33
Truman, D-MO	1.00	Overton, D-LA	1.33
Bilbo, D-MS	1.00	Gillette, D-IA	1.33
Barkley, D-KY	1.00	Brown, D-MI	1.33
Ellender, D-LA	1.00	Miller, D-AR	1.33
Russell, D-GA	1.00	George, D-GA	1.33
Hatch, D-NM	1.00	Smith, D-SC	1.33
Guffey, D-PA	1.00	Herring, D-IA	1.33
Hayden, D-AZ	1.00	Byrd, D-VA	1.33
Stewart, D-TN	1.00	Andrews, D-FL	1.50
Hughes, D-DE	1.00		

N = 45; D = 44; R = 0; I = 1

TABLE 1-6

76th CONGRESS - FOREIGN POLICY DIMENSIONS

MEDIUM SUPPORT

O'Mahoney, D-WY	1.67	Bone, D-WA	2.00
Reynolds, D-NC	1.67	Pittman, D-NV	2.00
Maloney, D-CT	1.67	Chavez, D-NM	2.00
VanNuys, D-IN	1.67	Wheeler, D-MT	2.00
Adams, D-CO	1.67	Donahey, D-OH	2.00
Hale, R-ME	1.67	Bridges, R-NH	2.00
Gerry, D-RI	1.67	King, D-UT	2.00
White, R-ME	1.67	Gurney, R-SD	2.00
Glass, D-VA	1.67	Townsend, R-DE	2.00
Murray, D-MT	2.00		

N = 19; D = 14; R = 5
Coastal = 9 (47%); Interior = 10 (53%)

LOW SUPPORT

Ashurst, D-AZ	2.33	Holt, D-WV	2.67
Davis, R-PA	2.33	Danaher, R-CT	2.67
Walsh, D-MA	2.33	Taft, R-OH	2.67
Bulow, D-SD	2.33	Tobey, R-NH	2.67
Clark, D-MO	2.33	LaFollette, I-WI	3.00
Holman, R-OR	2.33	Shipstead, I-MN	3.00
Barbour, R-NJ	2.33	Nye, R-ND	3.00
Lodge, R-MA	2.33	Frazier, R-ND	3.00
Austin, R-VT	2.50	Lundeen, I-MN	3.00
Gibson, R-VT	2.50	Wiley, R-WI	3.00
Downey, D-CA	2.67	McNary, R-OR	3.00
Clark, D-ID	2.67	Reed, R-KS	3.00
McCarran, D-NV	2.67	Johnson, R-CA	3.00
Johnson, D-CO	2.67	Vandenberg, R-MI	3.00
Capper, R-KS	2.67		

N = 29; D = 9; R = 17; I = 3
Coastal = 13 (45%); Interior = 16 (55%)

Senate Republicans, because they comprised only 25% of the upper house's membership, were again limited to a supporting role in the 76th Congress. When Democratic conservatives chose to support the Administration, GOP conservatives simply lacked the votes to influence the political agenda.

In light of political developments in 1938 and 1939, most studies of Congressional politics have understandably emphasized the growing power of the conservative coalition. It would be difficult to deny the power of the right wing in this era, yet such emphasis appears to draw an incomplete portrait of Senate alignments. For embedded in the political affairs in 1939 was evidence of the forces that were reshaping the conservatism of some senators. A clear sign of the transformation beginning in Senate conservatism was the presence of James J. Davis in the medium support category for both the 75th and 76th Congresses. Davis was a Republican and so largely immune to the partisan pressures affecting Democrats. Unlike the three other Republicans who scaled in the medium support level in these Congresses, moreover, Davis was not a western Pro-

TABLE 1-7

76th CONGRESS - DOMESTIC POLICY DIMENSIONS

HIGH SUPPORT

Downey, D-CA	1.13	Smathers, D-NJ	1.43
Schwartz, D-WY	1.22	Hill, D-AL	1.44
Neely, D-WV	1.22	Bilbo, D-MS	1.44
Wagner, D-NY	1.22	Norris, I-NE	1.44
Murray, D-MT	1.22	Schwellenbach, D-WA	1.44
LaFollette, I-WI	1.22	Andrews, D-FL	1.44
Lee, D-OK	1.29	Chavez, D-NM	1.44
Thomas, D-UT	1.33	Clark, D-ID	1.44
Sheppard, D-TX	1.33	Slattery, D-IL	1.50
Mead, D-NY	1.33	Truman, D-MO	1.50
Minton, D-IN	1.33	Frazier, R-ND	1.50
Pepper, D-FL	1.33	Lundeen, I-MN	1.50
Bone, D-WA	1.33	Barkley, D-KY	1.56
Green, D-RI	1.38	Hayden, D-AZ	1.56
O'Mahoney, D-WY	1.38	Wheeler, D-MT	1.56
Pittman, D-NV	1.38	McCarran, D-NV	1.56
Caraway, D-AR	1.40	Nye, R-ND	1.57
Thomas, D-OK	1.43	Ellender, D-LA	1.63

N = 36; D = 31; R = 2; I = 3

TABLE 1-7

76th CONGRESS - DOMESTIC POLICY DIMENSIONS

MEDIUM SUPPORT

Russell, D-GA	1.67	Donahey, D-OH	2.00
Hatch, D-NM	1.67	Wiley, R-WI	2.00
Guffey, D-PA	1.67	Lucas, D-IL	2.13
Hughes, D-DE	1.67	Walsh, D-MA	2.22
Shipstead, I-MN	1.67	Bulow, D-SD	2.22
Ashurst, D-AZ	1.67	Harrison, D-MS	2.25
Overton, D-LA	1.71	George, D-GA	2.25
Stewart, D-TN	1.75	Herring, D-IA	2.25
Reynolds, D-NC	1.75	VanNuys, D-IN	2.25
Maloney, D-CT	1.75	Clark, D-MO	2.25
Bankhead, D-AL	1.78	Smith, D-SC	2.29
Johnson, D-CO	1.78	McNary, R-OR	2.29
Connally, D-TX	1.88	Miller, D-AR	2.33
Byrnes, D-SC	1.88	Austin, R-VT	2.33
McKellar, D-TN	1.89	Johnson, R-CA	2.33
Capper, R-KS	1.89	Davis, R-PA	2.38
Gillette, D-IA	2.00	Adams, D-CO	2.38
Brown, D-MI	2.00		

N = 35; D = 28; R = 6; I = 1
Coastal = 13 (37%); Interior = 22 (63%)

LOW SUPPORT

Holman, R-OR	2.44	Glass, D-VA	2.75
Holt, D-WV	2.44	Bridges, R-NH	2.75
Reed, R-KS	2.44	Lodge, R-MA	2.75
Burke, D-NE	2.50	Taft, R-OH	2.75
Barbour, R-NJ	2.50	Gurney, R-SD	2.78
Gibson, R-VT	2.50	Townsend, R-DE	2.78
Danaher, R-CT	2.56	Bailey, D-NC	2.80
Radcliffe, D-MD	2.57	Tydings, D-MD	2.80
Hale, R-ME	2.67	King, D-UT	2.83
Gerry, D-RI	2.67	Tobey, R-NH	2.89
Vandenberg, R-MI	2.67	Byrd, D-VA	3.00
White, R-ME	2.75		

N = 23; D = 9; R = 14
Coastal = 17 (74%); Interior = 6 (26%)

gressive, but came from Pennsylvania, an orthodox Republican state that supported Herbert Hoover in 1932. Yet Pennsylvania was also a state with substantial urban and industrial interests that had been seriously affected by the Depression. That Davis scaled in the medium support position by 1938, and voted for such New Deal domestic initiatives as the Spend-Lend bill or the Fair Labor Standards Act, is an indication that he, like other conservatives, was moving toward a new conservatism that acknowledged the interdependency of individuals in the urban, industrial nation and accepted, consequently, an expanded role for the federal government.

Another indication of a transformation in Senate conservatism were the internecine squabbles within the GOP. Many Republicans, stressing the comeback their party had made in 1938 following its disastrous defeat two years earlier, continued to voice loud objections to the New Deal's active use of government power. Warren Austin of Vermont complained in March, for example, that the only way to bring about permanent economic recovery was to reduce government spending, cut taxes, and lower the budget deficit. "Government," he continued in terms that would have found favor with William McKinley, "should not intervene directly in industry beyond that minimum degree of regulation which tends to secure the maximum of competition." The same year, Vermont's governor, Republican George Aiken, who in 1940 would begin a long career in the Senate, expressed a more accommodating attitude on the positive state. Aiken, who had shocked many in the nation in 1937 when he castigated the GOP as an outdated party largely oblivious to the needs of the American people, explained to readers of the *Christian Science Monitor* that his support for the New Deal's basic social welfare principles was neither a case of political apostasy nor radicalism. Rather, it stemmed from an earnest desire to modernize his ideology. Just as the introduction of the power looms in England in the 1830s had created social upheaval and poverty, so too, he insisted, had America's industrial revolution of the late nineteenth and early twentieth centuries created human problems with which governments had to catch up. Those who resisted those changes could not be seen as conservatives; rather, he asserted, they were fools.[37]

While the ideas expressed by Aiken and the votes of Davis were undoubtedly influenced by the politics of an opposition party, it is also clear that each was struggling to define a new political ideology that adjusted traditional conservative values to the demands of the modern industrial state. That their views were not simply a case of "me-tooism" was made clear by Aiken. The Vermont Republican argued that as they weighed questions of social improvement, opponents of the New Deal had to consider carefully all proposed legislation and reject any that infringed too heavily on individual freedom or the free enterprise system.[38] It was equally clear that their views were also not a refurbished version of progressivism. In the late 1930s Robert and Phillip LaFollette, sons of one of the leading Progessives of the early 1900s, mounted an effort to revive the Progressive party. But their ideology, as *The Nation* made clear, stressed "frontier Populism" and individualism, thereby rejecting wholeheartedly the collective assumptions of the New Deal in favor of basic laissez faire notions.[39] Thus, Aiken's views, like the scale position of James J. Davis, it seems clear, were the beginning of a new conservatism in American politics.

2

The Nation at War, 1940–1942

THE DETERIORATING INTERNATIONAL CONDITIONS, CULMINATING with an American declaration of war in December 1941, dominated political affairs from 1940 to 1942. With American entry into World War II imminent in 1940 and 1941, the U.S. Senate increasingly concentrated its efforts on issues of national preparedness and defense. The patriotic fervor that swept the nation in this era temporarily altered the contours of Senate politics that had been evident in the late 1930s. Senate conservatives, and especially those from the Democratic side of the aisle, proved more willing in this time of national crisis to support the initiatives of their commander-in-chief. Thus, between 1940 and 1942 the stress lines that had begun to appear in Senate conservatism in previous sessions temporarily disappeared.

Of the many legislative measures approved during this period of war-bred unity, the First and Second War Powers Acts adopted in early 1942 were arguably most important to the transformation of Senate conservatism. For although these acts were designed to achieve a high degree of coordination in the defense effort, they realized this goal by allowing the President to organize the government as he saw fit. Most agencies that directed the war effort, then, were established by Executive order. If Senate conservatives in the late 1930s worried about the centralization of power in the White House, American participation in World War II greatly intensified these concerns.[1] Consequently, tensions between the Executive and Legislative branches formed the subtext of many debates in 1940 and 1941, and flared occasionally in 1942, though mainly on non-war issues. If the immediate effect of the international crisis was to temporarily close the developing fissures within conservatism, suspicions about FDR's leadership remained strong among Senate conservatives. In the long run, these suspicions, combined with a GOP resurgence in the 1942 elections, helped guarantee that conservative opposition to the Roosevelt Administration was only temporarily suppressed by the war. By war's end, the corrosive suspicions conservatives harbored about Franklin Roosevelt erupted into open warfare and allowed the stress lines within the right wing to reappear and deepen.[2]

I

The year 1940 was one of dramatic developments in international affairs. The Nazi blitzkrieg against western Europe in the spring shocked most Americans. By early June Adolf Hitler had conquered all of western Europe, leaving Great Britain as the last bulwark separating the United States from the armies of the Third Reich. The rapid change in the European war intensified concern in America over national preparedness and the outpouring of patriotism forged a sense of national unity, which quieted the incipient congressional rebellion.

It was also a presidential election year, which added considerably to the forces reshaping the political landscape. The major question that dominated domestic politics was Franklin Roosevelt's intentions regarding a third term. Although he refused to reveal his plans well into the spring, the possibility that the President might stand for re-election made most Senate Democrats, as had been true in 1938, reluctant to challenge their party's leader. Throughout 1940, the combination of election-year politics and the deteriorating international situation tended to override Senate conservatives' concerns with reducing federal expenditures and limiting the President's discretionary power.

That thoughts of the upcoming elections and the worsening international conditions overrode conservatives' concerns with the growth of Executive power was evident in the spring when the Senate considered bills to extend reciprocal trade and to reorganize the Civil Aeronautics Authority. In late March the Senate focused its attention on the President's request to extend the Reciprocal Trade Act for three years with no changes. Reciprocal trade had been criticized in the past by conservatives who charged that it gave the President power both to negotiate and to ratify treaties, thereby undermining the separation of power intended by the Constitution. Typical of their complaints were remarks made by Arthur Capper in February 1940. "No one man, nor any executive department," the Kansas Republican asserted, "should be given the power to negotiate trade agreements that affect so vitally the interests of American producers of farm commodities and other raw materials. . . ."[3]

In 1940, however, extension of reciprocal trade became a partisan issue that found only Senate Republicans voting to limit expansion of Executive power, while most conservative Democrats, who had opposed FDR on the 1937 Court-Packing bill and the 1938 Reorganization bill, voted to preserve their president's power.

The strongest test on reciprocal trade came on 29 March when a Key Pittman amendment requiring Senate ratification for all trade agreements was narrowly rejected, 44 to 41. Six days later additional amendments, including an O'Mahoney amendment requiring majority approval by both houses of Congress for all trade agreements and an Adams amendment requiring simple "approval" by the Senate of all new trade agreements were rejected handily. The following day after a Walsh amendment to limit extension of reciprocal trade to only one year was defeated 46–34, the three-year extension of the program was adopted by a 42–37 margin. All of the votes on reciprocal trade testified to the impact that an election year had on voting alignments. The Senate's twenty-three Republicans, including the normally internationalist Warren Austin, consistently ignored the desires of businessmen for lower tariffs and were, according to *Time,* united in opposition to reciprocal trade largely because it was advocated by Franklin Roosevelt. Similarly, the Democratic bloc, which fought off all attempts to limit extension of the trade program, was a mixture of economic self-interest and party politics. While concern for their states' economic development was undoubtedly a major factor leading many to favor reciprocal trade, the fact that the Administration was supported on this issue by such conservative Democrats as Guy Gillette, Bennett Clark, Frederick Van Nuys, George Radcliffe, Harry Byrd, Ellison D. "Cotton Ed" Smith, James Byrnes, Walter George, and Richard Russell, who in the past had often voted against expansion of Executive power, suggests that a desire to avoid embarrassing the President in an election year figured prominently in the voting alignments.[4]

The international crisis also appeared to alter the attitude of some conservatives on reciprocal trade. Some senators viewed the trade program as an American response to the Nazi blitzkrieg then raging across Europe. Democrat Pat Harrison of Mississippi, for example, supported extension in the belief that low tariffs would enable the U.S. to continue to trade with Western Europe, thereby strengthening those countries economically and reducing the possibility of American involvement in the war.[5] Regardless of their motivation, however, the vote to extend reciprocal trade indicated that Senate Democrats in 1940 were less inclined to oppose the Administration.

The same combination of election-year politics and foreign policy worries also explained the Senate's adoption of an Executive reorganization plan in the spring. In mid-April, Franklin Roosevelt surprised many on Capitol Hill by submitting a plan to change the Civil Aeronautics Authority from an independent government agency to a board within the Department of Commerce. Although the new board would continue to supervise the training of pilots, as the CAA had, the President's plan, by giving to the secretary of commerce control of the board's budget and personnel, raised fears that the new aviation authority would be susceptible to White House manipulation.[6] When the White House submitted a similar reorganization plan in 1938, concern over the expansion of Executive authority had produced a firestorm of opposition. Yet in 1940 the Senate gave easy approval to the changes in the CAA.

Although the House voted by a wide margin on 8 May to rescind the transfer of the aviation authority to the Commerce Department, the upper house on 14 May defeated a resolution offered by Patrick McCarran of Nevada to reject the reorganization plan. Senate Republicans again demonstrated their partisan determination to oppose the Administration's initiatives by offering unanimous support for the McCarran resolution. But numbered among the opponents of the resolution were such conservative Democrats as Guy Gillette, George Radcliffe, Millard Tydings, Carter Glass, Josiah Bailey, James Byrnes, Richard Russell, Pat Harrison, and Alva Adams, most of whom had voted against the expansion of Executive authority proposed in the 1938 Reorganization bill.[7]

The increased partisanship and more loyal party voting among Senate Democrats intensified in the summer of 1940 when Franklin Roosevelt's long-rumored attempt for a third term became official. The start of the German Luftwaffe's savage air war against Great Britain in August only added to these trends. Because the Battle of Britain raised doubts about the survival of the last European buffer between America and the Nazi blitzkrieg, it had a decisive impact on the way Americans viewed the war. As late as June, public opinion polls revealed that two-thirds believed it was more important for the U.S. to stay out of the war than it was to prevent Britain from being defeated. Polls taken in the midst of the Battle of Britain, however, revealed that one-half of those surveyed now believed it more important for the U.S. to aid Britain, even at the risk of American involvement, than it was to remain aloof from the European war.[8] Under such circumstances, then, it was not surprising that when the Senate turned its attention to preparedness measures in August, conservatives were largely powerless to thwart the Administration's agenda.

The first measure, a draft bill sponsored by Democrat Edward R. Burke of Nebraska in the Senate and by Republican James Wadsworth of New York in the House, reached the upper chamber in early August. Requiring all men between the ages of twenty-one and thirty-five to register for the country's first peacetime draft, the Burke-Wadsworth bill was immediately attacked along two fronts. By subjecting America's young men to one year's military service, some charged that the draft bill necessarily brought the country closer to war. Other critics charged that a peacetime draft was antithetical to the very principles upon which the nation was founded. Democrat Burton Wheeler argued, for instance, that passage of the bill "will slit the throat of the last Democracy still living."[9]

Despite the harshness of the opponents' rhetoric, the Burke-Wadsworth bill survived three weeks of Senate debate with little change. An amendment proposed by Democrats Richard Russell and John Overton, authorizing the President to seize and operate any company he deemed vital to the national defense, demonstrated how dramatically the international crisis had transformed Senate politics. Although both Russell and Overton had voted frequently in the late 1930s to lessen government's intrusion into the free enterprise system and to reduce the Executive's discretionary power, both felt in the summer of 1940 that the nation's defense was of paramount importance. As the Georgia Democrat explained to the president of the Jackson, Mississippi, Typographical Union, "I believe the principle of my amendment, which asserts that every resource of this country should be equally available to defend it, is as eternally right as any principal [sic] of democracy. . . . I could never accept the philosophy that any industry should be permitted to refuse to cooperate in the defense program while we are drafting men to serve for a dollar a day." Most Senate conservatives seemed to agree with Russell, for on 28 August the upper house voted 69–16 to add the Russell-Overton amendment to the draft bill. Included in the winning majority were such conservative Democrats as George Radcliffe, James Byrnes, Millard Tydings, Richard Russell, Joseph O'Mahoney, Carter Glass, Harry Byrd, and Josiah Bailey, as well as such eastern Republicans as Charles Tobey, Warren Austin, and Henry Cabot Lodge. Shortly after adoption of the Russell-Overton amendment, the draft bill was given final approval in a vote that again saw conservatives from both parties back the Administration.[10]

Further evidence of the alteration in the political agenda came in

September when the Senate, after less than two weeks of debate, approved the Second Revenue Act of 1940. The need for additional revenue to pay for the defense build-up and the concern that such spending created wartime profiteering seemed to overwhelm conservatives' previous opposition to the Administration's antibusiness course. For chief among the features of the Senate's tax bill adopted on 19 September were an excess profits tax, a 3.1% increase in all brackets of the regular corporate tax rate, and a 10% surtax on any portion of the excess profits a corporation derived directly from defense contracts. Although the final version of the Senate's tax bill eased the computation of the tax burden favored by the House, the upper chamber had nevertheless approved a tax on excess profits, over the protests of businessmen, that was similar to the measure that had spawned open rebellion against the Administration in 1938.[11] The vote on final passage of the tax bill again revealed that the desire of conservatives for legislation that reduced government's intrusion into the free enterprise system had been at least temporarily superseded by their concern with national preparedness.[12]

Taken collectively, Senate action in 1940 revealed the ephemeral nature of conservatives' power at the start of the war. Despite their success in the late 1930s, when faced with the deteriorating international situation and FDR's re-election campaign, voting alignments reverted to patterns reminiscent of the early New Deal. Senate Democrats in 1940, for the most part, voted out of mixture of patriotism and party loyalty to uphold most White House initiatives. Republicans in the upper house, on the other hand, reverted to the strongly partisan behavior that had characterized the GOP in the early 1930s.

Table 2–1 reflects the changes that occurred in the 1940 Senate. Although the scale scores are somewhat distorted because the 76th Congress spanned two years: 1939, which saw an increase in Democratic independence until the outbreak of war; and 1940, which was dominated by preparedness, patriotism, and national unity, the increased partisanship is apparent. Ten Democrats who had served in the 75th Congress increased the level of support they gave the Administration in the 76th. Seven of them, Russell of Georgia, Chavez of New Mexico, O'Mahoney of Wyoming, Andrews of Florida, Pittman of Nevada, Connally of Texas, and Caraway of Arkansas, moved from the medium support scale position in the 75th to the high support group in the 76th. Perhaps testifying more powerfully to the influence exerted by party loyalty in 1940 was the movement of three strong critics of the New Deal, Bailey of North Carolina,

TABLE 2-1

76th CONGRESS

Name	Policy Dimensions	Score
	1 2 3 4 5 6 7 8 9 10 11 12	

HIGH SUPPORT

Name	Policy Dimensions	Score
Schwartz, D-WY	1 1 2 1 1 1 1 1 2 1 1 1	1.17
Neely, D-WV	2 2 1 1 1 1 1 1 1 1 1 1	1.17
Lee, D-OK	2 1 1 0 0 1 1 1 2 1 1 1	1.20
Wagner, D-NY	1 1 1 1 1 1 1 1 3 2 1 1	1.25
Thomas, D-UT	2 1 1 1 1 1 1 1 3 1 1 1	1.25
Sheppard, D-TX	2 1 1 2 1 2 1 1 1 1 1 1	1.25
Mead, D-NY	2 2 1 1 1 1 1 1 2 1 1 1	1.25
Caraway, D-AR	2 2 1 0 0 0 1 0 1 1 1 1	1.25
Minton, D-IN	3 1 1 2 1 1 1 1 1 1 1 1	1.25
Green, D-RI	2 1 1 0 1 1 1 3 1 1 1 1	1.27
Thomas, D-OK	3 1 1 1 0 1 1 0 2 1 1 1	1.30
Smathers, D-NJ	3 1 1 0 0 1 1 2 1 1 1 1	1.30
Slattery, D-IL	3 0 0 2 1 1 0 1 1 1 1 1	1.33
Pepper, D-FL	3 1 1 2 1 1 1 1 1 2 1 1	1.34
Hill, D-AL	3 1 1 2 1 1 1 2 1 1 1 1	1.34
Truman, D-MO	2 0 1 2 2 2 1 1 1 1 1 1	1.36
Bilbo, D-MS	3 1 1 2 1 1 1 2 1 1 0 1	1.36
Norris, I-NE	1 1 2 1 3 1 1 2 1 1 2 1	1.42
Barkley, D-KY	2 1 1 2 2 2 1 1 2 1 1 1	1.42
Murray, D-MT	3 1 1 1 1 1 1 1 3 2 1	1.42
Schwellenbach, D-WA	3 1 2 1 1 1 1 1 2 1 2 1	1.42
O'Mahoney, D-WY	1 0 2 1 1 1 1 1 3 3 1 1	1.45
Andrews, D-FL	2 1 1 3 2 1 1 1 1 0 2 1	1.45
Ellender, D-LA	3 2 1 2 1 1 0 2 1 1 1 1	1.45
Russell, D-GA	2 1 1 2 2 2 2 2 1 1 1 1	1.50
Hatch, D-NM	2 1 2 2 1 2 1 2 2 1 1 1	1.50
Guffey, D-PA	3 2 1 2 1 1 1 1 3 1 1 1	1.50
Bone, D-WA	0 0 2 0 2 1 1 1 1 2 2 0	1.50
Downey, D-CA	1 0 2 1 1 1 1 1 1 3 2 3	1.55
Pittman, D-NV	2 1 2 1 1 1 2 0 1 3 2 1	1.55
Hayden, D-AZ	3 1 1 2 1 2 1 2 1 1 1 1	1.55

Name	Policy Dimensions	Score
	1 2 3 4 5 6 7 8 9 10 11 12	

HIGH SUPPORT continued

Name	Policy Dimensions	Score
Stewart, D-TN	3 1 1 2 2 2 0 2 1 1 1 1	1.55
Chavez, D-NM	3 1 2 1 1 1 1 1 2 2 1 3	1.58
Hughes, D-DE	3 2 1 2 1 1 1 3 1 1 1 1	1.58

MEDIUM SUPPORT

Name	Policy Dimensions	Score
Wheeler, D-MT	2 2 2 1 2 1 2 1 1 0 2 2	1.64
Connally, D-TX	3 2 1 2 0 2 2 2 1 1 1 1	1.64
Bankhead, D-AL	3 2 1 3 1 2 1 2 1 1 0 1	1.64
Byrnes, D-SC	3 0 2 2 1 2 1 2 2 1 1 1	1.64
LaFollette, I-WI	1 1 2 1 1 1 1 1 2 3 3 3	1.67
Overton, D-LA	2 2 1 3 0 0 2 1 1 1 1 2	1.67
McKellar, D-TN	3 1 1 2 2 2 2 3 1 1 1 1	1.67
Reynolds, D-NC	2 1 2 2 0 2 2 2 1 1 2 2	1.73
Maloney, D-CT	3 1 2 1 0 1 1 2 3 2 2 1	1.73
Clark, D-ID	2 1 2 2 1 1 1 2 1 2 3 3	1.75
Shipstead, I-MN	2 2 3 1 1 2 2 1 1 3 3 3	1.75
Gillette, D-IA	2 0 1 2 1 3 3 2 2 1 2 1	1.82
Brown, D-MI	3 1 2 1 1 2 0 3 3 1 2 1	1.82
Lucas, D-IL	3 0 2 2 1 2 2 3 2 1 1 1	1.82
McCarran, D-NV	1 2 2 1 2 2 2 1 1 3 2 3	1.83
Ashurst, D-AZ	2 0 2 1 0 2 0 1 2 3 2 2	1.89
Nye, R-ND	1 0 2 1 0 2 1 1 2 3 3 3	1.90
Frazier, R-ND	2 2 0 1 2 1 1 1 2 3 3 3	1.91
Harrison, D-MS	2 3 1 3 0 2 3 2 2 1 1 1	1.91
Lundeen, I-MN	0 2 3 1 2 1 1 1 1 3 3 3	1.91
Miller, D-AR	3 2 2 3 2 2 2 2 1 1 1 2	1.92
Johnson, D-CO	2 1 2 3 2 1 2 2 1 3 3 2	2.00
George, D-GA	2 0 2 3 2 3 3 2 1 1 2 1	2.00
Smith, D-SC	2 0 2 3 2 3 3 0 1 1 2 1	2.00
Donahey, D-OH	3 2 2 0 0 1 0 0 2 1 2 3	2.00
Herring, D-IA	3 0 2 3 1 3 2 2 2 1 2 1	2.00
Capper, R-KS	1 2 3 1 3 2 3 1 1 2 3 3	2.08
VanNuys, D-IN	2 0 2 2 2 3 3 1 3 2 2 1	2.09
Radcliffe, D-MD	0 0 2 3 3 2 3 3 2 1 1 1	2.10
Bailey, D-NC	3 0 2 3 3 3 0 0 0 1 1 1	2.13

Name	Policy Dimensions	Score
	1 2 3 4 5 6 7 8 9 10 11 12	

MEDIUM SUPPORT continued

Davis, R-PA	1 3 3 1 3 2 0 1 3 3 2 2	2.18
Adams, D-CO	3 0 2 1 2 3 2 3 3 2 2 1	2.18
Walsh, D-MA	2 2 2 1 3 2 3 2 3 2 2 3	2.25
Bulow, D-SD	3 3 2 3 2 3 2 1 1 2 2 3	2.25
Clark, D-MO	2 0 2 2 2 2 3 2 3 1 3 3	2.27

LOW SUPPORT

Burke, D-NE	1 0 3 3 2 3 3 2 3 0 1 1	2.30
Austin, R-VT	1 3 3 2 3 2 3 1 3 3 2 0	2.36
Wiley, R-WI	1 0 3 0 0 0 3 2 1 3 3 3	2.38
Holman, R-OR	1 2 3 3 3 3 3 1 3 3 1 3	2.42
Hale, R-ME	1 2 3 3 3 3 3 3 2 1 2	2.42
Gerry, D-RI	2 3 3 1 3 3 3 3 3 2 1 2	2.42
White, R-ME	1 3 3 3 3 0 3 3 3 2 1 2	2.45
Tydings, D-MD	2 3 3 3 3 3 3 0 3 1 1 2	2.45
Barbour, R-NJ	2 3 3 0 3 2 2 2 3 3 2 2	2.45
Glass, D-VA	3 2 2 3 0 3 3 3 3 2 1 2	2.45
McNary, R-OR	1 2 3 0 0 3 3 2 2 3 3 3	2.50
Holt, D-WV	2 2 3 1 3 3 3 2 3 3 2 3	2.50
Gibson, R-VT	0 3 3 2 2 3 3 1 3 3 0 2	2.50
Reed, R-KS	1 3 3 3 3 3 3 1 2 3 3 0	2.55
Bridges, R-NH	1 0 3 3 3 3 3 3 3 3 1 2	2.55
Johnson, R-CA	1 2 3 2 0 3 0 0 3 3 3 3	2.56
King, D-UT	3 3 3 0 3 3 2 0 0 3 2 1	2.56
Danaher, R-CT	1 3 3 1 3 3 3 3 3 2 3 3	2.58
Gurney, R-SD	1 3 3 3 3 3 3 3 3 3 1 2	2.58
Byrd, D-VA	3 3 3 3 3 3 3 3 3 1 1 2	2.58
Townsend, R-DE	1 3 3 3 3 3 3 3 3 2 0 2	2.64
Lodge, R-MA	1 3 3 0 3 3 3 3 3 3 1 3	2.64
Taft, R-OH	1 3 3 2 3 3 3 3 3 3 3 2	2.67
Vandenberg, R-MI	2 3 3 1 3 3 3 3 3 3 3 3	2.75
Tobey, R-NH	2 3 3 3 3 3 3 3 3 3 2 3	2.83

Policy Dimension Key:

0　　denotes that a senator did not scale on the dimension

1.　Extension of Federal Authority

2.　Public Power

3.　Extension of Executive Power

4.　Labor

5.　Business Regulation

6.　Social Welfare

7.　Economy in Government Spending

8.　Fiscal Policy

9.　Agriculture

10.　Reciprocal Trade

11.　National Defense

12.　Foreign Aid

76TH CONGRESS (N=94)

HIGH SUPPORT (N=34 or 36%)

Democrats	= 33 (97%)
GOP	= 0 (0%)
Independents =	1 (3%)

MEDIUM SUPPORT (N=35 or 37%)

Democrats	= 28 (80%)
GOP	= 4 (11%)
Independents =	3 (9%)

LOW SUPPORT (N=25 or 27%)

Democrats	= 7 (28%)
GOP	= 18 (72%)
Independents =	0 (0%)

Burke of Nebraska, and Maloney of Connecticut, from low support in the 75th to medium support in the 76th. Indeed, Bailey acknowledged to a constituent the change wrought on his voting behavior by the war. "I am very much inclined to sustain the President in the war effort. . . . If he asks for anything in the name of National Defense or . . . foreign policy, it is my disposition to sustain him. . . . We must have unity in our country in order that its power may be fully manifest in this day of ultimate trial."[13]

Table 2–1 indicates, on the other hand, that partisan politics continued to be the strongest influence on the other side of the aisle. Of the twenty-two GOP senators who scaled in the 76th Congress, eighteen continued to offer only low support to Administration initiatives in the 76th Congress. Of the four Republicans who scaled in the medium support categories, moreover, all but Davis of Pennsylvania were midwestern Progressives.

With patriotism and partisanship sharply delineating political alignments throughout 1940, there were few overt signs of the transformation of Senate conservatism that had begun in the late 1930s. The 1940 elections did see the replacement of several obstructionist conservatives with legislators who would espouse the principles of the "new" conservatism in the 1940s, including Republicans George Aiken of Vermont, who replaced Ernest Gibson; Ralph O. Brewster of Maine, who replaced Frederick Hale; and Harold Burton of Ohio, who succeeded Democrat A. Victor Donahey. Yet among the new members elected to the upper house in 1940 were also C. Wayland "Curly" Brooks of Illinois, Hugh Butler of Nebraska, and Raymond Willis of Indiana, who throughout their Senate careers would continue the obstructionist conservative battle against the New Deal. Similarly, some of the most conservative Democrats of the 1930s, including Harry Byrd of Virginia, Peter Gerry of Rhode Island, and Francis Maloney of Connecticut, were returned to the Senate in 1940 by the voters of their states.

If the election returns offered little new evidence of the transformation of Senate conservatism, other developments in 1940 pointed to the long-term forces that were reshaping the political right. In March 1940 a committee of 216 men and women led by Dr. Glenn Frank, former president of the University of Wisconsin, released the results of its two-year analysis of GOP voters' opinions. Based on its findings that rank and file Republican voters had become more liberal than they had been in 1936, the Frank Committee recommended that the party of Lincoln had to modify its total opposition to the New Deal in order to restore true two-party competition to U.S. politics.[14] Although the GOP was unable to escape its third

TABLE 2-2

Regional Divisions in Medium and Low Support Groups

MEDIUM SUPPORT (N=35)

Coastal (N=9 or 26%)

Byrnes, D-SC	Maloney, D-CT	Smith, D-SC
Reynolds, D-NC	Walsh, D-MA	Radcliffe, D-MD
George, D-GA	Davis, R-PA	Bailey, D-NC

Interior (N=26 or 74%)

Wheeler, D-MT	Connally, D-TX	Bankhead, D-AL
LaFollette, I-WI	Overton, D-LA	McKellar, D-TN
Clark, D-ID	Shipstead, I-MN	Gillette, D-IA
Brown, D-MI	Lucas, D-IL	McCarran, D-NV
Ashurst, D-AZ	Nye, R-ND	Frazier, R-ND
Harrison, D-MS	Lundeen, I-MN	Miller, D-AR
Johnson, D-CO	Donahey, D-OH	Herring, D-IA
Capper, R-KS	VanNuys, D-IN	Adams, D-CO
Bulow, D-SD	Clark, D-MO	

LOW SUPPORT (N=25)

Coastal (N=18 or 72%)

Austin, R-VT	Holman, R-OR	Hale, R-ME
Gerry, D-RI	White, R-ME	Tydings, D-MD
Barbour, R-NJ	Glass, D-VA	McNary, R-OR
Holt, D-WV	Gibson, R-VT	Bridges, R-NH
Johnson, R-CA	Danaher, R-CT	Byrd, D-VA
Townsend, R-DE	Lodge, R-MA	Tobey, R-NH

Interior (N=7 or 28%)

Burke, D-NE	Wiley, R-WI	Vandenberg, R-MI
Reed, R-KS	King, D-UT	
Gurney, R-SD	Taft, R-OH	

consecutive defeat in the presidential election of 1940, the changing nature of the electorate signaled by the Frank Committee provided additional impetus to Republican conservatives of the need to modernize their ideology.

II

The central dilemma facing the 77th Congress, which convened in January 1941, was how best to protect America's interests in a world fraught with peril. At the start of the new year, the nation's attention was focused on Britain, which had barely survived the Nazi blitzkrieg of the previous summer. If, as most observers expected, the Germans renewed their attack in spring, many argued that American aid was essential for Britain's survival. The strong patriotic feelings evoked by the international crisis again tended to paralyze Senate conservatives in 1941, as few were willing publicly to dissent from Administration measures aimed at preparing the nation for war. Although the 77th Congress generally proved to be a tractable one, many legislators were privately troubled by the actions taken to meet the crisis. These concerns, in turn, helped produce open rebellion against the Roosevelt Adminstration by war's end.

To meet the international challenge, the President in his annual message urged the new Congress to approve a massive program of aid to the democracies of the world, coupled with a rapid expansion of American weapons of war. The centerpiece of the President's defense program was the Lend-Lease measure, empowering him to lend or lease to Great Britain whatever war materiel he deemed necessary for its survival. Serving as the arsenal of democracy, FDR asserted to the assembled legislators, was the best way for America to protect its national interests without becoming entangled in the European war.[15] While Congressional response to the principle of aid for Britain was generally favorable, Senate debate indicated that many in the upper house believed that the Lend-Lease bill granted too much discretionary power to Franklin Roosevelt. The aging isolationist Hiram Johnson, who had led the opposition to revision of the Neutrality Act in 1939, again spoke out vehemently against Lend-Lease. Insisting that he desired to see Britain triumph over Germany, the California Republican asserted nonetheless that the President's proposal would do irreparable harm to the nation's democratic government and challenged Congress to resist what he believed was a drift toward totalitarianism. Similarly, Henry Cabot

Lodge Jr., who had voiced a more moderate position in the 1939 struggle over neutrality revision, denounced H.R. 1776 as a dictatorial bill that would weaken American democracy. Even the internationalist Warren Austin of Vermont, in announcing his support for the major goals of Lend-Lease on 11 January, advocated that the bill be modified to place a definite time limit on the powers granted to the Executive.[16]

The strong concern with Executive power was also reflected in two substitutes, proposed thirteen days after Lend-Lease had been introduced. While Democrat Edwin Johnson's plan simply authorized the President to turn over $2 billion worth of war materiel to Britain, provided that she make full reports to the U.S. on its effectiveness in warfare, Robert Taft's substitute was more specific. Under the Ohioan's proposal, the RFC was authorized to lend $1 billion to Britain, $500 million to Canada, and $50 million to Greece, whenever the President and the federal loan administrator certified that those countries had no funds to purchase war supplies. Additionally, Taft's proposal required that the recipients post security for the loans, unless the federal loan administrator found it to be impractical. Defending his substitute as a means to get aid to England more quickly than Lend-Lease, Taft emphasized that his goal was to ensure that Britain, and not FDR, was the sole beneficiary of this effort.[17]

Before either substitute attracted much support, however, the House Foreign Affairs Committee attached four amendments to Lend-Lease, which effectively eliminated the issue of Executive power from the debate. Acting with the tacit approval of the White House, as well as the full support of the liberal community, the House committee on 29 January placed a two-year limit on the act; required the President to report to Congress every ninety days on Lend-Lease; mandated that materiel to be transferred had first to be certified by the Army and Navy as unnecessary to U.S. defense; and prohibited the use of American ships as convoys.[18]

The House amendments appeared to allay Senate conservatives' fears about presidential power. For when the upper house finally began voting on 8 March, fifty-eight days after H.R. 1776 had been introduced, most conservatives voted consistently with Administration forces to reject all limiting amendments. Among the defeated proposals were an O'Mahoney amendment prohibiting the use of U.S. convoys outside the western hemisphere, a Walsh amendment barring further transfer of American naval ships to Britain, and the Taft amendment authorizing the President to lend a total of $2 billion to Britain, Canada, and Greece. Conservatives who voted with the White House to reject the Taft amendment, for example, included Democrats Walter George, James Byrnes, George Radcliffe, Richard Russell, John Bankhead; and Republicans Warren Barbour, Joseph Ball, and Wallace White. When the voting on final passage of H.R. 1776 was completed well past dinnertime, the 60 to 31 victory won by the Roosevelt Administration was again accomplished with the support of most Senate conservatives. The winning majority on final passage included a core of Administration supporters, such as Alben Barkley, Tom Connally, Claude Pepper, and Elbert Thomas, together with a bipartisan assortment of conservatives such as Warren Barbour, Harold Burton, Ralph Brewster, Henry Cabot Lodge, Wallace White, James Byrnes, Walter George, Joseph O'Mahoney, George Radcliffe, and Richard Russell, who in the past had often been critical of White House policies.[19]

The wide margin of the Administration's victory on Lend-Lease can easily distract attention away from the long-range impact the debate had on Senate voting alignments. Contemporary political observers viewed the vote as a sign that the Roosevelt Administration had been revived and revitalized by the emergency.[20] This analysis was, perhaps, accurate for the short term. Less apparent to contemporary observers, however, was that beneath the surface of national unity many senators continued to harbor suspicions about FDR's leadership. Writing in his diary the night the Senate gave final approval to Lend-Lease, Republican Arthur H. Vandenberg of Michigan complained bitterly about the implications of the act. "When H.R. 1776 passed the Senate . . . ," he noted angrily, "we did vastly more than to 'aid Britain.' . . . We have said to Britain: *'We will see you through to victory. . . .'* And we have said to the President . . . *'You* pick our allies; *you* pick our enemies; . . . *you* lend, lease or give away what you please. . . ; *you* are *monarch of all you survey.*"[21]

If Vandenberg's opinion was colored by his partisanship and his determined opposition to Lend-Lease, the same was not true of Richard Russell. Since his election to the Senate in 1932, the Georgia Democrat had often loyally supported Franklin Roosevelt and the New Deal. By the late 1930s, however, Russell, like many of his southern colleagues, had grown disenchanted with the pace and the direction of reform and had begun to vote more independently. Despite his doubts, Russell had stood stalwartly behind the Administration on Lend-Lease. Yet in a letter written to his mother early in the Senate debate, Russell revealed a private skepticism that was at odds with his voting record. "I am scared to death of this bill," he wrote to his mother on 5 February, "and have worried over it more than I ever have any piece of legislation. We have gone so far though, in 'Aid to Britain' that I don't guess we can stop. . . . I cannot but feel that in the future we will find out that the Congress has been deceived by half-truths by some of our high officials but in the circumstances we cannot get facts from any other source." The doubts voiced by Russell and Vandenberg continued to fester beneath the surface of public debate in the early war years and, once the air of crisis had passed, made many in the Senate willing to challenge the Administration's initiatives.[22]

In a broader sense, the final vote on Lend-Lease pointed to an emerging realignment of Senate voting patterns that sheds additional light on the transformation of Senate conservatism. The vote giving final approval to H.R. 1776 revealed two sectional blocs in the upper house. One bloc of senators from the twenty-five states consisting of New England, Atlantic seaboard, Ohio, and the South, supported Lend-Lease by a 6-to-1 margin, while the other bloc, composed of senators from the remaining twenty-three states, cast an absolute majority of votes against the bill.[23] Support for Lend-Lease, in other words, was strongest in the industrial and urban sections of the country, which were learning through the Depression and the world war that their security and their economic well-being were intimately tied to the international community. Opposition to Lend-Lease, on the other hand, came disproportionately from the rural, agrarian regions of America, whose existence was centered on farms and small businesses and which, as a consequence, felt no direct threat from European fascism nor any direct benefit from foreign trade. For similar reasons, throughout the 1940s support for governmental activism in domestic policy was also rooted in the urban, industrial regions.[24]

The effect of the international crisis on political alignments was further demonstrated in July 1941 when the Senate considered extension of Selective Service. One million young men had been inducted into the armed forces under the 1940 Burke-Wadsworth Act, but were scheduled to be released in September 1941. The steadily deteriorating international conditions during the first six months of 1941 convinced the Roosevelt Administration that retention of those inductees was critical to national defense. The Administration's case for draft extension was made by General George Marshall in testimony before the Senate Military Affairs Committee in July. Noting that draftees constituted anywhere from 50% to 85% of most Army divisions and that only two divisions were comprised of fewer than 30% draftees, Marshall warned that if the current German invasion of the Soviet Union succeeded, Hitler's troops would be within 100 miles of Alaska. For these reasons, Marshall urged Congress to extend the tenure of draftees for the duration of the national emergency, and to lift the ban on the use of national guardsmen and trainees outside of the western hemisphere and U.S. posessions.[25]

Several days after Marshall's testimony, Robert Reynolds of North Carolina, chairman of the Military Affairs Committee, introduced three resolutions embodying the Administration's position. The Reynolds resolutions extended the draft for the duration of the national emergency, permitted the President to use American troops anywhere in the world, and required national guardsmen and regular soldiers to serve until six months after the end of the national emergency. The three resolutions provoked intense debate in the upper house, in part, because suspicions that the Administration was using the national emergency as a pretext for expanding its power were heightened by Roosevelt's 7 July announcement that U.S. naval forces had occupied Iceland.[26] Pointing to the degree of concern over Executive power was Reynolds' unusual decision, announced on 12 July, to oppose the draft resolutions he had introduced only several days earlier. The North Carolina Democrat explained that he had sponsored the resolutions only at the behest of the War Department, but was now convinced that they conferred far too much power on the President. Republicans in both houses were similarly reported to be united in opposition to the resolution allowing the President to use American troops anywhere in the world.[27]

The debate over draft extension was altered somewhat on 14 July when, after a meeting with a group of Congressional leaders that included Sam Rayburn, Alben Barkley, Walter George, Robert Reynolds, and Warren Austin, Roosevelt agreed to shelve the resolution on the use of American troops anywhere in the world. Although the decision was made to mollify those concerned with the expansion of presidential power and hence speed passage of the two remaining resolutions, the effort failed.[28] Indeed, the extent of the Senate's distrust of FDR became apparent on 26 July when the Military Affairs Committee summarily rejected by a 9 to 1 vote a proposal from Secretary of War Henry Stimson to declare a national emergency. Under the order, the President would automatically have the power to extend the draft and to lift the 900,000-man limit on draftees. Concerned that the White House might use the emergency powers to lift the ban on the use of U.S. troops outside the Western Hemisphere, the Military Affairs Committee instead approved a resolution declaring a state of national peril to be met by a simple extension of the draft. Explaining the resolution to the press, Lister Hill, a liberal Democrat from Alabama on the committee, argued forthrightly that the declaration of a national emergency had been rejected because the committee was not prepared to confer such vast powers on the President.[29]

In an effort to overcome the mounting suspicion of Roosevelt's motives, the Administration offered an amendment on the third day of Senate debate. Introduced by the draft bill's floor manager, Elbert Thomas of Utah, the amendment extended draftees' term of service for eighteen months beyond the initial year, rather than for the duration of the emergency. That compromise still failed to appease all Senate critics. Burton Wheeler continued to insist on the Senate floor that the Thomas amendment actually repudiated the "contract" made by the 1940 Selective Service Act to limit service to one year, while Robert Taft prepared a new amendment, reducing draft extension to only six months.[30]

The first test of the Senate's sentiment on draft extension came on 5 August when a coalition of internationalists and conservatives handily rejected the Taft amendment. Moments later, Taft's Ohio colleague, Harold Burton, introduced another plan extending the draft by twelve months. Because Democratic leaders on the Military Affairs Committee, as well as Elbert Thomas, all voiced their approval, passage of the Burton amendment seemed certain until Majority Leader Alben Barkley exerted a new form of pressure the following day. Speaking on the Senate floor, Barkley disclosed that the War Department believed that anything less than an eighteen-month extension would impede national defense and used this revelation to implore his colleagues to support the President. The majority leader's plea apparently succeeded in convincing most Democratic conservatives to support the President, for when the Senate voted on the Burton amendment on 6 August, Administration forces prevailed easily by a vote of 50 to 21. Until Barkley's plea for national unity, for example, Democrats Josh Lee of Oklahoma and "Happy" Chandler of Kentucky, both vigorous Administration supporters on draft extension, were prepared to accept the Burton amendment. They subsequently voted against it.[31]

Following defeat of the Burton amendment, action on draft extension was anticlimactic. In a night session on 7 August, the Thomas amendment to extend Selective Service by eighteen months was adopted by a 44 to 28 vote and then the Senate quickly approved the revised bill, 45–30. On both votes most Senate conservatives, apparently convinced that the international crisis warranted a limited extension of the draft, joined with internationalists to hand the Roosevelt Administration yet another important foreign policy victory.[32]

The vote approving draft extension, like the earlier adoption of Lend-Lease, provided solid proof of Franklin Roosevelt's continuing ability to lead Congress on foreign policy questions. When acceptance of the Administration's demand for an eighteen-month extension of selective service seemed doubtful, the President had skillfully used the air of crisis engendered by the international situation to appeal to the patriotism and party loyalty of wavering senators. FDR's tactics helped to overcome concerns with the expansion of Executive power and in the end, many Senate conservatives decided not to challenge the President's judgment in a time of national peril. Yet as was true in the case of Lend-Lease, distrust of FDR's leadership had been submerged only temporarily. One indication of the residue of suspicion that remained in the Senate came in the frustration Republican Charles Tobey expressed to a constituent on the day Majority Leader Barkley had made his plea for national unity. "Some day," he sputtered, "the common people of this country will wake up and realize what the President has done to our democratic way of life here; his dissipation of power; giving only lip service to the Constitution. . . . When one has this in mind, together with the fiscal situation of the nation and the broken promises which were made to the mothers and fathers of the country, it is difficult not to at least have righteous indignation."[33]

The ability of the national emergency to redraw the political landscape was demonstrated a third time in 1941 by the question of neutrality revision. The worsening international situation throughout the fall, highlighted by the 4 September attack of a German submarine on an American destroyer, the USS *Greer*, convinced the Roosevelt Administration that more stringent measures were necessary to defend national security. To enhance America's defense, on 11 September the President issued "shoot-on-sight" orders to American naval forces, and in early October announced that he would seek major revisions in the 1939 Neutrality Act. The Administration's modifications, introduced in late October by Tom Connally, the chairman of the Foreign Relations Committee, called for repeal of those sections of the 1939 act that forbade American merchant ships from arming themselves and that banned U.S. ships from belligerent ports.[34]

Even before the Connally Resolution had been formally introduced, Senate sentiment on neutrality revision was divided into liberal, moderate, and conservative groupings that had often characterized previous foreign policy debates. An AP poll taken of the Senate on 4 October, for instance, revealed three distinct groups. Twenty-nine senators, including Alben Barkley, Tom Connally, Robert Wagner, and Warren Austin, indicated that they would vote for either the Connally Resolution or total repeal of the Neutrality Act. Twenty other senators responding to the poll, including such isolationists as Hiram Johnson, Bennett Clark, Burton Wheeler, and Gerald P. Nye, were opposed to any modification of the Neutrality Act. Between the internationalists and the isolationists was a small group of moderates, including Walter George, George Radcliffe, Clyde Herring, Francis Maloney, and Henry Cabot Lodge, who were willing to allow U.S. merchant ships to arm themselves, but were opposed to any other change. Explaining his position during Senate debate, Lodge maintained that because evidence suggested American goods were reaching Britain, the Administration's request to allow U.S. ships to call on belligerent ports went beyond shoring up the nation's defense.[35]

The attack on the USS *Reuben James* in the north Atlantic in late October, however, swiftly altered previous alignments. Although opposition to revision of the major sections of the Neutrality Act had mounted steadily throughout October, the attack on the *Reuben James,* which killed 100 Americans, brought home the gravity of the international crisis. In this atmosphere of heightened danger, the middle ground on neutrality revision disappeared. Most of the moderates on neutrality revision followed the path taken by Walter George. Two days after the attack, the Georgia Democrat told his constituents in a radio address that he was now prepared to vote for total repeal of the Neutrality Act. Warning that the current neutrality legislation tied the hands of U.S. policymakers, George contended that the 1939 law was no longer relevant to the international threat posed in late 1941. A few of the moderates responded differently to the *Reuben James* incident. Democrat Francis Maloney of Connecticut who, like George, had supported only limited revision in early October, announced during floor debate on 3 November that he would vote against the Connally Resolution. Arguing that the sinking of the *Reuben James* had convinced him that any change in the neutrality laws would lead quickly to war, Maloney insisted that neutrality revision at the present time was simply unnecessary and unwise.[36]

The effect the *Reuben James* incident had on Senate alignments was even more evident in the votes on neutrality revision. On 7 November, after eleven days of debate, the upper house lost little time in rejecting two amendments that would have retained portions of the 1939 Neutrality Act, before giving final approval to the Connally Resolution by a margin of 50 to 37. Thus, for a third time in 1941 the Roosevelt Administration had prevailed on a foreign policy issue. Voting alignments on neutrality revision indicated that Senate conservatives were sharply polarized. Many, like George Radcliffe, Walter George, Richard Russell, Warren Barbour, and Wallace White, voted to support the Administration's foreign policy as they had throughout the session. But some, such as Francis Maloney, Henry Cabot Lodge, Harold Burton, Frederick Van Nuys, and Charles McNary, joined the isolationists in dissent.[37]

The intensifying threat to American security throughout 1941 forged a national unity that temporarily suppressed many legislators' concern with the expansion of Executive power and their personal distrust of FDR. In the air of crisis that infused Senate debate in 1941, patriotism and party loyalty became powerful forces leading many conservatives to support the Administration's foreign policy. But as was true in the earlier debates, conservatives' suspicion of Roosevelt, though largely unspoken, was not forgotten. During Senate debate on the Connally Resolution, political analyst Mark Sullivan argued that support for the Administration's foreign policy would be stronger were there not continuing suspicions that FDR had ulterior motives. Many in the nation he wrote on 29 October, believed that some ardent New Dealers were exploiting the international emergency as a means to expand presidential power, not in the interest of national defense, but to advance domestic reforms.[38] The formal entry of America into World War II on 8 December increased these trends. For while the declaration of war enhanced feelings of national unity, the substantial expansion of Executive power during the war deepened conservatives' distrust of Franklin Roosevelt, thereby laying the foundation for a full-scale congressional rebellion once the crisis had passed.

III

The Japanese attack on Pearl Harbor, which thrust America into the world conflagration, ended, at least for the short term, the foreign policy debate that had dominated political discourse in 1940 and 1941. Critics of the Administration's foreign policy fell silent and the demands imposed by the war galvanized Congress into action throughout 1942. Arthur Vandenberg, one of the Senate's leading isolationists, declared on 8 December, for example, that although opponents of the Administration could have reacted to the attack by shouting "we told you so!," they chose instead to "shout 'let's win the war!' " The conviction that America was engaged in an "all-out" offensive stifled most dissent and enabled Franklin Roosevelt to win approval for almost every piece of legislation he sought. Indeed, one seasoned observer of Senate affairs noted in 1942 that only thirty-four bills were debated for more than thirty minutes.[39] Yet by substantially augmenting Executive power and expanding the federal role in economic affairs, the war in the long run intensified the concerns of Senate conservatives. Legislative action in 1942, by adding to the distrust between Congress and the White House, helped revive conservative opposition once the air of crisis had dissipated.

The impact of the war on Executive-Congressional relations was illustrated by Senate consideration of price control legislation in January 1942. Six months earlier, in July 1941, Franklin Roosevelt had asked Congress for the power to establish price ceilings to control the spiraling inflation brought on by defense spending. The President's message did not, however, advocate wage ceilings, but merely suggested that wages in defense plants would not be allowed to "substantially exceed" those in nonwar plants. The House's version of price control, approved in November 1941, granted all but one of the Administration's requests. As a concession to the nation's farmers who objected to the absence of wage controls, the House bill set the ceiling price for farm products at 110% of parity, instead of 100% as desired by the White House. The Senate bill, delayed by the attack on Pearl Harbor, closely followed the House measure.[40]

The action of both houses of Congress to omit wage ceilings aroused the ire of farm-state senators who charged that the price control bill would deprive America's farmers of their fair share of the expanding national income.[41] To address these concerns, John Bankhead of Alabama, one of the leaders of the Senate farm bloc, proposed in early January to give the secretary of agriculture veto power over all farm price ceilings. Although Franklin Roosevelt lobbied against the Bankhead Amendment via a telegram to Majority Leader Alben Barkley, the Senate farm bloc proved to be too strong. On 9 January, in action that erased party lines, the Senate voted 48–37 to approve the Bankhead amendment. The following day the upper house again heeded the farm bloc when it voted 55 to 31 to add an amendment sponsored by Joseph O'Mahoney tying parity to increases in industrial wages and nonfarm prices, a move that many feared could raise farm prices by 25%. With the farmers' interests thus protected, the Senate approved its version of price control with only Gerald P. Nye of North Dakota dissenting.[42]

Despite the near unanimity of the Senate vote, many in the nation reacted unfavorably to the price control bill. Newspapers throughout the nation charged that farmers had acted out of utter selfishness and complained that the Senate bill would actually aggravate inflation. But the most important criticism came from Franklin Roosevelt. Speaking to reporters on 13 January, the President's criticism of the bill was so strong and so harsh that all observers were convinced he would do everything possible to influence the conference committee deliberations.[43] The depth of the President's reservations became clear the next day when he chose to meet with only the House members of the conference committee and threatened that unless the O'Mahoney amendment were removed from what he contemptuously termed "the bill to compel inflation," he would veto the measure.[44]

White House lobbying appeared to influence the Senate, for on 27 January, less than three weeks after it had overwhelmingly approved its version of price control, the upper house reversed itself and voted 65 to 14 to accept the conference bill that closely adhered to the President's position. Although the conference report preserved farm ceiling prices at 110% of parity, it vested price control in the hands of a single administrator, omitted wage controls and, most importantly, deleted the O'Mahoney amendment. Many of those who voted for the report did so apparently with the recognition that their personal reservations had to yield to the larger effort of winning the war. Despite feeling that it was a weak and unsatisfactory bill that would need revision within six months, Bennett Clark of Missouri voted for the final bill so that the price administrator would have a legal basis for controlling inflation. Roosevelt again succeeded by his personal intervention with the conference committee. But when the Senate paused briefly in mid-January from its debate over price control, clear evidence surfaced of the resentment that FDR's tactics were breeding among legislators.[45]

In a special message on 14 January, the President requested that for efficiency's sake, various Executive agencies should be empowered to act for Congress in such minor matters as allowing the War Department to control the construction and maintenance of bridges throughout the nation. Such delegations of power, Roosevelt argued, would allow Congress to turn its full attention to the war effort. This latest request for power, coming as it did so soon after FDR's effort to defeat the Bankhead amendment and his decision to meet only with the House conferees on the price control bill, snapped the last strands of Clyde Reed's patience. The normally even-tempered Kansas Republican interrupted Senate debate on the special message to denounce the President's meddling in Congress's affairs. The Administration's attempts to influence pending legislation, Reed insisted, was improper and disrespectful of the American tradition of separation of powers.[46]

Eleven days later, another instance of presidential interference provoked a similar outburst from Democrat Guy Gillette. On 25 January, during Senate debate of a bill to forbid the Commodity Credit Corporation from selling government-owned crops below parity, the Iowa Democrat denounced a message FDR had sent to Vice President Henry Wallace urging defeat of the measure because of what he believed were the farmer's selfish motives. Noting that he was extremely upset by the letter, Gillette questioned the propriety of the President's interference with the legislative process.[47]

The tension in Executive-Legislative relations reflected by Reed and Gillette was aggravated considerably in the spring of 1942 by the resumption of the price control debate. In spite of the inflation control bill Congress approved in January 1942, the upward spiral in the cost of living had continued. Because the OPA was initially empowered to set maximum prices only for key commodities, food prices rose nearly 5% in the first three months of 1942 and clothing prices advanced nearly 8%. Faced with continuing inflation, Franklin Roosevelt proposed a seven-point anti-inflation measure on 27 April, which demanded substantially higher taxes; a salary limitation of $25,000; "stabilization" of wages; rationing of scarce commodities; and a reduction in the ceiling price for farm products to 100% of parity. The following day, in a further effort to control inflation, the President issued the General Maximum Price Regulation ("General Max"), expanding price control to all commodities and freezing prices at the highest level attained in March 1942.[48] After announcing his seven-point plan, however, the President made no further effort to get the measure enacted, and Congress, with its legislative calendar crowded with war bills, took no action on it.

Without additional anti-inflation measures, prices continued to rise throughout the summer, largely because of the difficulty of enforcing the "General Max" regulations. One of the chief methods used by merchants to evade the general freeze was simply to change the brand name or the style of their product.[49] The continuing escalation in the cost of living finally led Franklin Roosevelt on 7 September to give Congress an ultimatum. Arguing that congressional inaction was to blame for inflation, the President threatened Congress that if it failed to enact by 1 October new price control legislation raising taxes and reducing farm ceiling prices to 100% of parity, he would act unilaterally under the authority granted to him by the War Powers Act.[50]

Roosevelt's ultimatum stunned Congress and the nation. To the partisan *Chicago Tribune*, the President's threat was tantamount to a *coup d'etat*. Robert Taft concurred. The Ohio Republican charged that if Congress allowed the President to alter the price control law by Executive order, there would be no limits on the actions he could take. But it was Robert LaFollette who best grasped the significance of the ultimatum. By his threat of unilateral action, the Wisconsin Progressive noted bluntly, Franklin Roosevelt had "placed a pistol at the head of Congress."[51]

The Senate, thus challenged, worked feverishly throughout September to meet the President's deadline. Although several attempts were made during debate to restrict the President's discretionary power to control prices and wages, the bill as finally adopted conformed closely to the Administration's desires. The most serious attempt to narrow the President's range of action came on 22 September when the farm bloc rallied behind an amendment offered by Elmer Thomas of Oklahoma, requiring the inclusion of all farm labor costs in the calculation of parity prices. Most observers predicted that the Thomas amendment would increase farm price ceilings to 112% of parity, thereby adding to the inflationary pressures in the economy. After Roosevelt expressed his complete opposition to the Thomas amendment, however, a substitute motion was approved that merely directed the President to weigh all production costs, including labor, in determining price ceilings.[52] Other compromises written into the bill further expanded the President's discretionary powers. Although the bill lowered farm price ceilings to 100% of parity, Roosevelt was allowed to adjust ceilings whenever necessary to spur production. Similarly, despite the requirement that wages and salaries be stabilized at their 15 September 1942 level, the President could modify them as he saw fit to prevent "gross inequities." Notwithstanding the ill will generated by the debate on price control, as finally approved by the Senate on 30 September, the Stabilization Act of 1942 granted to Franklin Roosevelt most of the sweeping powers he had requested in his ultimatum.[53]

Through the pressure exerted by his ultimatum, FDR had again prevailed over Congress, but it proved to be a Pyrrhic victory. The President's challenge deepened concern in Congress over the rapid expansion of Executive power and again raised questions about his motives. *The New York Times* quoted "informed sources" on 22 September, for example, who charged that the President's measure would actually increase some commodity prices above current levels and thus could not truly be considered a measure to curb inflation. These sources pointed out that although the OPA director had been empowered by Congress in January to put ceilings on farm products at 110% of parity, the prices of those commodities that exceeded 110% had not been capped. On 22 September, for example, cattle were selling for 135% of parity and hogs for about 125% of parity. Under the President's plan, moreover, those commodities whose price exceeded parity were to be capped at the highest price attained between 1 January and 15 September 1942. Thus, under the Stabilization Act adopted in September the ceiling price for 100 pounds of beef could be set as high as $16.90. The January 1942 Price Control Act, on the other hand, would have permitted rolling back the price of that beef to $12.91. Given these conditions, many senators undoubtedly concluded, as did *Newsweek's* business editor, Ralph Robey, that since the Administration had failed to use the powers granted to it in January 1942, the principal purpose of the 7 September ultimatum had not been to control inflation.[54]

Wartime fiscal policy offered a final point of contention between the Senate and the Administration in 1942. Because Treasury Secretary Henry Morgenthau aimed to finance the war largely through taxation in an effort to restrain inflation, the $59 billion budget for fiscal 1943 presented to Congress in mid-January was accompanied by a request for a $9 billion dollar tax increase.[55] Debate on the tax bill, however, revealed substantial differences between the Administration and Congress over how best to raise the additional revenue. The Treasury Department believed that additional revenue should come from well-to-do Americans and thus advocated sharp increases in tax rates on upper-income brackets and corporations, combined with a spending tax designed to discourage non-essential consumption. Congress, on the other hand, believed that additional revenue was most easily raised by targeting Americans in the lower-income brackets who were far more numerous than the small number of taxpayers at the top. The Legislature proposed, therefore, to broaden the tax base by lowering exemptions, and to implement a national sales tax.[56] Because of the differing opinions, there was almost constant sniping between the Administration and Congress as the revenue measure moved through the Legislature. The Treasury Department, for example, dismissed as wholly insufficient the House's version of the bill, which raised $6.3 billion dollars in new revenue and pressured the Senate Finance Committee to rewrite the tax bill in order to produce a minimum of $8.7 billion in additional revenue. In turn, the Senate Finance Committee summarily rejected the Treasury's spendings tax in favor of a 5% "Victory Tax" to be withheld from all incomes in excess of $624. In the Administration's eyes, however, because the Senate bill yielded only $830 million more than the House measure, it was still inadequate. Thus, on the day the Revenue Act of 1942 was formally introduced into the Senate, Treasury Secretary Morgenthau, in a step perceived by some observers as demonstrating his contempt for Congress, announced that he would immediately prepare a new bill asking for an additional $6 billion in tax revenue.[57]

Despite the controversy it provoked, the tax bill was ultimately adopted by nearly unanimous votes in both houses of Congress. Yet as was often the case on war-related issues in 1942, the White House effort to obtain higher taxes deepened long-standing Congressional concern with the expansion of Executive power and increased distrust of FDR's leadership. The Administration's treatment of Congress throughout the revenue debate seemed to many legislators to be one more example of Franklin Roosevelt's determination to run the war effort as he saw fit. Democrat Joseph O'Mahoney complained in a radio address on 8 December, for instance, that the President had issued five hundred Executive orders between 7 January 1941 and 12 April 1942. "They were written in private by anonymous experts," he continued. "They were not subject to public hearing nor were they analyzed in public debate. They did not become known to the public until issued—and then they were effective." Republican Charles Tobey was similarly disturbed by the President's actions. "The Congress is no longer a separate branch of government," he complained in a letter to a constituent. "It is being pushed about and swept about like chaff on the barn floor by the Presidential will. It is a far cry from allocation of powers under the Constitution to almost complete domination of the government today."[58]

Although the anger expressed by O'Mahoney and Tobey was largely confined to private discourse because of the immediacy of the war effort, by the end of 1942 cracks were beginning to appear in the national unity. Since 1940 legislators had viewed the rapid expansion of Executive authority with growing alarm. Many of the major wartime agencies had been established as advisory committees prior to Pearl Harbor under authority granted to the President by the 1916 National Defense Act. After the U.S. declared war, these committees generally assumed more power from the President's pool of delegated authority and consequently, "Congress was never called upon to establish an over-all organizational plan for administering the war."[59] Coming on the heels of a decade of unprecedented growth in presidential power necessitated by the Great Depression, the international crisis heightened conservatives' concern with the constitutional separation of power. In the early years of the war, however, these concerns were usually subsumed by the larger effort of winning the war. But as the war progressed and an Allied victory became more certain, conservatives' desire to challenge FDR's policies and to reverse the erosion of Congressional power steadily mounted. Thus, while the war's immediate effect was to create a tractable Congress, it helped in the long run to revive and intensify the conservative rebellion, which had been building in the late 1930s.

Both the short- and long-term effect of the international crisis on Senate politics is plainly evident in the statistical analysis of the 77th Congress. When senators were assigned a scale position based on all the scalable policy dimensions (table 2–3) important changes were evident in the voting alignments. While the high support group continued to be composed almost entirely of Democrats (88% Democratic in the 77th, compared with 97% in the 76th), the number of senators who scaled in the low support category was 53% lower than in the previous Congress. This sharp reduction undoubtedly reflects the heightened patriotism of the early war years.

The ability of patriotism and partisanship to distort voting alignments was more apparent when senators were assigned two separated scale scores, one reflecting their votes on only foreign policy dimensions and the other reflecting their voting record on domestice issues. Table 2–5, the foreign policy scales, is a study in contrasts. Only three of the forty votes that comprise the foreign policy dimensions in the 77th Congress, for example, were cast after Pearl Harbor. That so few foreign policy votes in 1942 were scalable indicates at least in part that fewer than 10% of the senators dissented from the majority, a strong indication of the unity forged by the war emergency. On the other hand, the partisanship of the preparedness debate throughout 1941 is apparent in senators' scale positions in table 2–5. When only foreign policy votes were considered, conservative Democrats such as Josiah Bailey, Carter Glass, Millard Tydings, Peter Gerry, Ellison D. "Cotton Ed" Smith, Harry Byrd, George Radcliffe, Walter Geroge, Richard Russell, Frederick Van Nuys, and Francis Maloney, who formed the core of the 1930s conservative coalition, scaled in either the high or medium support categories. Indeed, 85% of the scalable Democrats gave either high or medium support to Franklin Roosevelt's foreign policy in the 77th Congress. In contrast, the low support group on foreign policy consisted of 79% of the scalable Republicans, together with such west-

TABLE 2-3

77th CONGRESS

Name	Policy Dimensions	Score
	1 2 3 4 5 6 7 8 9 10 11	

HIGH SUPPORT

Name	Policy Dimensions	Score
Pepper, D-FL	1 1 0 1 1 1 1 1 2 1 1	1.10
Schwartz, D-WY	0 1 2 0 1 1 1 1 1 1 1	1.11
Wagner, D-NY	1 0 0 0 0 1 1 1 2 1 1	1.14
Tunnell, D-DE	1 1 1 1 1 2 1 1 2 1 1	1.18
Mead, D-NY	1 1 0 1 1 2 1 1 2 1 1	1.20
Thomas, D-UT	0 1 3 0 1 1 1 1 1 1 1	1.22
Chandler, D-KY	2 0 2 1 0 0 1 1 2 0 1	1.25
Downey, D-CA	0 1 1 2 0 2 0 1 1 1 1	1.25
Rosier, D-WV	0 2 1 1 1 2 1 0 1 0 0	1.29
Thomas, D-OK	1 1 0 1 2 0 2 1 1 1 2	1.33
Lee, D-OK	0 1 1 0 3 0 1 1 2 1 1	1.38
Hughes, D-DE	0 2 1 0 2 0 1 1 2 1 1	1.38
Smathers, D-NJ	0 1 2 1 2 3 1 1 1 1 1	1.40
Norris, I-NE	1 2 0 2 1 1 1 2 2 0 1	1.44
Truman, D-MO	2 2 0 0 1 3 0 1 2 1 1	1.44
Bilbo, D-MS	3 1 2 0 1 0 1 1 1 1 2	1.44
Murdock, D-UT	2 2 0 2 2 0 0 1 1 1 1	1.50
Ellender, D-LA	3 1 3 1 1 0 1 1 2 1 1	1.50
Stewart, D-TN	2 2 3 1 1 2 2 1 1 1 1	1.55
Kilgore, D-WV	1 1 1 0 3 2 2 2 0 2 1 1	1.56
Hill, D-AL	3 2 3 1 1 0 1 0 1 1 1	1.56
Overton, D-LA	3 0 3 1 1 0 2 1 1 1 1	1.56
Brown, D-MI	0 2 0 2 3 1 1 1 2 1 1	1.56
Bankhead, D-AL	3 1 3 1 2 0 1 1 1 2 1	1.60
Caraway, D-AR	3 2 3 1 2 0 1 1 1 1 1	1.60
McFarland, D-AZ	0 3 1 1 3 2 2 1 1 1 1	1.60
O'Mahoney, D-WY	2 2 2 0 2 0 2 1 1 0 1	1.63
Chavez, D-NM	2 2 0 1 2 0 0 1 2 1 2	1.63
Nye, R-ND	0 1 1 0 1 0 1 3 1 2 3	1.63
LaFollette, I-WI	1 1 1 2 1 1 1 3 1 3 3	1.64

Name	Policy Dimensions	Score
	1 2 3 4 5 6 7 8 9 10 11	

HIGH SUPPORT continued

Name	Policy Dimensions	Score
McNary, R-OR	2 2 1 2 1 1 1 2 1 3 2	1.64
Bulow, D-SD	3 0 1 0 1 0 1 2 1 3 3	1.67
Guffey, D-PA	0 2 3 0 1 3 1 1 2 1 1	1.67

MEDIUM SUPPORT

Name	Policy Dimensions	Score
Bunker, D-NV	3 2 2 2 3 0 1 1 1 1 1	1.70
Hayden, D-AZ	0 2 3 1 2 3 2 1 1 1 1	1.70
VanNuys, D-IN	2 2 3 1 1 3 2 1 1 1 2	1.73
Andrews, D-FL	3 2 3 1 1 3 2 1 1 1 1	1.73
Davis, R-PA	1 0 2 0 0 1 1 2 1 3 3	1.75
Gurney, R-SD	0 2 0 2 2 0 1 2 2 2 1	1.75
Langer, R-ND	2 1 1 0 2 0 1 3 1 2 3	1.78
Barkley, D-KY	2 0 3 0 2 3 1 1 2 1 1	1.78
Bone, D-WA	0 1 0 2 2 1 1 3 2 2 2	1.78
Russell, D-GA	3 2 1 0 1 3 3 2 1 1 1	1.80
Capper, R-KS	1 2 1 2 1 1 2 3 1 3 3	1.82
Reed, R-KS	1 0 0 0 0 1 2 3 1 3 0	1.83
Hatch, D-NM	0 2 3 0 2 0 0 0 2 1 1	1.83
Tobey, R-NH	0 0 1 0 0 1 1 3 1 3 3	1.86
Ball, R-MN	0 2 0 3 3 0 1 2 2 1 1	1.88
Herring, D-IA	2 0 3 1 3 3 2 0 1 1 1	1.89
Lucas, D-IL	0 2 3 1 2 0 1 2 3 2 1	1.89
Bailey, D-NC	0 2 3 0 2 3 3 1 1 1 1	1.89
Aiken, R-VT	2 1 1 2 2 0 1 3 1 3 3	1.90
Connally, D-TX	3 2 3 1 2 3 3 1 1 1 1	1.91
Green, D-RI	2 2 3 2 0 3 1 0 3 1 1	2.00
Gillette, D-IA	2 0 0 1 2 0 0 3 0 2 2	2.00
McKellar, D-TN	3 3 2 1 3 3 2 1 1 0 1	2.00
McCarran, D-NV	0 2 1 2 1 1 3 3 1 3 3	2.00
Thomas, R-ID	0 2 1 3 1 1 2 3 1 3 3	2.00
Clark, D-ID	0 0 1 2 1 3 1 3 2 2 3	2.00
George, D-GA	3 3 3 1 3 3 3 1 1 1 1	2.09
Burton, R-OH	1 2 2 2 2 0 1 2 3 3 3	2.10
Maloney, D-CT	0 2 2 3 3 1 3 1 3 1 2	2.10
Holman, R-OR	0 3 2 2 1 2 2 2 1 3 3	2.10

Name	Policy Dimensions	Score
	1 2 3 4 5 6 7 8 9 10 11	

MEDIUM SUPPORT continued

Name	Policy Dimensions	Score
Brewster, R-ME	1 0 2 0 3 1 2 2 0 3 3	2.13
Glass, D-VA	0 0 0 0 3 3 3 1 3 1 1	2.14
Reynolds, D-NC	0 0 0 0 0 2 2 3 2 3 3	2.14
White, R-ME	2 2 0 3 3 1 3 2 2 2 2	2.20
Brooks, R-IL	0 0 1 2 3 1 3 3 1 3 3	2.22
Johnson, D-CO	0 0 3 2 2 2 1 2 1 3 2	2.22
Shipstead, I-MN	2 0 0 3 0 0 1 3 1 3 3	2.29

LOW SUPPORT

Name	Policy Dimensions	Score
Willis, R-IN	1 3 0 3 3 1 2 3 1 3 3	2.30
Radcliffe, D-MD	2 3 3 0 3 3 3 1 3 1 1	2.30
Smith, D-SC	3 0 3 1 2 3 3 2 0 2 2	2.33
Tydings, D-MD	0 3 3 0 3 3 2 1 3 1 2	2.33
Wiley, R-WI	1 0 2 0 3 1 2 3 1 3 3	2.34
Walsh, D-MA	1 3 3 2 3 1 2 3 3 2 3	2.36
Austin, R-VT	3 0 3 0 3 0 3 2 2 2 1	2.38
Vandenberg, R-MI	1 3 1 3 3 1 3 3 3 0 3	2.40
Wheeler, D-MT	0 1 0 0 3 0 1 3 3 3 3	2.43
Butler, R-NE	0 0 2 3 2 0 0 3 1 3 3	2.43
Lodge, R-MA	0 0 1 3 3 1 3 2 3 3 3	2.44
Taft, R-OH	1 3 2 3 3 1 2 3 3 3 3	2.45
Gerry, D-RI	2 3 3 2 3 3 3 2 3 2 1	2.45
Byrd, D-VA	3 3 3 1 3 3 3 2 3 0 2	2.60
Danaher, R-CT	0 2 2 3 3 1 3 3 3 3 3	2.60
Clark, D-MO	0 3 2 0 3 3 3 3 2 3 3	2.78

Policy Dimension Key:

    0   denotes that a senator did not scale on the dimension

    1. Civil Rights/Civil Liberties

    2. Social Welfare

    3. Fiscal Policy

    4. Labor

    5. Economy in Government Spending

    6. Extension of Federal Authority

    7. Business Regulation

    8. National Defense

    9. Agriculture

    10. Extension of Executive Power

    11. Foreign Aid

77TH CONGRESS (N=86)

HIGH SUPPORT (N=33 or 38%)

    Democrats   = 29 (88%)
    GOP   = 2 (6%)
    Independents = 2 (6%)

MEDIUM SUPPORT (N=37 or 43%)

    Democrats   = 22 (59%)
    GOP   =14 (38%)
    Independents = 1 (3%)

LOW SUPPORT (N=16 or 19%)

    Democrats   = 8 (50%)
    GOP   = 8 (50%)
    Independents = 0 (0%)

TABLE 2-4

Regional Divisions in Medium and Low Support Groups

MEDIUM SUPPORT (N=37)

Coastal (N=15 or 41%)

Andrews, D-FL	Davis, R-PA	Holman, R-OR
Bone, D-WA	Russell, D-GA	Glass, D-VA
Tobey, R-NH	Bailey, D-NC	White, R-ME
Aiken, R-VT	Green, D-RI	Brewster, R-ME
George, D-GA	Maloney, D-CT	Reynolds, D-NC

Interior (N=22 or 59%)

Bunker, D-NV	Hayden, D-AZ	Thomas, R-ID
VanNuys, D-IN	Gurney, R-SD	Burton, R-OH
Langer, R-ND	Barkley, D-KY	Johnson, D-CO
Capper, R-KS	Reed, R-KS	Clark, D-ID
Hatch, D-NM	Ball, R-MN	Brooks, R-IL
Herring, D-IA	Lucas, D-IL	Shipstead, I-MN
Connally, D-TX	Gillette, D-IA	
McKellar, D-TN	McCarran, D-NV	

LOW SUPPORT (N=16)

Coastal (N=9 or 56%)

Radcliffe, D-MD	Smith, D-SC	Gerry, D-RI
Tydings, D-MD	Walsh, D-MA	Danaher, R-CT
Austin, R-VT	Lodge, R-MA	Byrd, D-VA

Interior (N=7 or 44%)

Willis, R-IN	Wiley, R-WI	Clark, D-MO
Vandenberg, R-MI	Wheeler, D-MT	
Butler, R-NE	Taft, R-OH	

ern Progressive isolationists as Robert LaFollette, Gerald Nye, Henrik Shipstead, and Burton Wheeler. Partisanship, as these figures indicated, went far toward defining a senator's stance on foreign policy issues prior to Pearl Harbor.

If the influence of partisan politics is evident in scale positions in table 2–5 the impact of patriotism on Senate voting alignments is readily apparent in table 2–6. The domestic policy dimensions represent a broad cross section of votes taken both before and after Peral Harbor. Immediately apparent in this table is the large medium support group, constituting 53% of all scalable senators in the 77th Congress. The twelve Republicans who gave medium support to the Administration's domestic policies, together with their eight

TABLE 2-5

77th CONGRESS - FOREIGN POLICY DIMENSIONS

HIGH SUPPORT

Pepper, D-FL	1.00	Hayden, D-AZ	1.00
Schwartz, D-WY	1.00	Andrews, D-FL	1.00
Wagner, D-NY	1.00	Barkley, D-KY	1.00
Tunnell, D-DE	1.00	Hatch, D-NM	1.00
Mead, D-NY	1.00	Herring, D-IA	1.00
Thomas, D-UT	1.00	Bailey, D-NC	1.00
Chandler, D-KY	1.00	Connally, D-TX	1.00
Downey, D-CA	1.00	Green, D-RI	1.00
Radcliffe, D-MD	1.00	McKellar, D-TN	1.00
Lee, D-OK	1.00	George, D-GA	1.00
Hughes, D-DE	1.00	Glass, D-VA	1.00
Smathers, D-NJ	1.00	Bunker, D-NV	1.00
Truman, D-MO	1.00	Norris, I-NE	1.50
Murdock, D-UT	1.00	Bilbo, D-MS	1.50
Ellender, D-LA	1.00	Chavez, D-NM	1.50
Stewart, D-TN	1.00	VanNuys, D-IN	1.50
Kilgore, D-WV	1.00	Gurney, R-SD	1.50
Hill, D-AL	1.00	Russell, D-GA	1.50
Overton, D-LA	1.00	Ball, R-MN	1.50
Brown, D-MI	1.00	Lucas, D-IL	1.50
Bankhead, D-AL	1.00	Maloney, D-CT	1.50
Caraway, D-AR	1.00	Tydings, D-MD	1.50
McFarland, D-AZ	1.00	Austin, R-VT	1.50
O'Mahoney, D-WY	1.00	Gerry, D-RI	1.50
Guffey, D-PA	1.00	Thomas, D-OK	1.50

N = 50; D = 46; R = 3; I = 1

TABLE 2-5

77th CONGRESS - FOREIGN POLICY DIMENSIONS

MEDIUM SUPPORT

McNary, R-OR	2.00
White, R-ME	2.00
Johnson, D-CO	2.00
Smith, D-SC	2.00
Byrd, D-VA	2.00

N = 5; D = 3; R = 2
Coastal = 4 (80%); Interior = 1 (20%)

LOW SUPPORT

Bulow, D-SD	2.50	McCarran, D-NV	3.00
Davis, R-PA	2.50	Thomas, R-ID	3.00
Bone, D-WA	2.50	Clark, D-ID	3.00
Gillette, D-IA	2.50	Reynolds, D-NC	3.00
Burton, R-OH	2.50	Brooks, R-IL	3.00
Holman, R-OR	2.50	Shipstead, I-MN	3.00
Brewster, R-ME	2.50	Willis, R-IN	3.00
Lodge, R-MA	2.50	Wiley, R-WI	3.00
Nye, R-ND	3.00	Walsh, D-MA	3.00
LaFollette, I-WI	3.00	Vandenberg, R-MI	3.00
Langer, R-ND	3.00	Wheeler, D-MT	3.00
Capper, R-KS	3.00	Butler, R-NE	3.00
Reed, R-KS	3.00	Taft, R-OH	3.00
Tobey, R-NH	3.00	Danaher, R-CT	3.00
Aiken, R-VT	3.00	Clark, D-MO	3.00

N = 30; D = 9; R = 19; I = 2
Coastal = 10(33%); Interior = 20 (67%)

bretheren who offered high support, constituted fully 83% of the scalable Republicans in the 77th Congress, a sharp increase over the 36% who offered similar levels of support in the previous Congress. The greater willingness of Republicans to support the Chief Executive's domestic policies in 1941–1942 was certainly influenced by the strong patriotism unleashed by the war, or at the very least, by their intensified fear of voters' reprisals against any legislator who failed to rally to the President's support in this time of crisis.

The large increase in the degree of Republican support for domestic policies in the 77th Congress also seems to point to the long-term forces reshaping Senate conservatism. While several Republicans in the medium or high support group, such as Arthur Capper, Gerald Nye, and Charles McNary, were old western Progressives, most were senators who represented states that had a strong urban industrial base, a coastal location, or both. The presence of George Aiken, Charles Tobey, James Davis, Harold Burton, Wallace White, and Ralph Brewster in the high or medium support groups on domestic issues in the 77th Congress also suggests that they perceived more clearly than their colleagues from the agrarian, interior states that individuals in modern America were increasingly interdepen-

TABLE 2-6

77th CONGRESS - DOMESTIC POLICY DIMENSIONS

HIGH SUPPORT

Pepper, D-FL	1.13	Langer, R-ND	1.43
Schwartz, D-WY	1.14	Lee, D-OK	1.50
Nye, R-ND	1.16	Hughes, D-DE	1.50
Wagner, D-NY	1.20	Smathers, D-NJ	1.50
Tunnell, D-DE	1.22	Davis, R-PA	1.50
Mead, D-NY	1.25	Aiken, R-VT	1.50
Thomas, D-UT	1.29	McNary, R-OR	1.56
Rosier, D-WV	1.29	Capper, R-KS	1.56
Thomas, D-OK	1.29	Bone, D-WA	1.57
Downey, D-CA	1.33	Reed, R-KS	1.60
LaFollette, I-WI	1.33	Chandler, D-KY	1.60
Tobey, R-NH	1.40	Ellender, D-LA	1.63
Norris, I-NE	1.43	Kilgore, D-WV	1.63
Bilbo, D-MS	1.43	Hill, D-AL	1.63

N = 28; D = 18; R = 8; I = 2

TABLE 2-6

77th CONGRESS - DOMESTIC POLICY DIMENSIONS

MEDIUM SUPPORT

Murdock, D-UT	1.67	Barkley, D-KY	2.00
Stewart, D-TN	1.67	Hatch, D-NM	2.00
Chavez, D-NM	1.67	Ball, R-MN	2.00
Bulow, D-SD	1.67	Herring, D-IA	2.00 ·
Overton, D-LA	1.71	Lucas, D-IL	2.00
Brown, D-MI	1.71	Burton, R-OH	2.00
Clark, D-ID	1.71	Holman, R-OR	2.00
Bankhead, D-AL	1.75	Brewster, R-ME	2.00
Caraway, D-AR	1.75	Brooks, R-IL	2.00
McFarland, D-AZ	1.75	Johnson, D-CO	2.00
Gillette, D-IA	1.75	Shipstead, I-MN	2.00
McCarran, D-NV	1.75	Connally, D-TX	2.11
Thomas, R-ID	1.75	Green, D-RI	2.13
VanNuys, D-IN	1.78	Willis, R-IN	2.13
Andrews, D-FL	1.78	Bailey, D-NC	2.14
Truman, D-MO	1.83	Wheeler, D-MT	2.20
O'Mahoney, D-WY	1.83	Butler, R-NE	2.20
Gurney, R-SD	1.83	Walsh, D-MA	2.22
Guffey, D-PA	1.86	McKellar, D-TN	2.25
Bunker, D-NV	1.88	Maloney, D-CT	2.25
Hayden, D-AZ	1.88	Reynolds, D-NC	2.25
Russell, D-GA	1.88	White, R-ME	2.25
Wiley, R-WI	1.88	Vandenberg, R-MI	2.25

N = 46; D = 33; R = 12; I = 1
Coastal = 11 (24%); Interior = 35 (76%)

LOW SUPPORT

George, D-GA	2.33	Austin, R-VT	2.67
Taft, R-OH	2.33	Gerry, D-RI	2.67
Smith, D-SC	2.43	Clark, D-MO	2.71
Lodge, R-MA	2.43	Byrd, D-VA	2.75
Danaher, R-CT	2.50		
Tydings, D-MD	2.57	N = 12; D = 8; R = 4	
Glass, D-VA	2.60	Coastal = 10(83%); Interior = 2 (17%)	
Radcliffe, D-MD	2.63		

dent and consequently, were more willing to embrace actions that involved expansions of government power.

On domestic dimensions in the 77th Congress, Senate Democrats offered less support for Administration policies. In 1941 and 1942, 70% of the scalable Democrats only mustered medium or low support for domestic dimensions, compared to 54% in the previous Congress. Most of that increase, moreover, was explained by senators falling from high support for the Administration in the 76th Congress to medium support in the 77th. Two factors seem to explain this decline. As the war emergency escalated, some senators certainly believed that preparedness and mobilization measures had to take precedence over many of the less essential domestic matters. Undoubtedly, however, the decline in the degree of Democratic support reflected the growing doubts that many senators harbored about FDR's leadership, such as the reservations over Lend-Lease that Richard Russell expressed privately to his mother. The surge of patriotism that filled the nation in these years appears to have made it difficult for most Senate Democrats to give anything less than high support to their commander-in-chief on issues directly related to the war, as the foreign policy scale scores indicate. As the domestic policy scale scores suggest, however, it appears to have been easier for Senate Democrats to register their doubts about FDR by offering less than full support on issues less central to the international emergency.

If the immediate effect of the wartime emergency was measured in heightened partisanship and patriotism, in the long term the experience of girding for war and, after 7 December 1941, actually fighting that war added much to the lessons many conservatives and, indeed, the American electorate had begun to sense in the 1930s. The ability of defense spending to revive the still sluggish economy increased their appreciation for government intervention into the free enterprise system. As Josiah Bailey acknowledged ruefully to U.S. News even before the major wartime buildup had begun, high levels of government spending since 1933 made it doubtful that the federal budget could balanced in the near term. Years of deficit spending by the New Deal, he concluded, had encouraged more and more Americans, from the unemployed to business, increasingly to turn to Washington for assistance.[60] Similarly, the mobilization effort, accomplished largely through a vast expansion of the federal bureaucracy, taught many conservatives about the array of beneficial powers at government's disposal, and renewed their concerns about the perils posed by that power to individual liberty. Finally, the international threat of the early war years, when America and Britain had stood alone against a larger, more powerful alliance of hostile powers, undoubtedly underscored for conservatives the dangers of pursuing an isolationist course in the modern world. In this sense, then, the experience of the nation at war was a critical ingredient in the transformation of Senate conservatism.

3

The Senate in Revolt, 1943–1944

THE SENATE THAT CONVENED IN JANUARY 1943 PROVED FROM THE start to be more truculent and independent than any legislative body Franklin Roosevelt had encountered. What to contemporary observers was a sudden and unexpected eruption of defiance by the upper house was explained in part by the 1942 elections. Those elections saw the defeat of a number of long-time supporters of the New Deal, including Josh Lee of Oklahoma, William Smathers of New Jersey, Prentiss Brown of Michigan, Matthew Neely of West Virginia, and George W. Norris of Nebraska. Their replacements, in turn, were often staunch Republican conservatives, who began Senate careers in 1943 marked by determined opposition to the positive state, including E. H. Moore, Albert Hawkes, Chapman Revercomb, and Kenneth S. Wherry.[1] A second and perhaps more important factor explaining the political rebellion was that in 1943 and 1944, with the defeat of the Axis powers ever more certain, senators from both parties, angry with FDR's near unilateral control of the war effort, began to reassert the Legislative branch's prerogative. In these years, for example, the upper house repealed Roosevelt's 1942 Executive order limiting salaries to $25,000. It ignored his position in fashioning a withholding plan for income taxes and banned the use of subsidies to roll back commodity prices. Most dramatically, however, the Senate reasserted its independence by overriding presidential vetoes of the 1943 Smith-Connally Act and the Revenue Act of 1943.

One consequence of the Senate rebellion was the revival of conservative opposition to the Roosevelt Administration that had frequently influenced political debates in the late 1930s. Freed from the political constraints created by the sense of crisis in the early war years, conservatives from both parties increasingly ignored Administration requests and pleas for party loyalty to vote, instead, as their consciences dictated. The conservative revival in 1943 and 1944, in turn, allowed the fault lines that had been developing within the right wing to reappear and intensify. For as the approach of an Allied victory steadily directed legislators' attention to the shape of the postwar world, internecine squabbles between obstructionist conservatives and the new conservatives were ignited over the extent to which New Deal reform should resume at war's end, as well as the degree to which America should maintain an internationalist foreign policy. Political developments in the 78th Congress offered strong evidence, then, that as conservatives continued to grapple with the implications of the Great Depression and the world war, many of them concluded that their political philosophy had to be adjusted to account for the tremendous changes that had occurred in twentieth century American life.

I

Anger with the President's interpretation of the 1942 Economic Stabilization Act produced the first instance of Senate defiance in 1943. Claiming that the clause in the 1942 act authorizing the President to adjust wages and salaries to correct gross inequities also empowered him to limit salaries, Franklin Roosevelt had, on 3 October 1942, issued an Executive order limiting individual net income to $25,000. That order, however, directly contradicted Congress's understanding of the act. Twice in 1942 the Legislative branch had explicitly rejected White House requests for the power to limit salaries, and throughout the debate on price control legislation, Administration supporters in Congress had agreed that the power to correct gross inequities could not be used to limit individual income. The new Senate, determined to resist further encroachments on its power, lost little time in attacking Roosevelt's order and by March had completed action on a bill rescinding the salary limitation.[2]

Congress defended its authority a second time in early 1943 in another dispute over the interpretation of the price control act. The point of controversy again centered on the President's 3 October Executive order, which had also directed the OPA to deduct all subsidy and soil conservation payments from the parity prices paid to farmers. Although Congress had yielded to the White House demand that ceiling prices for farm products be reduced to 100% of parity in 1942, the effect of the Executive order, which regarded all benefit payments as farm income, was to reduce farm ceilings below 100% of parity. The new Senate on 25 February, in another slap at government by Executive order, voted 78–2 to approve a bill sponsored by Alabama's John Bankhead repealing that section of the 3 October order that affected farm ceiling prices. Most observers believed that the wide margin of approval was evidence of the Senate's determination to uphold its integrity. As Kansas Republican Clyde Reed argued, the chief concern was not support for the farmers, but who would control farm policy—Congress or Franklin Roosevelt.[3]

Despite its wide margin of approval, when Franklin Roosevelt vetoed the Bankhead bill in early April, insisting that it would inhibit the government's ability to control inflation, the Senate was unable to muster sufficient votes for an override. The failure of the override effort, however, did not signal renewed Congressional subservience. Rather, by the time of the veto, many legislators had linked the issue of parity prices to the mounting problems with organized labor. In early April, John L. Lewis of the United Mine Workers had threatened to strike for higher wages. Lewis's demands outraged many in the nation who felt that the miners were putting their self-interest ahead of the war effort. Thus, Administration leaders urged the Senate to sustain the veto of the Bankhead bill (which would have resulted in higher crop prices) as a way of strengthening the President's ability to resist the wage demands of organized labor. Even the Administration's intense lobbying, however, failed to derail the Senate's drive to regain its power. For on 7 April, in a tactical move, the upper house voted to recommit the Bankhead bill to the Agriculture Committee. Rather than viewing recommittal as a defeat, supporters of the Bankhead bill defiantly argued that it was a weapon that could be used again should FDR yield to union demands for higher wages. "After all," John Bankhead told the *New York Times*, "we still have that cudgel behind the door. When the bill will come out again depends upon developments. We will be in no hurry."[4]

The Senate's concern with halting the drift of power to the Executive branch was again apparent in the spring when debate shifted to fiscal policy. The huge expenditures necessitated by the war had steadily revealed the inadequacy of the existing tax system. Because Americans paid their federal income tax in four installments in the year after the income was earned, critics complained that the system failed to provide the government with a predictable source of revenue. Others charged that the installment plan enabled many, especially new taxpayers and those with small incomes, to evade paying taxes entirely. As a result, support developed for a withholding tax which, its proponents argued, would solve both of these problems and also control inflation, because money would be immediately taken out of circulation. The biggest obstacle slowing the adoption of a withholding tax, however, was what to do with 1942 income taxes which, under the existing system, were to be paid in 1943. If taxpayers had to pay their 1942 taxes the same year they were subject to a withholding tax, they would, in effect, pay double taxes in 1943. Most supporters of a withholding tax proposed, therefore, to "forgive" some or all of the 1942 taxes. The "pay-as-you-go" plan that attracted most attention was devised by Beardsley Ruml of the R. H. Macy Company. It forgave all of the 1942 income taxes and simply began withholding taxes on 1943 incomes which, its supporters maintained, was merely a bookkeeping change that would result in no revenue loss.[5]

The Roosevelt Administration objected to the Ruml plan, however, arguing that complete abatement of 1942 taxes would be a huge windfall for the wealthy that could cost the Treasury as much as $200 million in lost revenue. In response to White House complaints, Congress developed several alternatives. The Administration threw its weight behind a proposal from the Ways and Means Committee to forgive 50% of 1942 taxes and to amortize the remainder over three years, but both the full House and the Senate spurned the measure. An alternative, the Forand-Robertson Act, approved by the House in early May, forgave 75% of 1942 taxes but scaled tax abatement progressively to favor the lower income brackets. The Senate's bill, which canceled 100% of the tax owed either in 1942 or 1943, whichever was lower, was still expected to raise $2 billion more revenue than either the existing tax system or the Forand-Robertson bill.[6]

That the dispute over the Ruml plan was more than a difference of opinion over taxation was made obvious by subsequent developments. When conferees appointed to reconcile the differences in the tax bills were unable to compromise, FDR reiterated his opposition to 100% tax abatement. In a stern letter to the conference committee chairmen, Walter George and Robert Doughton, the President threatened to veto any bill that contained such a provision. Although the conferees ultimately gave in to Administration pressure, approving a compromise that forgave 75% of the 1942 tax on all whose tax liability exceeded $50 and 100% for all who owed less than $50 in taxes, the conference contained a distinct anti-Administration flavor. Walter George insisted defiantly, for instance, that the unforgiven portion of the 1942 taxes, to be paid in equal installments in 1944 and 1945, was tantamount to an additional income tax and thus placed Congress in a position to spurn requests for higher taxes for at least two years.[7]

As George's comments revealed, Senate suspicions of Roosevelt reached new heights in the spring of 1943. The President's actions during debate of the tax bill seemed to many legislators yet another example of his determination to ignore Congress's constitutional role in lawmaking. Even before the tax controversy erupted, conservative Democrat Bennett Clark charged angrily in a radio address that "the Treasury has obstinately set its head against it [the Ruml plan] because it did not originate it. It is the business of the Congress under our Constitution to write revenue bills. The Treasury is trying to usurp this function."[8] The remarks of Clark and George, then, revealed how the unity of the early war years was, by 1943, giving way to growing bitterness between Congress and the Chief Executive.

Executive-Legislative tensions flared even more intensely in 1943 when the Senate dealt with the problems of organized labor and price subsidies. Although the issue of price subsidies was a relatively new issue in 1943, demands to restrict the power of organized labor had mounted steadily throughout the war. In spite of an antistrike pledge made by organized labor at the start of the war, some unions, particularly John L. Lewis's United Mine Workers, had periodically threatened to strike for higher wages to compensate for the higher cost of living. Most in the nation viewed these demands unsympathetically, believing that labor was either behaving selfishly at a time when all were called upon to sacrifice or acting treasonously to impede the war effort. Several times prior to 1943 Congress had been ready to adopt comprehensive legislation barring labor stoppages, but each time FDR had prevented such action by arguing that wartime labor policy was most efficiently directed by the Executive branch.[9]

The issue of labor relations came to a head in the spring of 1943 when a nationwide coal strike called by John L. Lewis idled more than 400,000 miners and brought coal production to a halt. The Senate lost little time dealing with the emergency and by early May had approved a tough antistrike bill. Sponsored by Democrat Tom Connally, the Senate bill provided for a thirty-day cooling-off period before strikes could be called, authorized the government to seize strike-bound plants, and made it illegal for anyone to interfere by lockout, strike, or slowdown with the production of war materials in a seized plant or mine.[10] The House quickly followed the Senate's action, and by mid-June the War Labor Disputes Act, known popularly as the Smith-Connally Act, was sent to the White House for the President's approval. When FDR vetoed the bill, claiming that the thirty-day cooling-off period would encourage strikes, Congress's drive to recapture its power could not be contained. Less than three hours after receiving the veto message on 25 June, the Senate and the House both overrode the veto by wide margins.[11]

Several factors explain the Senate's dramatic action on the Smith-Connally Act. Clearly, anger with organized labor was the major reason why many members of the upper house supported what was widely regarded as an antistrike bill. Reflecting the depth of public hostility to union labor in mid-1943 was a Gallup poll taken in June revealing that 81% favored a ban on strikes in *all* industries, not simply those seized by the government.[12] Many senators from both parties also viewed Roosevelt's veto as one more example of his determination to govern by Executive order. Republican Edward Robertson of Wyoming, for example, complained that even though the President had attempted to maintain White House control over all labor problems, when strikes developed, he was quick to shift the blame to Congress.[13] Finally, the bill's adoption also reflected the resumption of more independent voting among some Senate conservatives as an Allied victory became more apparent. Josiah Bailey of North Carolina, for example, regarded the wartime labor disputes as the logical culmination of the 1935 Wagner Act, and thus viewed the furor over John L. Lewis as an opportunity to dismantle a significant New Deal reform. In the midst of the 1943 debate, Bailey noted that he had voted against the 1935 measure and felt his opposition was fully vindicated by the wartime problems. "Undoubtedly it [the Wagner Act] does impose restrictions upon our people which are not good and ought not to be approved. I am for reforming that Act at the first opportunity."[14]

If resurgent conservatism played a role in the adoption of the 1943 Smith-Connally Act, the Congressional rebellion over the President's use of price subsidies pointed clearly to the means by which that conservatism was being transformed. Because of the continuing increase in the cost of living, FDR had issued an Executive order on 8 April creating a program of consumer price subsidies. Under the program, the government used monies from revolving funds in the Commodity Credit Corporation and the Reconstruction Finance Corporation to purchase farm commodities, which were then resold to consumers for less than the purchase price. Subsidies thus maintained low prices while simultaneously satisfying the demands of producers and processors for higher prices. Although the Administration defended the program as necessary to preserve the price-control and food-rationing systems, some in Congress saw it as another instance of Executive usurpation. Not only had Congress been neither informed nor consulted about the plan, but also, since subsidy payments were made from revolving funds in the RFC and the CCC, day-to-day administration of the program was beyond the control of the Legislature.[15]

Because of these concerns, both the House and Senate bills extending the life of the CCC for two years, prohibited the use of any funds for consumer price subsidies. The Senate ban, approved in late June following the override of the Smith-Connally veto, came in a motion sponsored by the conservative Democrat Bennett Clark. Defending his motion as a last-ditch effort to protect the free market economy, the Missouri Democrat warned that if the government gained control over farming through the subsidy program, government control of business and industry would quickly follow. FDR vetoed the CCC bill on 2 July, however, charging that it would intensify inflationary pressures and contribute to food shortages. Although the bill was killed when the House sustained the veto several days later, the controversy over consumer subsidies persisted because the veto left the CCC without funds at the start of a new fiscal year. New efforts to fund the agency reignited the battle over subsidies and power.[16]

When Senate debate on consumer subsidies resumed, support for continuation of the program came from a surprising source. Maryland Democrat George Radcliffe, who in the late 1930s had been one of the conservative voices demanding an end to the government's interference in the free enterprise system, spoke in favor of continued use of subsidies. Rejecting the position of such conservatives as Bennett Clark, who contended that inflation and consumer shortages would be solved by free market forces alone, Radcliffe defended this instance of government economic intervention. "Certainly no one can take such a position,[to end subsidies]," he argued in a radio address, "without realizing that runaway prices and inflation would bring on unbearable ills and make the costs of living prohibitive." Yet unlike many of his liberal Democratic colleagues, Radcliffe insisted that subsidies be viewed only as a temporary solution. "I am opposed to subsidies and roll backs, but [before they are eliminated] I must be sure that certain extraordinary and . . . temporary conditions . . . can be handled adequately without any resort to roll backs and subsidies."[17]

Radcliffe's position on subsidies suggests that by 1943 the ideology of some conservatives was being transformed. Rather than holding on to the talismans of rugged individualism and limited government, as many of his ideological brethren were doing, conservatives like Radcliffe were beginning to chart a new course. In a speech on the Senate floor in October 1943, Radcliffe offered clear insight into the forces transforming his philosophy. Despite the sentimental appeal of the Jeffersonian ideal of limited government, he maintained, "complexities of modern life have called for activities with which our ancestors did not have to reckon." Both the Depression and World War II had expanded government power at the expense of individual liberty, and although the day would come when there would be a demand to dismantle that power, Radcliffe urged caution. "Let us be vigilant lest we rush into hasty and ill-advised extensions of certain existing governmental activities or lest we make ruthless sacrifice of certain existing governmental policies which should in some form be preserved."[18] The more moderate brand of conservatism voiced by Radcliffe, then, together with the growing Congressional independence that had marked the first session of the 78th Congress, would grow more prominent in legislative affairs during 1944.

II

The revival of the conservative resistance that had flared in 1943 was accelerated in 1944 by differences over soldier voting, fiscal policy, and reconversion policies. The animosity that had formed an undercurrent in Executive-Legislative relations since the late 1930s boiled over when FDR vetoed the Revenue Act of 1943, and thereafter an angry and independent Congress approved only the most essential war measures. Yet beyond the harsh rhetoric, legislative action in 1944 offered further signs of the efforts made by some Senate conservatives to adapt their ideology to the changes in the nation made evident by the Depression and World War II. For although the upper house rejected the Administration's proposals on soldier voting and reconversion, the measures it ultimately approved with the help of conservatives' votes embraced an expanded role for the federal government that only several years earlier would have been unthinkable to all but the most liberal of the New Dealers.

Almost as soon as the second session of the 78th Congress convened, in early January 1944, the Senate became snarled over a bill enabling men and women in the armed forces to vote in the upcoming federal elections. The issue, which touched on both partisan politics and states' rights, provoked enormous controversy. Because public opinion polls indicated that a preponderant majority of those in the armed forces supported Franklin Roosevelt and the Democratic party, the Administration's bill, sponsored by Theodore Francis Green of Rhode Island and Scott Lucas of Illinois, sought to make it as easy as possible for inductees to vote. Instead of requesting absentee ballots from their states, as previous laws had mandated, every member of the armed forces under the Green-Lucas bill would automatically receive a ballot from Washington allowing them to vote for federal officials by writing-in either the candidate's name or the party of their choice.[19]

The Green-Lucas bill was opposed both by Republicans who saw it as a partisan measure engineered to elect Democrats, and by southerners who viewed increased federal control of elections as an overt threat to their Jim Crow laws. Because of these concerns, most Senate Republicans joined with southern Democrats in December 1943 to approve a substitute soldier-vote bill sponsored by James O. Eastland of Mississippi, Kenneth McKellar of Tennessee, and John McClellan of Arkansas, which merely encouraged state legislatures to enact measures permitting those in the armed forces to vote by absentee ballot.[20]

Particularly blunt comments from the White House reignited the soldier-vote controversy at the start of the second session of the 78th Congress. On 26 January, Franklin Roosevelt denounced the Senate's bill as fraudulent and chided the upper house for letting the soldiers down. Claiming that he spoke as Commander-in-Chief as well as an American citizen, the President urged Congress to adopt a measure that expanded federal control over soldier-voting. The effect of FDR's comments on already frayed tempers in the Senate was apparent to *New York Times* Capitol Hill correspondent, C. P. Trussell. The message, he observed, was resented by members of both parties, particularly in the Senate where twenty-four Democrats had supported the fraudulent measure.[21] The rancor felt by many in the upper house was also obvious in the remarks made by an unidentified senator to Allen Drury, then an AP correspondent:

> I'm as much for soldiers voting as the next man. . . . Roosevelt says we're letting the soldiers down. Why, God damn him. The rest of us have boys who go into the Army and Navy as privates and ordinary seamen and dig latrines and swab decks and his scamps go in as lieutenant colonels and majors and lieutenants and spend their off time getting medals in Hollywood. Letting the soldiers down! Why, that son of a bitch. I took my oath to defend the Constitution . . . and that's what I'm going to do. . . .[22]

In the end, the Senate refused to bow to White House pressure and instead voted on 8 February to attach a Barkley amendment adding federal ballot provisions to the Eastland-McKellar-McClellan bill. The Senate's bill, establishing a four-member federal commission that would send a federal ballot to all servicemen unable to obtain an absentee ballot from their state, was approved by a margin of 47–38.[23] Because the Senate rejected the Green-Lucas bill in favor of a measure that left the initiative for soldier voting with the states, most students of American politics have seen it as evidence marking the revival of a conservative coalition of Republicans and southern Democrats similar to that which had thwarted New Deal reform in the late 1930s. Roland Young in his study of Congressional politics during the war maintained, for example, that "the coalition between the Republicans and southern Democrats was the controlling factor in both the Senate and the House."[24]

But a close analysis of Senate action paints a more complex picture of the divisions. For among those voting for the federal ballot provisions of the Barkley amendment and for final passage of the amended bill was a handful of Republican and Democratic conservatives who either had been part of the anti–New Deal bloc in the 1930s, such as Guy Gillette of Iowa, George Radcliffe of Maryland, Arthur Vandenberg of Michigan, James Davis of Pennsylvania, and Charles Tobey of New Hampshire, or in the case of Burnet Maybank of South Carolina, Harold Burton of Ohio, and George Aiken of Vermont, were newly elected in the early 1940s. That these conservatives supported measures that expanded the federal government's authority, albeit in a limited way, into a matter which formerly had been the sole preserve of the states, further testifies to the transformation of Senate conservatism underway by the mid-1940s.

If the soldier-vote controversy offered a glimpse of the animosity that had developed between Congress and the President during World War II, a rancorous battle over fiscal policy in 1944 laid bare the full depth of that anger. Several weeks after Congress approved the withholding tax in May 1943, Treasury Secretary Morgenthau, in his continuing effort to control inflation, returned to Capitol Hill to request that Congress raise an additional $16 billion in new taxes as soon as possible, but no later than 1 January 1944. Fiscal developments over the remainder of 1943, however, led many in Congress to doubt the accuracy of the Administration's assumptions. Secretary Morgenthau, for instance, twice scaled down his demand for new taxes, suggesting in June that $12 billion was sufficient to restrain the cost of living, and then in October, requesting only $10.5 billion. The Treasury's demands also contradicted the general Congressional understanding that the recently adopted withholding tax, requiring that the 25% in "unforgiven" 1942 taxes be paid in two installments in 1944 and 1945, obviated the need for higher taxes. Making the Administration's demands for additional revenue seem even less essential was an announcement from General George Marshall in November that reduced military needs in the Mediterranean and the Caribbean would enable the Army to return more than $13 billion in appropriations to the Treasury by 1 July 1944.[25]

Perhaps most troubling to many in Congress, however, was the growing conviction that the Administration's fiscal policy was less concerned with controlling inflation than it was with redistributing wealth. In May 1943, the OPA released a report on civilian spending for the previous two years, showing that those earning more than $10,000 per year, though they constituted less than 2% of the population and controlled less than 16% of the national income, paid more than 72% of the total taxes. The report concluded that 98% of the population, accounting for more than 84% of the national income, paid less than 28% of the taxes. Thus, the report suggested to many that the only way to control inflation was to raise taxes on the lower income groups. But to many in Congress, the Administration's fiscal policy aimed to do the opposite. Although Secretary Morgenthau acknowledged that 80% of the inflationary oversupply of cash was in the hands of those earning less than $5000 annually, he still urged Congress to repeal the "Victory tax" and to implement a system of compulsory savings through a tax to be refunded at war's end. Yet as Arthur Krock of the *New York Times* estimated, Morgenthau's proposals would exempt from all income taxes approximately 23 million individuals who earned less than $5000 annually.[26] Thus, at the start of the second session in January 1944, Congress and the Executive were far apart on taxation. Although the Administration insisted that a tax hike of $10.5 billion was the minimum necessary to stave off inflation, Congress was prepared to grant no more than $2 billion in additional revenue.

Several fiscal reports released in early 1944 hardened Congress's resolve to resist White House revenue demands. In early January, *U.S. News* reported that most government officials aware of the war situation predicted that Germany would surrender by 30 June 1945 at the latest, and quite possibly as early as 1 July 1944. As a result, U.S. Budget Director Harold D. Smith had reduced the projected war costs for fiscal 1944 by $8 billion. By late January, moreover, the War Department had returned $14.25 billion in funds no longer needed by the Army, raising to $27.4 billion the total of appropriated funds returned to the Treasury in fiscal 1944 because of demobilization. Finally, in early February the Treasury Department announced that tax collections in 1943 had been nearly 100% higher than 1942 and that the number of taxpayers had increased sevenfold. It was thus widely believed in Congress that a tax increase of $10.5 billion was without justification.[27]

The revenue bill that emerged from Congress reflected these beliefs and proposed to raise taxes by only $2.1 billion. The President, unpersuaded, vetoed the bill on 22 February. Although the veto was not a complete surprise, its harsh criticism of Congress was unanticipated. FDR charged, for example, that the cancellation of the automatic increase in Social Security taxes (which Treasury Secretary Morgenthau favored) would cost the government $1.1 billion in lost revenue. There was no escaping the conclusion, he insisted petulantly, that the measure provides "relief not for the needy but for the greedy." The President also criticized Congress for the many forms required by the withholding tax, which, he predicted, would lead to confusion and frustration among the taxpayers.[28]

Most legislators of both parties, regardless of their previous attitude toward FDR and the New Deal, condemned the President's veto. The clearest demonstration of defiance came from Alben Barkley, the Senate's majority leader since 1937. The Kentucky Democrat, who had been a consistent opponent of the revenue bill, urged his colleagues on 23 February to uphold the Senate's integrity by overriding the veto, and then, to emphasize his independence from the White House, resigned as majority leader. Although Barkley was unanimously re-elected as majority leader the following day, the incident altered relations between the two branches of government for the remainder of Roosevelt's presidency. The significance of the incident was clear to Elbert Thomas. "By his one-vote margin in the 1937 contest when he was first elected [majority] leader," the Utah Democrat observed, "the impression was given, and it has been the impression ever since, that he spoke to us for the President. Now that he has been unanimously elected, he speaks for us to the President."[29]

On 25 February the Senate easily overrode FDR's veto of the Revenue bill in a vote that saw only fourteen New Deal Democrats sustain the President. The reasons for the wide margin by which FDR lost on this issue were evident in remarks made by a "liberal Democrat" to Allen Drury on 24 February. "Those of us who would have voted to sustain the veto, because we agree in general with the President's objections to the bill, cannot do so now," he admitted candidly. "The issue has gone beyond that. It has become an issue of the Executive versus the Congress, to determine once again which has the final say-so. Of course in the long run we do, and we shall vote in a way which will leave no doubt of it."[30]

The debate over reconversion policies in mid-1944 provided an additional glimpse of the shifting contours of Senate politics. To guard against the possibility of massive economic dislocation as the war drew to a close, two bills were introduced in August to ease anticipated employment problems. The more liberal of the two measures, supported by the Roosevelt Adminstration, was sponsored by Democrats Harley Kilgore and James Murray. It proposed to extend a variety of federal benefits to all defense workers idled by reconversion, including unemployment compensation for up to two years after the end of the war, transportation expenses to pay for the cost of relocation, and "maintenance allowances" of $50 to $100 per month for workers receiving free vocational training. Conservatives throughout the nation objected to the Kilgore-Murray bill. They saw in it all of the philosophical touchstones of New Deal reform, including direct payment to individuals, higher budget deficits, and government interference with the free enterprise system.[31]

Another reconversion measure, sponsored by Georgia's Walter George, proposed unemployment compensation for all defense workers, but allowed states to administer it. In addition, George's bill provided non–interest bearing loans to all states financially burdened by reconversion costs. During subsequent debate, two amendments were added to the Georgian's reconversion bill providing for the payment of defense workers' relocation costs and declaring that the federal government bore final responsibility for the retraining and reemployment of war workers. Despite these changes, the George bill's effort to preserve a measure of state autonomy ensured that it, rather than the Kilgore-Murray bill, won ultimate approval from a Senate determined to act independently of the White House.[32]

To contemporary observers, the reconversion debate provided additional evidence of a resurgent conservatism. Democrat Carl Hatch of New Mexico opined, for example, there was but one reason for the defeat of the Kilgore-Murray bill. "For the past two years," he told Allen Drury one day after adoption of the George bill, "the Republican minority aided by certain elements among the Democrats, has controlled the United States Senate."[33]

Yet a careful examination of the vote on the George bill points to a different conclusion. While partisan motives to support a measure opposed by FDR certainly explains some of the votes for the George bill, its promise of unemployment compensation for all defense workers also constituted a rejection of the free market principles conservatives had generally espoused in the 1930s. That the George bill won the support of Walter George, one of the prime targets of FDR's 1938 "purge," as well as southern Democrats George Radcliffe, Richard Russell, Burnet Maybank, and by such Republicans as Arthur Vandenberg, Robert Taft, Charles Tobey, and George Aiken, suggests the change occurring in the right wing.[34]

As the vote on the George bill indicates, the collapse of the national economy during the 1930s and its revival under the heavy defense spending in the early 1940s seemed gradually to convince some conservatives that the well-being of any economic group or region in America was tied to the health of the national community and that this demanded, in turn, a positive role for the federal government. A report issued in June 1944 by the Senate's Postwar Planning Committee, chaired by Walter George, emphasized that the enormous wartime expenditures had demonstrated the ability of government fiscal policy to stimulate consumer demand. Republican George Aiken had by 1944 also clearly grasped this lesson. The Vermont Republican reminded his Senate colleagues that returning veterans would not be the only ones to suffer from the failure to plan for postwar unemployment. "It would mean that people wouldn't buy shoes and wouldn't buy refrigerators and wouldn't buy radios and wouldn't have bathrooms and wouldn't have electric lights, and that manufacturers, consequently, wouldn't be called upon to produce as much."[35]

The 1944 presidential campaign of Republican Thomas E. Dewey provided further evidence that the attitudes reflected in George's and Aiken's position on reconversion was spread more broadly throughout the political party most closely identified with conservatism in the 1930s. Dewey's campaign left no doubt that the conservative philosophy, which had united the GOP in opposition to the New Deal during the 1930s, was giving way to bitter factional divisions within the party. Indeed, the New Yorker headed a wing of the party that by 1944 rejected total opposition to New Deal domestic reform and to an internationalistic foreign policy and sought instead to strike a balance between traditional conservative values and the needs of a modern, industrial society. During a campaign speech in Albany, New York on 13 July, for instance, Dewey criticized the New Deal for its tendency to centralize power in the Executive, but conceded that much of the recent growth in the size and scope of the federal government was a natural consequence of modern life. Those government functions that Dewey found essential to modern industrial life included stabilization of interest rates, creation of economic conditions that would provide full employment, protection of farmers against excessive price fluctuations, as well as unemployment compensation, minimum wage laws, and old-age pensions. The New York Republican embraced, furthermore, the Administration's postwar collective security plan and called also for extension of social security and unemployment compensation to farmers, domestic workers, and the self-employed.[36]

The factional dispute within the GOP was one aspect of the broader changes occurring in the 78th Congress. Years of White House disregard for the Legislature's prerogative, together with the dissipation of the national unity that had marked the early war years, revived conservative opposition to the Roosevelt Admininstration in 1943 and 1944. In these years, a sometimes rebellious Congress repealed the President's $25,000 salary limit, banned consumer price subsidies, approved its version of a withholding tax, and overrode vetoes of the Smith-Connally Act and the Revenue Act of 1943.

The revival of Congressional opposition is apparent in table 3–1, in which senators were assigned a scale position based on all scalable policy dimensions in the 78th Congress. Of the scalable senators, only 31% gave the Administration high support, compared with 38% in the 77th. Conversely, while only 19% of the scalable senators in the 77th Congress offered low support to the Administration, 31% did so in the 78th.

Partisan politics certainly played a role in the growing independence of the 78th Congress, as indicated by the surge in the number of Republicans scaling in the low support category (increasing from eight in the 77th to twenty-two in the 78th). Yet it also seems clear that ideological reasons contributed to the opposition of those in the third scale position. Oklahoma Republican E. H. Moore, who in 1942 was elected to the Senate seat held by New Deal Democrat Josh Lee, noted shortly after his victory that he subscribed to Jefferson's vision of a government of limited powers and vowed to undo most of the restrictions that the New Deal had placed on business since 1933.[37]

The Senate's growing rebelliousness and the effect of partisanship are both more apparent when senators were assigned separate scale positions for their support of foreign policy dimensions and for domestic policy dimensions (tables 3–3 and 3–4). Reflecting the continuing influence of patriotism on voting alignments during the war was FDR's ability to command high support on foreign policy dimensions from 57% of all scalable senators. On domestic pol-

TABLE 3-1

78th CONGRESS

Name	Policy Dimensions	Score
	1 2 3 4 5 6 7 8 9 10 11 12 13	

HIGH SUPPORT

Name	Policy Dimensions	Score
Bone, D-WA	1 1 1 1 1 1 1 1 1 1 1 1 1	1.00
Thomas, D-UT	1 1 1 1 1 1 1 1 1 1 1 1 1	1.00
Wagner, D-NY	1 1 1 1 1 1 1 1 1 1 1 1 1	1.00
Kilgore, D-WV	0 1 1 1 1 1 1 1 1 1 1 1 1	1.00
Downey, D-CA	0 0 0 1 0 1 1 1 1 1 1 1 1	1.00
Murdock, D-UT	2 1 1 1 1 1 1 1 1 1 1 1 0	1.08
Truman, D-MO	2 1 1 0 1 1 1 1 0 1 1 1 1	1.09
Walgren, D-WA	2 1 0 0 1 1 1 1 1 1 1 1 1	1.09
Green, D-RI	2 0 1 1 1 1 1 1 0 1 1 1 1	1.09
Murray, D-MT	0 1 1 1 1 1 1 1 0 1 1 1 2	1.09
Mead, D-NY	1 1 1 1 1 1 1 2 2 1 1 1 1	1.15
Guffey, D-PA	2 1 2 1 1 1 1 1 1 1 1 1 1	1.15
Pepper, D-FL	2 1 1 0 1 1 2 1 0 1 1 1 1	1.18
Barkley, D-KY	2 1 1 2 1 1 1 2 1 1 1 1 1	1.23
Lucas, D-IL	1 1 1 3 1 1 2 2 1 1 1 1 1	1.31
Tunnell, D-DE	2 1 1 3 1 2 1 1 1 1 1 1 1	1.31
Hayden, D-AZ	3 1 1 1 2 1 2 1 1 1 1 1 1	1.31
McFarland, D-AZ	3 2 1 1 2 1 1 1 1 1 1 1 1	1.31
Hatch, D-NM	1 2 0 2 1 1 3 1 0 1 1 1 1	1.36
Radcliffe, D-MD	1 1 1 3 1 2 2 2 1 1 1 1 1	1.38
LaFollette, I-WI	1 2 2 1 2 1 1 1 1 1 1 1 3	1.38
Ellender, D-LA	2 1 1 1 1 2 2 1 1 2 2 1 1	1.38
O'Mahoney, D-WY	2 2 2 0 1 1 0 0 1 1 1 1 3	1.50
Langer, R-ND	1 2 2 1 1 1 1 2 2 1 1 2 3	1.54
Andrews, D-FL	1 2 0 0 2 2 2 1 0 2 2 1 1	1.60
Hill, D-AL	1 2 1 1 2 1 2 2 1 3 3 1 1	1.62
Thomas, D-OK	3 2 1 1 2 2 2 1 3 1 1 1 1	1.62
Clark, D-ID	1 0 0 3 2 1 1 2 0 1 1 0 3	1.67
Scrugham, D-NV	2 2 0 0 0 1 1 0 2 2 2 0 3	1.67

Name	Policy Dimensions	Score
	1 2 3 4 5 6 7 8 9 10 11 12 13	

MEDIUM SUPPORT

Name	Policy Dimensions	Score
Stewart, D-TN	2 2 2 2 2 2 2 1 3 1 1 1 1	1.69
Caraway, D-AR	1 2 2 2 2 1 2 1 1 3 3 0 1	1.75
Danaher, R-CT	1 3 2 0 1 3 1 2 2 1 1 2 3	1.83
Walsh, D-MA	3 1 2 3 3 0 1 2 2 1 1 1 2	1.83
Russell, D-GA	3 2 2 1 2 1 2 1 1 3 3 0 1	1.83
Chandler, D-KY	2 2 3 3 1 3 3 2 1 1 1 1 1	1.85
Bilbo, D-MS	0 2 1 1 2 0 2 2 0 3 3 0 1	1.89
Bankhead, D-AL	1 2 2 2 2 0 2 1 0 3 3 0 1	1.90
Lodge, R-MA	1 3 2 3 2 2 2 2 1 0 0 0 1	1.90
VanNuys, D-IN	2 2 1 3 2 2 2 2 2 0 0 0 1	1.90
Aiken, R-VT	1 3 2 3 2 1 2 2 3 1 1 2 2	1.92
Austin, R-VT	1 3 2 3 2 2 2 3 3 1 1 1 1	1.92
Maloney, D-CT	3 1 2 3 3 3 0 1 1 1 1 1 3	1.92
Maybank, D-SC	3 2 2 1 3 2 3 1 3 2 1 1 1	1.92
Clark, D-MO	3 2 3 3 2 2 1 2 3 1 1 1 1	1.92
Ball, R-MN	1 3 0 3 2 3 3 1 0 2 2 1 1	2.00
Davis, R-PA	2 2 2 3 2 2 1 2 2 2 2 1 3	2.00
Chavez, D-NM	2 0 2 3 2 2 2 2 1 2 2 0 2	2.00
Gillette, D-IA	3 2 2 3 2 0 2 2 0 2 2 1 1	2.00
Burton, R-OH	1 3 2 3 3 2 3 2 1 2 2 2 1	2.08
Wheeler, D-MT	2 2 2 2 2 2 1 2 3 2 3 0 2	2.08
Johnson, D-CO	3 2 2 3 1 2 1 2 3 0 0 1 3	2.09
McNary, R-OR	2 0 2 3 2 0 2 2 0 0 0 0 2	2.14
Barbour, R-NJ	2 0 0 3 2 3 2 0 2 0 0 0 1	2.14
Capper, R-KS	2 2 2 3 2 2 2 2 3 2 2 1 2	2.15
George, D-GA	3 2 2 2 2 2 2 2 3 3 3 1 1	2.15
Tydings, D-MD	3 2 3 2 3 3 3 2 3 1 1 1 1	2.15
Eastland, D-MS	3 2 2 1 3 3 3 1 0 3 3 1 1	2.17
Nye, R-ND	0 0 2 3 3 2 1 3 1 2 2 0 3	2.20
Connally, D-TX	3 0 0 1 2 0 3 0 3 3 3 1 1	2.22
McCarran, D-NV	3 2 3 3 2 2 1 2 3 2 2 1 3	2.23
Vandenberg, R-MI	3 3 2 3 2 3 3 2 1 2 2 1 2	2.23
Shipstead, I-MN	2 3 0 2 2 2 1 3 3 2 2 3 2	2.25
McKellar, D-TN	3 2 2 1 2 3 2 2 3 3 3 0 1	2.25
Wiley, R-WI	3 3 0 3 3 0 3 2 2 2 2 2 2	2.25
Overton, D-LA	3 2 3 3 2 2 2 2 0 3 3 1 2	2.33

Name	Policy Dimensions	Score
	1 2 3 4 5 6 7 8 9 10 11 12 13	

LOW SUPPORT

Name	Policy Dimensions	Score
Gerry, D-RI	3 2 3 3 2 3 2 2 3 2 2 1 3	2.38
Bailey, D-NC	3 0 2 2 0 0 3 2 0 3 3 0 1	2.38
Reynolds, D-NC	2 2 0 3 2 3 2 0 3 2 0 3 0	2.44
White, R-ME	3 2 3 3 3 2 3 3 1 3 2 2 2	2.46
Tobey, R-NH	0 3 3 3 0 0 2 3 0 2 2 0 2	2.50
Taft, R-OH	2 3 3 3 3 3 3 3 1 2 2 2 3	2.54
Ferguson, R-MI	2 3 3 3 3 3 3 3 3 2 2 2 1	2.54
McClellan, D-AR	3 2 3 2 3 2 3 2 3 3 3 3 1	2.54
Byrd, D-VA	3 2 3 2 3 3 3 2 3 3 3 2 1	2.54
Hawkes, R-NJ	3 3 3 3 3 3 3 3 3 2 2 2 2	2.54
Thomas, R-ID	3 3 0 3 2 0 2 2 0 3 2 0 3	2.56
Brooks, R-IL	0 3 2 3 3 3 0 2 3 2 2 3 3	2.64
O'Daniel, D-TX	2 3 3 1 3 3 3 2 3 3 3 0 3	2.67
Gurney, R-SD	2 3 3 3 3 3 3 3 3 3 2 0 1	2.67
Reed, R-KS	3 3 2 3 3 3 3 3 2 3 3 0 2	2.67
Brewster, R-ME	3 3 0 3 3 2 3 0 0 2 3 2 3	2.70
Buck, R-DE	3 3 3 3 3 3 3 2 2 2 3 0	2.75
Smith, D-SC	3 0 0 0 0 3 3 3 3 3 3 0 1	2.75
Butler, R-NE	2 3 3 3 3 3 3 3 3 2 2 3 3	2.77
Holman, R-OR	3 3 3 3 2 3 3 3 3 3 2 2	2.77
Revercomb, R-WV	3 3 3 3 3 3 3 2 2 3 3 3	2.77
Robertson, R-WY	3 3 3 3 3 3 3 3 2 3 3 2 2	2.77
Bridges, R-NH	3 3 0 3 3 3 3 3 3 2 2 0 0	2.80
Wilson, R-IA	3 3 3 0 3 3 3 3 0 2 2 3 1	2.82
Wherry, R-NE	3 3 3 3 3 3 3 3 3 2 2 3 0	2.83
Willis, R-IN	3 0 3 3 3 3 3 3 3 2 2 3 3	2.83
Moore, R-OK	2 3 3 3 3 0 3 3 0 3 3 0 3	2.90
Bushfield, R-SD	3 3 3 3 3 0 3 3 0 3 2 3 3	2.91
Millikin, R-CO	3 0 3 3 3 3 3 3 3 3 3 3 3	3.00

Policy Dimension Key:

0   denotes that a senator did not scale on the dimension
1.   Public Power
2.   Extension of Executive Power
3.   Economy in Government Spending
4.   Fiscal Policy
5.   Business Regulation
6.   Social Welfare
7.   Labor
8.   National Defense
9.   Agriculture
10. Civil Rights/Civil Liberties
11. Extension of Federal Authority
12. Foreign Aid
13. Reciprocal Trade

78TH CONGRESS   (N=94)

HIGH SUPPORT (N=29 or 31%)   MEDIUM SUPPORT (N=36 or 38%)

Democrats   = 27 (93%)   Democrats   = 22 (61%)
GOP   = 1 (3.5%)   GOP   = 13 (36%)
Independents = 1 (3.5%)   Independents = 1 (3%)

LOW SUPPORT (N=29 or 31%)

Democrats   = 7 (24%)
GOP   = 22 (76%)
Independents = 0 (0%)

TABLE 3-2

Regional Divisions in Medium and Low Support Groups

MEDIUM SUPPORT (N=36)

Coastal (N=13 or 36%)

Danaher, R-CT	Walsh, D-MA	Barbour, R-NJ
Russell, D-GA	Lodge, R-MA	Tydings, D-MD
Aiken, R-VT	Austin, R-VT	George, D-GA
Maloney, D-CT	Maybank, D-SC	
Davis, R-PA	McNary, R-OR	

Interior (N= 23 or 64%)

Stewart, D-TN	Caraway, D-AR	Connally, D-TX
Chandler, D-KY	Bilbo, D-MS	Vandenberg, R-MI
Bankhead, D-AL	VanNuys, D-IN	McKellar, D-TN
Clark, D-MO	Ball, R-MN	Overton, D-LA
Chavez, D-NM	Gillette, D-IA	McCarran, D-NV
Burton, R-OH	Wheeler, D-MT	Shipstead, I-MN
Johnson, D-CO	Capper, R-KS	Wiley, R-WI
Eastland, D-MS	Nye, R-ND	

LOW SUPPORT (N=29)

Coastal (N=13 or 45%)

Gerry, D-RI	Bailey, D-NC	Holman, R-OR
Reynolds, D-NC	White, R-ME	Bridges, R-NH
Tobey, R-NH	Byrd, D-VA	Revercomb, R-WV
Hawkes, R-NJ	Brewster, R-ME	
Buck, R-DE	Smith, D-SC	

Interior (N=16 or 55%)

Taft, R-OH	Ferguson, R-MI	Willis, R-IN
McClellan, D-AR	Thomas, R-ID	Bushfield, R-SD
Brooks, R-IL	O'Daniel, D-TX	Moore, R-OK
Gurney, R-SD	Reed, R-KS	Millikin, R-CO
Butler, R-NE	Robertson, R-WY	
Wilson, R-IA	Wherry, R-NE	

TABLE 3-3

78th CONGRESS - FOREIGN POLICY DIMENSIONS

HIGH SUPPORT

Bone, D-WA	1.00	Mead, D-NY	1.33
Thomas, D-UT	1.00	Barkley, D-KY	1.33
Wagner, D-NY	1.00	Lucas, D-IL	1.33
Kilgore, D-WV	1.00	Radcliffe, D-MD	1.33
Downey, D-CA	1.00	O'Mahoney, D-WY	1.33
Murdock, D-UT	1.00	Hill, D-AL	1.33
Truman, D-MO	1.00	Chandler, D-KY	1.33
Walgren, D-WA	1.00	Clark, D-MO	1.33
Green, D-RI	1.00	Gillette, D-IA	1.33
Guffey, D-PA	1.00	George, D-GA	1.33
Pepper, D-FL	1.00	Tydings, D-MD	1.33
Tunnell, D-DE	1.00	Bilbo, D-MS	1.50
Hayden, D-AZ	1.00	Lodge, R-MA	1.50
McFarland, D-AZ	1.00	VanNuys, D-IN	1.50
Hatch, D-NM	1.00	McKellar, D-TN	1.50
Ellender, D-LA	1.00	Bailey, D-NC	1.50
Andrews, D-FL	1.00	LaFollette, I-WI	1.67
Thomas, D-OK	1.00	Walsh, D-MA	1.67
Stewart, D-TN	1.00	Austin, R-VT	1.67
Caraway, D-AR	1.00	Maloney, D-CT	1.67
Russell, D-GA	1.00	Burton, R-OH	1.67
Bankhead, D-AL	1.00	Johnson, D-CO	1.67
Maybank, D-SC	1.00	Capper, R-KS	1.67
Ball, R-MN	1.00	Vandenberg, R-MI	1.67
Eastland, D-MS	1.00	Overton, D-LA	1.67
Connally, D-TX	1.00	Byrd, D-VA	1.67
Murray, D-MT	1.33		

N = 53; D = 46; R = 6; I = 1

TABLE 3-3

78th CONGRESS - FOREIGN POLICY DIMENSIONS

MEDIUM SUPPORT

Aiken, R-VT	2.00	Gurney, R-SD	2.00
Chavez, D-NM	2.00	Smith, D-SC	2.00
Davis, R-PA	2.00	Langer, R-ND	2.33
Wheeler, D-MT	2.00	Danaher, R-CT	2.33
McNary, R-OR	2.00	White, R-ME	2.33
McCarran, D-NV	2.00	Hawkes, R-NJ	2.33
Wiley, R-WI	2.00	Holman, R-OR	2.33
Gerry, D-RI	2.00	Robertson, R-WY	2.33
Ferguson, R-MI	2.00	Wilson, R-IA	2.33
McClellan, D-AR	2.00		

N = 19; D = 6; R = 13
Coastal = 9 (47%); Interior = 10 (53%)

LOW SUPPORT

Tobey, R-NH	2.50	Reynolds, D-NC	3.00
Thomas, R-ID	2.50	Buck, R-DE	3.00
O'Daniel, D-TX	2.50	Butler, R-NE	3.00
Reed, R-KS	2.50	Revercomb, R-WV	3.00
Brewster, R-ME	2.50	Bridges, R-NH	3.00
Shipstead, I-MN	2.67	Wherry, R-NE	3.00
Taft, R-OH	2.67	Willis, R-IN	3.00
Brooks, R-IL	2.67	Moore, R-OK	3.00
Clark, D-ID	3.00	Bushfield, R-SD	3.00
Scrugham, D-NV	3.00	Millikin, R-CO	3.00
Nye, R-ND	3.00		

N = 21; D = 4; R = 16; I = 1
Coastal = 6 (29%); Interior = 15 (71%)

TABLE 3-4

78th CONGRESS - DOMESTIC POLICY DIMENSIONS

HIGH SUPPORT

Bone, D-WA	1.00	Pepper, D-FL	1.25
Thomas, D-UT	1.00	Lucas, D-IL	1.30
Wagner, D-NY	1.00	LaFollette, I-WI	1.30
Kilgore, D-WV	1.00	Langer, R-ND	1.30
Downey, D-CA	1.00	O'Mahoney, D-WY	1.38
Murray, D-MT	1.00	Hayden, D-AZ	1.40
Murdock, D-UT	1.10	McFarland, D-AZ	1.40
Mead, D-NY	1.10	Tunnell, D-DE	1.40
Truman, D-MO	1.13	Clark, D-ID	1.43
Walgren, D-WA	1.13	Hatch, D-NM	1.50
Green, D-RI	1.13	Radcliffe, D-MD	1.50
Guffey, D-PA	1.20	Ellender, D-LA	1.50
Barkley, D-KY	1.20		

N = 25; D = 23; R = 1; I = 1

MEDIUM SUPPORT

Danaher, R-CT	1.67	Davis, R-PA	2.00
Scrugham, D-NV	1.71	Chavez, D-NM	2.00
Thomas, D-OK	1.80	Nye, R-ND	2.00
Andrews, D-FL	1.88	Clark, D-MO	2.10
Walsh, D-MA	1.89	Wheeler, D-MT	2.10
Bankhead, D-AL	1.89	Shipstead, I-MN	2.11
Stewart, D-TN	1.90	Johnson, D-CO	2.13
Caraway, D-AR	1.90	Maybank, D-SC	2.20
Aiken, R-VT	1.90	Burton, R-OH	2.20
Russell, D-GA	2.00	McNary, R-OR	2.20
Chandler, D-KY	2.00	Capper, R-KS	2.20
Bilbo, D-MS	2.00	Gillette, D-IA	2.25
Lodge, R-MA	2.00	McCarran, D-NV	2.30
VanNuys, D-IN	2.00	Overton, D-LA	2.30
Austin, R-VT	2.00	Barbour, R-NJ	2.33
Maloney, D-CT	2.00		

N = 31; D = 20; R = 10; I = 1
Coastal = 12 (39%); Interior = 19 (61%)

TABLE 3-4

78th CONGRESS - DOMESTIC POLICY DIMENSIONS

LOW SUPPORT

Ball, R-MN	2.38	Buck, R-DE	2.70
Reynolds, D-NC	2.38	Butler, R-NE	2.70
George, D-GA	2.40	Brewster, R-ME	2.75
Tydings, D-MD	2.40	Wilson, R-IA	2.75
Vandenberg, R-MI	2.40	Bridges, R-NH	2.78
McKellar, D-TN	2.40	Willis, R-IN	2.78
Gerry, D-RI	2.50	Byrd, D-VA	2.80
White, R-ME	2.50	Hawkes, R-NJ	2.80
Tobey, R-NH	2.50	Gurney, R-SD	2.80
Taft, R-OH	2.50	Reed, R-KS	2.80
Eastland, D-MS	2.55	Revercomb, R-WV	2.80
Connally, D-TX	2.57	Wherry, R-NE	2.80
Thomas, R-ID	2.57	Moore, R-OK	2.88
Wiley, R-WI	2.63	Bushfield, R-SD	2.88
Brooks, R-IL	2.63	Holman, R-OR	2.90
Bailey, D-NC	2.67	Robertson, R-WY	2.90
Ferguson, R-MI	2.70	Millikin, R-CO	3.00
McClellan, D-AR	2.70	Smith, D-SC	3.00
O'Daniel, D-TX	2.70		

N = 37; D = 12; R = 25
Coastal = 14 (38%); Interior = 23 (62%)

icy dimensions, however, deemed by most to be less central to the war effort, only 27% of the scalable senators gave high support to Administration initiatives.

Tables 3–3 and 3–4 also testify to the continuing impact of partisanship on voting alignments. The 78th Congress culminated, of course, with the 1944 presidential election, and for many Senate Democrats, Franklin Roosevelt's decision to run for a fourth term exerted a strong influence on their voting behavior. Indeed, Democrats accounted for 92% of the high support offered on domestic policy dimensions in the 78th Congress. On foreign policy dimensions, Democrats comprised 87% of the high support group in the 78th Congress, down slightly from 92% in the previous Congress. But the unity Senate Democrats achieved in the 77th Congress on foreign policy dimensions is perhaps overstated because all scalable votes came during the highly charged preparedness debate in the months leading up to Pearl Harbor.

FDR's bid for re-election, on the other hand, encouraged the Senate GOP to unite more frequently during the 78th Congress, to thwart Administration efforts. In 1943 and 1944, for example, Republicans comprised 68% of the low support group on domestic policy dimensions, compared to only 33% in the previous Congress. Similarly, on foreign policy dimensions in the 78th Congress, Republicans accounted for 76% of the low support group, whereas in the 77th Congress the low support group had only been 63% Republican. As these statistics suggest, notwithstanding the calls for national unity to combat the enemy abroad, the pull of party politics in a presidential election year remained a powerful influence in Senate affairs throughout 1943 and 1944.

If the ebb and flow of Senate politics in the 78th Congress were often a product of the clash between war-bred unity and partisan politics, the statistical analysis also reveals the long-term forces that were transforming Senate conservatism. Indeed, if patriotism or electoral vulnerability explains why some in the right wing offered higher than usual support for Administration initiatives, deliberate adjustments of ideology seem also to have played a role.

As Allied battlefield success mounted steadily throughout 1943 and 1944, Americans came gradually to understand that the defeat of the Axis, once seemingly problematic, was inevitable. Particularly following the Allied landing on the Normandy beaches in June 1944, the only major unanswered question was the timing of the Axis defeat in Europe. As a result of this change in the nature of the war, the Senate in 1943 and 1944 devoted an increasing amount of its attention to the shape of the postwar world. Much of the legislation considered in these years, moreover, including the Ruml Tax, the Soldier-Vote bill, and the George Reconversion bill, signaled that the Administration intended to maintain a large role for the federal government once hostilities ended. Indeed, the degree of support given to those policy dimensions that had formed the core of the New Deal's domestic agenda tended to be the factor that divided the senators into the high, medium, and low categories. Almost all of the Democrats, for example, gave high or medium support to those policy dimensions connected most directly to the ongoing war, such as National Defense, Foreign Policy, and Reciprocal Trade. But while liberal Democrats in the high support category also gave strong support to those domestic policy dimensions that embraced the positive state, such as Extension of Executive Power, Business Regulation, Social Welfare, Labor, and Fiscal Policy, the twenty-two Democrats in the second scale position generally mustered no more than medium support on these issues.

Also testifying to the accommodation the Democrats in the medium support group were making to the positive state was their relative willingness to support the Extension of Federal Authority and Civil Rights/Civil Liberties. Since both policy dimensions were central to the changes introduced by the New Deal in 1933, it is perhaps no surprise that all seven Democrats who scaled in the low support category opposed the Administration in both of these dimensions, as many of them had in the 1930s. Many of the twenty-two Democrats in the medium support group, on the other hand, had also opposed the Admininstration in these areas in the 1930s, but by the 78th Congress had come to a more moderate position.

Similarly, scale divisions between Republicans in the 78th Congress also testify to a transformation of conservatism. Dividing the moderate Republicans in the medium support group from their colleagues in the low support group in table 3–1 was their respective attitude toward most of the domestic policy dimensions. On issues such as Public Power, Fiscal Policy, Business Regulation, Social Welfare, and Labor, the Republican senators divided into two groups. While those in the medium scale position generally provided moderate support on these dimensions, those in the low scale position continued on the staunch anti-Administration course their party had charted in the 1930s. Similarly, while the obstructionist Republicans in the third scale position were most supportive of issues designed to effect economy in government spending, the thirteen Republicans in the second scale position gave only moderate support to those measures.

Perhaps a more significant indication of the ideological forces transforming the Republican party was revealed when scale positions on domestic policy dimensions were separated from those on foreign policy. As Table 3–4 indicates, seven of the ten Republicans who offered medium support on domestic policy dimensions came from coastal states, which had often borne the full brunt of the industrial revolution. By contrast, seventeen of the twenty-five Republicans who scaled in the low support category on domestic dimensions represented interior states, which in the opening decades of the twentieth century had generally been less affected by industrialization and urbanization. As these intraparty divisions indicate, by the end of the 78th Congress the line separating new conservatives from obstructionists in the Senate was often a geographic line.

When the 78th Congress adjourned, the determination to win the war against fascism was giving way to a new set of concerns over the shape of the postwar world. This shift in concern, in turn, steadily dissolved the national unity bred by the war emergency, enabling partisan and ideological differences to resurface in Senate affairs. The intraparty divisions that appeared in the 78th Congress, and particularly those within the GOP, presaged the new conservatism that would play an important role in postwar political affairs.

4

The New Conservatism, 1945–1946

THE TRANSFORMATION OF SENATE CONSERVATISM, GAINING MOMEN-
tum gradually since the late 1930s, accelerated rapidly in 1945 and
1946. The end of World War II provided Americans with the necessary perspective to assess the full impact that conflict had on the
patterns of national life, and many drew from this analysis strong
new evidence of the interdependency of individuals and nations in
the industrial era. In this way, World War II, as the Great Depression earlier had done, convinced many in the nation that an expanded role for the federal government was both a necessary and
proper tool for the promotion of the general welfare. Results of the
1944 elections appeared to confirm this shift in national thinking as
voters unceremoniously removed from office some of the senators
most prominently identified with the right wing of the 1930s. Their
replacements, in turn, as legislative action in the 79th Congress
made clear, often embraced a different, more moderate brand of
conservatism. The lessons conservatives drew from the war, combined with the membership replacement effected by the 1944 elections, widened the fault lines in the Senate's right wing. The
distinction between obstructionist conservatives and the new conservatives, incipient since 1938, became a reality in 1945.

I

Two reports prepared in early 1945 by special Senate subcommit-
tees investigating the states of American health, education, and
housing provided compelling evidence of the degree to which
America had become a nation of interdependent individuals by the
1940s. A survey of wartime health and education prepared by a
subcommittee of the Senate Labor and Education Committee revealed that 40% of draft-age men in America were unfit for military
service because of physical or mental deficiencies. One of the prin-

cipal causes of this problem, the report argued, was the uneven quality and availability of health care throughout the nation. In 1945 the report found that 40% of American counties, representing a total population of 15 million, were without hospitals or full-time health officers. Such conditions, it concluded, created serious manpower problems that hindered the nation's defense as well as its industrial productivity.[1]

Seven months later a report from the subcommittee on Postwar Economic Policy and Planning detailed the poor condition of the nation's housing stock. Drawing on both 1940 census data and testimony given in late 1944, the subcommittee, chaired by Republican Robert Taft, found that almost one-quarter of the urban dwelling units in 1940 had no running water, private flush toilet, or bathing facilities, and that nearly one-half of the rural dwelling units lacked running water. Convinced that unequal housing conditions were a national problem that could be remedied only if a federal housing program supplemented the private sector's efforts, the subcommittee concluded that "in a country capable of our tremendous wartime production, there is no reason why hardship and extreme poverty cannot be prevented."[2]

In their effort to digest the changes made evident by the war and the Great Depression, many Senate conservatives undoubtedly found support in the subcommittee reports for their growing conviction that America was a nation of interdependent individuals. Both reports emphasized, for example, that although the inequality in health care, education, and housing touched some regions of the country more heavily than others, all were ultimately national problems. The obstacle these social problems posed to America's prosperity and national security presented the most immediate concern. But in a larger sense, the inability of some Americans to obtain adequate medical care or to live in a decent house convinced many Senate conservatives that their traditional philosophy of limited government could no longer satisfy the needs of modern industrial life. Republican George Aiken of Vermont explained in a December 1945 article on nutrition that, prior to World War II, most believed the American people were so well fed that even if supplies of food and fiber were expanded, consumption of them would remain stable. But per capita consumption of food had increased 11% during the war, primarily because higher incomes permitted individuals to buy food in both greater quantity and variety. Similarly, the high number of draft rejections related to malnutrition emphasized the inadequacy of the prewar American diet. "It is the fear that we may again slump back into pre-war malnutrition that has prompted me to become interested in corrective legislation," Aiken concluded. "I see no reason why, when we are making such progress in nutritional science, we should allow our chickens to be fed better than we feed our children, . . . [O]ur government is not without responsibility to protect the nutritional standards for the health of the nation."[3]

That the lesson about the role of government George Aiken drew from the wartime experience was shared more broadly throughout the nation was suggested by a letter the Vermont Republican received from a constituent in August. Writing in support of a pending bill to establish federal aid for education, the president of Vermont's League of Women Voters recounted how reports of 200,000 men disqualified by Selective Service because of illiteracy had convinced her organization that a federal role in education was vital for the national welfare. Because of the reports, she wrote:

Members [of the League] everywhere had become aware . . . that a state's educational standards are the concern of the entire country and not alone of that particular state. This national interest caused all of us to see the extreme inequality . . . of educational opportunity throughout the country. . . . Since then we have become aware that war expenses which will continue into the postwar period will leave poor communities in a worse position than before to support their school systems.[4]

The position taken by the League of Women Voters on federal aid to education in 1945 hints at the broad ideological reformulation that was taking place in American political thought by 1945. A bedrock belief that had held at least since the American Revolution was that as government power rose, individual liberty fell. When Franklin Roosevelt was inaugurated president in March 1933, most scholars have noted, the federal government still rarely touched the daily existence of most Americans. The New Deal and World War II, however, rapidly expanded the federal government's role, and in the eyes of most Americans, contributed to the successful resolution of those crises. Thus, by the end of World War II, perhaps a majority of Americans looked to the federal government for solutions to the problems of modern life. Thereafter, national political debate usually turned on the degree to which government's powers should be expanded, and the prominence of the U.S. role in world affairs.

That such a change had occurred in national political discourse by 1945 is also suggested by the effect of membership replacement on Senate conservatism. Steadily throughout the 1940s, many of the most conservative or most isolationist senators were removed through defeat or death. Indeed, only five of the fifteen Democrats listed by historian James T. Patterson as "most conservative" in 1939 (Millard Tydings, Peter Gerry, Harry F. Byrd, Edwin Johnson, and Josiah Bailey) remained in the Senate at the end of World War II. Senate isolationists fared no better. When the 79th Congress convened in January 1945, one scholar has noted, only two of the seven members of the Nye Committee, Walter George and Arthur Vandenberg, were still in the upper house.[5] The 1944 elections alone saw the defeat of such notable conservatives as Ellison D. "Cotton Ed" Smith of South Carolina, Bennett "Champ" Clark of Missouri, and Robert Reynolds of North Carolina. Among the new senators elected in 1944 were South Carolina's Olin Johnston, Missouri's Forrest Donnell, North Carolina's Clyde Hoey, Massachusett's Leverett Saltonstall, New Jersey's H. Alexander Smith, and California's William Knowland, all of whom espoused during their Senate careers a more moderate brand of conservatism. Clyde Hoey's views were typical of this new breed of conservative. In a speech to the Shelby, North Carolina Chamber of Commerce in March 1945, the freshman Democrat noted that, although it was natural to look to the nation's heritage for solutions to the many postwar problems, he warned that America could not rely solely on the past. "We are living in a changing world. . . . When victory comes we shall not be able to return to conditions which existed twenty years ago, or even before the war began. . . . The government can and should do much to help its citizens." Yet although the 5-point plan Hoey offered the Shelby Chamber of Commerce embraced such positive government functions as the development of economic projects to "supplement the efforts of private business and take up any slack in unemployment" he also stressed such traditional conservative dogma as lower taxes and balanced budgets to ensure national economic vitality. Hoey's political philosophy, then, like that of many other senators elected after 1938, was a new conservatism that sought to adapt traditional conservative values to the needs of the urban, industrial society of the twentieth century.[6]

This is not to suggest, of course, that senators espousing traditional conservative views of limited government and rugged individualism disappeared from the upper house in the 1940s. Indeed, some senators elected in this decade, including Kenneth Wherry, John Bricker, W. Lee "Pappy" O'Daniel, and Hugh Butler continued to denounce the "socialism" of the New Deal and to rail against American internationalism. But a careful reading of Senate politics indicates that by 1945 the right wing of both parties in the upper house had become deeply fragmented into the "obstruction-ists," who preferred to re-establish the America that had existed prior to 1933, and the new conservatives, who accepted the general principles of the New Deal welfare state and of American interna-tionalism, and sought only to limit their scope.

The differences separating the new conservatives from the ob-structionists were revealed clearly by the January 1945 debate over FDR's nomination of Henry Wallace as secretary of commerce. Be-cause the former Vice President had long been identified with the more liberal tendencies of New Deal reform, the nomination pro-voked intense debate. Liberal political commentator Richard L. Strout (T. R. B. of the *New Republic*) observed approvingly in the *Christian Science Monitor,* for example, that Wallace's nomination, together with the pledge in FDR's annual message to guarantee 60 million postwar jobs, meant that the American public should pre-pare for the return of New Deal reform. To the *Detroit Free Press,* however, the President's choice to head the cabinet department re-sponsible for leading the business community was incomprehensi-ble. "It would be difficult to imagine any man in all the United States," the newspaper opined on 24 January, "who is as thor-oughly distrusted and disliked by American business—big and lit-tle—as Henry Wallace. . . . American businessmen know . . . that Henry Wallace is a mystic who consults soothsayers, crystal gazers and Yogis."[7] Wallace's testimony before the Senate Commerce Committee in early January, moreover, did nothing to dispel these views. He called for a guaranteed annual minimum wage for all em-ployees, maintenance of high wartime wages in the postwar era, and automatic government pump-priming to be triggered whenever the number of jobs in the nation fell below 57 million. For both supporters and opponents, therefore, Wallace's nomination was a symbol of the Administration's intent to resume New Deal reform, with its emphasis on Executive leadership, at war's end.[8]

Because of widespread concern that Wallace, if confirmed, would use the broad financial powers of the Commerce Department to im-plement liberal New Deal reforms, Walter George proposed during committee hearings on the nomination to limit the Secretary's power to manage the economy. Under George's motion, the Federal Loan Administration was to be separated from the Commerce De-partment, thus removing the $32 billion lending authority of the Reconstruction Finance Corporation from the cabinet office's con-trol. The fears of some Senate conservatives, however, were not al-layed by the George bill. Harry Byrd and Josiah Bailey, for example, openly worried that if Wallace were confirmed to a circumscribed Commerce post, the President might later restore its lending authority by Executive order. Thus, when the issue moved into the full Senate, the obstructionists' strategy was to vote first on the nomination, in the belief that if the powers of the Commerce Department were not diminished, Henry Wallace would never win confirmation. A motion from Josiah Bailey on 1 February to proceed immediately to the nomination was defeated, however, by a 42–42 tie vote and then, before opponents could move to reconsider the vote, Walter George's bill was called up and summarily adopted.[9]

The votes on the Wallace nomination point directly to the change in voting alignments effected by the transformation of Senate conservatism. While contemporary observers attributed the powerful opposition to a resurgent conservative coalition, it is clear that the political divisions were more complex.[10] The 1 February vote on the Bailey motion revealed, for instance, that southern Democrats and Republicans were both deeply divided. Although eleven of the southern Democrats voted against Wallace, nine of them, including J. William Fulbright, Olin Johnston, Burnet Maybank, and Richard Russell, supported the Administration. Similarly, while most in the GOP voted for the Bailey motion, nine Republicans, including George Aiken, Warren Austin, Ralph Brewster, Harold Burton, Wayne Morse, and Leverett Saltonstall, deserted their party to back the Administration.[11] Later the same day, however, the southern Democrats and Republicans who had voted against the Bailey motion joined forces with conservatives to approve the George bill, but one month later threw their support behind Administration forces to confirm Henry Wallace to the circumscribed cabinet post.[12]

The factional divisions among southern Democrats and Republicans on the Wallace nomination point to the philosophical differences between the new conservatives and the obstructionists in the upper house. Many of the southern Democrats and Republicans who deserted their colleagues on these votes represented a new generation of conservatives, which understood that in the postwar era, government had to assume some responsibility for the national welfare. By supporting the George bill and then voting to confirm Wallace to the Commerce position, the new conservatives demonstrated that they were relatively untroubled by the principle of government economic intervention symbolized by the former Vice President, and questioned only the extent of that intervention. Indeed, as the statistical analysis of the roll call votes reveals, throughout the 79th Congress issues concerned with Business Regulation, as well as those in such related fields as Extension of

Federal Authority and Extension of Executive Authority, new conservatives and obstructionists were differentiated by the degree of support they provided. As they had demonstrated on the George bill and Wallace nomination, obstructionists with rare exception were unwilling to provide anything more than low support in these dimensions. Conversely, the new conservatives tended to give medium support and occasionally high support to those dimensions concerned with federal regulation of business and the extension of federal power.

The changing face of Senate politics was readily apparent to Josiah Bailey. Nine days after the adoption of the George bill, the North Carolina Democrat argued in a letter to Burton Wheeler, a leader of the anti–New Deal coalition in the late 1930s, that the Senate's action was more than an ordinary setback to his conservative principles. Rather, he argued, the imminent confirmation of Henry Wallace portended a sea change in political attitudes. "I recently made a study of what is going on," he noted plaintively, "and came to the conclusion that in the last several years this government has undergone a complete revolution. . . . Practically all the restraints upon Federal power have been removed and as matters stand the Congress assumes responsibility for the economic welfare of every group that demands it with sufficient votes. This is subversion itself and the consequences of it can hardly be foreseen. Certainly it means full regimentation of the entire population. . . . This is what Mr. Wallace is driving at."[13]

The issue of federal aid to education, debated throughout much of 1945, also revealed the wide philosophical differences dividing the Senate's right wing. Although proposals for federal aid had surfaced in the 1930s, conservatives, who objected to both the high cost and the federal encroachment of state power, were able to defeat the issue in the Senate. Robert Taft's comments in 1942 on S. 1313, a bill granting $300 million to the states for the general expenses of kindergarten and elementary schools, were typical of the obstructionist conservative position on this issue. Although his views on federal aid were transformed several years later, Taft maintained adamantly that not only were the states in better financial condition than the federal government but that the bill also "constitutes a further threat to local government which has already been weakened by the Federal Government in the last decade. . . . Education is purely a local affair . . . and requires no nursing along from Washington."[14]

By 1945, however, evidence accumulated during the war revealed wide variations in the quality of the American education system. Two economists at the University of South Carolina found in a 1942 study, for example, that although the national average of per capita wealth in 1940 was $573, South Carolina's average was only $281. At the same time, Connecticut's average per capita wealth was $864, while New Jersey's stood at $852, meaning that South Carolina, "is less than one-half as able to spend money for education as the nation as a whole and one-third as able as the more wealthy states of the nation." A survey released by the NEA in March 1945 contained similar conclusions. It found that although states in the Southeast and Southwest tended to have the highest proportion of school-age children, they generally had the least financial ability to meet those needs.[15] The high illiteracy rate that had forced Selective Service to reject more than 200,000 men during World War II stressed the significance of these figures. Education, like nutrition, health, or housing could no longer be regarded as simply a state or local problem.

The impact of this realization on Senate conservatism was apparent in the 1945 debates on federal aid to education. Although some conservatives continued to insist resolutely that federal aid would bankrupt the nation and lead to federal domination of the schools, others viewed the issue differently. North Carolina Democrat Josiah Bailey opposed the Ramspeck bill, extending limited federal aid to "poor" states, because he considered "it the primary duty of a state to provide fully for the education of the children within its borders."[16] Bailey's colleague from North Carolina, freshman Democrat Clyde R. Hoey, however, indicated that the great variation in education from state to state, together with the large number of draft rejections, had convinced him that education was an area for which the federal government had to assume some responsibility. Testifying in the spring of 1945 on behalf of the Ramspeck bill, Hoey maintained that "this bill goes a long way to equalize the matter of opportunities and to make available to the children in those states where the average income is lower and where the per capita wealth is smaller, the school facilities necessary and essential for the proper training, education and development of the children."[17]

The newly elected Republican senator from New Jersey, H. Alexander Smith, agreed fully with Hoey's conclusions. Although he recognized that his state was too "rich" to qualify for federal aid under the Ramspeck bill and admitted a "real difficulty in adjusting myself to a spending program that may take us into the billions of dollars after the war," Smith nevertheless confessed that "there are certain causes, like education and hospitals, that do appeal to me enormously because I do feel we must take care of equality of opportunity for our children in the schools without regard to race, creed or color."[18]

While the attitude toward federal aid to education displayed by Hoey, Smith, and other new conservatives in 1945 set them apart from obstructionist conservatives, their position was at the same time different from liberals' thinking on the issue. In contrast to some liberals who viewed federal aid as the first step toward a comprehensive national restructuring of the education system, the new conservatives in the Senate wanted to limit such aid carefully in order to hold down the cost and to retain local control of the schools.[19] H. Alexander Smith of New Jersey explained to a constituent in June 1945, for example, that although it was important to provide federal aid to poor states, "we must oppose widespread federal handouts which inevitably mean widespread federal controls, and we must try and get back to an appreciation of local responsibility." Clyde Hoey concurred fully. "The power to regulate the schools," he argued in testimony supporting the Ramspeck bill, "should remain under the jurisdiction of the sovereign states, free of regulations and restrictions, by the centralized government in Washington."[20]

The differences separating new conservatives from liberals on federal aid to education were typical of the policy differences that more broadly divided the two groups of legislators in the 79th Congress. The statistical analysis indicated that in all policy dimensions that most directly defined the New Deal's domestic agenda, such as Social Welfare, Civil Rights/Civil Liberties, and Agriculture, the new conservatives tended to offer no more than medium support throughout the 79th Congress, compared to the high support usually provided by liberals. The position adopted by the new conservatives in the Senate, then, suggested that they were searching for the middle ground between two extremes. While they rejected the obstructionists' belief that there was no need to employ federal power to solve society's problems, they also sought to limit the use of that power more sharply than the liberals. Vermont Republican George Aiken demonstrated the nature of his conservatism during 1945 Senate hearings on education. Although he recognized the need for federal aid, Aiken admitted that "I would prefer to see that States do it [increase spending on education], but if half the States won't do it, then I would rather see the Federal Government do it than not have it done at all."[21]

Another indication of the adjustment the new conservatives made in their political philosophy came in the debate of the Full Employment bill introduced in January 1945 by New Deal Democrats

James Murray and Robert F. Wagner. The bill in its original form sought, through a combination of Keynesian economic theory and New Deal liberalism, to establish the federal government's responsibility for postwar employment. It required the Executive branch to make annual estimates of the number of jobs needed to attain full employment, as well as the number of jobs likely to be created by the private sector. If the forecast indicated that the number of private sector jobs would be insufficient to attain full employment, then the President was to propose a program of positive federal action, which might include compensatory spending, to achieve full employment. Under the Murray-Wagner bill, in other words, the federal government would guarantee that jobs would exist for all Americans able and willing to work.[22]

Obstructionist conservatives throughout the nation opposed the Full Employment bill immediately, arguing that it would regiment American life and permanently commit the nation to deficit financing. The Committee for Constitutional Government, for example, charged that "this mislabelled 'Full Employment' bill (really bigger government—more debts—more taxes) may turn America permanently from constitutional private enterprise toward a system of collectivist statism."[23] C. Douglas Buck, a Republican senator from Delaware since 1942, viewed the bill similarly. Arguing that the principle of government-guaranteed jobs was incongruent with a free society, Buck insisted that more traditional fiscal policy was the key to full employment. "The remedy for unemployment," he contended, "is to balance the federal budget, reduce taxes on industry, remove government restrictions on business, and provide credit for small business, when venture capital will come out of hiding and full employment will become a reality."[24] To conservatives of this stripe, then, the Murray-Wagner bill, like Henry Wallace's nomination, was yet another sign of the Roosevelt Administration's determination to resume liberal New Deal reform at war's end.

Debate on the Murray-Wagner bill revealed, however, that not all Senate conservatives shared Buck's assessment. The new conservatives who had supported Henry Wallace's nomination and limited federal aid to education again acknowledged that the federal government had some responsibility for employment, but argued that such responsibility centered only on the need for a smooth reconversion of the American economy to peacetime production. H. Alexander Smith of New Jersey argued to a constituent in September 1945, for example, that "in this postwar period we are in a transition stage, really starting from scratch with many of our conceptions of industrial relationships, and . . . we cannot go back to just where we were before." Yet, unlike some liberals who viewed the Murray-Wagner bill as the first step toward a new era of central economic planning, Smith saw the bill as a limited method to assist the free enterprise system. "It is up to those of us who feel we have had some grounding in sound economics," Smith emphasized, "to see to it that our American set-up is protected from the dangerous consequences of the new-fangled thinking. I refer particularly to the Kaynes-Hansen [*sic*] theory that it makes no difference how much money we owe if we owe it to ourselves."[25]

The reasoning of the new conservatives on this issue was most clearly summarized by George Aiken. During a Senate speech in support of Henry Wallace's nomination, the Vermont Republican defended the need for government action in postwar employment, thereby indicating the common thread that the new conservatives saw in the two issues. The challenge facing postwar America, Aiken argued on 1 March, was to maintain world peace and prosperity. Yet the nation would fail in these endeavors unless it planned adequately for its own reconversion. "Let five million veterans become unemployed and we will see a demand for government operation of industrial plants," he warned. "When that time comes, those who now pursue a course which can only lead to the 'breadline and bayonet' method of dealing with unemployment will be very, very glad to vote for anything to satisfy the demands of these men." As Aiken and other new conservatives understood, then, an expanded role for the government over such matters as employment was necessary to meet the new conditions facing America. Yet in supporting such action, their goal was not to make fundamental changes in America, but simply to use new means to preserve its traditional values. Aiken was as clear on this point as Smith had been. "True conservatism," he concluded, "consists of maintaining the best in our institutions without obstructing progress. We must not confuse conservatism with obstructionism for the latter may lead to rifts in our social structure with undesirable consequences."[26]

The Murray-Wagner bill was modified substantially during Senate debate and the changes made in it reflected the philosophy of the new conservatives. The bill reported out of the Banking and Currency Committee, for example, continued to declare the federal government's responsibility for maintaining full employment. But in place of the bill's original stipulation that the President submit annually a detailed legislative program for expanding GNP to achieve full employment, the Committee's bill merely required him to offer a "general program" to maintain employment. This change, most observers agreed, reduced the bill's Keynesian emphasis on deficit spending to create jobs. The Murray-Wagner bill was further altered by a Hatch amendment, which declared that the federal government's responsibility for maintaining full employment had to be viewed within the context of the larger needs of national policy. This change was widely regarded as eliminating compensatory spending from the federal arsenal of economic weapons. Finally, a Taft amendment required that, beginning with fiscal 1948, all proposals to expand federal expenditures and investment to maintain full employment had to be accompanied by tax hikes to avoid increases in the national debt. The bill in its final form, then, established the federal government's responsibility for maintaining full employment, but eschewed any of the tendencies toward central economic planning and deficit spending that conservatives habitually associated with the New Deal.[27]

Because of the changes made to the Employment bill, many liberals were disenchanted with the final product that cleared the Senate on 28 September. Moments before the final vote, Alben Barkley asserted sarcastically that "if anything in connection with the program organized under . . . the pending bill is inconsistent with any part of the programs inaugurated under measures previously enacted, the program proposed under . . . this bill shall be abandoned." The journalist I. F. Stone, an ardent New Dealer, was even more disappointed. Writing while the upper house considered the amendments that would shear the bill of much of its Keynseian emphasis, Stone asserted that the Murray-Wagner bill was merely the first step the government had to take to ensure economic security. In the long run, he wrote, the federal government also had to develop a comprehensive economic plan to coordinate effectively industrial output with consumer demand.[28]

But to the new conservatives who had never completely accepted the active role for the federal government envisioned by the New Deal, the limited goals of the Senate's employment bill struck the right balance between the needs of the modern industrial state and America's traditional individualism. Employment of individuals in a modern industrial economy could no longer be entrusted solely to market forces, they reasoned. Government had to assist the private sector in creating stable, even economic growth. At the same time, the new conservatives recognized that if government assistance were not carefully limited, it could overwhelm individual initiative and free enterprise. In their minds, too much government intervention was as dangerous as no intervention at all. The limited view the new conservatives took of the Employment bill was clear in remarks Charles Tobey made to a constituent in November 1945. Far from attempting to guarantee jobs to all able-bodied Americans, the New Hampshire Republican contended, the purpose of the measure "is to use research to try and remain ahead, to determine what needs will be in the future, just as every large industry does." That such efforts by the government were necessary, Tobey had no doubts. "You know and I know," he concluded, "that the cataclysmic effect of this war has not come home to us until now. . . . [W]e have been through H—— as a nation, and now to get back to normal is going to be a task of tremendous size."[29]

If 1945 was a year that revealed a significant transformation in the domestic political philosophy of many Senate conservatives, it was also a year of important changes in foreign policy attitudes. Senate votes taken in the summer to extend reciprocal trade for three years, and to approve U.S. participation in both the Bretton Woods monetary agreements and the United Nations, offered evidence that the experience of the Depression and World War II had also convinced many in the Senate that in both an economic and a strategic sense, America's future was inextricably bound to the international community.

Of course, Senate isolationism did not disappear after 1945. But its adherents no longer commanded the broad-based support that had characterized prewar isolationism. Instead, Senate opposition to an internationalistic foreign policy after 1945 tended to be much more parochial, coming primarily from midwestern Republicans whose ideas were rooted in the same rural, agrarian traditions from which obstructionist conservatives on domestic policy drew sustenance.[30] After 1945, therefore, obstructionist conservatives and isolationists in the Senate tended to be one and the same. Unlike the new conservatives who attempted to adjust their political views to the demands of the modern industrial nation, the obstructionists, by opposing both the positive state and international entanglements, were united by their desire to resist change and to restore the preindustrial traditions of America.

The debate over extension of reciprocal trade in June illustrated the common link connecting the domestic and foreign policy philosophies of the obstructionists. Proponents of the extension bill, which continued reciprocal trade for three years and empowered the President to reduce tariff duties by as much as 50% in return for concessions from other countries, maintained that the program was essential for building postwar peace. They warned that if the United States, the richest nation in the world, pursued a course of economic nationalism, other countries would likely follow suit.

Although reciprocal trade had provoked strong opposition from conservatives in the 1930s who saw it as both entangling America too deeply in international affairs and granting too much discretionary power to the Executive, the 1945 extension bill encountered far less resistance. Indeed, new conservatives in the GOP frequently broke with their party's tradition of high protective tariffs to supply the votes needed to defeat crippling amendments to the extension bill. On 19 June, for instance, nine Republicans, including Aiken, Austin, Ball, Morse, Saltonstall, Smith, and Tobey (the other two Republicans were Buck and Ferguson) joined thirty-eight Democrats to defeat a Finance Committee amendment deleting the President's discretionary power to reduce tariffs up to 50%. The following day, the same seven Republicans, along with Homer Ferguson and George Wilson, again sided with the Democratic majority to help kill an O'Mahoney amendment requiring congressional approval for all future trade agreements. The winning majority by which reciprocal trade was extended on 20 June again included new conservatives as Aiken, Ball, Burton, Donnell, George, Hoey, Johnston, Radcliffe, Saltonstall, and Tobey.[31]

The factors transforming the foreign policy views of many senators were evident in the different analyses of the reciprocal trade debate offered by two Republicans. The traditional GOP attitude was reflected in criticism voiced by Kenneth Wherry of Nebraska. Wherry and other midwestern senators continued to regard reciprocal trade as a program that unfairly favored the industrial sector at the expense of the nation's farmers. In tones reminiscent of William Jennings Bryan, Wherry maintained during floor debate in June that "agricultural production is essential, and comes first, and is the basis of everything else. If we do not have a strong agricultural production structure the remainder of our economic structure is not strong. All industry is dependent on agriculture."[32] In contrast to Wherry and other traditional conservatives, Charles Tobey indicated that he had moderated his thinking on foreign policy. During debate on reciprocal trade, the New Hampshire Republican was particularly scornful of his party colleagues like Wherry who, he charged, heeded the call of special interests instead of the voice of the people. " 'You've got to understand people,' " he contended, " 'all the people, not just this group or that group. Damn it, what did Jesus say? . . . Love thy neighbor as thyself. And who is thy neighbor? It's everyone, all the people of this country and of all countries. We're all in this together . . . and we all rise and fall together.' "[33] Thus, just as Tobey and other new conservatives saw that an expanded role for government was necessitated by the interdependency of individuals in industrial America, so too did they see reciprocal trade as promoting the common welfare of all Americans.

The overwhelming approval the Senate gave to the Bretton Woods agreements and to the United Nations Charter in July underscored the change that was occurring in the foreign policy thinking of many senators in 1945. Voting to approve the system of international economic cooperation negotiated at Bretton Woods, for example, were six Republicans who scaled as new conservatives in the 79th Congress (Aiken, Cordon, Smith, Donnell, Tobey, and Ferguson), as well as four Republicans who scaled as new conservatives either in the previous or subsequent Congress but who had insufficient votes to scale in the 79th Congress. On the other hand, thirteen of the sixteen nay votes came from senators who scaled as obstructionists in the 79th Congress (O'Daniel, Brooks, Capper, Moore, Taft, Bushfield, Gurney, Milliken, Robertson, Wherry, Hawkes, Hart, and Revercomb). All but two of the sixteen opponents, moreover, represented interior states.[34] Although the Senate vote approving the United Nations charter on 28 July was far more lopsided, both votes suggested that, as had been true in the extension of reciprocal trade, a new consensus was beginning to emerge in the Senate, which recognized that some form of international cooperation was essential to the future prosperity and security of the United States.

While it is clear that the overwhelmingly favorable votes for Bretton Woods and the U.N. concealed a broad diversity of viewpoints, ranging from the "One World" philosophy to a limited commitment to cooperate with the nation's Allies in solving wartime problems, all proponents of these organizations differed from opponents in one important respect.[35] Supporters understood that, as a consequence of the Depression and the world war, America was part of an interdependent world and so could not resume the nationalistic foreign policy that had prevailed in the 1930s. Freshman Democrat Olin Johnston of South Carolina captured this point clearly in a 1946 Armistice Day speech:

> National isolation today is not humanly possible. Modern industrial nations cannot cut themselves off from commercial intercourse from the rest of the world and maintain an adequate standard of living. In these days of telegraph, radio and atomic energy, no nation can possibly isolate itself from the spread of ideas and beliefs and live completely unto itself.[36]

Opponents of Bretton Woods and the UN, on the other hand, seemed unable or unwilling to recognize the change that had occurred in America's relation to the world. This was plainly evident in the efforts of Robert Taft to delay consideration of the Bretton Woods agreement. On 14 July, the Ohio Republican joined three other Republicans on the Senate Banking and Currency Committee (Hugh Butler of Nebraska, Eugene Milliken of Michigan, and John Thomas of Idaho) in issuing a minority report assailing the Bretton Woods agreement because it invested taxpayers' money in international organizations over which the United States had little control and because it established a system of managed currency that would impair the flexibility of American economic action. In the eyes of the four GOP senators, therefore, Bretton Woods attempted to do in the international arena what such ardent New Dealers as Henry Wallace were trying to do domestically.[37]

Both the foreign and domestic policy debates in 1945, then, underscored the transformation occurring in Senate conservatism. As the debates on such seemingly diverse bills as the Full Employment bill and the Bretton Woods agreement revealed, a common thread uniting the new conservatism of the 1940s was the recognition that political views had to be adjusted to meet the needs of the predominantly urban, industrial nation that had emerged in the twentieth century. Senate action in the second session of the 79th Congress helped to further define the dimensions of the new conservatism.

II

As the Senate confronted the many problems associated with reconverting the nation to peace in 1946, the new conservatives continued to play a critical role. On issues of price control and labor, votes of the new conservatives helped preserve the expanded powers of the positive state. Yet as was true of their efforts in the previous session, the new conservatives sought in 1946 to limit carefully the expansion of federal power. A civil rights issue considered in the second session, however, demonstrated that there were distinct limits to the transformation occurring in Senate conservatism.

Although Senate debates in 1945 had frequently pointed to widening ideological differences among conservative southern Democrats, the first bill considered in 1946 demonstrated that issues of race relations continued to unify the South's right wing. On 17 January, despite an unofficial agreement that no controversial legislation would be considered before the President's annual message, Democrat Dennis Chavez of New Mexico introduced a bill establishing a permanent Fair Employment Practices Committee. Originally created in June 1941 by Executive order, the FEPC sought to prohibit racial discrimination in the employment practices of defense industries during World War II. From its inception, the FEPC had provoked loud criticism from conservatives, who saw in it every aspect of New Deal liberalism that they opposed (rule by Executive order, bureaucratic threats to individual liberty, and government interference with free enterprise), and from many southerners who perceived it as a threat to their segregated society. The Chavez bill, in addition to rekindling all these fears, was also seen by its opponents as a sign of liberals' determination, notwithstanding the death of FDR and the return of prosperity, to revive and expand New Deal reform in the postwar era.[38]

Debate on the Chavez bill indicated that however much the domestic politics of some southern Democrats had begun to moderate, regional considerations rather than ideology continued to the be the dominant force on civil rights issues. Josiah Bailey, an obstructionist conservative and a founding member of the Senate's anti–New Deal bloc in the 1930s, argued that "the FEPC . . . far from making for [more] liberty . . . will impose restrictions upon men who ought to be free to do as they please. Certainly," he concluded, "I would not permit any committee to require me to employ a colored clerk for private secretary." Olin Johnston of South Carolina, on the other hand, who unlike Bailey had supported the nomination of Henry Wallace and federal aid to education in 1945, denounced the Chavez bill in similar terms. "[T]he bill as written should . . . appeal to those people who believe in government by bureaus and commissions, who believe that the sovereign states should have no rights except as administered to them by Federal bureaus . . . ," he declared from the Senate floor in January. "This unfair employment practice act . . . ," he continued, "would be a great departure from the old and traditional American system of free enterprise, the right to choose and the right not to do certain things and would hamper . . . the right that has always been enjoyed by employers to utilize their own sound judgment in the selection of loyal and capable employees." Similarly, Johnston's colleague from South Carolina, Burnet Maybank, who had also disagreed with Bailey on many issues in 1945, regarded the FEPC bill in nearly identical terms. "I have been 100% and will continue to be 100% opposed to any F.E.P.C. law. . . . Private employers should have the right to employ whoever [sic] they desire." In the end, the nearly solid opposition of southern senators killed the 1946 effort to establish a permanent FEPC. A filibuster led by southern Democrats tied up the Senate for three weeks and ended only when Chavez, the bill's sponsor, agreed to table his measure so that more pressing legislation could be called up.[39]

If the conservatism of southern Democrats remained largely un-reconstructed on racial issues, it would be incorrect to conclude, as contemporary analysts often did, that their opposition to a federal role in civil rights mirrored more general opposition to the social reforms of the New Deal.[40] Rather, as this study argues and as an analysis of roll call votes shows, Senate debates on a wide range of social issues in the 79th Congress suggest that many of the southern Democrats frequently offered moderate support to measures geared to the needs of urban, industrial America. This view is also supported by the work of political scientist Hubert R. Fowler, who analyzed the roll call voting of southern senators between 1947 and 1960. He found that in the period, southern Democrats in the Senate were "torn asunder." While some continued to vote much like GOP conservatives, others voted increasingly as their nonsouthern colleagues did.[41]

The political moderation of the new conservatives from the South and elsewhere was displayed clearly in the summer of 1946 by Senate debate of a measure extending the life of the wartime Office of Price Administration. Although they had tolerated it as a wartime necessity, business leaders and conservatives alike viewed the price control agency as a symbol of the New Deal's attempt to manage the economy and to regiment individual life, which they had resisted since 1933. With the war over, however, many conservatives believed that immediate termination of the OPA should be an essential part of the nation's reconversion to peace.[42]

Conservatives' hopes were dashed in early 1946 when the Truman Administration asked for a one-year extension of OPA beyond its scheduled 30 June expiration. Citing the economic turmoil that hampered the reconversion process, the President maintained that extension of price controls was essential for the nation's welfare.

The differences that separated obstructionists from the Administration were apparent in Senate action of the Price Control bill. The measure that emerged from the Banking and Currency Committee on 11 June continued OPA for one year, but severely undermined its power to regulate the economy. Stripped from OPA, for example, was the power to place ceilings on meat, poultry, and dairy products. In addition, the Senate bill authorized either the Secretary of Agriculture or a special decontrol board to remove any other price ceilings if OPA refused to act. Most Senate liberals were so disenchanted with the bill that, notwithstanding its one-year extension of OPA, they were prepared to reject it.[43]

Many of the new conservatives in the Senate were careful to distance themselves from both the obstructionists and the liberals on OPA extension. While they maintained a healthy regard for the free enterprise system, many were convinced that some controls had to be continued at least temporarily to ease reconversion. Republican George Aiken of Vermont admitted to a constituent in June that "I want to get rid of it [OPA], but I am satisfied that prices will shoot up on many necessities of life if we remove all controls. This might start a series of labor troubles all over again." Democrat Olin Johnston was similarly willing only to modify OPA. "I, too, feel," he wrote to a state senator in April, "that we must have a continuation of price control in some form. However . . . it is imperative . . . that we correct the follies and discriminations which are causing confusion and distrust on the part of many of our people."[44]

New conservatives like Aiken and Johnston played a crucial role in shaping the OPA extension bill as it moved through the upper house. On 12 June, such new conservatives as Johnston, Walter George, Clyde Hoey, Burnet Maybank, Leverett Saltonstall, H. A. Smith, and Charles Tobey joined with such obstructionists as Kenneth Wherry, Albert Hawkes, W. Lee "Pappy" O'Daniel, E. H. Moore, C. Douglas Buck, and C. Wayland "Curly" Brooks to approve a Taft amendment designed to boost business's profits. The Taft amendment prohibited any ceiling price on a reconversion product that was less than its 1941 price plus any subsequent increases in production costs.[45] The following day nearly identical coalitions of new conservatives and obstructionists formed to expand the Taft amendment's provisions to apply to all consumer products, and to block an effort from liberal Democrat Claude Pepper to extend OPA for one year with no restrictions on its power. If the new conservatives had been concerned with restraining OPA's power to manage the economy throughout most of the price control debate, their differences with the obstructionists were apparent in the final vote. On 13 June the new conservatives deserted the obstructionists and instead joined with Administration forces to ensure passage of the amended bill, thereby guaranteeing that limited federal power over prices was continued into the postwar era.[46]

The OPA extension bill that emerged from conference committee on 24 June substantially modified the Senate's bill by restoring many of the price controls that had been eliminated by the upper house. In return for the House conferee's acceptance of a twelve-month extension of OPA (the House bill had extended OPA only nine months), Senate conferees agreed to retain price controls on meat, eggs, poultry, dairy products, tobacco, and petroleum.[47]

The changes made by the conference committee particularly disturbed obstructionist conservatives in the Senate who had sought to kill OPA entirely. Denouncing price controls as antithetical to American traditions, Texas Democrat W. Lee "Pappy" O'Daniel launched a filibuster on 26 June, hoping to prevent a vote on the conference report before June 30, thereby allowing OPA to die. The Senate, weary of the price control debate and under pressure to enact nine important appropriations bills before the start of the new fiscal year on 1 July, gave little support to the Texas Democrat's filibuster. In the end, therefore, the upper house voted 47–23 on 28 June to approve the conference report. Despite the changes made to the Senate's original bill, most of the new conservatives, including George Aiken, Walter George, Clyde Hoey, George Radcliffe, Richard Russell, H. Alexander Smith, and Charles Tobey, voted to approve the conference report, convinced that limited extension of price controls was necessary to ensure postwar economic health.[48]

Despite the changes made by the conference report, Harry Truman vetoed the bill on 29 June, claiming that the bill was inadequate to control prices effectively. When his veto was sustained, the House approved a stopgap resolution extending OPA for twenty days, but similar efforts were repeatedly blocked in the Senate by obstructionist conservatives, W. Lee "Pappy" O'Daniel and Kenneth Wherry. As a result, all price controls expired on 30 June. The rapid advance in consumer prices that followed, however, convinced Senate Majority Leader Alben Barkley to introduce a new bill on 3 July reviving the price control agency. Under the Barkley bill, which closely resembled the vetoed measure, OPA was continued until 30 June 1947 and price ceilings were required to reflect producers' profits in a prewar base period. The only major change was that, to assuage the President, who regarded the conference report as inflationary because it used 1941, a year of peak wartime production, as the base period to determine prewar profits, the Barkley bill established 1940, a more "normal" production year, as the yardstick to measure pre-war profits.[49]

Floor action on the Barkley bill revealed the voting alignments that distinguished new conservatives from both liberals and obstructionists. The new conservatives joined first with obstructionists to approve a series of amendments that removed price controls from such commodities as milk, petroleum, and soybeans, which all were in abundant supply.[50] Two days later, however, many of the new conservatives, including George Aiken, Clyde Hoey, Olin Johnston, H. Alexander Smith, and Charles Tobey, shifted their votes to the Administration to defeat an amendment offered by obstructionist conservative Edward Robertson of Wyoming that continued OPA for one year, but gave it only the power to control rents. Hours later they rejoined the obstructionists to defeat an amendment from Claude Pepper and nine other liberals that extended OPA for one year with no restrictions on its power. Finally, before the Senate adjourned, most new conservatives voted with the Administration to adopt the amended Barkley bill.[51]

Undoubtedly a number of factors influenced the new conservatives' votes during the long debate on price control extension. Certainly the new conservatives responded to pressure from home-state producers and consumers who had contended with OPA for a number of years. Concern about the approaching Congressional elections in November also helped to shape the response of the new conservatives. If southern Democrats were reluctant to oppose a measure their party's leader had deemed essential, limited extension of price control gave new conservatives in the GOP a chance to convince voters that theirs was not simply a party of nay-sayers. The votes of new conservatives on price control, however, also point to the philosophical accommodation some members of the right wing were making to the needs of the modern industrial state. That is, by voting to continue government price controls, the new conservatives acknowledged, as they had on earlier issues in the 79th Congress, that the complex conditions of life in the mid–twentieth century sometimes required positive action by the federal government. This point is underscored by the statistical analysis of the roll call votes. Throughout the 79th Congress, the degree of support given to those policy dimensions that had formed the core of FDR's expansion of the positive state, such as Social Welfare, Agriculture, Business Regulation, Extension of Executive Authority, Extension of Federal Authority, and Economy in Government Spending, formed the dividing line between the new conservatives and the obstructionists. By consistently providing low support in all of these dimensions, the obstructionists indicated that they were still adamantly opposed to the New Deal's domestic agenda as conservatives in the 1930s had been. In contrast, by offering medium and occasionally high support in these policy dimensions, the new conservatives demonstrated their understanding that neither individual action nor the unfettered operation of the free enterprise system was sufficient to meet the challenges of the modern urban, industrial nation.

If significant differences separated the new conservatives and the obstructionists in the 79th Congress, the roll call analysis also indicates important distinctions between the new conservatives and the liberals. As their effort to attach limiting amendments to the OPA bill suggested, the new conservatives throughout the 79th Congress were generally less supportive of an expanded federal role in modern life than liberals. Indeed, on all those policy dimensions where the new conservatives were more supportive of the positive state than obstructionists, they were with few exceptions consistently less supportive than liberals. While the new conservatives tended to provide medium support on such dimensions as Agriculture, Social Welfare, Civil Rights/Civil Liberties, Business Regulation, and even Extension of Executive Authority, most liberals gave consistently high support.

The aim of the new conservatives, then, was to expand the positive state cautiously, to use government power to assist the free enterprise system but not to supplant it. In a statement released in July 1946, following Truman's veto of the original OPA extension bill, Clyde Hoey aptly summarized the emerging philosophy of the new conservatives. The North Carolina Democrat noted that the recent debates had revealed the presence of three groups in the Senate. One group favored extension of OPA for one year with its full powers intact, while a second group sought to kill the price control agency entirely. The third group, Hoey observed, stood midway between these extremes and believed "that it would be wise to remove some controls now and to continue others for a while, with the distinct policy enforced on OPA of dealing justly and fairly with the producer, manufacturer, dealer and consumer." Hoey left no doubt, furthermore, that he was a member of this third group. "I believe the present bill will aid in preventing drastic inflation, and at the same time, serve to give the law of supply and demand a chance to become operative."[52]

Organized labor provided a final issue in 1946 that helped to define the nature of the new conservatism. Unlike the role they had played in extending price control, the new conservatives on this issue voted consistently with obstructionists to approve a bill restricting union power more substantially than liberals thought necessary. Throughout the debate, however, the new conservatives' rhetoric differentiated them from their obstructionist allies and made clear that their goal was to strike a balance between the legitimate rights of management and labor, not to reverse the gains organized labor had made since 1933.

Revision of the nation's labor laws received a great deal of attention throughout the first half of 1946 primarily because of the numerous strikes impeding the nation's reconversion efforts. Alarmed by the rising number of work stoppages, President Truman had asked Congress in late 1945 for legislation requiring a "cooling off" period before strikes could begin. By early February 1946, the House had responded with a tough labor bill authored by Representative Francis Case of South Dakota which, in addition to providing for a thirty-day cooling off period, also permitted the use of injunctions to halt various union practices, prohibited secondary boycotts, and made unions liable to breach of contract suits.[53]

Although the Senate was initially less inclined than the House to deal strictly with organized labor, by the time the full Senate began consideration of the Case bill in May, nationwide coal and railway strikes had hardened the attitude of many legislators. The coal strike in particular had forced a cutback in the nation's industrial production, seriously curtailed transportation (at this time about 75% of American railroads burned coal), and generally hindered the reconversion effort. In Illinois, where electric generating plants were heavily dependent on coal, for example, electricity was rationed, numerous industrial plants cut back to twenty-four-hour work weeks, and workers either had their hours reduced or were laid off entirely. The situation in Illinois was so severe that liberal Democrat Scott Lucas, previously considered a friend of organized labor, introduced legislation in May empowering the federal government to seize striking industries and compel workers to return to work or lose their rights guaranteed by the 1935 Wagner Act.[54]

The impact the coal and railroad strikes had on Scott Lucas's attitude was apparently mirrored in that of other senators, for the upper house moved quickly to attach a series of tough amendments to the Case bill. On 25 May, the Senate approved an amendment proposed by Joseph Ball, Robert Taft, and H. Alexander Smith, requiring both labor and management to bargain collectively and providing for a sixty-day cooling off period. Similarly, a Taft amendment creating fact-finding boards to make recommendations on wages and hours in labor disputes involving public utilities was added to the bill. When the Senate voted 49–29 to adopt the heavily amended version of the labor bill on 25 May, most new conservatives, including Donnell, George, Hoey, Johnston, Knowland, Russell, Saltonstall, Smith, and Tobey, voted with the obstructionists to restrict labor's power.[55]

Although the effort to reduce organized labor's power stalled when President Truman vetoed the Case bill on 11 June and was sustained by the House, the debate revealed the different political objectives dividing the new conservatives from the obstructionists.[56] To obstructionist conservatives, the wave of postwar labor unrest was the direct consequence of New Deal labor legislation, which in their eyes had unfairly elevated the interests of union labor above all others. Typical of the obstructionist view were comments Josiah Bailey made to the president of a North Carolina tanning company. "This government went over to the Labor Leaders some years ago as an act of legislation to suit them. There is no power now to prevent Labor agitators from going into plants like yours and others and organizing the workers. As you know," he concluded ruefully, "the policy of this government is to encourage the formation of Labor unions and the only debate now is . . . between the several organizations as to who shall get the dues."[57]

The new conservatives, in contrast, took a more charitable view of organized labor and sought legislation only to restore balance to labor-management relations. Bailey's colleague, Clyde Hoey, best described the balance new conservatives sought in labor legislation. Speaking to the Winston-Salem Junior Chamber of Commerce in November 1946, Hoey observed that:

> There was a time when business and management had too much power and the labor unions too little power. The pendulum has swung too far now and needs to be brought back nearer center. Labor should not be denied any rights, but should be required to observe and respect the rights of others. . . . The matter should not be approached in a punitive spirit, but rather with a view of correcting abuses.[58]

The debate on labor legislation emphasized, then, that the transformation of conservatism was incomplete. Although the new conservatives acknowledged rhetorically the government guarantees to organized labor begun by the New Deal, when they had to vote on this most controversial issue in the 79th Congress most voted to restrict labor's power. This behavior is underscored by the roll call analysis of the Labor dimension. On all other dimensions that dealt with the New Deal's domestic agenda, the new conservatives generally occupied a distinct middle ground between the liberals' high support and the obstructionists' low support. But on the Labor dimension, while all but nine of the scalable liberals continued to offer high support, thirty-five of the forty-six senators who scaled either as new conservatives or obstructionists offered low support. The Labor dimensions indicated that the new conservatives in the 79th Congress were moderate conservatives, rather than moderate liberals.

When the 79th Congress adjourned in July 1946, clear differences separated the new conservatives on all domestic policy dimensions save Labor, as well as on foreign policy dimensions. As the debates on such seemingly diverse issues as the Full Employment bill, the nomination of Henry Wallace as commerce secretary, federal aid to education, and the Bretton Woods agreements indicated, a common thread uniting the new conservatives of the 1940s was the recognition that America had become a mature, urban, industrial society of interdependent individuals. Republican Ralph Flanders of Vermont, appointed to the Senate when Warren Austin became the U.S. ambassador to the United Nations, recounted in late 1946 how a train ride he had taken in the summer of 1932 brought home this lesson to him. When his train was stoned by unemployed men outside Washington, D.C., Flanders understood that economic hardship could no longer be explained as an "act of God" as it had been in the nineteenth century. Instead, in twentieth-century industrial America, "we are tied together in a thousand ways—merchants, railroad people, industrial wage earners, farmers, bankers and professional men. No one class can cease its proper functions without harming and embittering the whole."[59]

Obstructionist conservatives, on the other hand, had a different vision of America in the mid–twentieth century. In their minds, America remained rooted firmly in its preindustrial, agrarian traditions. The view of America provided by Nebraska Republican Kenneth Wherry during Senate hearings on the oil industry in 1947 undoubtedly described the vision held by many obstructionists. "The small-town newspaper, the corner grocery store, the country baker, the smaller merchandiser or retailer, the independent oil dealer or the filling station operator," he observed, "are the strength of our communities, and the backbone of the American way of life." To conservatives of Wherry's stripe, therefore, the positive state was not only unnecessary, but actually antithetical to the traditional "rugged individualism" and limited government, which had for so long advanced America's welfare. A similar inability to recognize, or an unwillingness to acknowledge, the primacy of urban, industrial concerns in the mid–twentieth century usually produced in postwar obstructionists like Wherry a fierce oppostion to American internationalism. The common link binding the domestic and foreign ideologies of obstructionists has been ably established by historian Joan Lee Bryniarski. She has argued that "a man who believed any government interference with the free market was a further step down the road to socialism, and ultimately to totalitarianism, had little difficulty accepting the belief that Europe's problems were of no concern to Americans. Europe had always appeared decadent to most Americans."[60]

If the rhetorical differences between such conservatives as Flanders and Wherry had become more distinct by 1946, the statistical analysis of the roll call votes in the 79th Congress points to the broader forces responsible for the widening divisions. To be sure, partisan politics continued to be an important influence on senators' voting. As was true of previous Congresses, table 4–1 reveals that 91% of the high support group was composed of Democrats, whereas Republicans made up 92% of the low support group. But table 4–1 also indicates that the politics of the Republican party had moderated by the end of World War II. Indeed, the GOP accounted for 38% of the medium support offered to Administration policies in the 79th Congress, compared to only 11% in the 76th Congress and 15% in the 75th Congress. The gradual softening of the GOP's resistance to the initiatives of Roosevelt and Truman by the mid-1940s seems attributable, in part, to the pull of electoral politics. Public opinion polls had revealed steadily since the late 1930s that a majority of the electorate supported the broad outlines of both the New Deal's domestic agenda and American internationalism, and clearly some within the GOP attempted to adjust their party's politics to regain power. But the statistical analysis also underscores an ideological accommodation underway among conservatives in both parties.

Indeed, as table 4–2 indicates, of the twenty-one senators who scaled in the medium support or new conservative group in the 79th Congress, twelve of them or 57% represented coastal states. Conversely, eighteen of the twenty-five, or 72% of the senators who scaled in the low support or obstructionist group, were drawn from interior states. Table 4–3 demonstrates, moreover, that the proportion of senators representing coastal and interior states in these two groups was not distorted by strong support for foreign policy initiatives as the nation made the transition from war to peace. Rather, on both foreign and domestic policy dimensions in the 79th Congress, a majority of those senators who scaled as the new conservatives represented coastal states, and a majority of those who scaled as obstructionists represented interior states. The importance of the coastal/interior divisions between new conservatives and obstructionists as a factor in the transformation of Senate conservatism becomes even more apparent when the proportions for the 79th Congress are compared to earlier congresses. In fact, the coastal/interior divisions in the 79th Congress represent a direct reversal of the proportions in the earlier congresses. In the 76th Congress (1939–1940), the last full prewar Congress, 26% of the medium support group were senators drawn from coastal states, compared to 74% from interior states. Similarly, in the same congress, 72%

TABLE 4-1

79th CONGRESS

Name	Policy Dimensions	Score
	1 2 3 4 5 6 7 8 9	

HIGH SUPPORT

Name	Policy Dimensions	Score
Barkley, D-KY	1 1 1 1 1 1 1 1 1	1.00
Downey, D-CA	1 1 1 1 1 1 1 1 1	1.00
Guffey, D-PA	1 1 1 1 1 1 1 1 1	1.00
Mead, D-NY	1 1 1 1 1 1 1 1 1	1.00
Murdock, D-UT	1 1 1 1 1 1 1 1 1	1.00
Murray, D-MT	1 1 1 1 1 1 1 1 1	1.00
Myers, D-PA	1 1 1 1 1 1 1 1 1	1.00
Pepper, D-FL	1 1 1 1 1 1 1 1 1	1.00
Taylor, D-ID	1 1 1 1 1 1 1 1 1	1.00
Thomas, D-UT	1 1 1 1 1 1 1 1 1	1.00
Wagner, D-NY	1 1 1 1 1 1 1 1 1	1.00
Tunnell, D-DE	1 1 1 1 1 1 1 1 1	1.00
Briggs, D-MO	1 1 1 1 1 1 1 1 1	1.00
Kilgore, D-WV	1 1 1 1 1 1 1 1 2	1.10
Mitchell, D-WA	1 1 1 2 1 1 1 1 1	1.10
McMahon, D-CT	2 1 1 1 1 1 1 1 1	1.10
Green, D-RI	1 1 1 1 1 1 0 1 2	1.13
Chavez, D-NM	0 1 0 1 1 1 2 1 1	1.14
Huffman, D-OH	2 1 1 1 1 1 1 1 2	1.20
Magnuson, D-WA	2 1 1 1 1 1 1 1 2	1.20
Hayden, D-AZ	2 1 1 1 2 1 1 1 1	1.20
Morse, R-OR	2 2 1 1 1 1 1 1 1	1.20
Burch, D-VA	0 1 0 0 0 1 2 1 1	1.20
O'Mahoney, D-WY	2 2 1 1 0 1 1 1 1	1.25
Johnson, D-CO	0 0 1 1 1 1 1 1 3	1.29
Carville, D-NV	0 2 1 1 0 1 1 2 0	1.33
McKellar, D-TN	0 1 1 2 3 1 1 1 1	1.38
Hill, D-AL	1 1 2 1 3 1 2 1 1	1.40
LaFollette, I-WI	2 1 1 2 1 1 1 1 3	1.40
McCarran, D-NV	2 2 1 1 2 1 1 1 2	1.40
Fulbright, D-AR	2 2 1 1 3 1 1 1 1	1.40
Aiken, R-VT	2 3 1 2 1 1 1 1 1	1.40

Name	Policy Dimensions	Score
	1 2 3 4 5 6 7 8 9	

HIGH SUPPORT continued

Name	Policy Dimensions	Score
Walsh, D-MA	1 1 1 3 1 2 1 1 3	1.50
Gossett, D-ID	0 2 0 1 2 1 1 2 0	1.50
Maybank, D-SC	0 0 1 2 3 0 1 1 1	1.50

MEDIUM SUPPORT

Name	Policy Dimensions	Score
Radcliffe, D-MD	3 2 1 1 2 2 1 1 1	1.55
Hoey, D-NC	3 2 0 2 0 1 1 1 1	1.57
Thomas, D-OK	0 3 1 0 1 3 1 1 1	1.57
McFarland, D-AZ	1 0 1 0 2 0 1 0 3	1.60
Andrews, D-FL	2 0 0 1 3 1 2 1 0	1.66
Johnston, D-SC	3 2 1 1 3 1 1 1 3	1.78
Russell, D-GA	2 2 2 2 3 1 2 1 2	1.88
Knowland, R-CA	3 2 1 3 1 2 1 2 1	1.89
Tobey, R-NH	2 3 0 0 1 3 0 0 1	2.00
Overton, D-LA	3 2 3 1 3 1 2 1 0	2.00
Cordon, R-OR	3 3 2 0 1 2 1 X 2	2.00
Austin, R-VT	3 3 3 0 1 2 1 2 1	2.00
Ferguson, R-MI	3 3 2 2 1 3 2 2 1	2.11
Donnell, R-MO	3 3 3 3 1 2 1 2 1	2.11
Stewart, D-TN	2 2 0 2 3 2 0 1 3	2.14
Gerry, D-RI	3 2 3 2 0 2 2 0 1	2.14
George, D-GA	3 3 0 2 3 1 2 0 1	2.14
Langer, R-ND	2 3 1 3 1 0 0 0 3	2.17
Eastland, D-MS	3 3 2 2 3 2 2 2 1	2.20
Smith, R-NJ	3 3 3 3 1 2 2 2 1	2.22
McClellan, D-AR	3 2 2 3 3 2 2 1 3	2.33

LOW SUPPORT

Name	Policy Dimensions	Score
Willis, R-IN	2 3 0 3 1 3 2 2 3	2.38
Stanfill, R-KY	3 2 3 3 2 2 0 3 1	2.38
Byrd, D-VA	3 1 3 0 3 2 3 0 2	2.43
Capper, R-KS	3 3 3 2 1 3 1 3 3	2.44
Ball, R-MN	3 3 3 3 1 3 3 2 1	2.44
Hart, R-CT	3 3 3 3 2 2 3 2 1	2.44

Name	Policy Dimensions	Score
	1 2 3 4 5 6 7 8 9	

LOW SUPPORT continued

Name	Policy Dimensions	Score
Revercomb, R-WV	3 2 2 3 0 2 2 3 3	2.50
Wilson, R-IA	3 3 2 2 1 3 0 3 3	2.50
Taft, R-OH	3 3 3 3 1 2 3 2 3	2.55
White, R-ME	3 3 3 3 2 3 3 2 1	2.56
Bridges, R-NH	2 3 3 3 2 0 3 0 2	2.57
Young, R-ND	3 3 2 2 2 3 0 0 3	2.57
Reed, R-KS	3 3 3 2 0 3 3 3 1	2.62
Buck, R-DE	3 3 0 3 2 3 3 2 2	2.63
Brooks, R-IL	2 3 3 3 1 3 3 3 3	2.66
Gurney, R-SD	3 3 3 3 2 3 3 3 1	2.67
Moore, R-OK	3 3 3 2 0 3 3 2 3	2.75
Wiley, R-WI	3 3 3 3 0 3 3 3 1	2.75
Wherry, R-NE	3 3 3 3 1 3 3 3 3	2.78
Bushfield, R-SD	2 3 0 3 3 3 0 3 3	2.86
Millikin, R-CO	3 3 3 3 3 3 3 2 3	2.89
Robertson, R-WY	3 3 3 3 3 3 0 3 3	3.00
Capehart, R-IN	3 3 3 3 0 3 0 3 3	3.00
Hawkes, R-NJ	3 3 3 3 0 3 0 3 0	3.00
O'Daniel, D-TX	3 3 0 3 3 3 3 3 3	3.00

Policy Dimension Key:

0.   denotes that a senator did not scale on the dimension
1.   Labor
2.   Agriculture
3.   Social Welfare
4.   Extension of Executive Power
5.   Civil Rights/Civil Liberties
6.   Business Regulation
7.   Economy in Government Spending
8.   Extension of Federal Authority
9.   Foreign Aid

79TH CONGRESS   (N=81)

HIGH SUPPORT (N=35 or 43%)   MEDIUM SUPPORT (N=21 or 26%)

Democrats	= 32 (91%)		Democrats	= 13 (62%)
GOP	= 2 (6%)		GOP	= 8 (38%)
Independent	= 1 (3%)		Independent =	0 (0%)

LOW SUPPORT (N=25 or 31%)

Democrats	= 2 (8%)
GOP	= 23 (92%)
Independent =	0 (0%)

Table 4-2

Regional Divisions in Medium and Low Support Groups

MEDIUM SUPPORT (N=21)

Coastal (N=12 or 57%)

Andrews, D-FL	Johnston, D-SC	George, D-GA
Russell, D-GA	Knowland, R-CA	Radcliffe, D-MD
Tobey, R-NH	Cordon, R-OR	Smith, R-NJ
Austin, R-VT	Gerry, D-RI	Hoey, D-NC

Interior, (N=9 or 43%)

Overton, D-LA	Ferguson, R-MI	McClellan, D-AR
Donnell, R-MO	Stewart, D-TN	McFarland, D-AZ
Langer, R-ND	Eastland, D-MS	Thomas, D-OK

LOW SUPPORT (N=25)

Coastal (N=7 or 28%)

Byrd, D-VA	Hart, R-CT	Hawkes, R-NJ
Revercomb, R-WV	White, R-ME	
Bridges, R-NH	Buck, R-DE	

Interior (N=18 or 72%)

Willis, R-IN	Stanfill, R-KY	Wherry, R-NE
Capper, R-KS	Ball, R-MN	Millikin, R-CO
Wilson, R-IA	Taft, R-OH	Capehart, R-IN
Young, R-ND	Reed, R-KS	Bushfield, R-SD
Brooks, R-IL	Gurney, R-SD	Robertson, R-WY
Moore, R-OK	Wiley, R-WI	O'Daniel, D-TX

TABLE 4-3

79th CONGRESS - DOMESTIC POLICY DIMENSIONS

HIGH SUPPORT

Barkley, D-KY	1.00	Huffman, D-OH	1.00
Downey, D-CA	1.00	Magnuson, D-WA	1.00
Guffey, D-PA	1.00	Chavez, D-NM	1.17
Mead, D-NY	1.00	Hayden, D-AZ	1.25
Murdock, D-UT	1.00	Morse, R-OR	1.25
Murray, D-MT	1.00	Burch, D-VA	1.25
Myers, D-PA	1.00	LaFollette, I-WI	1.25
Pepper, D-FL	1.00	McFarland, D-AZ	1.25
Taylor, D-ID	1.00	O'Mahoney, D-WY	1.29
Thomas, D-UT	1.00	Carville, D-NV	1.33
Wagner, D-NY	1.00	McCarran, D-NV	1.38
Tunnell, D-DE	1.00	Walsh, D-MA	1.38
Briggs, D-MI	1.00	McKellar, D-TN	1.43
Kilgore, D-WV	1.00	Fulbright, D-AR	1.50
Green, D-RI	1.00	Aiken, R-VT	1.50
Johnson, D-CO	1.00	Gossett, D-ID	1.50
Mitchell, D-WA	1.13	Hill, D-AL	1.50
McMahon, D-CT	1.13		

N = 35; D = 32; R = 2; I = 1

MEDIUM SUPPORT

Maybank, D-SC	1.60	Cordon, R-OR	2.00
Radcliffe, D-MD	1.63	Stewart, D-TN	2.00
Johnston, D-SC	1.63	Langer, R-ND	2.00
Andrews, D-FL	1.66	Austin, R-VT	2.14
Hoey, D-NC	1.67	Tobey, R-NH	2.25
Thomas, D-OK	1.67	Ferguson, R-MI	2.25
Russell, D-GA	1.88	Donnell, R-MO	2.25
Knowland, R-CA	1.88	McClellan, D-AR	2.25
Overton, D-LA	2.00	Willis, R-IN	2.29

N = 18; D = 10; R = 8
Coastal = 10 (56%); Interior = 8 (44%)

TABLE 4-3

79th CONGRESS - DOMESTIC POLICY

LOW SUPPORT

Gerry, D-RI	2.33	Bridges, R-NH	2.67
George, D-GA	2.33	Buck, R-DE	2.71
Eastland, D-MS	2.38	Moore, R-OK	2.71
Smith, R-NJ	2.38	White, R-ME	2.75
Capper, R-KS	2.38	Wherry, R-NE	2.75
Revercomb, R-WV	2.43	Bushfield, R-SD	2.83
Wilson, R-IA	2.43	Reed, R-KS	2.86
Byrd, D-VA	2.50	Gurney, R-SD	2.88
Taft, R-OH	2.50	Millikin, R-CO	2.88
Young, R-ND	2.50	Wiley, R-WI	3.00
Stanfill, R-KY	2.57	Robertson, R-WY	3.00
Ball, R-MN	2.63	Capehart, R-IN	3.00
Hart, R-CT	2.63	Hawkes, R-NJ	3.00
Brooks, R-IL	2.63	O'Daniel, D-TX	3.00

N = 28; D = 5; R = 23
Coastal = 10 (36%); Interior = 18 (64%)

of the senators in the low support group represented coastal states, compared to 28% from interior states.

These figures suggest, then, that whatever role partisan consider-ations may have played in the moderation of some conservatives' politics, the transformation of Senate conservatism was also a re-sponse to the industrialization and urbanization the United States had experienced in the first half of the twentieth century. The col-lapse of the national economy in the 1930s, together with its revival under the New Deal and World War II, revealed to Americans the interdependency of individuals in a modern industrial society, as well as the benefits of the positive state. Similarly, the international crisis taught many Americans that the technology of modern war-fare rendered obsolete an insular foreign policy. Nowhere were these lessons understood more clearly than in those sections of the country where big business and industry predominated, such as the Northeast and parts of the West coast, and those regions that had been most directly exposed to the Axis threat, such as the states along the east and west coasts.

Residents of interior states, on the other hand, tended to be less aware of the changes the nation had undergone in the first half of the twentieth century. To be sure, the effects of the Great Depres-

TABLE 4-4

79th CONGRESS - FOREIGN POLICY DIMENSIONS

HIGH SUPPORT

Barkley, D-KY	1.00	Fulbright, D-AR	1.00
Downey, D-CA	1.00	Aiken, R-VT	1.00
Guffey, D-PA	1.00	Maybank, D-SC	1.00
Mead, D-NY	1.00	Radcliffe, D-MD	1.00
Murdock, D-UT	1.00	Hoey, D-NC	1.00
Murray, D-MT	1.00	Thomas, R-OK	1.00
Myers, D-PA	1.00	Knowland, R-CA	1.00
Pepper, D-FL	1.00	Tobey, R-NH	1.00
Taylor, D-ID	1.00	Austin, R-VT	1.00
Thomas, D-UT	1.00	Ferguson, R-MI	1.00
Wagner, D-NY	1.00	Donnell, R-MO	1.00
Tunnell, D-DE	1.00	Gerry, D-RI	1.00
Briggs, D-MO	1.00	George, D-GA	1.00
Mitchell, D-WA	1.00	Eastland, D-MS	1.00
McMahon, D-CT	1.00	Smith, R-NJ	1.00
Chavez, D-NM	1.00	Stanfill, R-KY	1.00
Hayden, D-AZ	1.00	Ball, R-MN	1.00
Morse, R-OR	1.00	Hart, R-CT	1.00
Burch, D-VA	1.00	White, R-ME	1.00
O'Mahoney, D-WY	1.00	Reed, R-KS	1.00
McKellar, D-TN	1.00	Gurney, R-SD	1.00
Hill, D-AL	1.00	Wiley, R-WI	1.00

N = 44; D = 28; R = 16

MEDIUM SUPPORT

Kilgore, D-WV	2.00	Russell, D-GA	2.00
Green, D-RI	2.00	Cordon, R-OR	2.00
Huffman, D-OH	2.00	Byrd, D-VA	2.00
Magnuson, D-WA	2.00	Bridges, R-NH	2.00
McCarran, D-NV	2.00	Buck, R-DE	2.00

N = 10; D = 7; R = 3
Coastal = 8 (80%); Interior = 2 (20%)

TABLE 4-4

79th CONGRESS - FOREIGN POLICY DIMENSIONS

LOW SUPPORT

Johnson, D-CO	3.00	Wilson, R-IA	3.00
LaFollette, I-WI	3.00	Taft, R-OH	3.00
Walsh, D-MA	3.00	Young, R-ND	3.00
McFarland, D-AZ	3.00	Brooks, R-IL	3.00
Johnston, D-SC	3.00	Moore, R-OK	3.00
Stewart, D-TN	3.00	Wherry, R-NE	3.00
Langer, R-ND	3.00	Bushfield, R-SD	3.00
McClellan, D-AR	3.00	Millikin, R-CO	3.00
Willis, R-IN	3.00	Robertson, R-WY	3.00
Capper, R-KS	3.00	Capehart, R-IN	3.00
Revercomb, R-WV	3.00	O'Daniel, D-TX	3.00

N = 22; D = 7; R = 14; I = 1
Coastal = 3 (14%); Interior = 19 (86%)

sion were no less severe than in other parts of the country. But because many of the interior states were still predominantly rural, agrarian societies, the hard times of the 1930s did not seem fundamentally different than those experienced by earlier generations. Similarly, although World War II exacted sacrifices from residents of interior states in equal proportion to those living elsewhere, the Axis threat was more remote from their daily lives. A resident of Kenneth Wherry's Nebraska, for example, could *read* about Nazi submarine warfare in the Atlantic; residents of H. Alexander Smith's New Jersey or Richard Russell's Georgia could occasionally *see* that warfare. Thus, when the new conservatives in the Senate voted in favor of extending price controls, or for federal aid to education, or for U.S. membership in international peacekeeping and economic agencies, they did so in the belief that the needs of their state and nation had changed. Action in the 79th Congress demonstrates, then, that by war's end the transformation of Senate conservatism was propelled both by the ongoing political accommodations senators made based on their partisan calculations and by the conscious effort made by some in the right-wing to modernize their philosophy.

5

The New Conservatism and Partisan Politics: The 80th Congress

THE CHANGE WROUGHT ON AMERICAN CONSERVATISM BY THE ECO-nomic collapse of the 1930s and the world war of the 1940s contin-ued to unfold throughout the 80th Congress, despite the heightened partisanship brought on by the GOP victory. Although the 80th Congress is usually regarded as the high-water mark of a postwar conservative, anti–New Deal resurgence, it is clear that political alignments in the new congress were more complex. To be sure, compared to its immediate predecessors, the 80th Congress saw a higher level of partisanship. Senators from both parties who had previously voted with the new conservatives were often led by the intense partisanship that prevailed in 1947 and 1948 to support or oppose the Truman Administration more strongly than they would have in ordinary times. Yet many members of the Senate's "class of 1946" joined ranks with the new conservatives, either immedi-ately in the 80th Congress or in subsequent Congresses when the partisanship surrounding the presidential election of 1948 had abated. The addition of more new conservatives, in turn, widened the gap between factions within the right wing, and particularly within the new Republican majority. This ensured that the legisla-tive outcomes of debates in the 80th Congress usually consolidated, rather than repealed, the foundations of the New Deal's domestic and foreign policy.

I

To many students of modern American politics, the 1946 election stands as a rare example of a truly decisive contest that swiftly and dramatically altered the contours of the political landscape. Since 1946 was the first election year in nearly a generation without the dominating presence of Franklin Roosevelt, the elections provided

162

the first test of the New Deal coalition's durability. The Republican campaign did much, furthermore, to sharpen partisan distinctions in voters' minds. By posing a simple, two-word question to voters, "had enough?", the GOP in 1946 skillfully linked the widespread public dissatisfaction with high taxes, wartime regimentation, and the economic difficulties of postwar reconversion to Democratic party policies and thereby created the impression that the Republicans' political philosophy was sharply different. The results seemed to confirm the voters' desire for an about-face in governmental policy, as the Democrats were roundly turned out of office and the Republicans were restored to majority-party status in both houses of Congress for the first time since Herbert Hoover's presidency. Removed from the Senate, for instance, were stalwart New Dealers such as Pennsylvania's Joseph Guffey, Washington's Hugh Mitchell, Ohio's James Huffman, Delaware's James Tunnell, and Utah's Abe Murdock. They were replaced, in turn, by such Republicans as Edward Martin, Harry Cain, John Bricker, John Williams, and Arthur Watkins, whose conservative political philosophy seemed to harken back to their party's heyday in the 1920s.[1]

Given the dramatic partisan reversal accomplished by the 1946 election, it is hardly surprising that observers see it as a conservative resurgence that aimed at undermining the foundations of the New Deal. *Newsweek* predicted on 25 November 1946 that by freeing southern Democrats from the burden of upholding New Deal reform, the election would produce a right wing resurgence. More recently, William Leuchtenburg has argued that following the elections "the 80th Congress set out to dismantle the New Deal brick by brick."[2]

A closer examination of the 1946 election, however, yields a more complex portrait of the political alignments it produced. Some of the Republicans elected to the 80th Congress, including Harry Cain in Washington, John Bricker in Ohio, William E. Jenner in Indiana, Arthur Watkins in Utah, Zales Ecton in Montana, James P. Kem in Missouri, and Joseph McCarthy in Wisconsin did indeed endorse a conservative political philosophy that sought largely to reverse the New Deal tide. For example, John Bricker's "views on domestic issues," his biographer has written, "never moved beyond a simplistic denial of the validity of the basic assumptions of the New Deal. . . . He was, in fact, only one of many prominent conservative Republicans of his generation who were incapable of coming to grips with a new era in American politics." But other members of the "class of 1946," such as Irving Ives of New York, Ralph Flanders of Vermont, Henry Cabot Lodge of Massachusetts, and

John Sherman Cooper of Kentucky, embraced a different, more modern brand of conservatism that accepted the major outlines of the political reforms accomplished since 1933. That Ives stood for principles different from those of John Bricker and of New Deal liberalism was made clear in his 1947 Lincoln Day speech in Queens, New York. Noting that the traditional emphasis Americans had always placed on individual freedom had given way in the 1930s and 1940s to a concern with economic security and a conviction that government could provide that security, Ives warned that necessary expansions in state power had to be monitored carefully lest they overwhelm indivdual liberty. "Too much or too little government," he concluded, "will inevitably bring the very results we are seeking to avoid. Therefore, our path must lie somewhere midway between these two extremes." Another member of the "class of 1946," Henry Cabot Lodge of Massachusetts, agreed fully with Ives's perspective. Dissenting from those in the GOP who saw the election as a mandate to repeal the New Deal, Lodge insisted that "we were not put back into office . . . to turn the clock back. We were . . . sent there in order to wind it up, get the crumbs and rats' nests out of the gears and get it going again."[3]

If the 1946 election brought to the 80th Congress more obstructionist conservatives who hoped to dismantle the New Deal, it also brought, as Ives's comments suggest, more new conservatives to the upper house who were committed to balancing the needs of the modern urban, industrial state against traditional conservative goals of individual freedom and free enterprise. Although the heightened partisanship of the 80th Congress often served in the short term to obscure its impact, the 1946 election helped in the long run to widen the developing divisions in the Senate's right wing. This ensured, in turn, that the 80th Congress marked the beginning of the New Deal's consolidation, rather than the start of its repeal. Even the normally partisan *Nation* predicted in early January 1947 that despite the harshness of the Republicans' recent rhetorical attack against big government, the split in the GOP between what it labeled liberals and conservatives guaranteed that the new Congress would not launch a frontal assault on the New Deal, but would selectively amend, retain, or repeal.[4]

The fault lines dividing the Senate's right wing became apparent in January when President Truman's budget proposal touched off a protracted debate on fiscal policy. Although the White House's proposal appeared to be the first balanced budget Washington had seen in years, many observers on Capitol Hill remained skeptical. Republican Styles Bridges of New Hampshire, the new chairman of the Senate Appropriations Committee, pointed out, for instance, that the President's budget was premised on the unlikely assumption that existing tax rates would yield more revenue in fiscal 1948 than they had in fiscal 1947. Because most economists predicted that national income would decline from its wartime peak, however, Bridges was convinced that federal expenditures would for yet another year exceed government revenues. Other critics charged that to balance the budget the President had asked Congress to maintain personal and corporate income taxes at their high wartime level and to retain all wartime excise taxes. Especially to Republicans who had pledged a 20% across-the-board tax cut to voters in the recent elections, this section of the budget message was unacceptable. Perhaps the most distressing feature to opponents of the budget was its level of projected expenditures. Except for a $3.4 billion reduction in defense expenditures, Truman's budget proposed to spend $9.7 billion more than had been spent in fiscal 1946, the last war year. Democrat Harry Byrd of Virginia, long an advocate of economy in government spending, scoffed that the President's budget had not even begun to take seriously the need to pare expenditures for every government agency.[5]

Although the President's critics focused their displeasure on different aspects of the budget, a common thread ran throughout their complaints. Whether their dissatisfaction was directed at the continuation of deficit spending, or at the high levels of taxation and spending envisioned by the budget, many of its critics viewed it as a New Deal wolf in sheep's clothing. That is, to obstructionist conservatives like Harry Byrd, fiscal 1948 presented the first real opportunity since 1933 to reduce both the domestic and international obligations of the federal government. Instead, they concluded, the President's budget, despite its appearance of fiscal restraint, actually intended to expand the New Deal agenda.

Obstructionist opposition, therefore, coalesced around a motion offered by Styles Bridges to slash $6 billion from the President's proposed expenditures, a sum they believed was the minimum necessary to commence government retrenchment. In the initial skirmish over fiscal policy in the 80th Congress, the obstructionists prevailed when the Joint Congressional Committee on the Budget voted 50–22 on 14 February to approve the Bridges motion. But when the budget debate moved to the full Senate, the obstructionists' position was attacked by two groups with somewhat different objectives.[6]

Most Senate Democrats, unaccustomed to their minority status, loyally supported the Administration's contention that any reduction of the President's proposed $37.5 billion in expenditures would impair vital domestic and international programs. Warren Magnuson, a liberal Democrat from Washington, contended on the Senate floor that budget cuts would undermine such important federal aid efforts as funds for public health and the school lunch program. Democrat Francis Myers of Pennsylvania agreed, noting on 21 February that such vital programs as flood control and soil conservation would also suffer.[7]

A second group fighting against the obstructionists' $6 billion reduction testified to the mixture of partisan politics and ideological accommodation that led senators to vote as new conservatives. This group, which proposed to reduce the President's budget by only $4.5 billion, was led by Republicans Robert Taft and Eugene Millikin. That Taft, who had scaled as an obstructionist in every previous Congress since his election in 1938, led a group seeking a middle ground between the Administration and the obstructionists, is probably the result of the difficult political position he occupied in the 80th Congress. One of the leaders of a party riven between those who were gradually accepting the fundamental outlines of the New Deal and others who completely rejected its statist assumptions, Taft, in order to capture the GOP presidental nomination in 1948, appeared to gravitate toward the center of American politics in the 80th Congress. Other members of the group supporting a $4.5 billion budget reduction, however, reasoned that the smaller figure would enable some tax relief without endangering the integrity of vital foreign and domestic policies. Arthur Vandenberg, the new chairman of the Foreign Relations Committee, maintained that the Bridges resolution, because it would pare $1 billion from the Army's budget and $750 million from the Navy's funds, threatened to impair efforts to maintain international peace. George Aiken similarly attacked the obstructionists' goals in a broad-ranging speech in the Senate on 19 February. The Vermont Republican acknowledged full support for the desire to lower taxes, but cautioned that such retrenchment should not be allowed to jeopardize the nation's security. Given such recent technological advances as atomic weapons, Aiken noted, national security was obviously threatened by foreign powers. But equally dangerous was the threat posed by the staggering national debt and by substandard health care and education in many parts of the country. The thousands of young men unfit for military service in World War II because their health and education had been neglected was a potent lesson that the national government's responsibility for the domestic welfare was much larger than previously recognized. "It should be the aim of the Congress," he argued in support of the Millikin proposal, "to reduce Government expenses to the lowest point consistent with national safety and national welfare and to pay a reasonable amount on the national debt."[8]

When the Senate finally voted on the budget resolutions in late February, the fractures within the right wing became more apparent. Convinced for either ideological or partisan reasons that some reduction in government expenditures was essential to national well-being, most new conservatives, including Aiken, Cooper, Hoey, Holland, Ives, Johnston, Saltonstall, Taft, and Thye, sided first with obstructionists on 24 February to table liberal Democratic motions to postpone any consideration of budget reduction until April. Two days later, however, most new conservatives switched to join with Administration forces to substitute the $4.5 billion Milliken motion for the more extreme Bridges resolution.[9]

The struggle between supporters of the Millikin and Bridges Resolutions was more than an intraparty scrap over the size of a tax reduction. Rather, it revealed clearly the fault line dividing the new conservatives, who generally accepted the positive state, from the obstructionists, who desired to restore the limited government that had prevailed in the past. The significance of the 1947 fiscal debate was apparent to the political commentator, Joseph Alsop. Writing in the midst of the debate, Alsop contended that the Republican divisions could not properly be regarded as a dispute between progressives and conservatives, as it was usually diagnosed. Rather, the struggle was between those who accepted the changes of modern life, and those who did not. Those who understood modern life, he continued, were those who had adjusted their politics to the conditions of American life in the 1940s. The "unadjusted" members of the party, he concluded, looked fondly back to the GOP's heyday in the 1920s.[10]

The widening divisions within the right wing, illustrated by the struggle over fiscal policy, were also evident in the major legislative effort of the 80th Congress, the effort to reform the nation's labor laws. But if the labor struggle revealed the ongoing transformation of conservatism, it also testified to the power exerted by partisan politics in the 80th Congress. By early 1947 the widespread labor unrest of the postwar period, highlighted by the 1946 coal and rail strikes, had created a powerful demand for change in the nation's labor laws. A letter written to South Carolina's Olin Johnston in February by the superintendent of a cotton mill was typical of the angry public mood. "The Congress," he wrote, "should *repeal* at once this damnable Wagner Act. It is both un-American and uncon-

stitutional and the rottenest piece of legislation ever put on our stat-
ute books."[11] Also suggesting the antilabor sentiment that pervaded
public opinion was a Gallup poll taken in November 1946, indicating that 50% of those surveyed favored a law forbidding all strikes
and lockouts for one year.[12]

To curb the spate of strikes, four separate bills were introduced in
the Senate in early January. The first measure, cosponsored by Joseph Ball, Robert Taft, and H. Alexander Smith, modified the 1946
Case bill vetoed by the President. It provided for a sixty-day cooling off period, during which a Mediation Board within the Labor
Department would attempt to reconcile differences between labor
and management. In addition, the bill made unions liable for breach
of contract suits and prohibited both secondary boycotts and jurisdictional strikes. The three remaining bills, each proposed by
Joseph Ball, banned the closed shop, forbade industrywide bargaining, and permitted the dismissal of striking workers who refused
employers' invitations to return to work. That he regarded his bill
as merely an attempt to adjust the nation's laws to account for the
substantial growth in labor's power since 1935 was evident in remarks made by H. Alexander Smith. Noting that the nation was increasingly polarized between those who sought to punish labor for
its abuses and those who acknowledged no problem at all in labor-
management relations, the New Jersey Republican argued in a letter
to the mayor of Newark that "both of these views are wrong. . . .
The union movement is here to stay and I believe profoundly in it.
. . . But the unions must not abuse the strength of their position.
They should on their own initiative recognize the evils that may
come from the power of sheer numbers and . . . correct their own
abuses before the Government is compelled to. Above all, they
should not look with the eyes of suspicion on those of us who are
trying to solve this problem without jeopardizing the legitimate as-
pirations of labor, but with the end in view that labor, like anyone
else, must be made to conform to the welfare and needs of our entire people."[13]

After the four bills were referred to the Senate Labor Committee,
they were combined into one omnibus bill at the insistence of the
chairman, Robert Taft. Although Taft's motives seem to have been
influenced in part by partisan politics, he also appeared to reason
that this action increased the likelihood that Congress would adopt
a labor bill in 1947, because the House also was considering only
one bill.[14] The committee hearings on the omnibus bill revealed the
depth of the conviction in the Senate that some changes had to be
made in the nation's labor laws. The testimony of AFL President

William Green and CIO President Phillip Murray, for instance, both of whom opposed any change in the Wagner Act, provoked sharp rebukes from some pro-labor members of the committee. Irving Ives, former dean of the Cornell School on Industrial and Labor Relations, complained to the labor leaders that they were foolish to object to all proposed changes in labor relations law. Even Wayne Morse of Oregon, perhaps the staunchest friend of labor among the Senate Republicans, warned the union leaders that if he had to choose between an antilabor bill or no bill, he would chose the former.[15]

Action in the Senate Labor Committee presaged the effort the new conservatives would make in the upper house to modify the Wagner Act without crippling organized labor's power. Five amendments proposed by the committee's chairman, Robert Taft, to strengthen the bill were defeated by votes from new conservatives and Democratic liberals. Three of the amendments, proposing to prohibit the involuntary check-off of union dues, ban the payment of production royalties to unions, and eliminate industrywide bargaining, were defeated by identical 7–6 margins when Vermont's George Aiken voted with such New Deal liberals as Elbert Thomas, James Murray, and Claude Pepper. Two subsequent amendments, allowing employers to seek injunctions against jurisdictional strikes and to seek triple damages in suits involving jurisdictional strikes, were similarly rejected on 14 April when Republican H. Alexander Smith joined with Aiken and the New Deal Democrats. After all strengthening amendments had been defeated, however, Aiken and Smith joined with Taft and other amendment supporters in voting to report the omnibus labor bill to the full Senate.[16]

The speech made by Robert Taft on 23 April, opening Senate debate on the omnibus labor bill emphasized the need for balance in labor-management relations. Arguing that his bill was not antilabor, the Ohio Republican insisted that it was intended to preserve the rights of unions to strike for such basic issues as wages and working conditions. The wave of postwar work stoppages had convinced him, however, that the administration of the Wagner Act "has been completely one-sided." The Labor Committee's one goal, he stressed, was "to get back to the point where, when an employer meets with his employees, they have substantially equal bargaining power so that neither side . . . can make an unreasonable demand and get away with it."[17]

Throughout Senate debate the new conservatives repeatedly shifted their votes between the obstructionists and the liberals to

fashion a labor bill that achieved balance in labor-management relations. On 2 May, for example, such new conservatives as Cooper,
Flanders, George, Holland, Hoey, Ives, Lodge, Russell, Saltonstall,
Smith, Taft, Thye, and Tobey voted with obstructionists to approve
a Taft amendment declaring it an unfair labor practice for unions to
"coerce" individual workers into joining unions. The victory was
not unexpected, for much of the opposition dissolved when Taft
agreed to delete from the amendment union "interference" as an
unfair labor practice.[18] Four days later, however, when Senate debate turned to the second Taft amendment that would have prohibited NLRB certification of national unions as bargaining agents and
instead only allow local unions to call in a national union to represent it, many new conservatives shifted their votes to the liberals.
Although Taft insisted that his amendment was not designed to prohibit industrywide bargaining but merely to prevent national unions
or their leaders from dictating contract terms to locals, new conservatives were skeptical. Irving Ives contended, for example, that the
Taft amendment would enable "chiseling employers" to entice locals away from national unions, thereby weakening organized labor
as a whole. Many new conservatives appeared to share Ives's concerns, for the 44–43 vote by which the second Taft amendment was
defeated showed that Aiken, Cooper, Flanders, Ives, Johnston,
Knowland, Lodge, Maybank, Saltonstall, Thye, and Tobey had
voted with the liberals to preserve the bargaining power of organized labor. The vote thus indicated that, while the new conservatives did want to curb the power of unions, they would resist
measures that risked crippling organized labor.[19]

The following day most new conservatives again voted with liberals to defeat a Ball amendment 62–26 that would have permitted
either the NLRB or employers to seek injunctions to halt secondary
boycotts and jurisdictional strikes. But then they shifted their votes
to the obstructionists to secure passage of a milder version sponsored by Taft that permitted only the NLRB to seek such injunctions.[20] When Senate debate ended on 13 May with adoption of the
Taft omnibus bill by the comfortable margin of 68–24, the new
conservatives were again aligned with the obstructionists in favor
of modifying the nation's labor-management legislation.[21]

Just how effective the new conservatives had been in steering the
Senate bill along a middle path became clear when the major provisions of the Taft bill were compared to those of the House's Hartley
bill. Although the Hartley bill flatly prohibited industrywide bargaining, the Taft bill did not touch the subject; where the House bill
permitted employers to seek injunctions against secondary boycotts

and jurisdictional strikes, the Taft bill allowed such action only when requested by the NLRB. The Hartley bill, moreover, abolished the NLRB and made every strike illegal unless approved by a majority of the union, whereas the Senate bill retained the NLRB and put no limitation on the right to strike except in "public interest" cases.[22]

Although substantial differences separated the Taft and Hartley bills, a conference committee took just two weeks to produce a compromise that closely followed the outlines of the milder Senate bill. Among the major provisions of the Taft-Hartley bill were a required eighty-day cooling off period before strikes affecting the public interest could begin, a ban on closed shops and the involuntary check-off of union dues, and an expansion of the definition of unfair labor practices to include such union actions as the refusal to bargain collectively, as well as the use of jurisdictional strikes and secondary boycotts. The only major provision of the conference report that followed the outlines of the Hartley bill was section 14b, the so-called right-to-work clause, that permitted individual states to outlaw the union shop. While section 14b was undeniably harsh, given the intense hostility many Americans appeared to have for organized labor in 1947, the conference report's overall tendency to preserve, and indeed consolidate, the federal guarantees extended to labor in 1935 testifies to the new conservative's determination to modify, rather than repeal, the Wagner Act.[23]

The conference report on Taft-Hartley was adopted overwhelmingly by both houses of Congress in early June and the Senate vote again revealed that most new conservatives had sided with the obstructionists to approve a measure that trimmed the power of organized labor. Then, after President Truman vetoed the Taft-Hartley bill on 20 June, claiming that it threatened to undo the important progress made in national labor policy, new conservatives in the Senate joined forces with obstructionists once more to override the veto. The Senate vote approving the conference report and overriding Truman's veto was supported by such new conservatives as Aiken, Cooper, George, Hoey, Holland, Ives, Lodge, Maybank, Russell, Saltonstall, and Smith, together with such obstructionists as Buck, Byrd, Cain, Dworshak, Hawkes, McCarthy, Moore, O'Daniel, Revercomb, and Wherry.[24]

If the debate over the Taft-Hartley Act again revealed the role played by the new conservatives in fashioning legislation that found the middle ground between policy extremes, it also testified to the power of partisan politics in the 80th Congress. Because Republican candidates in 1946 had frequently played to the voters' frustration over strikes, many in the party undoubtedly felt the need to deliver on their promises. Thus, many of the Republicans who scaled in the medium support or new conservative position in the 80th Congress, such as H. Alexander Smith, John Sherman Cooper, Ralph Flanders, and Irving Ives, offered only low support on the Labor dimension. Testifying to the pull of partisanship in the labor debate were the comments H. Alexander Smith recorded in his diary during committee hearings on the bill. Although he voted for a Taft amendment that prohibited NLRB certification of national unions as bargaining agents, Smith confessed on 8 May that "I believe I voted wrong yesterday on the 'industry wide' amendment. But it was defeated for which I am thankful. . . . Taft and Ball have been definitely wrong in pushing these amendments. I only stand with them out of a sense of loyalty."[25]

Conversely, many of the Democrats who offered medium support on the Labor dimension in the 80th Congress and who had scaled as new conservatives in previous Congresses, such as Clyde Hoey, Spessard Holland, Walter George, and Burnet Maybank, scaled in the high support or liberal group when all policy dimensions were considered. Unexpectedly reduced to the minority party by the 1946 elections, many Democrats in the 80th Congress appeared to put aside their ideological convictions to vote to defend their embattled President.

The elevated partisanship of the debate over labor policy in 1947 often obscured the true nature of the changes made in the nation's labor laws. The harsh rhetoric used by supporters of organized labor who denounced Taft-Hartley as a slave-labor law suggested to many in 1947 that the advocates of punitive legislation had realized their objectives. Following the Senate's override of Truman's veto, for instance, a Ford Motor Company employee bitterly asserted that the labor law stripped working people of all their freedom. Liberal Democrat Claude Pepper similarly predicted that the American people were now wholly subservient to the power of big business.[26] The new conservatives, however, were more sanguine about the measure. Democrat Clyde Hoey of North Carolina maintained that the new bill "is not anti-labor and it does not take away any substantial or legitimate rights of the unions. It does remove some of the discriminations which exempted labor unions from the laws which other people and organizations are required to obey, and it does put labor and management on an equal basis." Republican George Aiken agreed, arguing "that the bill is just and equitable to both labor and management. It amends the Wagner Act to correct injustices that have existed. By banning the closed shop and secondary boycotts, the bill goes far toward equalizing relations between labor and management."[27]

The role played by the new conservatives in fashioning the Taft-Hartley Act in 1947 reveals much about the transformation of Senate conservatism. While the highly charged issue of labor-management relations revealed differences among the new conservatives that were more substantial than on most other public policy issues in the postwar era, they were differences largely in degree. Some proposals to curb unions, which seemed reasonable and necessary to an H. Alexander Smith or a Leverett Saltonstall, were rejected by an Irving Ives or a George Aiken, who feared they might cripple organized labor. Whatever differences that divided the new conservatives, they were united by the belief that the basic rights guaranteed to labor by the 1935 Wagner Act had to be preserved. By that conviction they demonstrated that yet another facet of their conservative ideology had been modernized to meet what they regarded as the challenges of the modern corporate state.

Prior to the rise of large-scale industry, labor had been generally viewed as a commodity that was "purchased" and "sold" in free and equal negotiations between employers and employees. The rough parity that was presumed to exist between employer and employee in this pre-industrial system left little room for any sort of government intervention. Workers and owners alike, for example, viewed action taken by the state to establish minimum wages or safe working conditions as both unnecessary and paternalistic. Despite the tremendous changes wrought in the scale and power of business by the industrialization of the late nineteenth and early twentieth centuries, the role of government in labor relations on the federal level largely continued to reflect these pre-industrial concepts until the 1935 Wagner Act and the 1938 Fair Labor Standards Act.[28]

The 1947 debate on the Taft-Hartley Act also reveals the fundamental nature of the differences separating Senate conservatives. The efforts of the obstructionist conservatives, for example, seem to have been guided by pre-industrial concepts of labor. Their efforts to sharply modify or repeal the Wagner Act were intended not simply to offer a solution to postwar labor problems, but to reverse the direction federal labor policy had taken after 1932. In their minds, the postwar labor problems were not caused by a supposed imbalance in labor-management relations. Rather, the source of the problem was the Wagner Act itself which, together with such measures as the Fair Labor Standards Act, established an expanded federal role in labor relations. Indeed, the biographer of one of the

Senate's most strident critics of organized labor, Kenneth Wherry, argues that the source of the Nebraskan's extreme conservatism was his inability to see beyond the values of his rural, agrarian upbringing. "He felt that the entire trend toward an increasingly greater role of the Federal Government in the life of the citizen was somehow antithetical to the traditional values and virtues. . . . His whole scheme of values and attitudes were those of the rural nineteenth century America into which he was born and from which he never departed."[29]

The arguments advanced by the new conservatives, on the other hand, suggest that they viewed labor largely in modern corporate terms. Because business in the twentieth century had grown so large and powerful, they acknowledged that government had to intervene to protect the rights of individual workers. Such intervention was not paternalistic in their eyes, but essential to preserve the freedom and opportunity of workers in a corporate economy. At the same time, however, the wave of postwar strikes indicated to them that the 1935 Wagner Act could not be regarded as the last word on labor-management relations. Thus, during the 1947 labor debate the new conservatives had voted to mandate an eighty-day cooling off period as a way to minimize crippling work stoppages, and similarly had supported bans on the closed shop and the involuntary check-off, which they believed had contributed to the growth of excessive union power. But they resisted all efforts to impair the fundamental federal guarantees of organization and collective bargaining established in 1935.

If debates on domestic policy in 1947 exposed the changes that had occurred in Senate conservatism, action on the Truman Doctrine pointed to the equally significant changes that had taken place in foreign policy attitudes. President Truman's request in March for $400 million in economic and military aid to help the governments of Greece and Turkey resist communist subversion stirred considerable uneasiness in Congress. Coming at a time when growing tension in United States–Soviet relations seemed to threaten the nation's interests, Truman's request for assistance was, on one hand, difficult for many legislators to oppose. On the other hand, the principle established by the Truman Doctrine "that it must be the policy of the United States to support free peoples who are resisting attempted subjugation by armed minorities or outside pressures," appeared to be a quantum leap in American internationalism that many in Congress were not prepared to accept. In the end, most new conservatives in the upper house bowed to the imperatives of the Cold War and voted reluctantly to approve the Truman Doctrine, demonstrating thereby how lessons learned during World War II had influenced their political philosophy.[30]

Before the Greek-Turkish aid bill reached the Senate floor in early April, modifications made to it in the Foreign Relations Committee headed off much of the potential opposition. At the insistence of the committee's chairman, Arthur Vandenberg of Michigan, the bill was amended to invite the United Nations to modify or to end the American aid program when the international security agency either substituted its own aid package or found that such assistance was no longer required. The Vandenberg amendment went far toward allaying the concerns of those who feared that unilateral action taken by the U.S. would undercut the fledgling U.N., and those who worried that the bill might establish a precedent for unlimited U.S. foreign aid wherever communism threatened. On the latter point, Vandenberg argued vigorously, if not always convincingly, that the Greek-Turkish aid bill should not be seen as part of a doctrine or a long-range policy, but simply as a short-term plan aimed at protecting America's interests by defending two noncommunist governments.[31] The arguments of Vandenberg, together with the seeming gravity of the international situation, overwhelmed the doubts of most senators, including the new conservatives, for on 22 April thirty-five Republicans joined thirty-two Democrats to ratify the Truman Doctrine by a vote of 67–23.

The vote revealed that opposition to the measure had come from an unusual coalition of obstructionist conservatives, such as Bricker, Brooks, Buck, Butler, Byrd, Kem, Moore, O'Daniel, Revercomb, and Wherry, who believed that the United States' interests were best served by a course of noninvolvement, and three extreme left-wing Democrats Claude Pepper, James Murray, and Glen Taylor, who viewed the aid package as a threat to world peace because it was unduly provocative toward the Soviet Union. Despite the disclaimers made by sponsors of the bill that it was not precedent-setting, most contemporary observers grasped the significance of the measure. James Reston of the *New York Times* argued, for example, that the Senate's action reversed the long-standing American faith in nonintervention. Similarly, *Newsweek* viewed Senate approval as a rejection of the nation's traditionally insular foreign policy.[32]

In addition to the historic change that approval of the Truman Doctrine meant for American foreign policy, the debate also revealed that the differences separating supporters and opponents, like the divisions on domestic policy, turned on the acceptance or rejection of America as a modern industrial state. That is, opposition to the Truman Doctrine came largely from obstructionist conservatives who viewed international entanglements as a threat to the traditions of rural, agrarian America. American internationalism, they feared, would necessarily entail large government expenditures, a permanent bureaucracy to administer the policies, and additional enhancements of Executive power. Chapman Revercomb of West Virginia explained during Senate debate on 18 April that he opposed the Truman Doctrine because it would, in his judgment, establish a precedent for unlimited U.S. aid throughout the world. The consequence, he predicted, would be an "abdication" by Congress of its constitutional duty to concur or reject on future foreign actions, as well the preclusion of any chance for tax reduction and debt retirement. Democrat Millard Tydings viewed the issue similarly. Although the Maryland Democrat, who was an outspoken critic of the positive state, voted for the Truman Doctrine, he based his support for it on a hard-nosed calculation of economic costs. Given the tension in United States–Soviet relations, Tydings reasoned, "the rejection of aid to Greece and Turkey . . . would probably delay still further an agreement on Germany's future. The net result would be to keep our Army overseas longer and to put an expense on our government far in excess of the amount of aid suggested for Greece and Turkey."[33]

Thus, opponents of postwar American internationalism, like those who resisted the expansion of governmental power symbolized by New Deal domestic reform, tended to be cut from the same cloth. That postwar legislators such as Kenneth Wherry, Hugh Butler, John Bricker, Chapman Revercomb, Albert Hawkes, W. Lee "Pappy" O'Daniel, and James P. Kem opposed such seemingly diverse legislation as the Truman Doctrine, reciprocal trade, or the Wagner Act can be explained only in that they saw all as obstacles to the restoration of a self-reliant America of rugged individuals which, they believed, had been under constant assault since 1933. The common denominator in the resistance offered by some postwar senators to the domestic and foreign policies of the Truman Administration was evident in the argument Hugh Butler of Nebraska advanced against the Truman Doctrine. He would vote against the Greek-Turkish aid bill, he maintained, because it was "a return to the basic philosophy of the New Deal—that the way to meet any problem is to spend Government money."[34]

Support for the Truman Doctrine, on the other hand, came from those who recognized that America, in both an economic and strategic sense, was an interdependent part of the international community. Some supporters, of course, had been committed to an internationalistic foreign policy long before World War II. But others who voted for the Greek-Turkish aid bill had learned this lesson only through the economic collapse in the 1930s and the destruction of the world order in the 1940s. Democrat Spessard Holland of Florida explained to a friend in April 1947 that, despite his strong hatred for war, he had decided reluctantly to vote for the Truman Doctrine. In a direct reference to the 1938 Munich Conference, Holland asserted that "if we permitted Russia by infiltration and threats to accomplish all the expansion which she wants . . . , it would be practicing a kind of appeasement that would be more apt to get us into trouble than to frankly go to the aid of the Greeks and Turks. I am, of course, not happy about the situation, but this seems to me to be soundest course to follow." Clyde Hoey of North Carolina drew the same comparison. Writing to a Methodist minister in April, the moderate Democrat argued "if Great Britain and France had stopped Germany at the beginning, I think we could have avoided the second World War. Just as I believe now that if we stop Russia we will not have to fight a third World War; whereas if we let her take charge of all surrounding countries, then the third World War is inevitable."[35]

Although the air of crisis generated by the Truman Administration over the Greek-Turkish aid bill tended to obscure differences among supporters of the measure, new conservatives, such as Holland and Hoey, would strive to limit the degree of America's international commitments during foreign policy debates in 1948 and 1949. In this sense, therefore, a common thread also bound the political philosophy of the new conservatives on domestic and international questions. Recognizing that America had been irrevocably transformed into an urban, industrial nation, they adjusted their conservatism to accept an expanded role for government and an internationalistic foreign policy as essential components of the transformation that had occurred. At the same time, they sought to preserve as much self-sufficiency and individual initiative as was compatible with the demands of the modern industrial state.

II

The fall presidential election cast a long shadow over the legislative debates in the second session of the 80th Congress. As each party jockeyed for votes, partisanship increased materially. Indeed, despite his decision to de-emphasize social reforms throughout

1947 in an attempt to cooperate with the Republican Congressional majority, Harry Truman's 1948 State of the Union Address was widely regarded as the first shot of the presidential campaign. Calling for such reforms as an expansion of social security, a comprehensive federal civil rights program, an increase in the minimum wage, federal health care and education programs, as well as a $40 "cost-of-living tax credit" for every taxpayer and all dependents to be funded by an increase in corporate taxes, Truman made a concerted effort to abandon his middle-of-the-road course to fight for re-election as a New Deal liberal.[36]

The Republicans were similarly affected by election-year politics. Although Truman's unpopularity presented the GOP with its best chance since 1932 for capturing the White House, the internal disputes over political philosophy, gaining momentum since the early 1940s, prevented the party from offering to the electorate in 1948 a distinct political identity. Riven between obstructionists who desired to return to pre-1932 America in both domestic and foreign policy, and new conservatives who accepted the fundamental domestic and foreign policy requirements of urban, industrial America, GOP Congressional leaders usually were forced to search for the lowest common denominator of policy which, in the end, satisfied neither group and contributed ultimately to the defeat of the party's nominee in November.[37]

The heightened partisanship of the election year also determined that controversial legislation was generally put aside in favor of politically popular measures or truly urgent matters of public policy. For instance, the Republican majorities in both houses of Congress easily enacted over Truman's veto a measure to reduce voters' income taxes by $4.7 billion. Fear of a protracted and bitter debate, on the other hand, led Congress to substitute a voluntary enlistment program, providing one year of military training for up to 161,000 eighteen-year-old Americans for a White House proposal calling for universal military training. Similar partisan concerns encouraged Congress to reject the President's demand for a temporary draft that would have required the registration of all men between the ages of eighteen and forty-five, in favor of a temporary measure that affected only those nineteen to twenty-five years of age. As Congress rushed toward adjournment before the national party conventions in summer, however, several important measures were enacted that underscored the transformation in Senate conservatism.[38]

Perhaps the clearest sign of the change in the Senate's right wing in 1948 was provided by the adoption of the Marshall Plan. The idea for the European Recovery Plan, as it was formally known, was introduced by Secretary of State George Marshall in a June 1947 commencement address at Harvard University. But the formal request for a four-year, $17-billion package of economic aid to rebuild war-torn Europe was not transmitted to Congress until 19 December 1947. The Truman Administration's case for the urgent necessity of the aid package was made forcefully by Marshall, himself, in testimony before the Foreign Relations Committee in early January 1948. Adopting the scare tactics that had helped persuade Congress to approve the Truman Doctrine a year earlier, the secretary of state warned that if the foreign aid package were rejected, Europe would be plunged into totalitarian dictatorship. To emphasize the urgency felt by the Administration, Marshall challenged Congress to provide the entire $6.8 billion requested for the first fifteen months of the program, or to reject it outright. Arguing that it was futile to attempt to economize on so vital a program, he insisted that less than full funding would simply squander U.S. resources without achieving the objectives.[39]

Opposition to the European Recovery Plan surfaced among obstructionist conservatives in the Senate even before the Administration had made its formal request. As had been true of their criticism of previous foreign policies, obstructionists' complaints about the Marshall Plan centered on both its cost and the degree to which it would deepen America's international involvement. Missouri Republican James P. Kem contended in October 1947, for instance, that the program would devastate the American economy. If the Marshall Plan were adopted, he declared, "this country risks a price inflation and price debacle that may shake the country to its foundations." Hugh Butler of Kansas agreed that the program risked bankrupting the country, but also raised the specter of permanent foreign entanglements. "Europe was always self-supporting before the war and even under Hitler," he wrote in August 1947. "There should be some hope, therefore, that it can be self-supporting again withough [sic] going on a *permanent* dole from the United States." Beneath these specific concerns, however, obstructionists generally resisted the Marshall Plan, as they did other forms of postwar foreign policy, because it symbolized to them the fundamental assault on traditional American values, which they believed had begun in 1932. Asserting that foreign aid would sap the initiative of European countries, just as New Deal relief had undermined individual initiative in America, Republican William Jenner of Indiana dismissed the Marshall plan as a "boondoggling PWA." Jenner's Indiana colleague, Homer Capehart, was more pointed in his criticism. "This is the fundamental basis of socialism," he asserted, "and I oppose socialism."[40]

The attitude of the new conservatives in the Senate toward the Marshall Plan fell between the Administration's demand for all-or-nothing and the obstructionists' unrelenting opposition. While most accepted the need for American assistance in rebuilding Europe, the new conservatives were unhappy with the Administration's approach for several reasons. To Democrat Walter George, who had endured years of FDR's expansion of the Executive perogative, Marshall's unyielding insistence that nothing less than the full $6.8 billion in aid would suffice seemed to be another attempt to browbeat Congress. Vowing to look for small reductions in the funds Marshall had requested, the Georgia Democrat angrily denounced what he regarded as an Administration ultimatum.[41]

Those new conservatives elected during the 1940s, on the other hand, seemed less concerned with the Administration's methods than with the amount of foreign aid it had requested. New conservatives such as Spessard Holland and Burnet Maybank understood, in contrast to the obstructionists, that the Marshall Plan aid would ultimately further America's self-interest. But they were not convinced that the full amount requested by the Administration was vital to achieve the plan's objectives. In early February 1948, for example, Holland contended that "I feel that it is for the best interest of our nation to assist the countries of Western Europe to rehabilitate themselves but in doing so we . . . must take every precaution not to impair our own economy." Burnet Maybank viewed the matter similarly. In a speech to postal clerks in late January, the South Carolina Democrat emphasized the link that the new conservatism saw between the well-being of industrial America and that of the international community. One of the chief benefits of American economic aid, he argued, was that it would create customers for U.S. products, especially tobacco, lumber, and cotton, the chief exports of South Carolina. These benefits had to be balanced carefully, however, against the cost of such foreign aid. "I'll support the Marshall Plan only insofar as it will build strength against Russia, preserve our kind of political stability in Western Europe, help anti-Communist governments to their feet industrially so they can walk alone and buy from us. . . . Beyond that I cannot go. Sound politics, sound economics, sound morality, all demand that the United States remain strong. If we weaken ourselves trying to help others, no matter how noble our motives, we'll be doing disservice to ourselves and to others."[42]

The concerns of the new conservatives were addressed by several modifications written into the bill by Arthur Vandenberg, chairman of the Foreign Relations Committee, before it was reported out in February. The most significant alteration was that only $5.3 billion was to be allocated for twelve months of aid, instead of the $6.8 billion requested by the Administration for fifteen months. Although this change, since it provided the same amount of aid per month as the Administration's request, appeared to be only a cosmetic change, its significance to the new conservatives was great. First, by limiting the initial allocation to only twelve months, Vandenberg reduced the amount of America's financial commitment. More importantly, by restricting the initial outlay of aid to twelve months, Vandenberg's change also permitted the new Congress to be elected in November to determine the future of the program, thereby limiting the commitment of American aid to only one year. That Vandenberg's modification had provided the necessary reassurance for some senators was evident in remarks made by Robert Taft. Although he made an unsuccessful effort during Senate debate to reduce Marshall Plan funds below $5.3 billion, the Ohio Republican voted for final passage of the bill with the understanding that it committed America to only one year of aid. Additionally, Vandenberg's modifications made continuation of American aid contingent upon the total cooperation of recipients, a change directed at those who feared that the program would jeopardize America's sovereignty and established a "Congressional Watch-Dog Committee" that would oversee the operation to guarantee that the legislative branch maintained its voice over this important foreign policy.[43]

The success of Vandenberg's strategy to head off potential opposition from new conservatives before reporting out the bill was borne out by Senate action. Formally introduced on 1 March amid heightened concerns over the threat of communism because of recent developments in Czechoslovakia and Finland, the Marshall Plan won easy approval in the upper house only two weeks later by a margin of 69–17.[44] Only two serious efforts were made during Senate debate to modify the committee's bill. An amendment offered on 8 March by Republicans Joseph Ball and Kenneth Wherry, for example, was widely regarded by Marshall Plan defenders as a subtle effort to discourage countries from applying for U.S. foreign aid. The Ball-Wherry amendment required aid recipients to stop pegging their currency at levels below the free market value. Instead, the value of foreign currencies would be determined by the free market, which in most cases in 1948 would have overvalued foreign currencies relative to U.S. dollars. The net result of the Ball-Wherry amendment was, therefore, to discourage Americans from

TABLE 5-1

80th CONGRESS

Name	Policy Dimensions	Score
	1 2 3 4 5 6 7 8 9 10 11 12 13	

HIGH SUPPORT

Name	Policy Dimensions	Score
Hill, D-AL	1 1 1 1 1 1 1 1 1 1 1 1 1	1.00
Kilgore, D-WV	1 1 1 1 1 1 1 1 1 1 1 1 1	1.00
McGrath, D-RI	1 1 1 1 1 1 1 1 1 1 1 1 1	1.00
McMahon, D-CT	1 1 1 1 1 1 1 1 1 1 1 1 1	1.00
Sparkman, D-AL	1 1 1 1 1 1 1 1 1 1 1 1 1	1.00
Downey, D-CA	1 1 1 1 1 1 1 0 0 1 1 1 1	1.00
Wagner, D-NY	1 0 1 1 0 1 1 0 1 1 1 1 1	1.00
Myers, D-PA	1 1 1 2 1 1 1 1 1 0 1 1 1	1.08
Maybank, D-SC	2 2 1 1 1 1 0 1 1 1 1 1 1	1.08
McFarland, D-AZ	1 1 1 1 1 1 2 1 1 1 0 1 1	1.09
Hayden, D-AZ	1 2 1 1 1 1 0 1 0 1 1 1 1	1.09
Murray, D-MT	1 1 1 1 1 1 1 3 1 1 1 1 1	1.15
Magnuson, D-WA	1 2 1 2 1 1 1 0 1 1 1 1 1	1.17
Chavez, D-NM	1 2 2 1 0 1 1 0 1 1 1 1 1	1.18
Taylor, D-ID	1 1 1 1 1 1 0 0 1 0 1 1 3	1.20
Barkley, D-KY	1 0 1 0 2 1 1 0 1 2 1 1 1	1.20
Fulbright, D-AR	2 1 1 1 1 2 2 1 1 1 1 1 1	1.23
Pepper, D-FL	1 1 1 1 2 1 1 3 0 1 1 1 1	1.25
Thomas, D-OK	2 1 1 1 2 1 2 1 0 1 1 1 1	1.25
Lucas, D-IL	2 2 1 1 2 1 1 1 1 0 1 1 1	1.25
Thomas, D-UT	1 0 1 3 0 1 1 1 1 2 1 1 1	1.27
Green, D-RI	0 2 1 2 1 1 1 0 2 1 1 1 1	1.27
Johnston, D-SC	1 1 1 1 1 1 3 1 1 1 1 1 3	1.31
Russell, D-GA	2 1 1 1 2 1 3 1 1 1 1 1 1	1.31
Holland, D-FL	2 1 1 2 1 1 3 1 1 1 1 1 1	1.31
Hatch, D-NM	2 2 1 3 1 1 1 1 1 1 1 1 1	1.31
Umstead, D-NC	2 2 2 1 1 1 2 1 1 1 1 1 1	1.31
Hoey, D-NC	2 2 1 2 1 1 3 1 1 1 1 1 1	1.38
McCarran, D-NV	1 2 2 1 1 1 0 0 0 0 3 1 1	1.44
Connally, D-TX	2 1 2 1 1 1 3 1 2 1 2 1 1	1.46

Name	Policy Dimensions	Score
	1 2 3 4 5 6 7 8 9 10 11 12 13	

HIGH SUPPORT continued

Name	Policy Dimensions	Score
George, D-GA	2 1 2 2 0 2 3 1 1 1 2 1 1	1.46
O'Conor, D-MD	2 2 2 2 2 2 1 1 1 1 1 1 1	1.46
McClellan, D-AR	2 1 1 1 1 0 3 1 2 1 3 1 1	1.50
Stewart, D-TN	2 1 2 1 2 2 3 0 1 1 3 1 1	1.54
Tydings, D-MD	2 2 2 1 1 2 2 0 0 2 1 1 1	1.55
Johnson, D-CO	1 2 2 2 1 1 1 3 2 2 2 1 1	1.62
Eastland, D-MS	3 2 1 2 0 2 3 1 0 1 1 1 1	1.64
Morse, R-OR	2 3 1 1 1 1 1 3 1 3 1 3 1	1.69

MEDIUM SUPPORT

Name	Policy Dimensions	Score
Aiken, R-VT	2 0 2 1 1 2 1 3 1 3 1 3 1	1.75
Robertson, D-VA	3 0 2 3 2 2 3 1 1 1 1 1 1	1.75
Tobey, R-NH	3 0 2 0 0 2 1 0 1 3 1 1 0	1.75
McKellar, D-TN	0 1 2 1 2 2 3 1 2 2 3 1 1	1.75
Ellender, D-LA	2 2 2 3 1 2 3 1 3 1 1 1 1	1.77
Overton, D-LA	3 2 1 0 2 2 3 1 2 1 3 3 1	2.00
Cooper, R-TN	3 3 2 3 0 2 1 3 1 1 2 2 1	2.00
Byrd, D-VA	3 2 2 0 2 2 3 1 2 0 3 1 2	2.09
Saltonstall, R-MA	3 2 3 3 1 3 1 3 1 3 0 3 1	2.25
Smith, R-NJ	3 3 3 3 3 3 1 3 1 2 1 3 1	2.31
Lodge, R-MA	3 3 3 3 3 3 1 3 1 3 1 3 1	2.38
Robertson, R-WY	3 2 2 3 2 0 1 0 3 3 0 3 0	2.44
Langer, R-ND	2 3 1 0 0 1 3 3 3 3 2 3 3	2.45
Bridges, R-NH	3 0 3 3 2 3 1 0 2 3 3 3 1	2.45
Ives, R-NY	3 3 3 3 2 3 1 3 3 3 1 3 1	2.46
Taft, R-OH	3 3 3 3 3 3 1 3 2 3 1 3 1	2.46
Flanders, R-VT	3 3 3 3 2 3 2 3 1 3 0 3 1	2.50
Thye, R-MN	3 3 3 3 3 3 2 0 2 3 1 3 1	2.50

LOW SUPPORT

Name	Policy Dimensions	Score
Baldwin, R-CT	3 3 3 2 3 3 2 3 3 2 2 3 1	2.54
Watkins, R-UT	3 3 3 3 2 3 2 3 3 3 1 3 1	2.54

Name	Policy Dimensions	Score
	1 2 3 4 5 6 7 8 9 10 11 12 13	

LOW SUPPORT continued

Name	Policy Dimensions	Score
O'Daniel, D-TX	3 3 3 3 2 3 3 1 2 1 3 3 3	2.54
Ball, R-MN	3 3 3 3 3 3 1 3 2 3 1 3 2	2.54
Moore, R-OK	3 3 3 3 3 3 0 1 3 1 3 0 2	2.55
Cordon, R-OR	3 3 3 3 2 3 3 2 2 3 0 3 1	2.58
Donnell, R-MO	3 3 3 3 2 3 3 0 2 3 2 3 1	2.58
Brewster, R-ME	3 0 3 3 3 3 1 3 2 3 3 3 1	2.58
Knowland, R-CA	3 3 3 3 2 3 3 3 2 3 2 3 1	2.62
Gurney, R-SD	3 3 3 3 3 3 3 1 3 3 2 3 1	2.62
Wilson, R-IA	3 3 2 3 0 3 2 0 2 3 0 3 0	2.67
Hickenlooper, R-IA	3 3 3 3 3 3 3 1 3 3 0 3 1	2.67
Ferguson, R-MI	3 3 3 3 3 3 1 3 3 3 3 3 1	2.69
Vandenberg, R-MI	3 3 3 3 3 3 2 3 3 3 2 3 1	2.69
McCarthy, R-WI	3 3 3 3 2 3 3 3 3 3 0 3 1	2.75
Wiley, R-WI	3 3 3 3 2 3 0 3 3 3 3 3 1	2.75
Young, R-ND	3 3 3 3 3 3 3 2 3 3 0 3 1	2.75
Brooks, R-IL	3 3 3 3 3 3 1 3 3 3 3 3 2	2.77
Ecton, R-MT	3 3 3 3 3 3 3 3 3 2 3 3 1	2.77
Capper, R-KS	3 3 3 3 3 3 3 3 3 3 2 3 1	2.77
Millikin, R-CO	3 3 3 3 3 3 3 3 3 3 2 3 1	2.77
Revercomb, R-WV	3 3 3 3 3 3 3 3 3 2 0 3 2	2.83
Martin, R-PA	3 3 3 3 3 3 3 3 0 3 3 3 1	2.83
Malone, R-NV	3 3 3 3 3 3 3 0 2 2 3 3 3	2.83
Bricker, R-OH	3 3 3 3 3 3 3 0 3 3 3 3 1	2.83
Dworshak, R-ID	3 3 3 3 3 3 3 2 3 3 3 3 2	2.85
Cain, R-WA	3 3 3 3 3 3 3 3 3 3 3 3 1	2.85
Butler, R-NE	3 3 3 3 2 3 3 3 3 3 3 3 2	2.87
Wherry, R-NE	3 3 3 3 2 3 3 3 3 3 3 3 2	2.87
Bushfield, R-SD	3 3 3 3 2 3 3 0 0 3 0 3 0	2.89
Reed, R-KS	3 3 3 3 0 3 3 0 3 0 3 3 2	2.90
Buck, R-DE	3 3 3 0 0 3 3 3 2 3 3 3 0	2.90
Capehart, R-IN	3 3 3 0 0 3 3 3 3 2 3 3 3	2.91
Kem, R-MO	3 3 3 3 3 3 3 2 3 3 3 3 3	2.92
Jenner, R-IN	3 3 3 3 3 3 3 3 3 3 3 3 3	3.00
Hawkes, R-NJ	3 3 3 3 3 3 3 3 3 3 3 3 3	3.00
Williams, R-DE	3 3 3 3 3 3 3 3 3 3 3 3 0	3.00
White, R-ME	3 3 3 3 3 3 0 0 0 0 3 3 0	3.00

Policy Dimension Key:

    0   denotes that a senator did not scale on the dimension
    1.   Labor
    2.   Extension of Executive Power
    3.   Fiscal Policy
    4.   Extension of Federal Authority
    5.   Social Welfare
    6.   Economy in Government Spending
    7.   Displaced Persons
    8.   National Defense
    9.   Business Regulation
    10.   Agriculture
    11.   Public Power
    12.   Reciprocal Trade
    13.   Foreign Aid

80TH CONGRESS (N=94)

HIGH SUPPORT (N=38 or 40%)   MEDIUM SUPPORT (N=18 or 20%)

        Democrats = 37 (97%)   Democrats =   5 (28%)
        GOP   = 1 (3%)   GOP   = 13 (72%)

                LOW SUPPORT (N=38 or 40%)

                Democrats = 1 (3%)
                GOP   = 37 (97%)

Table 5-2

Regional Divisions in Medium and Low Support Groups

MEDIUM SUPPORT (N=18)

Coastal (N=10 or 56%)

Aiken, R-VT	Byrd, D-VA	Tobey, R-NH
Saltonstall, R-MA	Ives, R-NY	Bridges, R-NH
Flanders, R-VT	Smith, R-NJ	
Lodge, R-MA	Robertson, D-VA	

Interior (N=8 or 44%)

Ellender, D-LA	Langer, R-ND	McKellar, D-TN
Overton, D-LA	Robertson, R-Wy	Thye, R-MN
Cooper, R-TN	Taft, R-OH	

LOW SUPPORT (N= 38)

Coastal (N=11 or 29%)

Baldwin, R-CT	Cordon, R-OR	White, R-ME
Knowland, R-CA	Martin, R-PA	Brewster, R-ME
Cain, R-WA	Hawkes, R-NJ	Buck, R-DE
Williams, R-DE	Revercomb, R-WV	

Interior (N=27 or 71%)

Wilson, R-IA	Watkins, R-UT	O'Daniel, D-TX
Butler, R-NE	Wherry, R-NE	McCarthy, R-WI
Donnell, R-MO	Bushfield, R-SD	Wiley, R-WI
Hickenlooper, R-IA	Ferguson, R-MI	Brooks, R-IL
Vandenberg, R-MI	Gurney, R-SD	Ball, R-MN
Dworshak, R-ID	Kem, R-MO	Young, R-KS
Ecton, R-MT	Capper, R-KS	Millikin, R-CO
Jenner, R-IN	Malone, R-NV	Bricker, R-OH
Moore, R-OK	Reed, R-KS	Capehart, R-IN

purchasing imported goods by increasing their prices. The Ball-Wherry amendment was defeated 53–19, however, when most new conservatives joined with liberals against a small phalanx of obstructionists. The second challenge came four days later in the form of a Taft amendment proposing to reduce the first year of Marshall Plan aid from $5.3 billion to $4 billion. It was rejected by a margin of 56–31 in a vote that again saw most new conservatives vote with liberals.[45]

The votes on both the Ball-Wherry and Taft amendments, as well as on final passage of the Marshall Plan, revealed that Senate conservatives had consistently divided into two groups. A bloc of new conservatives composed of Aiken, Cooper, Flanders, George, Hoey, Ives, Lodge, Saltonstall, H. Alexander Smith, Thye, and Tobey regularly voted with the liberals to deepen America's entanglement in international affairs. Opposition to the Marshall Plan, on the other hand, came largely from such obstructionist conservatives as Hugh Butler, Harry Cain, Homer Capehart, William Jenner, John Bricker, James Kem, C. Wayland "Curly" Brooks, Kenneth Wherry, Chapman Revercomb, and W. Lee "Pappy" O'Daniel. Their opposition to the internationalism represented by the Marshall Plan was certainly rooted in their conviction that the nation's interests were best promoted by continued avoidance of entangling foreign alliances, as the nation had sought to do since George Washington's time. But the frequent comparisons they made between the Marshall Plan and Franklin Roosevelt's New Deal suggests that they resisted American internationalism also because of its tendency to promote deficit spending and expand federal power.

While the new conservatives' rhetoric during the Marshall Plan debate clearly differentiated them from the liberals and the obstructionists, the roll call analysis on all foreign policy dimensions (table 5–3) testifies to the persistent power of partisan politics to shape voting alignments. Because 1948 was a presidential election year, few Democrats were willing to disagree publicly with their commander-in-chief. Indeed, thirty-eight of the forty Democrats (88%) who scaled on foreign policy dimensions gave high support to initiatives of the Truman Administration, and only one Democrat, O'Daniel of Texas, offered low support.

On the other hand, Republicans, facing their best prospects in the presidential sweepstakes since 1932, were of two minds on foreign policy. While only two of the fifty scalable Republicans (4%) mustered high support for the Administration, twenty-five of fifty (50%) provided medium support, and twenty-three of fifty (46%) offered low support. Clearly, some members of the party of Lincoln believed that moderate support for internationalism was the key to electoral success, while others believed that resistance to American internationalism was the road that would take the party to the White House. Viewed another way, the foreign policy dimensions reveal partisan patterns of voting not evident since before World War II. Democractic votes in the 80th Congress accounted for 95% of the high support on all foreign policy dimensions, whereas 96% of the low support came from Republicans. Thus, although many within the GOP majority in the 80th Congress could be counted on to offer moderate support for American internationalism, politics in 1948 clearly did not stop at the water's edge.

Two domestic issues addressed by the 1948 Senate, federal aid to education and public housing, offered further evidence of the gap separating the new conservatives from the obstructionists. Although the need for federal assistance in both areas had been revealed by earlier congressional investigations, by 1948 the burgeoning postwar population had exacerbated the problems. Faced with overcrowded schools and an inadequate housing stock, the new conservatives worked to fashion bills in 1948 that provided federal assistance in both areas, thus distinguishing themselves from obstructionists who continued to denounce the programs as "socialistic." At the same time, by seeking to limit the amount of aid provided as well as the role of the federal government in administering that aid, the new conservatives distinguished themselves from liberals in the upper house.

The Senate addressed the crisis in the nation's educational system first. By 1948 the migration of the population during World War II, together with the postwar surge in the birth rate, had produced serious overcrowding in many parts of the country. The complaints from a principal of a rural school district in Florida were typical. "This district has more than doubled in school enrollment since the beginning of the war," he wrote to Spessard Holland. "Our school facilities are inadequate to educate our 1,000 children. Consequently, all of the junior high has been transferred to the over-crowded Tampa district, and approximately 100 grammar school children are in school in another district."[46] In addition, low salaries had forced many of the best individuals out of the teaching profession, producing critical shortages of qualified teachers in many of the nation's schools. The long-standing American practice of financing education solely through state and local tax revenues, moreover, served only to complicate the search for a solution to these problems, for given the wide variation in the size and prosperity of the states in the Union, the amount each was able to commit to education differed substantially. While New York spent $184 per pupil in 1947, South Carolina was able to allot only $25.50. As a result, many states, particularly those in the South, were faced with problems they could not solve by themselves. In a letter to President Truman, Olin Johnston of South Carolina summarized the plight of many states in late 1947. "We in the South would be able to greatly improve the quality of our teaching and training aids and facilities through assistance from the Federal Treasury. At the present time because of our relatively low financial wealth and the abundance of youth in our population, we are required to devote a disproportionate [*sic*] burdensome share of our state and local revenue to the maintenance of a barely adequate school system."[47]

To address the developing crisis in the nation's schools, Republican Robert Taft in March introduced a $300 million dollar federal aid to education bill. That Taft sponsored the bill was perhaps another indication that partisan considerations had pushed the Ohio Republican toward the center in the 80th Congress. For, as late as 1944 Taft had opposed federal aid as an unwarranted intrusion into state affairs. Taft's bill also offered a good example of the efforts made by postwar new conservatives to expand federal authority without usurping the liberty of individuals or the power of state governments. In contrast to previous education bills that had proposed blanket grants of aid to all states, regardless of their need, Taft's bill simply used federal funds to ensure that all states spent at least $50 annually per pupil. Because the average national expenditure was $125 per pupil, Taft emphasized that federal aid would be directed solely at those states with the greatest need. In addition, to prevent Washington from dominating the nation's schools, the bill also stipulated that all federal funds were outright grants to be administered and distributed exclusively by the individual states.[48]

Despite the limited nature of the Education bill, obstructionist conservatives criticized it as a measure designed to continue the flood tide of power coursing into the nation's capital since 1933. Democrat Harry Byrd of Virginia charged, for instance, that "there is no element of Home Rule about it. . . . Senators who vote for this Bill on the theory that they are getting a direct gift from the Federal Government with no strings tied to it are adopting a very dangerous procedure." The conservative *Chicago Tribune* agreed completely, noting that as long as federal funds were involved, Washington would have some voice in educational policy.[49]

The Senate's new conservatives, on the other hand, generally supported the bill as the only way to overcome the tremendous variation in the quality of America's schools. Contending that the need for federal assistance had been made obvious by the overcrowding, the teacher shortage, and the large number of draft rejections for educational deficiencies during the war, Democrat Burnet Maybank of South Carolina defended the Education bill, maintaining that "with this legislation, we have the opportunity to better equalize the situation. Where this opportunity [for a sound education] is now within the reach of only a few . . . by virtue of having been born or moved to a more fortunate geographic location, under this Federal assistance these increased educational facilities would be made available to every child in this great land." H. Alexander Smith viewed the issue identically. Explaining his support of the bill to a friend who had charged that federal aid was socialistic, the New Jersey Republican also revealed his differences with postwar liberalism. "I am the last one in the world who wants the hand of the Government in anything," he admitted, "but I think there are some areas where we have to act to smooth out the inequalities . . . [to] protect . . . the equality of opportunity. The evidence showed clearly that in the States in the Deep South, there were not adequate financial resources to give the children of those states a minimum of education."[50]

Most new conservatives were confident, furthermore, that obstructionists' fears that the bill would lead to federal domination of education were unfounded. Olin Johnston explained in May to the City Attorney of Lake City, South Carolina, that the measure "specifically and definitely reserves to the states the right to control educational policy and methods and allows the Federal Government no right or privilege of intervention or interference in any manner." In the end, the solid support of most new conservatives helped to provide the margin of victory for Senate approval of the first measure granting federal aid for education. The 58–22 vote on 1 April revealed that such new conservatives as Aiken, Cooper, Flanders, George, Hoey, Holland, Ives, Russell, Saltonstall, Smith, Thye, and Tobey had joined with most liberals against a bipartisan assortment of obstructionists, including Bricker, Buck, Byrd, Ecton, Hawkes, Kem, McCarthy, Moore, O'Daniel, and Wherry.[51]

The support given by Senate new conservatives to this social reform was certainly influenced by home-state needs, but it also reflected their awareness of the interdependency of individuals' welfare in the modern industrial state. Not only was a sound education important to national security, as the wartime experience with Selective Service had demonstrated, but it also affected America's economic health. Education, George Aiken maintained, is the principal means by which individuals gained the ability to be self-sufficient. Thus, to the new conservatives, the limited commitment of federal aid in the 1948 bill did not undermine the American way of life; it conserved it. Federal aid was simply a new means, made necessary by the changes the nation had experienced in the twentieth century, to preserve American democracy and capitalism.[52]

The new conservatives' recognition that new means had to be employed to preserve traditional ends was again evident during Senate debate of public housing legislation. The only previous housing measure enacted was the 1937 Wagner Housing Act which, despite its concern with low-cost public housing and slum clearance, was viewed by many of its supporters more as a way to stimulate the economy than as a social reform. Public housing measures languished throughout the early 1940s, receiving cautious backing from the White House and from liberals, but repeatedly encountering bitter opposition from the housing industry, real estate interests, and conservatives in general. A public housing bill sponsored by Robert Wagner, Allen Ellender, and Robert Taft passed the Senate in 1946 without a roll call vote, for example, but died in the House Banking and Currency Committee. As a result of this inaction, by 1948 the nation's housing, like its educational system, was confronted by critical problems. The economic imperatives of the Depression and World War II had largely prevented both the construction of new housing and the maintenance of the nation's existing housing stock. Following the war, when the wave of returning veterans and the rapid increase in the birth rate combined to create a powerful demand for housing, the nation's builders chose mainly to concentrate on more profitable middle- and upper-income housing. The conditions described by the mayor of Tampa, Florida, in May 1948 were typical of many regions throughout the nation. "There are thousands of families of low-income, including families of veterans," he noted, "who are in desperate need of housing but they cannot pay the exorbitant prices charged for dwellings presently constructed. Tampa also, like other cities, is greatly in need of slum clearance but we are financially unable to eliminate slums."[53]

Given the extent of the problems, President Truman revived the issue of public housing legislation in his 1948 State of the Union message, and by early April the three sponsors of the 1946 bill had introduced a new measure in the Senate. The Taft-Ellender-Wagner Housing bill, which envisioned spending up to $1 billion per year for housing and slum clearance, included a commitment to use federal funds to construct 500,000 public housing units over a five-year period. Although liberals such as Wagner would have preferred a more extensive federal commitment to public housing, they supported the bill as the best obtainable in the GOP-dominated 80th Congress. Obstructionist conservatives, on the other hand, denounced the measure vehemently, charging that the public housing section, by bringing the federal government into direct competition with private enterprise, was both an inefficient use of taxpayers' revenue and a threat to America's democratic capitalistic heritage. Nebraska Republican Kenneth Wherry maintained, for instance, that "public housing has been consistently opposed by those who believe that government should be confined to the role of assisting and not superseding private initiative." James Kem of Missouri reacted more bluntly, charging that the T-E-W bill was socialistic and aimed to subvert American capitalism.[54]

Most of the new conservatives in the Senate rejected the obstructionists' position, arguing instead, as they had on federal aid to education, that the T-E-W bill would not supersede America's traditions, but was in fact necessary to preserve those traditions. Indeed, they contended that a federal program of public housing and slum clearance was needed precisely because the private sector had failed to meet the nation's needs. As long as the construction industry concentrated on the more profitable market for middle- and upper-income housing, the new conservatives warned that a class of Americans was being left behind. "Equality of opportunity does not exist today in the slums and bad housing conditions of this country," Republican Ralph Flanders charged in May 1948. "Private initiative and freedom cannot thrive under home conditions which create warped minds and warped bodies." Viewing the housing problem from the perspective of slum clearance, Robert Taft concurred with Flanders' bleak judgment. "It is clear," he maintained at the 1948 National Public Housing Conference, "that private building alone has not eliminated slums in the past. . . . The system which has been followed for the past hundred years just does not work to eliminate slums without some government intervention."[55]

The new conservatives also maintained that if the private sector by itself was incapable of meeting the nation's housing needs, so too, was the scope of the problem beyond the resources of local and state governments. Public housing, they insisted, like aid to education or policies promoting full employment, was a national responsibility. During Senate debate of the T-E-W bill, Charles Tobey of New Hampshire dismissed assertions from the bill's critics that some states might not receive their fair share of housing funds. Such concerns were irrelevant, he declared. "Our small individual States are not all-important after all. The whole is greater than any part. . . . This is a national problem. It is a cancer spot on the economic body of the country." That all Americans did not live in decent housing, the new conservatives contended, posed a far more serious threat to the maintenance of American democracy and capitalism than the public housing bill. "We must . . . give a real hope to those whom private enterprise is not now serving," Ralph Flanders opined, "a hope that they will be lifted out of the slum environments . . . , a hope that will sustain their faith in American institutions." To the Senate's new conservatives, then, public housing was, like federal aid to education, another responsibility government had to shoulder in mid-twentieth century America to guarantee that all citizens continued to enjoy equality of opportunity. Defending federal aid to education and public housing before a "mock" GOP convention in 1948, Irving Ives of New York emphasized the differences between the new conservatives and the obstructionists. "Some may say that these ideas are socialistic," the New York Republican admitted. "I deny it. . . . Far from being socialistic, it offers the only antidote for socialism of which I am aware."[56]

The fundamental change in the new conservatives' attitude was reiterated on 21 April when obstructionist conservatives led by Harry Cain of Washington moved to delete all public housing provisions from the T-E-W bill. New conservatives such as Aiken, Flanders, Ives, Lodge, Russell, Saltonstall, Smith, Thye, and Tobey joined with liberals to defeat the amendment by the narrow margin of 49–35. Although the public housing bill was approved by voice vote in the Senate the following day, it ran into stiff opposition in the House, and died in the Rules Committee. Attempts to revive the measure in the Special Session called by President Truman in July were similarly unsuccessful, largely because Taft and many other Republicans withheld their support, fearful that another House rejection would fix blame for the failure on the GOP.[57]

In the end, then, although Congress failed to enact a public housing measure in 1948, Senate approval of the T-E-W bill offered further evidence of the deliberate effort made by the new conservatives to adapt their political philosophy to the conditions of modern America. In a speech given in September 1948, George Aiken succinctly summarized the forces that had transformed many conservatives' views. People in Vermont, he observed, no longer grew, harvested, or prepared their own food, as they had forty years earlier. Rather, in 1948 most bought packaged foods and ready-made clothes. As a result, individuals were more dependent on one another. "It is not a neighborhood interdependency any longer,"

Aiken added, "but we find that our welfare is inextricably linked with that of others, both economically, nationally and internationally." This lesson had been graphically demonstrated, Aiken argued, by recent events. "The great depression of the early Thirties was precipitated by a collapse in farm prices which reduced the purchasing power of the farmers, throwing millions of industrial workers out of their jobs, thus further depressing the market for farm products." Prosperity was not restored until farm prices were supported by the federal government, thereby boosting farmers' purchasing power and increasing demand for products of business and industry. Although he recognized that some Vermonters desired to return "to the rule of survival of the fittest," Aiken insisted it was futile. "We either keep pace with changes in this world of ours, adapting ourselves to the necessities of the hour, or we find ourselves inextricably enmeshed . . . and hopelessly out of place."[58]

While new conservatives like Aiken agreed with liberals on the need for a more active government and an international foreign policy, they were generally more concerned than liberals with limiting the expansion of government power, as well as the degree of America's overseas involvement. During the 80th Congress, for example, the new conservatives supported federal aid for education and public housing bills that were aimed solely at helping the neediest elements of society. They cast their votes for the Truman Doctrine and Marshall Plan, believing that neither established precedents for unlimited foreign aid, but simply offered limited aid aimed at specific purposes. Similarly, votes from new conservatives helped enact the Taft-Hartley Act which, they argued, protected the fundamental rights of labor but balanced those rights more equally with the rights of management. They remained conservatives, in other words, but conservatives who had modernized their political philosophy.

However much new conservatives like Aiken adjusted their political philosophy to the demands of the industrial era, the roll call analysis of votes in the 80th Congress reveals the power that partisanship in a presidential election year had in influencing voting alignments. The Democratic party, for example, which faced its first presidential election as a minority party since 1928, rallied behind their Chief Executive to a degree rarely seen in peace time. As table 5–1 reveals, forty-two of forty-three scalable Democrats gave Harry Truman's policy high or medium support. Seven Democrats who had generally scaled as new conservatives in previous Congresses (Russell, Hoey, Stewart, Johnston, McClellan, George, and Eastland) moved up to the high support group in the 80th Congress.

Even Virginia's Harry Byrd, usually one of the Senate's most obdurate obstructionists, scaled in the medium support group in the 80th Congress, clearly suggesting the ability of electoral politics to overwhelm ideological conviction.

If party loyalty often encouraged Democrats like Harry Byrd to stand by their president throughout the 80th Congress, it often tended to drive the Republican majority in the opposite direction. Although deep disagreements surfaced periodically within the GOP over how broadly to interpret the mandate for change that voters had given them in 1946, most Republicans, enjoying majority party status for the first time since 1930 and confident that the White House was truly within their grasp, often could not resist the opportunity to make Harry Truman appear ineffectual to the electorate. Indeed, fifty of the fifty-one scalable Republicans gave either low or medium support to Administration initiatives on all policy dimensions (table 5–1).

TABLE 5-3

80th CONGRESS - FOREIGN POLICY DIMENSIONS

HIGH SUPPORT

Hill, D-AL	1.00	McFarland, D-AZ	1.25
Kilgore, D-WV	1.00	Murray, D-MT	1.25
McGrath, D-RI	1.00	Fulbright, D-AR	1.25
McMahon, D-CT	1.00	Thomas, D-OK	1.25
Sparkman, D-AL	1.00	Umstead, D-NC	1.25
Downey, D-CA	1.00	Stewart, D-TN	1.25
Wagner, D-NY	1.00	Tydings, D-MD	1.33
Myers, D-PA	1.00	Pepper, D-FL	1.50
Maybank, D-SC	1.00	Russell, D-GA	1.50
Hayden, D-AZ	1.00	Holland, D-FL	1.50
Magnuson, D-WA	1.00	Hoey, D-NC	1.50
Chavez, D-NM	1.00	Connally, D-TX	1.50
Barkley, D-KY	1.00	George, D-GA	1.50
Lucas, D-IL	1.00	McClellan, D-AR	1.50
Thomas, D-UT	1.00	Johnson, D-CO	1.50
Green, D-RI	1.00	Eastland, D-MS	1.50
Hatch, D-NM	1.00	Robertson, D-VA	1.50
McCarran, D-NV	1.00	McKellar, D-TN	1.50
O'Conor, D-MD	1.00	Ellender, D-LA	1.50
Tobey, R-NH	1.00	Moore, R-OK	1.50

N = 40; D = 38; R = 2

TABLE 5-3

80th CONGRESS - FOREIGN POLICY DIMENSIONS

MEDIUM SUPPORT

Bridges, R-NH	1.67	Brewster, R-ME	2.00
Cooper, R-KY	1.75	Gurney, R-SD	2.00
Byrd, D-VA	1.75	Hickenlooper, R-IA	2.00
Taylor, D-ID	2.00	Ferguson, R-MI	2.00
Johnston, D-SC	2.00	Flanders, R-VT	2.25
Morse, R-OR	2.00	Baldwin, R-CT	2.25
Aiken, R-VT	2.00	Watkins, R-UT	2.25
Overton, D-LA	2.00	Ball, R-MN	2.25
Saltonstall, R-MA	2.00	Cordon, R-OR	2.25
Smith, R-NJ	2.00	Vandenberg, R-MI	2.25
Lodge, R-MA	2.00	Young, R-ND	2.25
Robertson, R-WY	2.00	Brooks, R-IL	2.25
Ives, R-NY	2.00	Wiley, R-WI	2.33
Taft, R-OH	2.00	Bricker, R-OH	2.33
Thye, R-MN	2.00	Donnell, R-MO	2.34

N = 30; D = 4; R = 26
Coastal = 13 (43%); Interior = 17 (57%)

LOW SUPPORT

O'Daniel, D-TX	2.50	Butler, R-NE	2.75
Knowland, R-CA	2.50	Wherry, R-NE	2.75
Wilson, R-IA	2.50	Kem, R-MO	2.75
McCarthy, R-WI	2.50	Malone, R-NV	3.00
Ecton, R-UT	2.50	Bushfield, R-SD	3.00
Capper, R-KS	2.50	Buck, R-DE	3.00
Millikin, R-CO	2.50	Capehart, R-IN	3.00
Martin, R-PA	2.50	Jenner, R-IN	3.00
Dworshak, R-ID	2.50	Hawkes, R-NJ	3.00
Cain, R-WA	2.50	Williams, R-DE	3.00
Reed, R-KS	2.67	White, R-ME	3.00
Revercomb, R-WV	2.75		

N = 23; D = 1; R = 22
Coastal 8 (35%); Interior = 15 (65%)

When separate scale scores were calculated for foreign and domestic policy dimensions, however, the full effect of partisanship on voting alignments was more apparent. As table 5–3 indicates, twenty-eight of the fifty (56%) Republicans who scaled on foreign policy dimensions gave either high or medium support to Truman's international initiatives. Despite their frequently harsh rhetoric, in other words, a majority of Republican senators either believed sincerely that the unfolding policy of containment was the best approach to safeguard national security, or were reluctant to risk the voters' wrath by resisting too intently the Administration's efforts to deal with the challenges of the Cold War.

When domestic policies were considered, on the other hand, most Republicans seemed to decide that their party's time-worn stalwart opposition to the positive state was the best way to present a united front to the voters. For, as table 5–4 reveals, only five of the fifty-one (10%) Republicans who scaled on domestic policy dimensions gave high or medium support to Harry Truman's policies. Such Republicans as Leverett Saltonstall, H. A. Smith, H. C. Lodge, Irving Ives, and Ralph Flanders, whose voting record and rhetoric usually distinguished them from their obstructionist counterparts, scaled in the low support group in the 80th Congress, reflecting their apparent decision to place electoral considerations ahead of ideological conviction.

Nowhere was the tension between partisanship and ideological conviction in the 80th Congress more evident than in the politics of Ohio's Robert Taft. Since his election in 1938, Taft had been one of the Senate's most consistent, and occasionally the shrillest, critics of Franklin Roosevelt's and later, Harry Truman's policies. Yet as Senate majority leader in the 80th Congress, the politics of the Ohio Republican seemed to change. Not only did he take leadership roles in finding a middle ground on such controversial issues as fiscal policy and labor, but he also cosponsored important advances in social policy, such as federal aid to education and public housing. Seeming to underscore this change is Taft's appearance in the medium support group on all scalable policy dimensions (table 5–1). Despite these appearances of moderation, this study maintains that "Mr. Republican" gravitated toward the center in 1947 and 1948 mainly as a way to maintain leadership of a badly splintered party and as a way to advance his presidential ambitions. Thus, although Taft ranked as a new conservative on all scalable policy dimensions in the 80th Congress, he remained at heart an obstructionist conservative. Indeed, when domestic policy dimensions were separated from the more voter-sensitive foreign policy dimensions, Robert

TABLE 5-4

80th CONGRESS - DOMESTIC POLICY DIMENSIONS

HIGH SUPPORT

Hill, D-AL	1.00	Holland, D-FL	1.22
Kilgore, D-WV	1.00	Chavez, D-NM	1.25
McGrath, D-RI	1.00	Thomas, D-OK	1.25
McMahon, D-CT	1.00	Barkley, D-KY	1.29
Sparkman, D-AL	1.00	Umstead, D-NC	1.33
Downey, D-CA	1.00	Hoey, D-NC	1.33
Wagner, D-NY	1.00	Lucas, D-IL	1.38
McFarland, D-AZ	1.00	Green, D-RI	1.38
Murray, D-MT	1.00	Thomas, D-UT	1.43
Taylor, D-ID	1.00	Hatch, D-NM	1.44
Johnston, D-SC	1.00	Connally, D-TX	1.44
Myers, D-PA	1.13	McClellan, D-AR	1.50
Hayden, D-AZ	1.13	Morse, R-OR	1.56
Pepper, D-FL	1.13	McCarran, D-NV	1.57
Maybank, D-SC	1.22	George, D-GA	1.63
Magnuson, D-WA	1.22	Tydings, D-MD	1.63
Fulbright, D-AR	1.22	Aiken, R-VT	1.63
Russell, D-GA	1.22	McKellar, D-TN	1.63

N = 36; D = 34; R = 2

MEDIUM SUPPORT

O'Conor, D-MD	1.67
Stewart, D-TN	1.67
Johnson, D-CO	1.67
Eastland, D-MS	1.71
Robertson, D-VA	1.88
Ellender, D-LA	1.89
Tobey, R-NH	2.00
Overton, D-LA	2.00
Cooper, R-KY	2.13
Langer, R-ND	2.14
Byrd, D-VA	2.29

N = 11; D = 8; R = 3
Coastal = 4 (36%); Interior = 7 (64%)

TABLE 5-4

80th CONGRESS - DOMESTIC POLICY DIMENSIONS

LOW SUPPORT

Saltonstall, R-MA	2.38	Revercomb, R-WV	2.88
Smith, R-NJ	2.44	Gurney, R-SD	2.89
Lodge, R-MA	2.56	Vandenberg, R-MI	2.89
O'Daniel, D-TX	2.56	Wiley, R-WI	2.89
Robertson, R-WY	2.57	Ecton, R-MT	2.89
Flanders, R-VT	2.63	Capper, R-KS	2.89
Ives, R-NY	2.67	Millikin, R-CO	2.89
Taft, R-OH	2.67	Butler, R-NE	2.89
Thye, R-MN	2.67	Wherry, R-NE	2.89
Baldwin, R-CT	2.67	Hickenlooper, R-IA	3.00
Watkins, R-UT	2.67	Ferguson, R-MI	3.00
Ball, R-MN	2.67	Young, R-ND	3.00
Donnell, R-MO	2.67	Brooks, R-IL	3.00
Knowland, R-CA	2.67	Martin, R-PA	3.00
Wilson, R-IA	2.71	Bricker, R-OH	3.00
Bridges, R-NH	2.75	Dworshak, R-ID	3.00
Cordon, R-OR	2.75	Cain, R-WA	3.00
Malone, R-NV	2.78	Reed, R-KS	3.00
Moore, R-OK	2.78	Kem, R-MO	3.00
Buck, R-DE	2.86	Jenner, R-IN	3.00
Capehart, R-IN	2.86	Hawkes, R-NJ	3.00
Bushfield, R-SD	2.86	Williams, R-DE	3.00
Brewster, R-ME	2.88	White, R-ME	3.00
McCarthy, R-WI	2.88		

N = 47; D = 1; R = 46
Coastal = 17 (36%); Interior = 30 (64%)

Taft once again scaled with the obstructionists, as he did in every other Congress in this study.

If elevated partisanship in the 80th Congress frequently distorted voting alignments, evidence continued to point to the ongoing transformation of conservatism. In addition to the role they played in steering much of the major legislation between liberal and obstructionist extremes, the determination of Republicans such as George Aiken, Wayne Morse, Charles Tobey, and John Sherman Cooper to defy their party's leadership by offering high or medium support for the domestic initiatives of Harry Truman offered clear

evidence that ideological conviction had not been completely sur-
rendered to the partisan imperatives of an election year. Thus, if
electoral politics sometimes obscured the divisions within the right
wing during the 80th Congress, it did not arrest the transformation
of Senate conservatism. For when Congressional politics returned
to more "normal" patterns following Harry Truman's unexpected
triumph in 1948, the divisions within Senate conservatism intensified.

6

The New Conservatism and the Fair Deal

THE SURPRISING VICTORY HARRY TRUMAN AND THE DEMOCRATS won over the Republicans in the 1948 elections sharpened the divisions within the right wings of each party and thereby accelerated the transformation of Senate conservatism. In the Democratic party, for instance, which was splintered by the Dixiecrat rebellion led by South Carolina's Strom Thurmond, Truman's victory appeared to bolster the confidence of many new conservatives. For although the challenge by the States' Rights Democrats initially spawned fears that southern Democrats would revert to the obstructionist path they had followed in the 1930s, party leaders expressed confidence after the election that on all issues save civil rights, eight to twelve younger, more progressive southern Democrats could be counted on to support Administration initiatives with a fair degree of regularity.[1]

The repercussions of the 1948 elections were far more acute in the Republican party. In the GOP, where confidence had been high that 1948 would bring the election of the first Republican president in twenty years, the defeat of Thomas E. Dewey, coupled with the loss of control of Congress won only two years earlier, produced bitter recriminations between the party's factions. The new conservatives, who in the 80th Congress had occasionally muted their criticism of party policy for the sake of unity, blamed their party's defeat squarely on the obstructionists whose philosophy, they complained, was out of step with the thinking of the American electorate. Republican obstructionists, on the other hand, blamed the 1948 debacle on the new conservatives' efforts to mimic the Democrats, and thus approached the 81st Congress determined to return the GOP to its course of unyielding opposition to the domestic and foreign policies of the New Deal.

Election results, however, appeared to lend credibility to the beliefs of new conservatives in both parties that voters in 1948 had rejected the ideology of extreme reaction. Of the five incumbents defeated in the elections, four were individuals prominently associated with obstructionist conservatism. They were: C. Wayland "Curly" Brooks of Illinois, who was defeated by Paul H. Douglas; W. Lee "Pappy" O'Daniel of Texas, replaced by Lyndon Johnson; Albert Hawkes of New Jersey, replaced by Robert Hendrickson; and C. Douglas Buck, replaced by J. Allen Frear. An analysis of the election returns prepared by pollster Elmo Roper in March 1949 underscored this impression. Roper concluded that nearly all of the GOP gubernatorial and senatorial candidates identified with what he labeled the party's "liberal" wing consistently ran equal to or better than the national ticket, while those candidates associated with "Old Guard conservatism" ran behind the party's standard bearers. Thomas Dewey lost Illinois by 31,000 votes, for example, but senatorial candidate C. Wayland "Curly" Brooks lost by 369,000 votes. "Liberal" Republican candidates, such as Leverett Saltonstall of Massachusetts, on the other hand, ran 365,000 votes ahead of Dewey. Rightly or wrongly, then, the 1948 election results appeared to convince new conservatives of both parties that a majority of American voters had rejected the policies of extreme reaction represented by the Dixiecrats and Republican obstructionists. Throughout the domestic and foreign policy debates of the 81st Congress, therefore, they mounted a determined effort to modernize Senate conservatism.[2]

I

As the first presidential election following Franklin Roosevelt's death, the 1948 contest was widely regarded as a test of the durability of the Democrats' New Deal coalition. Throughout the year, most observers confidently predicted that the coalition would dissolve into the disparate groups that composed it, dooming any chance for Harry Truman's re-election. On the one hand, some left-wing Democrats were convinced that Truman, a border-state Democrat with an uneven record of support for the New Deal, was insufficiently liberal to inherit FDR's mantle of reform. Led by Henry A. Wallace, they bolted the Democratic party to form the Progressive party in 1948. At the other end of the ideological spectrum was a group of conservative Democrats, mostly from the south, that also bolted from the party when it decided to include a strong civil rights plank in the 1948 platform.[3]

Because a disagreement over civil rights prompted the States' Rights Democratic party, usually referred to as the "Dixiecrats," to walk out of the Democratic party in 1948, they were usually dismissed by their contemporaries simply as a group of segregationists. Clare Booth Luce, speaking to the GOP national convention in July 1948, for example, labeled them "a Jim Crow wing [of the Democratic party], led by lynch-loving Bourbons." While continued segregation of the races was certainly of great importance to the States' Rights Democrats, a close reading of their 1948 campaign suggests that they were also generally obstructionist conservatives determined to resist the creeping influence of modern industrial American values, symbolized most clearly by the New Deal's use of the positive state. The keynote speaker at their 1948 convention, former Alabama governor Frank M. Dixon, insisted, for example, that "the issues are not purely sectional. Fundamentally, they are the ancient issues of a highly centralized police state, as opposed to local self-government." Similarly, the Dixiecrats' "Declaration of Principles" maintained that to guard "against the onward march of totalitarian government," it was necessary to uphold the Bill of Right's tenth amendment, reserving to the states all powers not specifically delegated to the federal government. Similarly, Robert Ferrell has recently argued that the Dixiecrats' nominee, Strom Thurmond, "truly believed in the Federalism of 1787. Unvoiced was the southerners' lingering resentment of FDR's New Deal, which, they felt, had infringed upon state prerogatives and encouraged southern blacks to be 'uppity.' "[4]

Despite strong hopes in July 1948 that their rebellion could deny Truman's re-election by forcing the presidential election into the House of Representatives, the efforts of the States' Rights Democrats failed to attract widespread support in November. One of the key factors explaining their weak showing was the decision of many influential southern Democrats, including Richard Russell, Walter George, John Overton, James O. Eastland, and even Harry F. Byrd, to remain loyal to the national party, notwithstanding their doubts over Truman's leadership. While a combination of party loyalty and reluctance to risk losing their seniority by openly challenging Truman appear to have been the main factors leading these southern Democrats to spurn the Dixiecrats, ideological differences almost certainly made that decision easier. That in the four congresses, culminating with the 81st, Russell, George, and Overton had scaled as new conservatives three of the four times suggests that they had largely come to terms with the expansion of federal power begun with the New Deal. The Dixiecrats' goal, in contrast, was aimed at restoring the federal-state relationship that had prevailed prior to 1933. Following the voters' rejection of the Dixiecrats in 1948, any doubts held by the new conservatives in the Democratic party about the ideological course they had been pursuing were undoubtedly eased.[5]

Among Republicans the efforts made by new conservatives to modernize their party's political philosophy got underway even before the 81st Congress convened. Convinced that their party had been defeated because of its long record of opposition to the policies of the New Deal, a "rump caucus" of fourteen Republicans, led by Irving Ives and Edward Thye, nominated Henry Cabot Lodge in late December to oppose Robert Taft for the chairmanship of the GOP Policy Committee and chose William Knowland to run against obstructionist conservative Kenneth Wherry for the post of minority leader. Despite the risks they ran by challenging the party leadership, all members of the caucus believed that the soul of the GOP was at stake. One of the caucus participants, H. Alexander Smith of New Jersey, noted ruefully in his diary on 30 December that "if the matter [of choosing party leaders] went by default we would have . . . Taft, Millikin and Wherry. This with the House [leadership] lineup would be fatal to the future of the party." In an interview with Arthur Krock, Henry Cabot Lodge expressed similar concern over the party's future. Noting that the GOP, having failed in the past by adopting both a "me-too" approach and an obstructionist approach, the Massachusetts Republican insisted it was time for the party to change tactics. Yet the assessment made of the "rump caucus" by the *Chicago Tribune* reflected the wide gap that divided the new conservatives and the obstructionists within the GOP. In the view of the right-wing newspaper, it was the renegades in the GOP, such as Lodge and Smith, that were responsible for the party's losses. To the *Tribune,* salvation would come for the Republicans only when the moderates were run out of the party.[6]

The GOP new conservatives ultimately failed in their effort to change the party leadership when Senate Republicans voted 28–14 on 3 January to re-elect Taft and Wherry to their posts. Although the votes were taken by secret ballot, the names of thirteen of Lodge's supporters were revealed by the *New York Herald Tribune,* and the list included many of the new conservatives who had voted together on many issues throughout the 80th Congress. They were Lodge, Ives, Knowland, Young, Saltonstall, Morse, Aiken, Flanders, Tobey, Baldwin, H. A. Smith, Thye, and Gurney.[7]

The effort made to unseat Robert Taft has long puzzled observers of Senate affairs. A number of his contemporaries noted at the time of the rebellion that the Ohioan's voting record was practically identical to that of most of the insurgents. In 1948, for example, Taft's voting record tied him with Lodge and Knowland. His rhetoric on specific issues such as labor, federal aid to education, and public housing, moreover, as this study has noted, indicated an awareness of the need to modernize his political principles that was shared by the new conservatives. Overall, however, the statistical analysis of roll call votes done for this study indicates a significant difference between the voting behavior of Taft and the Republicans who tried to unseat him. As table 6–1 indicates, through the 81st Congress Taft's average scale score was 2.57. On the other hand, the combined average scale score of his opponents was 2.20.

Thus, despite the occasional rhetorical congruence between Taft and the new conservatives in the GOP, the voting behavior of "Mr. Republican," whether for partisan or ideological reasons, placed him squarely within the obstructionists' orbit. The effort of the Republican new conservatives to unseat Taft in 1949 seems, then, to have been a deliberate effort to reorient the party's political philosophy in the wake of their 1948 defeat.[8]

Despite their defeat, the GOP insurgents remained optimistic about the ability of their group to influence legislation in the upcoming Congress. Irving Ives, one of the leaders of the revolt,

TABLE 6-1

Average Scale Scores of Taft and GOP Insurgents

Taft	2.57
Lodge	2.35
Ives	2.23
Knowland	2.37
Aiken	1.73
Morse	1.52
Tobey	2.12
H. A. Smith	2.15
Young	2.61
Saltonstall	2.08
Flanders	2.21
Baldwin	2.54
Thye	2.25
Gurney	2.39

Average Insurgent Score: 2.20

maintained that the vote demonstrated there was a core of thirteen Republicans in the Senate who would work for change. Wayne Morse agreed, observing that the entire effort had forged durable bonds among the insurgents that would influence the party well into the future. Thus, the 1948 defeat forged a strong *esprit de corps* among the GOP insurgents and made them more inclined to support expansions of federal power and American internationalism, regardless of the consequences to party harmony. Throughout the 81st Congress, then, the determination of the GOP insurgents to chart a new course for their party helped substantially to advance the new conservatism.[9]

The progress of the new conservatism was blocked until March, however, by a protracted filibuster over civil rights. Following President Truman's 1949 State of the Union Address, which largely laid out the liberal agenda of the Fair Deal, the upper house became snarled in a parliamentary tangle over Senate rules. In February, Senate Republicans, acting primarily for partisan reasons, attempted to force immediate consideration of a rules change designed to expand the use of cloture petitions to halt debate. The controversy centered on Senate Rule 22, by which cloture could be invoked during debate on a bill whenever two-thirds of the senators voting approved. Because Rule 22 applied only to debate on a bill, southern Democrats in the past had filibustered against a motion to bring up a bill, rather than the bill itself, and so had been immune to the cloture provisions of the rule. Senate Republicans in 1949 sought to broaden Rule 22 to apply to both situations, but southern Democrats fought vehemently against the change, indicating, as had the 1946 debate over a permanent FEPC, that civil rights continued to be an issue that united southern senators of all ideological stripes. Finally, on 16 March a compromise was reached that permitted cloture to be invoked during debate on either a bill or a motion to bring up a bill, provided that two-thirds of the Senate membership agreed. In effect, by requiring the vote of sixty-four senators (two-thirds of the ninety-six members) to end debate, the compromise made it more difficult to invoke cloture. Rule 22, which had specified that cloture could be invoked simply by two-thirds of the senators voting, theoretically allowed debate to be stopped with as few as thirty-three votes (two-thirds of a quorum).[10]

Public housing and federal aid to education were two substantive issues to which the Senate turned in spring, following the end of the civil rights filibuster. In both cases, the new conservatives fought to ensure that federal aid was directed only to the poorest elements of society whose needs, they believed, were being met by neither free enterprise nor state and local government. The unique philosophy of the new conservatives on such social issues was evident in a speech given by Democrat Clyde Hoey to the North Carolina Building and Loan League in June. Arguing that the need for an expanded role for government was a product of the complexity of modern life, he insisted that:

> I do not share the view that government participation is essentially bad. ... There is a happy medium between those who would have no government control, regulation or supervision and those ... wishing the government to exercise a full measure of regulation, supervision and control to the end that the individual will be practically eliminated. ... The golden mean between those extremes is for the government to render assistance in those fields where it is essential ... to maintain business, industry, agriculture, education and health upon a basis that insures a fair opportunity for the individual and makes it possible to have profitable operations and achievements under our free enterprise system.[11]

The 1949 debate over public housing provided solid evidence of the new conservatives' struggle to apply Hoey's "golden mean" to legislation. Although the lack of adequate housing was a problem considered by previous Congresses, by 1949 the rapid escalation in postwar construction costs, together with the low level of construction during the Depression and World War II, had produced a crisis of major proportions. High construction costs, Robert Taft pointed out during Senate debate in 1949, made it difficult to build a four-room house for less than $7000. Yet the income earned by 44.6% of American families, he noted, was insufficient to enable them to afford even such minimal housing.[12]

Although new conservatives had fought for public housing in the previous session of Congress, they balked initially at the Administration's 1949 bill, fearful that it would supplant rather than supplement the private sector's efforts. Introduced by Allen Ellender on 5 January, the Administration's bill proposed to construct 1.05 million public housing units over seven years, or twice the number of units projected in the 1948 T-E-W bill, and to allot $1.5 billion for slum clearance and urban redevelopment. In the eyes of many new conservatives, the Administration's bill made the federal commitment to public housing too broad and failed to limit sufficiently the role of the federal government in administering the program. Under the Ellender bill, for example, public housing would comprise about 25% of total annual housing construction, in contrast to the 10% envisioned by the 1948 T-E-W bill. The new conservatives emphasized that any public housing measure had to limit carefully the cost of the program, preserve local or state administration of public housing, and restrict federal aid only to those who could not afford decent housing. The following day these principles were embodied in a substitute housing bill introduced by Robert Taft, Irving Ives, and Ralph Flanders, which proposed the construction of only 500,000 public housing units.[13]

The differences between the Ellender and Taft bills were reconciled in the Banking and Currency Committee, and a compromise housing measure was reported out in late February that addressed many of the new conservatives' concerns. The compromise bill, sponsored by a coalition of liberal Democrats and new conservatives from both parties, proposed to construct 810,000 public housing units by 1955, with the federal government supplying $308 million in direct assistance and $1 billion in loans. Local authority over housing was carefully preserved by the compromise, which specified that federal aid for slum clearance and urban redevelopment would be supplied only to those local authorities who requested it and only after they had demonstrated that private enterprise could not solve the problem. One of the new conservative cosponsors of the bill, Republican Charles Tobey, emphasized the limited nature of the bill to a wary constituent. "The proposed Housing Act is not a public housing measure in the strict sense of the term," he maintained. "The bill is based on the theory that while housing is a problem of national concern, it is fundamentally a local problem to be worked out by the local community."[14]

Despite the limited view new conservatives such as Tobey held of the committee's bill, obstructionists were quick to denounce it as a measure that continued the assault on traditional American values of self-suffiency and individual initiative. Republican Kenneth Wherry of Nebraska complained in April, for example, that "it is not the responsibility of the Federal Government to provide a decent home for each and every American family. . . . Federally subsidized housing is part and parcel of the ideology that the Government owes everybody a living—abundance—prosperity—security—and happiness from cradle to grave. This . . . is not the kind of stuff that made America strong and great."[15] Obstructionists' attempts to kill what they regarded as a socialistic measure, however, were repeatedly rejected by a coalition of new conservatives and liberals. On 21 April, for instance, hours before the Senate was to vote on the housing bill, obstructionist Republican John Bricker made a desperate effort to scuttle the bill when he proposed an amendment forbidding segregation and discrimination in all housing units constructed with federal funds. Bricker's amendment, which most saw as a transparent attempt to alienate southern support for the bill, was rejected 49–31 when new conservatives, such as Flanders, George, Hoey, Holland, Morse, and Tobey, joined forces with liberals. Moments later, a practically identical coalition formed to beat back another Bricker amendment barring only discrimination in public housing units. Then, with all crippling amendments defeated, new conservatives and liberals united again to ensure adoption of the housing bill by a margin of 57–13.[16]

Although most new conservatives sided consistently with liberals throughout the public housing debate, each group clearly viewed the housing problem differently. While Senate liberals supported the Ellender-Taft bill, many would have preferred an expanded program that was not limited to the neediest members of society, but that also enabled most Americans in the lower economic classes to become home owners. Indeed, in 1950 the Truman Administration would propose a plan of federal assistance for middle-income housing. The new conservatives, on the other hand, accepted the need for federal assistance in housing, but insisted that it should be a limited reform designed only to supplement the free enterprise system. Defending his vote for the bill, Spessard Holland of Florida argued that "none of the construction which we have had since the war, at least in the cities, has tended to make housing facilities available for the really poor people. Construction costs have been so high that no private agency has been able to make any approach whatever towards low cost housing construction." Republican Henry Cabot Lodge insisted, on the other hand, that the obstructionists' desire to rely solely on the private sector to meet the nation's housing needs posed a greater danger to free enterprise than the 1949 bill. "[U]ntil building costs are radically lowered," he asserted to the president of a lumber company, "it will remain impossible for private enterprise . . . to supply adequate housing at a price within reach of veterans or others of low income. The bill . . . helps our whole free system by making housing available to citizens who would assuredly not be enthusing about private enterprise if forced to live under unsatisfactory housing conditions." Lodge's colleague, Charles Tobey, viewed the measure similarly. "I am confident," he wrote in May, "that this bill is very carefully drawn to preserve our liberties and local autonomy and yet give a minimum of hope to thousands of extremely low-income families who cannot help themselves under the present diseased conditions of our slums."[17]

Similar ideological divisions developed in early May when the Senate turned its attention to the crisis in the nation's schools. As was true of housing, America's educational system had deteriorated rapidly after World War II because of the sharp increase in the birth rate, the high construction costs, and the general lack of school construction during the Depression and World War II. A survey made of the nation's schools by the *New York Times* in April 1949 found that only 18% of the country's school buildings were in good condition, while 82% were in fair or poor condition, and none were regarded as excellent. Compounding the problem was that most states were able to spend far less than was needed. The survey reported, for instance, that Arkansas planned to spend $5.5 million on school construction in 1949–1950, though it acknowledged that $50 million was needed, while Florida had committed only $15 million out of an estimated $150 million required to improve its school system. Because of these deficiencies, millions of children across the nation in 1949 were forced to attend classes in a wide variety of sub-standard settings.[18]

To address the education crisis, Republican Robert Taft joined with New Deal Democrats Elbert Thomas and Lister Hill in the spring to sponsor a bill providing $300 million in federal aid for education. As had been true of the public housing bill, however, the education bill was designed to funnel most aid to the poorest states whose need was greatest. Under the bill, federal aid was to be distributed on a graduated basis, with thirty states, regarded as wealthier than average, receiving the minimum allotment of $5.00 per pupil, and the remaining "poorer" states receiving aid ranging from $5.38 per pupil in Vermont, to $29.18 per pupil in Mississippi. To guard against the possibility that the bill would lead to federal domination or devolve simply into a system of federal hand-outs, it further stipulated that all states had to spend annually a minimum of $55 per pupil in order to qualify for assistance.[19]

Throughout debate on the education bill, a coalition of new conservatives and Administration supporters defended the measure against obstructionist criticism. Their concerns focused on two general aspects of the bill. First, obstructionists argued that the bill expanded the power of the federal government into an area previously controlled by the states. Second, they regarded federal aid for education as a continuation of the economic policies that had prevailed since 1933. Harry Byrd of Virginia, for example, complained that the education bill "would open up a Pandora's box . . . that would be only a beginning, the entering wedge, and would amount to millions and even billions of dollars in the years to come."[20] Efforts to alter the bill were largely futile, however, because of the solid support it received from the new conservatives and liberals. On 2 May, for example, such new conservatives as Aiken, Flanders, George, Hoey, Holland, Russell, M. C. Smith, Thye, and Vandenberg joined with liberals to reject a Lodge amendment 68–11 that proposed to distribute federal aid uniformly to all states at a rate of $10 per pupil.

Although supporters of the education bill opposed the Lodge amendment out of fear that it would undermine the measure's goal of establishing greater equality in public education, the Massachusetts Republican insisted that he supported the principle of federal aid. His amendment's sole goal, he added, indicating the power of home-state interests, was to increase the share of aid that his state would receive.[21] Three days after rejecting the Lodge amendment, a similar coalition voted 65–11 against a substitute from John Bricker that would have granted $250 million to states solely for school construction and then voted 58–15 to approve the education bill.[22]

National labor policy was another domestic issue in 1949 that revealed the efforts of the new conservatives to chart a new ideological course. Because of continuing objections raised by organized labor and its supporters to the Taft-Hartley Act, the Democrats had pledged during the 1948 campaign to restore the Wagner Act as the basis for labor-management relations. Following the Democrats' victory, the party moved quickly to honor its promise. On 6 January Elbert Thomas, a liberal Democrat from Utah, introduced a bill repealing the entire Taft-Hartley Act, except for its provision fixing the NLRB's membership at five. Three weeks later the Administration transmitted to Congress its idea of national labor law in the form of a modified version of the Wagner Act that retained only Taft-Hartley's definition of jurisdictional strikes and secondary boycotts as unfair labor practices. Stripped from the 1947 labor relations act by the Administration's bill were the use of injunctions to halt strikes endangering the general welfare, the ban on closed shops, the requirement that unions sign noncommunist affadavits, and the restrictions on the use of welfare funds. Indeed, so completely did the Administration's proposal change existing labor law that most observers could see no vestiges of Taft–Hartley in it.[23]

Although organized labor praised the Administration's bill as a measure that would restore the basic rights of workers, the new conservatives in the Senate viewed the issue differently. Republican H. Alexander Smith contended, for instance, that he would not vote to reinstate the Wagner Act because organized labor had abused the powers given to it by that act. While he agreed that some of Taft-Hartley's provisions required modification, the New Jersey Republican insisted that any new labor bill had to preserve the major principles established by the 1947 act, particularly government's protection of individual workers from exploitation by big business or big labor, and the "responsibility of government to protect the health and safety of all of our people from the defiant autocracy of bigness whether it is big business or big labor." Democrat Richard Russell held a similar attitude. Admitting that he would support efforts to eliminate such "inequities" in the 1947 labor law as the requirement that only unions sign anticommunist affidavits, the Georgia Democrat argued nonetheless that Taft-Hartley had to be preserved in principle because it was "an honest attempt to retain the legitimate protections of the Wagner Act while correcting the abuses that had arisen."[24]

The new conservatives' opposition to the Administration's labor bill was echoed, furthermore, by many voices throughout the United States. A writer who identified himself only as an "employee" exhorted Burnet Maybank to resist the Administration's plans. "I urgently request that you support such legislation as will be fair to both Management and Labor," he wrote; "certainly we do not want to go back to the one-sided Wagner Act. . . . Being an employee I feel that labor as well as management should shoulder their responsibility, and that the public welfare transcends both." Leading newspapers throughout the nation offered similarly harsh judgments of the bill. The *Washington Post* charged on 31 January that the bill would restore the uneven conditions in labor relations that had prevailed before 1935. The *Atlanta Constitution* agreed, pointing out that none of the bill's defenders had identified any specific flaws in Taft-Hartley. A survey of public opinion published in February by the Opinion Research Corporation of Princeton revealed, moreover, that support for the major provisions of the 1947 act was practically as high as when the act was adopted.[25]

Because of the widespread public support for major provisions of Taft-Hartley, the Administration's bill was modified substantially when it reached the full Senate. Approved on 15 June with broad bipartisan support, for instance, were three amendments requiring both labor and management to bargain collectively and to file annual financial reports, as well as guaranteeing each freedom of speech.[26] By late June, Senate debate had narrowed to a single divisive question posed by an amendment concerning the President's injunctive power. The Taft amendment sought to maintain Taft-Hartley's solution for halting strikes endangering the national welfare by authorizing the President either to seek injunctions or to seize strike-bound plants.

The Administration's position was complicated by partisan political considerations. Even though Harry Truman had used injunctions on six previous occasions and had requested extension of such power in the 1949 act, the Administration ultimately bowed to intense lobbying from organized labor, who feared that injunctions could be used to crush unions. The Administration's stance, embodied in an amendment offered by Majority Leader Scott Lucas on 23 June, proposed to eliminate the President's injunctive power and rely instead solely on seizure of strike-bound plants to end work stoppages endangering national welfare.[27]

Shortly after the Lucas amendment was introduced, Spessard Holland of Florida offered a third alternative to the debate by proposing to delete the President's seizure power, and to rely only on injunctions as a solution to crippling national strikes. The highly charged emotions that surrounded the 1949 debate distorted political perception of the three amendments. While the Lucas amendment was widely regarded as pro-labor, the Holland amendment, given union labor's intense opposition to injunctions, was regarded by organized labor and its supporters as harshly antiunion, despite the fact that it narrowed the President's power to stop strikes. The Taft amendment, even though it continued a major provision of the 1947 "slave labor" bill, was seen somewhat ironically as occupying the middle ground in this debate.[28]

Given the intense public concern with organized labor in 1949 and the odd circumstances surrounding the debate over the President's injunctive and seizure power, it was perhaps to be expected that the new conservatives were more divided than on most other issues in the 81st Congress. The votes by which both the Holland and Lucas amendments were defeated on 28 June, for instance, revealed that the new conservatives were split rather evenly. But when faced with a choice of continuing the use of injunctions and seizures as prescribed by the Taft amendment or eliminating those powers entirely, most new conservatives, including Aiken, Flanders, George, Hoey, Holland, Lodge, Russell, Saltonstall, M. C. and H. A. Smith, and Vandenberg, voted to retain the modifications in labor-management relations made by the 1947 act. The following day, practically the same coalition formed first to substitute for the Administration's bill a measure introduced earlier by Robert Taft that made some minor, technical modifications in the 1947 law, and then voted 51–42 to approve that substitute.[29]

Although twenty-eight changes were made in the existing law, both friends and foes of the 1949 measure were in substantial agreement with Claude Pepper's assessment that by leaving intact the basic structure of labor-management relations established in 1947, the new labor act was a carbon-copy of Taft-Hartley. If the upper house's action revealed the shallowness of the Truman Administration's support in Congress, it also testified to changes that had occurred in Senate conservatism in little more than a decade. Whereas most Senate conservatives in the 1930s had opposed the reforms of the Wagner Act as an unwarranted intrusion by the federal government into the free enterprise system, by the late 1940s Senate conservatism was of two minds on national labor policy. Obstructionist conservatives appeared to view Taft-Hartley as the first victory in a continuing war to repeal all government guarantees to union labor, which perhaps helps to explain why organized labor viewed the 1947 measure with such hostility. But to the new conservatives, Taft-Hartley was a evolutionary step taken to preserve the free enterprise system under the new conditions posed by modern corporate capitalism. Spessard Holland wondered in a January 1949 letter, for example, why unions regarded his support for Taft-Hartley as contrary to their interests. "[I]t is my judgment," he maintained, "that the abuses in the field of industry-labor relations . . . manifested during the war period were so great as to justify a constructive and moderate effort to work out amendments to the Wagner Act which would strike a sounder balance between industry and labor, give much better protection to the individual member of a labor union, and above all give much greater consideration and sounder protection to the general public." Irving Ives saw national labor policy in similar terms. In testimony during hearings on the 1949 bill, the New York Republican argued that national labor law should emulate the careful balancing of interests achieved by the U.S. Constitution. "In our economic workaday life we must evolve a similar balance of powers between organized business, organized labor, and the national general interest."[30]

Debates on three foreign policy issues in 1949, funding for the second year of the Marshall Plan, ratification of the North Atlantic Treaty Organization, and extension of reciprocal trade, provided additional evidence of the transformation that had occurred in Senate conservatism. In early April, for instance, most of the new conservatives sided consistently with Administration forces to approve the President's request for $5.6 billion for the second year of the Marshall Plan. Opponents of the plan, citing reports that the first year of economic assistance had enabled production in many European countries to approximate prewar levels, argued for reductions in aid because American taxpayers, as Republican Homer Capehart observed, should not be expected to raise any nation above its prewar condition. But most new conservatives, continuing to believe, as they had a year earlier, that the Marshall Plan made a substantial contribution both to world peace and American prosperity, joined with Administration forces to defeat a Wherry amendment that would have cut 15% from the Marshall Plan's authorization, as well as a Taft-Russell amendment that sought to reduce funding by 10%.[31]

Similar patterns developed in July when the upper house turned to the NATO pact. The mutual security agreement, which had its origins in provisions of the United Nations charter, had been signed in Washington in April to bolster Western defenses against Soviet communism. Opposition came largely from obstructionist conservatives, who complained that Article 5 of the pact pledging U.S. assistance, including the use of armed force, to all signatories in the event of attack, departed significantly from traditional American foreign policy. Typical of the obstructionist attack were the efforts of Arthur Watkins, who petitioned the Senate for the right to attend Foreign Relations Committee hearings on NATO to ensure that tough questions were asked. The Utah Republican proposed on 1 June that the treaty be amended to forbid specifically the use of any U.S. military force without direct and advance authorization by Congress. Without the amendment, he continued, the treaty unconstitutionally usurped Congress's power to declare war.[32] In the end, however, most new conservatives seemed to agree with Spessard Holland's view of NATO as "a necessary and logical step in the international movement to preserve the peace." For on 21 July, before the pact was ratified by a vote of 82–13, new conservatives joined with Administration forces to reject the Watkins amendment, 84–11, and also to defeat a Wherry amendment 74–21, which explicitly disavowed any American obligation to supply arms to signatories.[33]

Extension of reciprocal trade provided a final example of the transformation that had occurred in the new conservatives' foreign policy views by 1949. Although the trade program had been a controversial issue in the 1930s, the 1949 debate on the Administration's request for a two-year extension revealed that a substantial majority in the upper house supported the general principle of reciprocal trade and that most questions focused only on the means of implementation. Indeed, much of the debate centered on whether reciprocal trade should be bound by "peril points" advocated by the GOP, or unrestricted as the Truman Administration preferred. "Peril points," which had been added to reciprocal trade by the GOP majority in the 80th Congress, required the President to fix tariff duties within guidelines established independently by the U.S. Tariff Commission to ensure that American business would not be hurt by any change in trade duties. Republican sponsors of the "peril point" provision in 1949 emphasized that it was not aimed at returning to the highly protectionist course previously pursued by the party, but was intended simply, in Eugene Millikin's view, as an attempt to maintain vigilance in the protection of American producers. The Administration lobbied intensely against peril points, however, charging that they would unduly emphasize protectionism at a time when free trade was critical to improving the world economy and urged all Democrats to stand by the President. By transforming the issue into a question of party loyalty, the White House tactics apparently succeeded, for the peril point amendment was narrowly defeated on 15 September by a 43–38 margin, in a vote that saw most Democratic new conservatives side with the Administration.[34]

Obstructionist conservatives continued to fight against a program they viewed as unnecessarily generous and one that they believed undermined the Constitution's separation of powers. Hugh Butler of Kansas, for example, asserted that future trade agreements should reflect the principles espoused by William McKinley, which required approval by the upper house and which demanded equal concessions from the nations with whom we negotiated trade agreements. Conservatives of Butler's ilk, therefore, coalesced around a substitute sponsored by Nevada Republican George Malone aimed at ending reciprocal trade entirely in favor of a system to protect domestic industry. Charging that the Administration's trade policy gave up much for little in return, Malone's substitute sought to tie tariffs to the production costs of the exporting countries and to have an independent trade authority adjust those rates to account for fluctuations in the costs. Many of the new conservatives on the GOP side of the aisle, who had earlier voted in favor of peril points, shifted their votes back to the Administration to help defeat Malone's substitute, and to ensure passage of the reciprocal trade extension bill.[35]

The 1949 Senate debates on foreign policy revealed clearly, then, that a bipartisan consensus had formed in support of American internationalism. While the postwar fears of communism had made it difficult for most senators to oppose such aid programs as the Truman Doctrine or the Marshall Plan, reciprocal trade had continued to be a divisive, partisan issue through the 80th Congress. But the statistical analysis of roll call votes in the 81st Congress revealed that, although all but two of the thirty senators who scaled as obstructionists continued to offer only low support on reciprocal trade, twenty-three of the twenty-four new conservatives gave either medium or high support to the issue.

The change in Senate conservatism was also apparent to *Newsweek*'s political commentator, Ernest K. Lindley. He argued in May 1949 that neither the President nor the conservative coalition controlled Congress. Rather, he suggested, Congress was best viewed as a group of shifting coalitions that changed as the issues varied. In addition to the growth of a bipartisan coalition supporting a more international foreign policy, Lindley discerned a bipartisan group supporting the expansion of social services, which was to the right of Fair Deal liberals, but to the left of Old Guard conservatives. Similarly, he asserted that a bipartisan coalition held the balance of power on labor legislation which, while definitely not antilabor, was intent on maintaining a balance between the rights of labor and management. Congressional politics in 1949, Lindley concluded, had moved considerably beyond the conservatism of the 1930s.[36]

II

Until the outbreak of the Korean War in June, political affairs in the second session of the 81st Congress closely resembled the pattern established in the first session. New conservatives in the Senate continued to pursue an increasingly independent political path that expanded the ideological differences between themselves and the obstructionist members of their parties. As a result, the Truman Administration was able to secure passage in 1950 of a new public housing initiative, as well as funding for a third year of the Marshall Plan. Similarly, the votes of new conservatives helped preserve Taft-Hartley as the basis for the nation's labor policy. The outbreak of the Korean War, however, coming less than five months before the fall Congressional elections, concentrated the Republican criticism of the Truman Administration's foreign policy that had been mounting steadily throughout the late 1940s. The intense partisanship that surrounded the war polarized the new conservatives and temporarily rekindled a sense of party loyalty on both sides of the aisle. In contrast to the national unity spawned by U.S. entry into World War II in 1941, Administration initiatives in the last six months of 1950 received enthusiastic support from most Democratic senators, but only grudging cooperation from GOP members.

The legislative victories won by the Truman Administration in the first six months of 1950 were largely attributable to the ongoing transformation of Senate conservatism. The *New York Times*'s political analyst William S. White argued in May, for example, that although the power of the Senate's twenty southern Democrats had never been more formidable, it was incorrect to see them as a unified, retrogressive bloc. Except for civil rights issues to which all were still opposed, White maintained that some southern senators were in the forefront of support for various aspects of the Truman Administration's domestic and foreign policy agenda. Burnet Maybank and John Sparkman, he noted for example, were leaders in public housing efforts. The southern Democrats, White concluded, were likely to be swing votes, alternately siding with Republicans and liberal Democrats as issues changed.[37]

The factional dispute that had simmered in the Republican party throughout the 1940s finally erupted into open warfare in 1950. The little progress the United States had made in containing communism in the Cold War was for many Americans powerfully emphasized in 1949 by the "loss" of China and the Soviet detonation of an atomic bomb. Members of the GOP, who had often criticized aspects of the Truman Administration's foreign policy, used the 1949 reverses to mount a broad partisan attack on the Democratic party. Beginning with Joe McCarthy's February 1950 speech in Wheeling, West Virginia, many Republicans sought to lay at the feet of Democratic party policies and policymakers all of the problems confronting the nation. America's precarious international position, the GOP insisted, was the result of "twenty years of treason." To buttress their charges of Democratic disloyalty, the Republicans also heaped abuse on the liberal domestic policies of the New Deal and Fair Deal, asserting frequently that they came directly from the Soviet constitution. At their traditional Lincoln Day dinners in February 1950, for example, the GOP national leadership issued declarations portraying the divisions between the Republicans and the Democrats as a battle between freedom and socialism and expressed blanket opposition to the entire Fair Deal.[38]

The Republican party declarations were absolute folly to the new conservatives within the GOP. Convinced that voters had steadily abandoned their party because of its outdated political philosophy, the new conservatives in the GOP broke openly with their leadership in March. Led by Henry Cabot Lodge and Margaret Chase Smith in the Senate, and by Jacob Javits in the House, the GOP new conservatives drafted their own "Declaration of Republican Principles" that emphasized the profound policy differences separating the warring factions of the party. Calling for a broad civil rights program, expanded social security, equality in labor-management relations, reduced taxes, and a balanced budget, the Declaration emphasized the substantial role government had to play in promoting what it termed "the Right to Life." Indicating clearly that the Great Depression had been a major formative experience, leading the Republican new conservatives to embrace the positive state, the Declaration contended "in an industrial society, in which men and women are dependent for their livelihood upon economic factors wholly beyond their control, the . . . Right to Life becomes largely an *economic* matter. It gives rise to certain rights . . . which can be implemented only by providing protection from economic hazards against which the individual cannot hope adequately to insure himself. These hazards include unemployment, old age, accident, ill health, disabilities, etc."[39]

The split in the GOP was widened in the summer, when Maine's Margaret Chase Smith and six other Republicans issued a "Declaration of Conscience," protesting the anticommunist tactics utilized by right-wing Republicans led by Joe McCarthy. As the *New York Times*'s Cabell Phillips recognized, however, Smith's protest was aimed not simply at the red-baiting techniques of her colleagues, but was also a reiteration of the new conservatives' demand for an end to the party's obstructionist course. The new conservatives, Phillips concluded, understood that conditions of modern life had changed substantially which, in turn, required significant alterations in the role of government.[40]

The effect of the increased independence of the new conservatives on policy debates was made apparent in March 1950 when the Truman Administration proposed a new federal housing program. Although public housing continued to be a controversial subject, Title 3 of the new measure provoked even more heated argument because it proposed to create a $100 million government corporation to make long-term loans to private housing cooperatives at low interest rates for the construction of middle-income housing. Asserting that the nation's housing program had largely ignored the middle class, the bill's sponsor, Alabama Democrat John Sparkman, explained that the government assisted upper income brackets through FHA mortgages and lower income groups through public housing, but had ignored the real housing needs of the middle third of the country's income range. Title 3 called for the government to appropriate $100 million to fund a National Mortgage Corporation that would make loans to housing cooperatives or non-profit associations. The loans, to be repaid over a fifty-year period at an annual interest rate of 3½%, sought to provide housing that would rent at a median rate of $69 per month for families with incomes between $2840 and $4425.[41]

Although the Truman Administration and its supporters in Congress defended the bill as a logical extension of the government's effort to solve the postwar housing crisis, obstructionist conservatives in the Senate assailed Title 3 as a further step down the road to socialism. Republican Harry Cain of Washington maintained, for instance, that Title 3 would encourage communal living, while John Bricker predicted that it "will have a completely unjustifiable effect on individual effort and individual investment, serving as a deterrent to individual thrift and initiative." To address their concerns, Bricker and Cain cosponsored an amendment on 10 March, which proposed to delete Title 3 from the housing bill.[42]

The new conservatives in the Senate also attacked Title 3, albeit for different reasons. They contended that the controversial program was inflationary and that it unfairly discriminated against other income groups in the country. The new conservatives pointed out that a householder buying a home through Title 3 cooperatives would be able to borrow money at 3% and have fifty years, or almost an entire lifetime, to repay the loan. Homeowners taking out a mortgage through the FHA, on the other hand, had to pay 4½% interest and had only twenty to twenty-five years to repay the loan. Even veterans, they noted, had to pay 4% on FHA mortgages. The unhappiness many new conservatives felt toward Title 3 was voiced by Charles Tobey on 10 March. The New Hampshire Republican, who had been outspoken in his support for previous public housing measures, argued on the Senate floor that the bill was a dangerous experiment that would add to the size of the federal government and increase the federal deficit. Together with fellow Republican Irving Ives, Tobey introduced a substitute on 10 March, which proposed to stimulate the construction of middle-income housing simply by requiring the FHA to insure loans to housing cooperatives at interest rates currently available to private builders.[43]

Before the Senate gave final approval to the housing measure on 15 March, it was altered substantially by a coalition of new conservatives and obstructionists. The Bricker-Cain amendment, eliminating Title 3 entirely, was narrowly approved 43–38, when new conservatives from both parties, including George, Hoey, Holland, Russell, Saltonstall, H. A. Smith, and Thye joined with obstructionists to provide the margin of victory. Then, reflecting the mounting partisanship of an election year, the Tobey-Ives substitute was easily defeated 66–14, when most Democratic new conservatives and Administration supporters, apparently preferring no loaf to half a loaf, joined forces with obstructionists to defeat the more modest proposal. The final housing bill, approved by voice vote, merely provided $2.5 billion in further government incentives for the construction of middle-income housing. The 1950 housing debate, therefore, emphasized the distinctiveness of the new conservatives' political philosophy. Through their opposition to Title 3, the new conservatives demonstrated that they were determined to draw more narrow boundaries around government's role in the private sector than were most liberals. Yet their support for public housing and federal aid to education in previous sessions indicated that the new conservatives believed that government did have an obligation to assist those groups in society who were left behind by the conditions of modern industrial life.[44]

In late spring, the new conservatives further demonstrated their independence when the upper house voted to preserve two previously adopted policies, Taft-Hartley and rent control. The nation's labor law was the first challenge faced by the Senate. In early 1950, President Truman submitted to Congress a series of reorganization plans based on recommendations made by a commission headed by former President Herbert Hoover. One of the plans, number 12, proposed to streamline the National Labor Relations Board by abolishing its Office of General Counsel, and naming its chairman as the sole chief administrative officer. The general counsel position had been established by the 1947 Taft-Hartley Act specifically to share the administrative functions of the labor board, because of the widespread perception then that the NLRB was dominated by organized labor. Although the White House contended that the present division of administrative control had produced numerous intra-agency confrontations that undermined the NLRB's efficiency, defenders of Taft-Hartley suspected that there were other motives. Citing organized labor's long-standing campaign to eliminate the general counsel post, Robert Taft charged on 11 May that the President was attempting to change provisions of national labor law approved only recently by Congress. In the end, new conservatives from both parties, including Flanders, George, Hoey, Holland, Saltonstall, H. A. and M. C. Smith, and Thye, ignored a direct appeal from the White House to join instead with obstructionists in rejecting Reorganization Plan Number 12.[45]

Twice in 1950 votes of new conservatives also helped to preserve the nation's rent control laws, but unlike their role on Taft-Hartley, on this issue they sided consistently with the Administration. In January, the White House, citing the continuing shortage of available housing, had asked Congress to appropriate $3.6 million to keep rent control alive until 30 June. Obstructionists on the Senate Appropriations Committee, however, led by Harry Cain, who had long regarded rent control as unwarranted government interference with the free market, approved a bill alloting only $2.6 million and stipulated that all funds be used to terminate the program by 30 June. A confrontation between the White House and Senate obstructionists was avoided when a compromise, engineered by Democrat Joseph O'Mahoney, appropriating only $2.6 million for rent control but using the funds to continue operation through 30 June, was adopted by the Senate on 9 March by a 44–28 margin.[46]

Three months later, as the 30 June expiration neared, the Truman Administration made a new request for a simple one-year extension of the program. When the Senate Banking and Currency Committee balked at this new appeal and instead reported a bill to continue rent control for only six additional months, the Administration intensifed the partisan pressure on its Congressional followers. At a Democratic Congressional conference held on 8 June, Senate Democratic leaders stressed that failure to enact at least a six-month extension of rent control might cost the party the election and control of Congress. The Administration's warning, combined with the sincere belief of some senators that extension of rent control was necessary to ensure affordable housing for many Americans, assured adoption of the measure. On 12 June, after the obstructionists' effort to recommit the bill was rejected, the Senate voted 36–28 to approve the six-month extension of rent control. Importantly, all three votes dealing with rent control in 1950 showed that most new conservatives had consistently supported the principle that government had a necessary role to play in regulating this aspect of the free enterprise system.[47]

Foreign policy debates in May underscored that the new conservatives' ideological independence was not limited to domestic issues. A Truman Administration request in January for $3.4 billion in foreign aid, most of which was earmarked for the third year of the Marshall Plan, sharply polarized the upper house. On one side were loyal Administration Democrats, such as Texas's Tom Connally, who maintained that the European aid plan was the best way to provide strength against Soviet treachery. Opposition to the foreign aid bill came largely from Republican obstructionists like Bourke Hickenlooper of Iowa who railed that the government had to stop its deficit spending. The new conservatives filled in the middle ground between these two extremes, agreeing with the White House that the Marshall Plan was essential to American national defense, but also supporting the obstructionists' contention that the size of the appropriation could be reduced for the sake of greater economy in government.[48]

When the Senate began voting on the foreign aid bill in early May, the new conservatives saw that neither the Administration nor the obstructionists realized their full objectives. An amendment sponsored by Republican James Kem to slash $1 billion from the Marshall Plan was rejected 62–17, for example, when all new conservatives voting united with Administration forces. Shortly thereafter, a Taft amendment that would have reduced Marshall Plan funds by $500 million failed on a 40–40 tie vote, when such new conservatives as Aiken, Flanders, Hoey, Holland, Lodge, Saltonstall, H. A. Smith, and Thye continued to vote with the Administration against any reduction. Before the foreign aid bill was approved by a 60–8 margin, however, most of the new conservatives shifted their votes to the obstructionists to ensure passage of a Styles Bridges amendment paring $250 million from the funds for the European Recovery Plan. By shifting their votes, therefore, the new conservatives helped to ensure that the Marshall Plan would survive for a third year, despite the wishes of the obstructionists, but would do so with somewhat less funding than the White House had requested.[49]

The ideological independence of the new conservatives diminished markedly, however, following the outbreak of the Korean war in June. The shock of fighting another war, so close on the heels of World War II, appeared initially to engender a national unity that silenced partisan debate in Congress. When the Truman Administration in late July requested emergency allocation and priority controls to prevent hoarding of essential goods, the Senate, after only two weeks of debate, approved a bill that not only granted those powers, but also permitted the White House to impose standby wage and price controls, and to ration scarce commodities. During Senate debate on the bill, moreover, when Robert Taft objected to its extreme delegation of power to the Executive and demanded that the measure be amended to require Congressional concurrence to any wage and price ceilings, he was shouted down by members of his own party.[50]

Once the initial shock of war had worn off, however, the communist invasion of South Korea, coming only six months after the fall of China, seemed to many Americans to be one more example of the Truman Administration's failure to contain international communism. Because this perceived failure also occurred in an election year, the Korean War quickly proved to be an irresistible partisan weapon for the GOP. During the third week of August, for example, all Republican members of the Senate Foreign Relations Committee (H. A. Smith, Lodge, Hickenlooper, and Wiley) charged publicly that Democratic errors were responsible for the Korean War. Three days later, Republican Kenneth Wherry considerably escalated the partisan discourse when he angrily contended on the Senate floor that "the blood of our boys today is on his [Secretary of State Dean Acheson's] shoulders, and not on the shoulders of anyone else."[51]

Partisanship even colored the debate in September over Truman's nomination of George Marshall to be secretary of defense. Because the 1947 Military Unification Act, which created the post of secretary of defense, forbade any commissioned officer from holding the office within ten years of active service, the Senate had to approve a bill exempting Marshall before acting on his nomination. Senate Republicans argued vehemently against the exemption, contending publicly that it would contravene the long-standing American tradition of civilian control of the military. Privately, they admitted, however, that their opposition was grounded in the belief that Marshall's great public prestige would strengthen the Truman Administration against GOP charges that it was soft on communism. Although the bill granting Marshall a special exemption was ultimately adopted, much of the Republican rhetoric during debate shredded whatever bipartisanship the Korean War had engendered. On 15 September, for example, the Senate sat in stony silence while Indiana's William Jenner denounced Marshall. "General Marshall is not only willing, he is eager to play the role of a front man for traitors. . . . General Marshall has either been an unsuspecting, well-intentioned stooge," the Indiana Republican contended, "or an actual co-conspirator with the most treasonable array of political cutthroats ever turned loose in the Executive branch of the Government."[52]

The effect of this rancorous debate was to polarize the upper house along party lines to a much greater extent than was normally seen in an election year, a development which, in turn, led most new conservatives to emphasize party loyalty, rather than ideological independence for the remainder of the second session. As the harsh attacks launched by obstructionist Republicans against the Truman Administration's foreign policy found an increasingly receptive public audience, new conservatives within the party became less inclined to dissent from what seemed to be a winning political issue. Democratic new conservatives, on the other hand, felt increasingly compelled to defend their party's record.

Although the 81st Congress ended with a heightened sense of partisanship that blurred the political alignments that had prevailed throughout most of 1949 and 1950, it continued to sharpen the contours of the new conservatism. The new conservatives' support for public housing and federal aid to education, for example, remained steadfast, so long as the aid was aimed at lifting the poorest members of society up to minimum acceptable standards. When expansions of the positive state beyond this principle were proposed, as with the 1950 Title 3 housing program, the new conservatives drew the line. Similarly, both in 1949 and 1950 the new conservatives reaffirmed their support for the basic rights established for labor by the Wagner Act. But they were equally adamant that the balance injected into labor-management relations by the 1947 Taft-Hartley Act be preserved. Finally, in foreign affairs, the new conservatives continued their support for American internationalism by voting to extend the Marshall Plan and reciprocal trade, and by committing the U.S. to NATO. At the same time, however, in the interests of holding down the tax burden on Americans, they were generally willing to commit fewer dollars to foreign aid than liberals, and as their position on NATO revealed, more determined to draw narrower interpretations of the nation's international obligations.

The new conservatives, then, were still conservatives who believed strongly in individual freedom and private enterprise, but were convinced that unless new means were sometimes used to achieve these goals, the conditions of modern life would ultimately destroy them. This was apparent in a statement made by Henry Cabot Lodge in defense of a bill he cosponsored with Connecticut Democrat Brien McMahon. "This bill is . . . an attempt to induce our free [enterprise] system to yield all the benefits which it is capable of yielding. If the free system does not do all the good of which it is capable, increased governmental services are inevitable. In fact . . . either we make the most of our present system and develop all its latent strength—or we can expect a succession of policies which will progressively sap its vigor and thus eventually make lower living standards for everyone."[53] In contrast, in 1950 the *New York Times*'s William S. White still found Republican Kenneth Wherry in 1950 to be a conservative who, with the exception of federal price supports for farmers, wanted to repeal all of the social and economic powers granted to the federal government since 1933.[54]

The sharpening divisions between liberals, new conservatives, and obstructionists in the 81st Congress are plainly evident in the statistical analysis of the roll call votes. As table 6–2 reveals, when all scalable policy dimensions were considered, a bipartisan group of senators, representing roughly one-third of the upper house, voted as new conservatives. More importantly, many of the same senators whose voting records had placed them in between liberals and obstructionists in Congresses throughout the 1940s, again

TABLE 6-2

81st CONGRESS

Name	Policy Dimensions	Score
	1 2 3 4 5 6 7 8 9 10 11 12 13	

HIGH SUPPORT

Name	Policy Dimensions	Score
Green, D-RI	1 1 1 1 1 1 1 1 1 1 1 1 1	1.00
Hill, D-AL	1 1 1 1 1 1 1 1 1 1 1 1 1	1.00
Kilgore, D-WV	1 1 1 1 1 1 1 1 1 1 1 1 1	1.00
Lucas, D-IL	1 1 1 1 1 1 1 1 1 1 1 1 1	1.00
Murray, D-MT	1 1 1 1 1 1 1 1 1 1 1 1 1	1.00
Myers, D-PA	1 1 1 1 1 1 1 1 1 1 1 1 1	1.00
Neely, D-WV	1 1 1 1 1 1 1 1 1 1 1 1 1	1.00
O'Mahoney, D-WY	1 1 1 1 1 1 1 1 1 1 1 1 1	1.00
Sparkman, D-AL	1 1 1 1 1 1 1 1 1 1 1 1 1	1.00
Humphrey, D-MN	1 1 1 1 1 1 1 1 1 1 1 0 1	1.00
Kefauver, D-TN	1 1 1 1 1 1 1 0 1 1 1 1 1	1.00
Hunt, D-WY	1 1 1 0 1 1 1 1 1 1 1 1 1	1.00
Graham, D-NC	1 0 1 1 1 1 1 1 1 1 1 1 1	1.00
Downey, D-CA	1 0 1 1 0 1 1 0 0 1 0 1 1	1.00
McMahon, D-CT	0 1 1 1 1 1 1 1 1 1 1 1 1	1.00
Pepper, D-FL	1 1 1 1 1 1 1 1 1 1 1 2 1	1.08
Magnuson, D-WA	1 1 1 2 1 1 1 1 1 1 1 1 1	1.08
Hayden, D-AZ	1 2 1 1 1 1 1 1 1 1 1 1 1	1.08
Thomas, D-OK	1 1 1 2 1 1 0 1 1 1 1 0 1	1.09
McKellar, D-TN	1 1 1 1 1 1 3 1 1 1 1 1 1	1.15
Thomas, D-UT	1 1 1 2 1 1 2 1 1 1 1 1 1	1.15
Anderson, D-NM	1 1 2 2 1 1 1 1 1 1 1 1 1	1.15
McFarland, D-AZ	0 2 1 2 1 1 1 1 1 1 1 1 1	1.17
Long, D-LA	1 1 1 2 1 1 2 0 0 1 1 1 1	1.18
Johnston, D-SC	1 1 1 1 1 1 3 2 1 1 1 1 1	1.23
Connally, D-TX	1 1 2 1 1 1 3 1 1 1 1 1 1	1.23
Chavez, D-NM	1 2 2 1 1 1 1 2 1 1 1 1 1	1.23
Douglas, D-IL	3 1 1 1 1 1 1 1 1 1 2 1 1	1.23
Taylor, D-ID	1 1 1 1 1 1 1 1 0 1 2 1 3	1.25
Kerr, D-OK	1 1 2 2 1 1 0 1 2 1 1 1 1	1.25
Fulbright, D-AR	2 1 3 1 1 1 0 1 1 1 1 1 1	1.25

Name	Policy Dimensions	Score
	1 2 3 4 5 6 7 8 9 10 11 12 13	

HIGH SUPPORT continued

Name	Policy Dimensions	Score
Gillette, D-IA	1 1 1 1 1 1 2 3 1 1 1 2 1	1.31
Withers, D-KY	1 1 1 1 1 2 3 1 0 2 1 1 1	1.33
Johnson, D-TX	1 1 3 2 1 2 0 1 1 1 1 1 1	1.33
Chapman, D-KY	1 1 2 1 2 1 3 1 1 2 1 1 1	1.38
Maybank, D-SC	1 1 3 1 1 1 3 2 1 1 1 1 1	1.38
Stennis, D-MS	2 2 1 1 1 1 3 2 1 1 1 1 1	1.38
Frear, D-DE	2 1 2 2 1 1 0 0 1 1 2 2 1	1.45

MEDIUM SUPPORT

Name	Policy Dimensions	Score
Ellender, D-LA	1 1 3 2 1 1 3 2 1 1 1 1 0	1.50
O'Conor, D-MD	2 2 2 1 1 2 1 1 1 1 0 3 1	1.50
Tydings, D-MD	2 2 2 1 1 2 1 1 1 0 2 2 1	1.50
Hoey, D-NC	2 2 3 1 2 2 0 1 1 1 1 1 1	1.50
Eastland, D-MS	0 2 3 1 0 0 3 1 1 1 1 1 1	1.50
Russell, D-GA	1 2 1 1 2 2 3 2 1 2 1 1 1	1.54
Holland, D-FL	2 2 3 1 1 2 3 1 1 1 1 1 1	1.54
Benton, D-CT	2 2 2 2 0 1 0 0 0 1 0 0 1	1.57
Robertson, D-VA	2 2 1 1 2 1 2 1 1 2 0 3 1	1.58
Morse, R-OR	2 1 1 0 2 2 1 1 2 3 3 1 1	1.67
Aiken, R-VT	3 1 1 2 2 1 1 1 2 3 2 2 1	1.69
McCarran, D-NV	1 0 2 0 2 2 3 2 1 1 1 3 1	1.73
Tobey, R-NH	3 1 0 2 2 2 1 2 0 2 3 2 1	1.75
Johnson, D-CO	3 2 1 2 2 2 2 2 1 2 1 1 2	1.77
George, D-GA	3 2 3 1 2 2 3 2 1 1 1 1 1	1.77
Vandenberg, R-MI	3 2 3 1 0 3 1 1 0 2 0 0 1	1.89
Saltonstall, R-MA	0 2 2 0 2 3 1 2 2 2 3 3 1	1.91
McClellan, D-AR	2 2 3 2 2 2 3 2 1 2 1 2 1	1.92
Flanders, R-VT	3 1 2 2 2 2 1 1 2 3 2 2 2	1.92
Smith, R-NJ	3 2 2 1 3 2 1 1 2 2 3 2 1	1.92
Smith, R-ME	3 2 2 1 2 2 1 2 2 3 3 2 1	2.00
Thye, R-MN	3 3 1 3 3 2 1 1 2 2 3 1 1	2.00
Ives, R-NY	3 0 1 1 2 2 1 2 2 3 3 3 1	2.00
Lodge, R-MA	3 2 2 0 2 2 1 1 1 3 3 3 1	2.08

Name	Policy Dimensions	Score
	1 2 3 4 5 6 7 8 9 10 11 12 13	

LOW SUPPORT

Name	Policy Dimensions	Score
Gurney, R-SD	2 3 3 3 0 3 1 2 3 2 3 1 1	2.25
Millikin, R-CO	3 3 3 3 3 3 2 3 3 1 1 1 1	2.31
Langer, R-ND	2 3 1 3 2 1 3 0 3 3 3 1 3	2.33
Byrd, D-VA	3 2 3 1 3 0 3 2 0 2 2 3 2	2.36
McCarthy, R-WI	3 3 2 3 3 3 2 3 3 3 3 1 1	2.46
Hendrickson, R-NJ	3 3 3 3 2 3 1 2 2 3 3 3 1	2.46
Young, R-ND	2 3 3 3 2 3 0 2 3 3 2 1 2	2.50
Brewster, R-ME	3 2 2 0 3 3 1 3 3 2 3 3 2	2.50
Knowland, R-CA	3 3 3 3 2 3 1 3 0 2 3 3 1	2.50
Ecton, R-MT	3 3 0 3 3 3 3 3 2 3 2 1 1	2.50
Cordon, R-OR	2 3 3 3 3 3 3 2 2 2 3 3 2	2.54
Donnell, R-MO	3 3 3 2 3 3 3 2 3 2 1 2 3	2.54
Capehart, R-IN	3 3 2 3 3 3 2 3 3 3 0 2 1	2.58
Ferguson, R-MI	3 3 3 3 3 3 1 3 3 2 3 3 1	2.62
Mundt, R-SD	3 3 3 3 3 3 2 3 3 2 3 2 1	2.62
Bridges, R-NH	3 3 0 3 3 3 1 3 3 3 3 0 1	2.64
Hickenlooper, R-IA	3 3 3 3 3 3 2 0 2 3 3 3 1	2.67
Wiley, R-WI	3 0 3 3 3 3 3 2 2 3 3 3 1	2.67
Watkins, R-UT	3 2 3 3 3 3 3 2 3 3 3 1 3	2.69
Schoeppel, R-KS	3 3 3 3 3 3 3 3 3 3 2 1 2	2.69
Cain, R-WA	3 3 3 3 2 3 3 2 0 3 3 3 2	2.75
Taft, R-OH	3 3 3 0 3 3 1 3 3 2 3 3 3	2.75
Kem, R-MO	3 0 3 3 3 3 3 3 3 3 1 2 3	2.75
Williams, R-DE	0 3 3 3 3 3 3 3 2 3 3 3 2	2.83
Malone, R-NV	3 3 2 3 3 3 3 3 3 3 2 3 3	2.85
Jenner, R-IN	3 3 3 3 3 3 3 3 3 3 3 1 3	2.85
Butler, R-NE	3 2 3 3 3 3 3 3 3 3 3 3 3	2.92
Bricker, R-OH	3 3 3 3 3 3 3 3 3 3 3 3 2	2.92
Martin, R-PA	3 3 3 3 3 0 3 3 3 3 3 3 2	2.92
Wherry, R-NE	3 3 3 3 3 3 3 3 3 3 3 3 3	3.00

Policy Dimension Key:

0 denotes that a senator did not scale on the dimension
1. Economy in Government Spending
2. Social Welfare
3. Labor
4. Reciprocal Trade
5. Extension of Executive Power
6. Business Regulation
7. Displaced Persons
8. Foreign Aid
9. Civil Rights/Civil Liberties
10. Fiscal Policy
11. Agriculture
12. Public Power
13. National Defense

81ST CONGRESS (N=92)

HIGH SUPPORT (N=38 or 41%)   MEDIUM SUPPORT (N=24 or 26%)

Democrats = 38 (100%)   Democrats = 13 (54%)
GOP   = 0 (0%)   GOP   = 11 (46%)

LOW SUPPORT (N=30 or 33%)

Democrats = 1 (3%)
GOP   = 29 (97%)

ranked as new conservatives, suggesting that ideological affinity was an element that undergird this scale position.

When scale scores on domestic policy dimensions were separated from those on foreign policy, the change that had occurred in Senate politics since 1938 was even more apparent. The scale scores of foreign policy dimensions summarized in table 6–4 reflect the tumultous international events Americans faced in 1949 and 1950. To most observers, the "loss" of China and the Soviet detonation of an atomic bomb in 1949, followed by the start of the Korean War in 1950, substantially increased the threat to national security. The spy trials, both at home and abroad, added to the national sense of alarm. Believing that the nation faced imminent peril, remarkably few senators in the 81st Congress dissented from the rapid evolution of American internationalism. Indeed, as Table 6–4 indicates, 84% of the scalable senators gave either high or medium support to Harry Truman's foreign policies, a clear sign of the emerging Cold War consensus.

Comparisons with earlier periods of national peril further emphasize the significant transformation that had occurred in Senate attitudes on internationalism throughout the 1940s. At the start of the decade, as the United States faced the Fascist threat, resistance to American internationalism was still a viable position. For example, in the 77th Congress (1941–1942), the first war Congress, 35% of the scalable senators gave only low support to Franklin Roosevelt's initiatives, more than double the 16% who did so for Harry Truman's efforts in the 81st Congress. Clearly, as these figures suggest, by the middle of the twentieth century many Senate conservatives had been convinced by the experience of World War II, by the fear of communism, or by both, that an international foreign policy was vital to the nation's well-being.

Amid the escalating tensions of the Cold War, partisanship, to be sure, did not vanish from Senate debates over foreign policy. As table 6–4 indicates, only thirteen of the scalable Democrats gave anything less than high support to the Administration's policies. In contrast, all fifteen of the senators who scaled as obstructionists on foreign policy dimensions were Republicans, the vast majority of whom, moreover, represented interior states. While many of these GOP obstructionists undoubtedly had philosophical objections to American internationalism, the ferocity of the verbal attacks that some like William Jenner unleashed on Administration spokesmen suggests that they were sometimes consciously fishing for votes among an American electorate searching for simple answers to the complex international crisis.

Table 6-3

Regional Divisions in Medium and Low Support Groups

MEDIUM SUPPORT   (N=24)

Coastal (N=17 or 71%)

O'Conor, D-MD	Tydings, D-MD	Saltonstall, R-MA
Hoey, D-NC	Russell, D-GA	Smith, R-ME
Holland, D-FL	Benton, D-CT	Lodge, R-MA
Robertson, D-VA	Morse, R-OR	Smith, R-NJ
Aiken, R-VT	Tobey, R-NH	Ives, R-NY
George, D-GA	Flanders, R-VT	

Interior (N=7 or 29%)

Ellender, D-LA	Eastland, D-MS	Thye, R-MN
McCarran, D-NV	Johnson, D-CO	
Vandenberg, R-MI	McClellan, D-AR	

LOW SUPPORT (N=30)

Coastal (N=9 or 30%)

Byrd, D-VA	Hendrickson, R-NJ	Cain, R-WA
Brewster, R-ME	Knowland, R-CA	Martin, R-PA
Cordon, R-OR	Bridges, R-NH	Williams, R-DE

Interior (N=21 or 70%)

Millikin, R-CO	Langer, R-ND	Taft, R-OH
McCarthy, R-WI	Young, R-ND	Malone, R-NV
Ecton, R-MT	Gurney, R-SD	Butler, R-NE
Donnell, R-MO	Capehart, R-IN	Wherry, R-NE
Ferguson, R-MI	Mundt, R-SD	Kem, R-MO
Wiley, R-WI	Watkins, R-UT	Jenner, R-IN
Hickenlooper, R-IN	Schoeppel, R-KS	Bricker, R-OH

Voting alignments on domestic policy dimensions in the 81st Congress (table 6–5) are more revealing about the transformation of Senate conservatism. In the 81st Congress, as had been true of many previous Congresses, a bipartisan group of senators, drawn mainly from coastal states, supported Harry Truman's Fair Deal more strongly than obstructionists, but less strongly than liberals. Given their party's unexpected defeat in 1948, it is significant that twelve Republicans scaled as new conservatives in the 81st Congress. Nine of these Republicans, moreover, (Aiken, Morse, Tobey, Saltonstall, Flanders, H. A. Smith, Ives, Lodge, and Thye) were

TABLE 6-4

81st CONGRESS - FOREIGN POLICY DIMENSIONS

HIGH SUPPORT

Green, D-RI	1.00	Lodge, R-MA	1.00
Hill, D-AL	1.00	Robertson, D-VA	1.25
Kilgore, D-WV	1.00	Aiken, R-VT	1.25
Lucas, D-IL	1.00	Smith, R-ME	1.25
Murray, D-MT	1.00	Ives, R-NY	1.25
Myers, D-PA	1.00	Magnuson, D-WA	1.25
Neely, D-WV	1.00	Thomas, D-UT	1.33
O'Mahoney, D-WY	1.00	Anderson, D-NM	1.33
Sparkman, D-AL	1.00	McFarland, D-AZ	1.33
Humphrey, D-MN	1.00	Chavez, D-NM	1.33
Kefauver, D-TN	1.00	Saltonstall, R-MA	1.33
Hunt, D-WY	1.00	Kerr, D-OK	1.33
Graham, D-NC	1.00	Johnson, D-TX	1.33
Downey, D-CA	1.00	Taylor, D-ID	1.50
McMahon, D-CT	1.00	Flanders, R-VT	1.50
Pepper, D-FL	1.00	Thomas, D-OK	1.50
Hayden, D-AZ	1.00	Connally, D-TX	1.50
Douglas, D-IL	1.00	Withers, D-KY	1.50
Fulbright, D-AR	1.00	Chapman, D-KY	1.50
O'Conor, D-MD	1.00	Frear, D-DE	1.50
Tydings, D-MD	1.00	Eastland, D-MS	1.50
Hoey, D-NC	1.00	Holland, D-FL	1.50
Morse, R-OR	1.00	Benton, D-CT	1.50
Vandenberg, R-MI	1.00	Tobey, R-NH	1.50
Smith, R-NJ	1.00	Thye, R-MN	1.50

N = 50; D = 39; R = 11

TABLE 6-4

81st CONGRESS - FOREIGN POLICY DIMENSIONS

MEDIUM SUPPORT

McKellar, D-TN	1.67		McClellan, D-AR	2.00
Long, D-LA	1.67		McCarthy, R-WI	2.00
Johnston, D-SC	1.75		Knowland, R-CA	2.00
Gillette, D-IA	1.75		Ferguson, R-MI	2.00
Maybank, D-SC	1.75		Bridges, R-NH	2.00
Stennis, D-MS	1.75		Hickenlooper, R-IA	2.00
Russell, D-GA	1.75		Millikin, R-CO	2.25
George, D-GA	1.75		Capehart, R-IN	2.25
Gurney, R-SD	1.75		Mundt, R-SD	2.25
Hendrickson, R-NJ	1.75		Wiley, R-WI	2.25
Johnson, D-CO	2.00		Taft, R-OH	2.33
Byrd, D-VA	2.00		Young, R-ND	2.33
Brewster, R-ME	2.00		Ellender, D-LA	2.33
McCarran, D-NV	2.00			

N = 27; D = 13; R = 14
Coastal = 9 (33%); Interior = 18 (67%)

LOW SUPPORT

Ecton, R-MT	2.50		Bricker, R-OH	2.75
Cordon, R-OR	2.50		Langer, R-ND	3.00
Donnell, R-MO	2.50		Kem, R-MO	3.00
Cain, R-WA	2.50		Malone, R-NV	3.00
Martin, R-PA	2.67		Jenner, R-IN	3.00
Watkins, R-UT	2.75		Butler, R-NE	3.00
Schoeppel, R-KS	2.75		Wherry, R-NE	3.00
Williams, R-DE	2.75			

N = 15; D = 0; R = 15
Coastal = 4 (27%); Interior = 11 (73%)

among the rebels who attempted to unseat Robert Taft in 1949 as chairman of the GOP Policy Committee. Their support for the domestic agenda of a newly re-elected Democratic administration reflects the deliberate effort they made in 1949 and 1950 to break with their party's past record of obstruction in order to define a "modern Republicanism."

The Democrats in the medium support group in Table 6–5 continued to be a mixture of long-term southern senators elected prior to 1936, such as Walter George and Millard Tydings, together with a group of younger southerners elected in the 1940s, including Clyde Hoey, John McClellan, Herbert O'Conor, and A. Willis Robertson. These Democratic new conservatives, like their Republican counterparts, were committed to preserving the basic outlines of the New Deal/Fair Deal domestic policies from obstructionists' attacks. But they were equally determined that the growth of the positive state proceed more cautiously than the Truman Administration would have preferred.

Those senators who scaled in the low support category, on the other hand tended, as was the case in the 80th Congress, to be Republicans from interior states. The dominance of the GOP in this category, together with the Republicans in the medium support category, strongly supports the numerous contemporary reports of bitter intraparty conflict. The large number of interior-state Republicans in the low support category also testifies to a significant change in the regional composition of both parties that was largely complete by the late 1940s. Throughout the 1930s there had been sizable contingents of former Progressives from interior and western states in both parties, but particularly within the GOP, who were in the forefront of those forces challenging the status quo. Such senators as Robert LaFollette, Arthur Capper, Lynn Frazier, Gerald P. Nye, Alva Adams, Burton Wheeler, and Ernest Lundeen gave at least moderate support to the domestic agenda of the early New Deal. By the late 1940s, however, these "sons of the wild jackass" had disappeared almost completely from the Senate, replaced in most cases by obstructionist conservatives who were bitter opponents of the positive state and American internationalism. Democrat Edwin Johnson of Colorado was perhaps the last Progressive who appeared in the medium support category in the 81st Congress. By the late 1940s, in other words, as the composition of medium support category indicates, the locus of reform in each party had largely shifted to the coastal regions, and the nation's heartland had become, particularly for the GOP, the center of political reaction.

TABLE 6-5

81st CONGRESS - DOMESTIC POLICY DIMENSIONS

HIGH SUPPORT

Green, D-RI	1.00	Hayden, D-AZ	1.09
Hill, D-AL	1.00	Anderson, D-NM	1.10
Kilgore, D-WV	1.00	Connally, D-TX	1.10
Lucas, D-IL	1.00	Gillette, D-IA	1.10
Murray, D-MT	1.00	McFarland, D-AZ	1.11
Myers, D-PA	1.00	Chavez, D-NM	1.20
Neely, D-WV	1.00	Kerr, D-OK	1.20
O'Mahoney, D-WY	1.00	Maybank, D-SC	1.20
Sparkman, D-AL	1.00	Stennis, D-MS	1.20
Humphrey, D-MN	1.00	Withers, D-KY	1.22
Kefauver, D-TN	1.00	Ellender, D-LA	1.22
Hunt, D-WY	1.00	Douglas, D-IL	1.30
Graham, D-NC	1.00	Fulbright, D-AR	1.30
Downey, D-CA	1.00	Johnson, D-TX	1.30
McMahon, D-CT	1.00	Chapman, D-KY	1.30
Magnuson, D-WA	1.00	Taylor, D-ID	1.33
Thomas, D-OK	1.00	Frear, D-DE	1.40
McKellar, D-TN	1.00	Russell, D-GA	1.44
Thomas, D-UT	1.00	Eastland, D-MS	1.50
Long, D-LA	1.00	Holland, D-FL	1.56
Johnston, D-SC	1.00	Benton, D-CT	1.60
Pepper, D-FL	1.09	McCarran, D-NV	1.63

N = 44; D = 44; R = 0

MEDIUM SUPPORT

Hoey, D-NC	1.67	Langer, R-ND	2.11
Johnson, D-CO	1.67	Tobey, R-NH	2.14
O'Conor, D-MD	1.75	Thye, R-MN	2.22
Tydings, D-MD	1.75	Smith, R-NJ	2.33
Robertson, D-VA	1.75	Smith, R-ME	2.33
George, D-GA	1.78	Lodge, R-MA	2.33
Morse, R-OR	1.89	Millikin, R-CO	2.33
Aiken, R-VT	1.89	Saltonstall, R-MA	2.38
McClellan, D-AR	1.89	Ives, R-NY	2.38
Flanders, R-VT	2.11		

N = 19; D = 7; R = 12
Coastal = 14 (74%); Interior = 5 (26%)

TABLE 6-5

81st CONGRESS - DOMESTIC POLICY DIMENSIONS

LOW SUPPORT

Young, R-ND	2.44	Mundt, R-SD	2.78
Gurney, R-SD	2.50	Malone, R-NV	2.78
Ecton, R-MT	2.50	Jenner, R-IN	2.78
Donnell, R-MO	2.56	Wiley, R-WI	2.88
Byrd, D-VA	2.57	Cain, R-WA	2.88
Vandenberg, R-MI	2.60	Williams, R-DE	2.88
Kem, R-MO	2.63	Ferguson, R-MI	2.89
McCarthy, R-WI	2.67	Hickenlooper, R-IA	2.89
Brewster, R-ME	2.67	Taft, R-OH	2.89
Cordon, R-OR	2.67	Butler, R-NE	2.89
Watkins, R-UT	2.67	Bridges, R-NH	3.00
Schoeppel, R-KS	2.67	Bricker, R-OH	3.00
Knowland, R-CA	2.75	Martin, R-PA	3.00
Capehart, R-IN	2.75	Wherry, R-NE	3.00
Hendrickson, R-NJ	2.78		

N = 29; D = 1; R = 28
Coastal = 9 (31%); Interior = 20 (69%)

This geographical bifurcation among Senate opponents of the Truman Adminstration suggests, then, that while partisan considerations cannot be dismissed as an explanation for the voting behavior of the new conservatives, they do not seem to offer a full explanation. That the preponderance of new conservatives represented coastal states (74%), whereas a similar proportion (69%) of obstructionists represented interior states, suggests that each group had a different understanding of the United States at mid-century. While most new conservatives appeared to be sympathetic to the needs of an urban, industrial state, the obstructionists continued to draw on the lessons of the nation's rural, agrarian past. This transformation in Senate conservatism ensured, in turn, that by the 81st Congress the New Deal's domestic and international agenda had largely been consolidated in the American political system. For although the new conservatives, by combining their votes with obstructionists, could block major expansions of that agenda, they could also, by joining with liberals, fend off all efforts to repeal the changes begun by Franklin Roosevelt.

7

The New Conservatism in an
Era of Consensus

POLITICAL ALIGNMENTS IN THE 82ND CONGRESS RETURNED RATHER quickly to the patterns that had been established prior to the outbreak of the Korean War, and as a consequence, the new conservatism once again was a more visible force in Senate affairs. By early 1951 the air of crisis that had followed the start of war gave way to concern with the war's tendency to centralize power in the White House. Because of this concern, the pull of party loyalty that had especially influenced the voting behavior of Democratic new conservatives in the early months of the war abated markedly, to be replaced by a renewed sense of independence.

Partisan politics also influenced legislative affairs in the 82nd Congress. The mounting public frustration over the Cold War, symbolized graphically by the unresolved war in Korea, steadily eroded Harry Truman's popular support in 1951 and 1952. As a result, Democrats were given another reason to put distance between themselves and the White House. The declining popularity of the Truman Administration also removed whatever restraints that remained on Republican anticommunists such as Joe McCarthy. Their intensified partisan attacks on the Democratic Administration added to the political turmoil throughout the 82nd Congress. The climate of frustration, doubt, and partisanship that pervaded American politics in these years, then, offered wide opportunities for the new conservatives in the Senate to shape the policy agenda.

The major consequence of the new conservatism's revival was to demonstrate how thoroughly Senate conservatism had been transformed by the early 1950s. On most issues debated in the 82nd Congress, a broad consensus dominated Senate affairs. While the new conservatives often disagreed with liberals over means, there was general agreement between both groups that an internationalist foreign policy and an active role for government in domestic life were essential to promote the national welfare.

In these circumstances, obstructionist conservatives were reduced to a small and largely powerless force in the 82nd Congress. Unable to thwart administration initiatives alone, and dependent on the occasional votes of the new conservatives to have any influence on the policy agenda, obstructionists mainly had to fight rearguard actions that could limit, but not reverse, the gains made by American internationalism and the positive state.

I

By early 1951 the Korean War had ignited an intensive re-evaluation of postwar American foreign policy. In December 1950, former President Herbert Hoover had fired the first salvo when he called for major changes in the nation's international obligations. Charging that America had overextended itself, the Republican leader proposed immediate withdrawal of all U.S. forces from Korea and western Europe so that the nation could concentrate its resources on a smaller defensive perimeter. He argued that the western frontier for this defensive perimeter should be the British Isles, but only if they cooperated with the U.S. The eastern border would be formed by Japan, Formosa, and the Phillipines. Hoover's plan recommended, moreover, that no additional aid be given to the western European nations until they strengthened their own defenses against communism. Most observers agreed that Hoover's plan, though it never mentioned the Marshall Plan, implicitly advocated an end to the aid program.[1]

Several weeks later, Harry Truman joined the debate. In his State of the Union address, the President stated unequivocally that he would dispatch four additional divisions of American troops to bolster NATO forces in Europe. By countering Hoover's neo-isolationist proposal with a plan that expanded America's international commitment, the President's address sparked a lengthy foreign policy debate that occupied the Senate's attention through the spring of 1951. When the "Great Debate" finally ended in early April, the impact that the transformation of Senate conservatism had on the policy agenda was plainly evident.[2]

That a new consensus in support of American internationalism had been forged both by sincere national security concerns and anticommunist paranoia was made evident in a speech Robert Taft delivered on the Senate floor in early 1951. Although the Ohio Republican had given grudging support to an international foreign policy in the past, the developing Cold War, together with his ambitions to capture the GOP presidential nomination in 1952, appeared to push him toward the center of the political spectrum on this issue. Taft announced to his colleagues that he was opposed to Truman's dispatch of troops presently, but refused to rule out the future stationing of additional U.S. forces in Europe. More importantly, however, Taft rejected Herbert Hoover's advice that the United States withdraw to the western hemispere. Instead, he fully accepted the extension of foreign aid to America's allies, and declared that he was prepared to go to war if Russia attacked any member of the NATO alliance. In the course of his speech, the Ohio Republican also argued that, although he did not object in principle to sending more U.S. troops to Europe, he believed that any such action required Congressional approval.[3]

By 1951, as Taft's speech indicates, the Great Depression, World War II, the development of nuclear weapons, and the unfolding Cold War had convinced a majority in the Senate that America was an integral part of the international community. The nation's interests, most understood, could not be secured by isolating itself from the world, and therefore, the central question facing American foreign policy was no longer whether the U.S. should participate in international affairs, but how it should participate. Although he sometimes disagreed with Robert Taft's position in the course of the Great Debate, Henry Cabot Lodge was quick to recognize the significance of his colleague's speech. Taft's speech indicated, he asserted in early January, that there was general agreement on the ends of American foreign policy and that all differences concerned only means. Thus, the point of controversy in the Great Debate centered on what role, if any, Congress should play in this matter.[4]

The obstructionists' position in the debate was defined on 8 January by Kenneth Wherry. His resolution proposed that no more troops could be sent to Europe without the express consent of Congress. Wherry denied that his measure was intended to bar the use of additional U.S. forces in Europe, and insisted that it was aimed only at preserving the same strict separation of powers between Congress and the President that obstructionists had sought on practically every foreign policy issue since World War II. Because the Nebraskan had been an outspoken critic of NATO in 1949, Administration forces were fearful that his resolution would spark lengthy debates that could undermine European confidence in America's commitment to the alliance.[5]

When President Truman fought back against the Wherry resolution, defiantly insisting at his weekly press conference on 11 January that, as commander-in-chief, he had a clear Constitutional right to dispatch U.S. troops anywhere in the world, the issue was transformed into a complex problem that also involved the prerogative of the Legislative Branch. Truman's statement provoked pointed criticism from a bipartisan group of senators that included most Republicans, as well as Democrats Walter George and Paul Douglas. To avoid a major constitutional debate, the White House gave its blessing to a new resolution, introduced on 23 January by Democrats Tom Connally and Richard Russell, that merely expressed Senate approval for the use of four more divisions in Europe without raising the question of Congress's role in the decision.[6]

As debate proceeded in the Senate, it became apparent that many of the new conservatives, including George Aiken, Ralph Flanders, Spessard Holland, Irving Ives, Henry Cabot Lodge, and H. Alexander Smith, were willing to support neither the Wherry resolution nor the Connally-Russell resolution. Two basic concerns informed their wariness. Most worried, for example, that if the President was free to commit troops throughout the world, there would truly be no limit to his control of foreign policy. Thus, Henry Cabot Lodge, together with William Knowland, advocated a cap on the number of American troops in Europe. Under their proposal, American troops would be committed to Europe on a strict ratio of one U.S. division to six European divisions until there were ten American divisions in the field. Democrat Spessard Holland was similarly concerned that the Connally-Russell resolution did not go far enough in protecting Congress's power. Noting in a weekly radio address to his Florida constituents that the international scene was so unstable that it was unwise to tie the President's hands, Holland nonetheless believed that it was desirable "to set up a definite pattern which will afford and require closer contact and more intimate consultation between Congress and the Chief Executive. Such a course should always assure a check against unsound Executive action, but will not prevent the President . . . from making promptly any vital strategic decisions . . . to safeguard the security of our nation."[7]

The new conservatives' position was also prominent during committee hearings on the Connally-Russell resolution. Before the resolution was reported out on 13 March by a joint Committee on Foreign Relations and Armed Services, two stipulations were attached reflecting the new conservatives' position. By identical 14–10 votes, a bipartisan coalition of new conservatives and obstructionists approved an amendment sponsored by H. Alexander Smith requiring the President to consult with both houses of Congress on all future troop commitments, as well as a Henry Cabot Lodge amendment stipulating that European nations be informed directly that they were expected to supply the bulk of the ground forces.[8]

Throughout the Senate debate, the new conservatives continued to shape the troops resolution to ensure that additional American forces would be sent to Europe, but that a role for Congress in such matters was also preserved. On 2 April, for instance, new conservatives joined with obstructionists to approve 49–43 a declaration proposed by John McClellan of Arkansas as a more precise substitute for the H. Alexander Smith stipulation. The McClellan declaration, which required the White House to obtain explicit Congressional approval to dispatch any ground troops in addition to the four divisions already planned, alienated some eastern Republican new conservatives, who feared it was too restrictive. But enough new conservatives from both parties, including Frear, George, Holland, Johnston, and Nixon continued to vote with the obstructionists to provide the margin of victory for a measure seen as upholding the constitutional role of Congress.[9] The following day, however, when obstructionists proposed three amendments aimed at giving Congress a veto power over the use of additional troops in Europe, the divisions among the new conservatives disappeared. On 3 April, for instance, when Ohio Republican John Bricker proposed to change the Connally-Russell resolution from a nonbinding, advisory measure into a joint resolution of Congress that would become law unless specifically vetoed by the President, most new conservatives joined with Administration forces to reject it. The same day a similar coalition of new conservatives and Administration backers rejected obstructionist amendments from Republican Karl Mundt that restrained the President from sending even the four planned divisions to Europe until Congress had given its express consent, and from Republican James Kem that prohibited the dispatch of any troops until the Joint Chiefs of Staff certified that U.S. air power was sufficient to protect the forces in western Europe. As their votes in early April indicated, then, while the new conservatives were unwilling to grant the President unilateral control over the nation's troops, they were determined to preserve the international direction of postwar American foreign policy.[10]

On 4 April the Great Debate came to an unceremonious conclusion when, after eighty-six days of debate, a coalition of Administration supporters and new conservatives formed one more time to adopt a modified version of the Connally-Russell resolution. In its final form, the resolution approved the President's decision to send more troops to Europe, but stipulated that the consent of Congress was necessary for any additional dispatches of American forces. Although the Truman Administration was left with a narrower troops-to-Europe resolution than it desired, the action helped to cement a change of historic proportions in America's foreign policy. The significance of the vote was clear to James Reston. Noting that only ten years earlier Congress had been thoroughly divided over the question of Lend-Lease aid to Britain and the need to build up the nation's armaments, the *New York Times* columnist found the unity of purpose in the 1951 debate remarkable. All major participants agreed, he observed, that it was in the nation's interest to defend far-flung overseas nations and to maintain a high level of defense spending.[11]

If most observers of the Great Debate were struck by the consensus it seemed to denote in Senate politics, closer analysis of it also yields clear evidence of the transformation in Senate conservatism. Throughout the debate the new conservatives demonstrated by their statements and their votes that they were less convinced than liberals that the state of world politics warranted the surrender of Congress's voice in the use of American troops. While twenty-three of the twenty-eight liberals gave high support to this dimension, only fifteen of the thirty new conservatives did so. At the same time, though they disagreed among themselves about the exact role Congress should play in this area, they were united by the conviction that some increase in presidential power was necessary to maintain national security in the midst of the Cold War. Where twenty-seven of the thirty new conservatives gave either medium or high support on this dimension, thirty of the thirty-seven obstructionists gave only low support.[12]

By 1951, in other words, the "Great Debate" revealed that the new conservatives occupied a distinct position on the American political spectrum that distinguished them from both liberals and obstructionists. The gulf separating them from the obstructionists was apparent in the comments John Bricker made defending his amendment to change the Connally-Russell resolution into a joint resolution of Congress. Warning that Congress was about to commit "legislative suicide," the Ohio Republican fumed that approval of the pending resolutions "would be tantamount to an admission that the President has the sole power to determine whether or not troops shall be sent, how many, and under what conditions. . . . If Congress grants this power," he warned, "It is but a short step to Executive direction and control of all phases of foreign policy, and, eventually, all phases of domestic policy. . . . The pending resolutions contain the seeds of dictatorship." To the obstructionists, then,

America's national security in 1951 was still chiefly influenced by events within, rather than outside of America's territorial borders. From their perspective, therefore, any measure like the Connally-Russell resolution that tacitly expanded the President's power invariably undermined the nation's safety.[13]

The new conservatives' concern for supporting American internationalism without surrendering Congress's voice in foreign affairs was again evident when the Senate considered the extension of Selective Service in the spring. At the urging of the armed forces, the Truman Administration requested in early 1951 that Congress lower the draft age from nineteen to eighteen and extend draftees' term of service from twenty-one to thirty months. These changes, which would increase the size of the armed forces and also create a pool of reserves that could be relied upon for a longer period of time, were necessary, the President argued, to ensure that the nation could fulfill its international obligations.[14]

The first major floor test of the draft bill came on 5 March when the Senate rejected an amendment offered by Wayne Morse that would have reduced the size of the armed forces by lowering the draft age only to eighteen and one-half years. The vote on the Morse amendment revealed that most of the new conservatives, including Aiken, Duff, Flanders, Frear, George, Hoey, Holland, Lodge, Maybank, Nixon, Robertson, Russell, Saltonstall, H. A. Smith, and Tobey, had joined with the Administration.[15] Two days later, however, many of the same new conservatives shifted their votes to the obstructionists to reaffirm Congress's control over the armed forces. Although Congress had voted less than seven months earlier to lift all troop ceilings until 1954, the tendency of the Korean War to expand Executive power caused many in the Senate to reassess that position. Thus, on 7 March when Wayne Morse proposed to cap the size of the armed forces at 3.5 million, the new conservatives shifted their votes to the obstructionists to defeat a substitute from Brien McMahon designed to forestall a vote on the Morse amendment. Moments later, many of the new conservatives rejoined Administration forces to approve a motion from Virginia's A. Willis Robertson raising the troop ceiling to 4 million. Then, the new conservatives swung back to the obstructionsts to attach the modified Morse amendment to the draft bill.[16]

Throughout the debate on the draft bill, the new conservatives had again attempted to balance the demands of America's postwar international role against conservatism's traditional emphasis on preserving liberty through a separation of power. By supporting efforts to reduce the draft age and lengthen inductees' term of service, the new conservatives demonstrated their willingness to provide the military force required to make America an effective force in international affairs. At the same time, though they disagreed with one another about the exact level at which the size of the armed forces should be capped, they were in general agreement that a Congressionally mandated ceiling was essential to reaffirm the Legislature's constitutional power over the armed forces.[17]

The new conservatives' concern with balancing the political imperatives of modern American life with traditional conservative values also underlay action on the extension of the Defense Production Act in June. The measure, adopted at the start of the Korean War, had broadly authorized the President to allocate and to ration scarce materials, and had given him standby authority to impose price and wage ceilings. Because that authority was scheduled to expire on 30 June 1951, the White House in late April requested a two-year extension of the act, and at the same time urged Congress to expand the President's economic powers in several important ways. Truman's request proposed that the Executive branch be authorized to impose ceilings on all farm products as soon as their prices touched the parity level prevailing at the start of each marketing season, thereby eliminating the need to recalculate ceiling prices throughout the season. Similarly, the President requested authority to grant subsidies to stimulate the production of nonfood items, and to impose controls on both residential and commercial rents. Arguing that the new powers would enhance government's efforts to check inflation, Truman insisted before a nationwide radio and television audience that ultimately extension of the Defense Production Act was vital to American security. Runaway inflation, the President warned, by damaging our economy, would make it far easier for the Soviet Union to achieve world domination.[18]

Most in the Senate were unconvinced by Truman's overblown rhetoric, and rather than grant even more power to the White House, new conservatives and obstructionists attacked the Administration's interpretation of the power conferred by the original act. After the Banking and Currency Committee turned back an effort to terminate all economic controls within one month, it reported a bill on 21 June extending the President's emergency powers for only eight months. More importantly, the committee's bill prohibited the Price Stabilizer from rolling back any prices to their prewar levels, and canceled all price rollbacks ordered earlier by the Administration. Despite the White House's warning that the ban on price rollbacks would add 6% to the cost of living, new conservatives and obstructionists, fearful that rollbacks would produce shortages and black markets as they had during World War II, defeated all efforts to repeal the ban.[19] On 27 June, for example, a bipartisan coalition of new conservatives and obstructionists including Aiken, Flanders, Frear, Hoey, Holland, Maybank, Nixon, Russell, Taft, Bricker, Bridges, Butler, Byrd, Kem, and Wherry formed to defeat an amendment offered by liberal Democrat Paul Douglas proposing to remove the ban on price rollbacks. The following day, a similar coalition rejected another Douglas amendment allowing price rollbacks of up to 10%. Finally, after more than sixteen hours of debate on 28 June, most new conservatives shifted their votes to the Administration to ensure approval of the modified bill, extending the Defense Production Act by a 71–10 margin.[20]

The votes cn extension of the Defense Production Act helps to explain why the new conservatism, fairly moribund in the last six months of 1950, was much more prominent in the affairs of the 82nd Congress. One year after the start of the Korean War, many of the Democratic new conservatives were no longer concerned with upholding every action of their commander-in-chief and instead had resumed the independent voting habits they had followed in the late 1940s. Political analyst Arthur Krock pointed out, for example, that on all of the key roll call votes on the extension bill, prominent Democrats including majority leader Ernest McFarland, party whip Lyndon Johnson, and Tom Connally had consistently voted against the Administration. While Krock recognized that some of their votes were to respond to the needs of home-state industries, he argued that many Democrats were upset with the lack of leadership displayed by the Administration on control of inflation. The anger of some within the Democratic party was manifest in the remarks Burnet Maybank made to Krock. Noting that Congress had approved the previous September stronger economic controls than requested by the White House, he complained that the Administration had made only a half-hearted effort to enforce them. Under these circumstances, Maybank indicated that few Democrats in the Senate felt any urgency to respond to the President's new requests.[21]

As Maybank's remarks also make clear, by mid-1951 many new conservatives were also determined to reaffirm the constitutional role of the Legislative branch in light of the war-driven escalation of Executive authority. Rather than continuing the President's emergency economic powers unchanged for two more years, the new conservatives voted to continue the Defense Production Act for only eight months, thereby ensuring that Congress's voice would soon be heard again on this issue. In addition, by voting to continue the President's emergency powers, but only after requests for additional powers had been eliminated, the new conservatives also indicated that, while they generally accepted the need for a mixture of public and private initiatives in the wartime economy, they wanted that mixing to go no further.

Foreign aid provided one final demonstration of the role of the new conservatives in the Legislative affairs of the 82nd Congress. By 1951, whatever bipartisanship that World War II had generated on foreign policy issues seemed to have evaporated entirely. Thus, a June request from the State Department for $8.5 billion in foreign aid for fiscal 1952 produced immediate controversy. Many in Congress objected to the size of the President's request. Democrat Walter George spoke for many in the Legislative branch when he pointed out in August that Marshall Plan recipients had by 1951 attained on average 144% of their prewar productivity and therefore should have largely achieved self-sufficiency. Given these sentiments, both houses of Congress lost little time in paring funds from the Administration's request. By mid-August the House had approved a foreign aid bill providing only $7.5 billion, and the Senate had begun debate on a bill raising $7.53 billion.[22]

As Senate consideration of the foreign aid bill proceeded, pressure mounted to reduce the funds still further. Most of the momentum for that effort was supplied by Democrat Tom Connally, who found himself on the horns of an especially delicate dilemma. The tall Texan, chairman of the Senate Foreign Relations Committee and normally a dependable supporter of the Administration's foreign policy, faced re-election in 1952. Many of his Texas constituents were, moreover, angry with the Truman Adminstration's foreign aid program, which they viewed as far too generous. Bowing to the partisan imperative, Connally announced on 25 August that he would support efforts to cut an additional $300 million from the bill. The following day, Republican Homer Ferguson increased the pressure by demanding that an additional $1 billion be slashed from the bill. Opposition to the bill thus united around an amendment introduced on 30 August by Republican Everett Dirksen and ten others, proposing an additional $500 million reduction in the funds reserved for economic assistance. Democratic liberals, on the other hand, argued that, given the great peril posed by communism, any reduction in aid inevitably endangered the freedom and lives of people throughout the world. Thus, led by Theodore Francis Green and Brien McMahon, liberals proposed an amendment on 28 August restoring the full $8.5 billion requested by the President.[23]

When the Senate began voting on the foreign aid bill, the new conservatives helped to strike a balance between the respective goals of the Administration and its opponents. Most new conservatives, for example, sided with the Administration to defeat the Dirksen amendment 41–31, but then switched to the obstructionists to help defeat the liberal Green-McMahon amendment by a vote of 56–17. Finally, before the foreign aid bill was overwhelmingly approved, two of the new conservatives who had voted against the first Dirksen amendment, Aiken and Maybank, shifted their support to the obstructionists to approve a new Dirksen amendment reducing funds for economic aid by $250 million.[24]

The debate on the foreign aid bill was thus symptomatic of the consensus that dominated American thinking on international affairs in the first session of the 82nd Congress. On all issues facing Congress in 1951, the new conservatives generally voted to uphold the basic principles of American internationalism. Whatever objections they raised, furthermore, were over the means by which policies were to be implemented, rather than with their ends. Thus, the new conservatives acceded to the Administration's desire to use additional troops to bolster the nation's commitment to NATO, but insisted that any additional use of troops required the consent of Congress. Similarly, they supported the White House's requests to lower the draft age, to extend emergency economic powers, and to continue the foreign aid program, but only after provisions for preserving Congress's role in each issue had been approved. Convinced by 1951 that the security and economic well-being of the nation were inextricably linked to the international community, and that as a consequence, some increase in Executive authority was unavoidable, the new conservatives worked only to ensure that the new needs of the nation did not completely circumvent Congress's constitutional role in foreign affairs.

II

The approach of the fall presidential elections strongly influenced legislative affairs in the second session of the 82nd Congress. Although the Senate finally ratified peace treaties with Japan and West Germany in March, seven years after hostilities had ended, and approved a bill in May giving the states sole title to offshore oil, debates tended to be curt as both houses rushed toward early adjournment before the national nominating conventions in July. The revelation in late 1951 of an influence-peddling scandal involving the President's trusted aide, Major General Harry Vaughan, plunged Harry Truman's popularity to its lowest level and largely eliminated the remaining political influence of the lame-duck President. As a result of these domestic political pressures, generally only the most pressing legislation was considered in 1952. This meant, in turn, because of the continuing irresolution of the Korean War, that foreign policy again occupied the attention of the second session of the 82nd Congress. But one issue of domestic policy thrust on the Senate in the spring, Truman's seizure of American steel mills, offered firm proof that however much the thinking of the new conservatives had been transformed, they were still fundamentally conservatives who cherished the free enterprise system and individual liberty.

Demands for higher wages made by America's steel workers produced a contentious debate on domestic policy in the spring. Wage disputes had been a continuing issue in postwar labor relations, but the combination of war-driven inflation and the wage restraints imposed by the Truman Administration exacerbated the problem in early 1952. The issue came to a head in April when steel workers called a strike following management's rejection of a recommendation from the Wage Mediation Board for higher wages. To prevent a work stoppage in an industry it deemed essential to national defense, the Truman Administration did not invoke Taft-Hartley, because it would allow the steel mills to shut down while a fact-finding board made a preliminary study. Instead, the President seized the steel mills one minute before the strike deadline.[25]

In spite of the Administration's claim that it was an issue of national security, the steel seizure provoked sharp debate in the Senate. Many liberal Democrats defended the President's action as necessary and appropriate. But most new conservatives joined with obstructionists in denouncing it as an action that endangered both the free enterprise system and the Constitutional separation of powers. Clyde Hoey, for example, a frequent supporter of the Truman Administration's expansion of federal power since 1945, refused to back the steel seizure. "The process of taking private property away from its owners by an executive order," he fumed, "becomes at once a dangerous policy for any free people and is a dire threat to the very basic principles of our liberty." Even those new conservatives who out of party loyalty or personal political ambition stood behind the Administration's action were clearly upset with the President's methods. Democrat Richard Russell of Georgia, an aspirant for the 1952 Democratic presidential nomination, denied that the President harbored any dictatorial motives. "Nevertheless," he admitted, "his action in relying on inherent powers . . . does furnish a blue-print to any future President who might take the position that the end justifies the means, and follow a course of action which could result in a dictatorship."[26]

Because nearly all of the Senate's new conservatives disagreed with the Administration on this issue, their votes, combined with those of the obstructionists, were effectively able to thwart the steel seizure. On 21 April, for instance, a bipartisan group of new conservatives, including Aiken, Hoey, Holland, Lodge, Maybank, Robertson, H. A. Smith, and Tobey, joined with obstructionists to approve 44 to 31 an amendment to a supplemental appropriations bill barring the use of any of the bill's funds to carry out the steel seizure order. The amendment was adopted, moreover, despite a direct appeal from the President, who claimed that the Senate's action threatened to paralyze the government in a time of emergency.[27]

When the President requested new seizure powers following the Supreme Court's 2 June ruling that his earlier order was unconstitutional, the new conservatives again played a crucial role in shaping the outcome. Only several hours after Truman requested the legislation on 10 June, the new conservatives voted first with the Administration to defeat what many regarded as an antilabor amendment proposed by South Carolina's Burnet Maybank, permitting government seizure of struck industries only after a 120-day cooling off period. Shortly thereafter, when Administration forces, led by Oklahoma's Mike Monroney, countered with an amendment allowing government seizure of struck industries after only seven days' notice, the new conservatives shifted their support back to the obstructionists to defeat it by a 52–28 margin.[28] Finally, a similar coalition of new conservatives and obstructionists held firm to ensure adoption of a Harry Byrd amendment requesting that the Taft-Hartley Act be invoked to solve the steel strike.[29]

Rarely had the Truman Administration suffered so thorough a defeat as it was dealt on the steel seizure case. Indeed, such complete Congressional rebellion was reminiscent of the waning days of Franklin Roosevelt's presidency. Several factors appeared to explain the new conservatives' behavior on the steel seizure case. Certainly, their attitudes were to a degree influenced by the partisan politics of an election year. Sensing an opportunity to embarrass the President and the Democratic party, most Republicans, regardless of their philosophical persuasion, voted consistently against the Administration's desire to seize the steel industry. The generally low esteem in which Harry Truman was held in 1952 was a second factor that made it easy for Democratic new conservatives to defy the Chief Executive. While Executive-Congressional relations had never been good during the Truman years, the fact that the President was a lame duck in 1952 tended to erode what little political clout he retained. William S. White of *The New York Times* observed in June, following the Senate's flat rejection of all steel seizure legislation, that Truman, though he enjoyed much greater personal popularity in Congress than Franklin Roosevelt, was able to instill less than one tenth of the political fear his predecessor had evoked.[30] But perhaps most importantly, the unwillingness of new conservatives to accede to the Administration's wishes was a reflection of their unique political philosophy that put careful limits on the expansion of the positive state.

If the controversy over the steel seizure revealed the boundaries dividing the new conservatism from liberalism, debates over foreign aid and extension of the Defense Production Act in 1952 again emphasized the distance separating the new conservatism from obstructionism. Indeed, the debates presented a near replay of those on each issue in 1951. When President Truman requested $7.9 billion in foreign aid in March, for instance, obstructionists immediately attacked the bill. Their concerns were typified in the remarks of Republican Styles Bridges who claimed that, in light of the already galloping inflation brought on by enormous federal expenditures, Congress would be in no hurry to enact new spending measures. Joined by Tom Connally, whose rightward tilt on the issue in the previous session was accelerated by the press of election-year politics, obstructionists like Bridges mounted a steady campaign from the committee hearings on the bill to floor debate to slash funds for foreign aid.[31]

On 28 April Connally and the obstructionists on the Foreign Relations Committee succeeded in paring $1 billion from the bill when they were joined by the new conservative members, Walter George, H. Alexander Smith, Charles Tobey, and Guy Gillette. Thereafter, however, the new conservatives voted consistently with Administration forces to resist further reductions in foreign aid.[32] Although the goal of the obstructionists in the foreign aid battle had been to come as close as possible to Tom Connally's goal of making severe reductions in all appropriations for foreign policy, the new conservatives, apparently convinced that a strong international presence was essential to postwar American national security, helped to preserve most of the White House's request.[33]

Action on extension of the Defense Production Act, scheduled to expire on 30 June, similarly revealed the ideological differences dividing the new conservatives and the obstructionists. Although the President had wrung an eight-month extension of the bill from a skeptical Congress in the previous session, few on Capitol Hill believed that his February request for two additional years of controls would be respected. Indeed, by 1952, as the air of crisis faded and the economy adjusted to wartime production, most congressmen believed that two more years of the Defense Production Act were neither necessary nor wise. Thus, the bill that emerged from the Banking and Currency Committee in May proposed to continue the economic controls a mere eight months past their expiration date. Even this bare-bones approach did not satisfy obstructionists, who charged that the broad regulatory powers of the act were the very antithesis of free enterprise. In a March radio address, for example, Nebraska Republican Hugh Butler decried the expansion of government power that had taken place during the Truman years. "It doesn't matter what names may be given to their programs by the Fair Dealers," he complained. "So long as they are just like the Socialist programs of other countries, we ought to call them Socialism."[34]

Obstructionists like Butler, therefore, coalesced around an amendment offered by Illinois's Everett Dirksen on 29 May to end all economic controls on 30 June. Most of the new conservatives, however, including Aiken, Frear, George, Hoey, Holland, Ives, Johnston, Maybank, Nixon, Robertson, Saltonstall, H. A. Smith, and Tobey, sided with the Administration to defeat the Dirksen amendment. Similarly, before adjourning on 4 June, the new conservatives again joined with the Administration to defeat a Homer Capehart amendment lifting all price and wage controls until either the consumer price index rose by three points or Congress declared the official end of the war.[35]

The bill extending the Defense Production Act, approved by the Senate on 12 June by a vote of 58–18, continued wage, price, and rent controls for eight additional months, while industrial regulations such as allocations, priorities, and production incentives were maintained for one more year. By voting to continue limited government regulation of the economy, then, the new conservatives again affirmed their philosophical differences with the obstructionists.

Political affairs in the 82nd Congress, concerned mainly with foreign policy matters because of the continuing war in Korea, did much to clarify the nature of the new conservatism at mid-century. Just as World War II had exacerbated the power struggle between the Legislative and Executive branches, so too did the "police action" in Korea heighten legislators' concern with the centralization of power in the White House. As a result, the new conservatives throughout the 82nd Congress repeatedly sought to draw narrower boundaries on the President's power to commit troops abroad or to regulate the wartime economy than liberals advocated. Similarly, by paring appropriations for foreign aid more extensively than liberals thought wise, the new conservatives reiterated their determination to preserve as much of the nation's traditional emphasis on individual liberty as was possible in the postwar era.

Yet throughout the foreign policy debates in the 82nd Congress, the new conservatives left no doubt that, whatever differences they had with liberals, they completely embraced the general principles inherent in postwar American internationalism. When he affirmed in June 1952 that there was no doubt the United States could only be secure through cooperation with the other noncommunist nations throughout the world, Richard Russell of Georgia undoubtedly spoke for most of the Senate's new conservatives.[36]

Russell's political views by 1952, like those of most other new conservatives in the Senate, reflected the impact of the Great Depression and World War II. Indeed, 63% of those who scaled as new conservatives on all policy dimensions represented coastal states. The cataclysms of the 1930s and 1940s served to convince these senators especially that, in both a strategic and an economic sense, the fate of their state and their nation was inextricably bound to the wider international community. As a result, the new conservatives were quick to reject all suggestions to restore a "Fortress America" foreign policy that Herbert Hoover advocated directly in the "Great Debate" or that was implied by the positions adopted by the obstructionists in many of the foreign policy debates of the 82nd Congress.

In a broader sense, the foreign policy debates of 1951 and 1952 point to a common thread that ran through the foreign and domestic policies of both the new conservatives and the obstructionists. As their votes and their rhetoric in the 82nd Congress revealed, the new conservatives were prepared to accept an increase in presidential power as a necessary by-product of the collective security arrangements they believed best safeguarded U.S. national interests in the modern world. In like fashion, the new conservatives' support for such programs as public housing, federal aid to education, and regulation of the economy also demonstrated by 1952 that they were willing to accept an increase in the power of government vis-a-vis the individual in domestic affairs, as a necessary adaptation to the interdependency of individuals in modern industrial America. They were in both cases, in other words, convinced that it was necessary to employ new means in order to preserve and promote the general welfare of the nation.

In contrast, the obstructionists in 1952 resisted the adjustments that had occurred in American political philosophy since 1933. In foreign affairs, obstructionists were generally opposed to any increase in presidential power, preferring instead to preserve the strict separation of power that had prevailed in the rural, agrarian republic. They continued, in other words, to work from a model of America that saw its national security threatened most severely by events occurring *within* U.S. territorial borders. Similarly, the obstructionists in 1952 still generally fought against any alteration in the traditional relationship between individuals and the state, believing instead that the fate of all individuals was influenced most strongly by their own decisions, rather than by external forces. Where the new conservatives saw the interdependency of individuals and nations as a hallmark of postwar life, the obstructionists continued to stress individual liberty and the sovereignty of all nations. As a result, the obstructionists saw no need to adjust their political philosophy, believing that, since both expanded government power, American internationalism and the positive state necessarily endangered the national welfare.

If the foreign policy controversy arising from the Korean War was one dominant influence in the 82nd Congress, partisan politics, culminating with the presidential election in 1952, was surely the other. As the first presidential election since 1928 where an incumbent did not seek re-election, the 1952 contest placed greater than usual stress on political affairs in the new Congress. Adding to that partisanship was the generally low public esteem in which the Truman Administration was held. The unresolved war in Asia, together with White House scandals, exposed the political vulnerability of Truman and the Democrats and thereby encouraged partisan attacks from Republicans.

The roll call analysis of votes in the 82nd Congress summarized in table 7–1 testifies to the partisanship that colored many of the debates. The analysis makes clear that, as in the previous Congresses, a rough consensus still held on the basic domestic and foreign policy agenda defined by the New Deal. Almost all senators who scaled as new conservatives could be counted on to add their medium to high support to the high support liberals generally provided on such policy dimensions as Social Welfare, Business Regulation, Foreign Policy, and even Extension of Federal Authority. But the National Defense dimension, which dealt with such issues as extension of Selective Service and troop ceilings, appeared to be a vehicle for partisan attacks on the Truman Administration. In the GOP, which used the "mess in Korea" as one of their prime argu-

TABLE 7-1

82nd CONGRESS

Name	Policy Dimensions	Score
	1 2 3 4 5 6 7 8 9 10 11	

HIGH SUPPORT

Name	Policy Dimensions	Score
Benton, D-CT	1 1 1 1 0 1 1 1 1 1 1	1.00
Green, D-RI	1 1 1 1 0 1 1 1 1 1 1	1.00
Humphrey, D-MN	1 1 1 1 1 1 1 1 1 1 1	1.00
Kilgore, D-WV	1 1 1 1 0 0 1 1 1 1 1	1.00
Lehman, D-NY	1 1 1 1 1 1 1 1 0 1 1	1.00
Magnuson, D-WA	1 1 1 1 1 1 1 1 0 1 1	1.00
Murray, D-MT	1 1 1 1 1 1 1 1 1 1 1	1.00
Hennings, D-MO	1 1 1 1 2 1 1 1 1 1 1	1.09
Hill, D-AL	1 1 1 1 2 1 1 1 1 1 1	1.09
O'Mahoney, D-WY	1 1 1 1 1 1 1 2 1 1 1	1.09
Sparkman, D-AL	1 1 1 1 2 1 1 1 1 1 1	1.09
Moody, D-MI	1 1 1 1 2 1 1 0 0 1 0	1.13
Anderson, D-NM	0 1 0 0 2 0 1 0 1 1 1	1.17
Neely, D-WV	1 2 1 1 2 1 1 1 1 1 1	1.18
Chavez, D-NM	3 1 1 1 0 1 2 1 0 1 1	1.20
Kerr, D-OK	3 1 1 0 0 1 1 1 1 1 1	1.20
Pastore, D-RI	2 1 1 1 2 1 1 0 1 1 1	1.20
Douglas, D-IL	1 1 2 1 1 1 1 1 1 1 3	1.27
Hunt, D-WY	2 1 1 1 2 2 1 1 0 1 1	1.30
Kefauver, D-TN	2 1 2 1 2 1 1 1 0 1 1	1.30
McMahon, D-CT	1 0 1 1 3 1 2 1 1 1 1	1.30
Clements, D-KY	2 1 1 2 3 1 1 1 1 1 1	1.36
Hayden, D-AZ	2 1 1 3 2 1 1 1 1 1 1	1.36
McFarland, D-AZ	2 1 1 3 2 1 1 1 1 1 1	1.36
Underwood, D-KY	2 2 1 1 2 1 2 1 1 1 1	1.36
Fulbright, D-AR	2 2 0 2 2 1 1 1 1 1 1	1.40
Monroney, D-OK	2 1 2 2 3 0 1 1 1 1 1	1.50
Morse, R-OR	1 2 0 1 1 1 3 2 1 2 1	1.50

Name	Policy Dimensions	Score
	1 2 3 4 5 6 7 8 9 10 11	

MEDIUM SUPPORT

Name	Policy Dimensions	Score
Gillette, D-IA	2 2 2 1 3 2 1 1 1 1 1	1.55
Johnson, D-TX	2 3 2 3 0 1 1 1 1 1 1	1.60
Long, D-LA	1 1 0 3 2 1 1 2 1 1 3	1.60
Maybank, D-SC	2 3 0 3 2 1 1 1 1 1 1	1.60
Connally, D-TX	3 1 2 3 3 1 1 1 1 1 1	1.64
Smathers, D-FL	2 3 2 3 2 1 1 1 1 1 1	1.64
Russell, D-GA	2 0 2 3 2 2 1 1 1 2 1	1.70
Holland, D-FL	2 3 2 3 2 1 2 1 1 1 1	1.73
Tobey, R-NH	0 2 2 1 1 2 2 0 2 2 0	1.75
Johnston, D-SC	3 2 2 3 2 1 2 0 1 1 1	1.80
McKellar, D-TN	3 1 2 3 3 0 1 2 1 1 1	1.80
Stennis, D-MS	2 3 2 3 2 1 0 2 1 1 1	1.80
Aiken, R-VT	2 2 2 1 1 2 2 2 2 2 2	1.82
Ellender, D-LA	3 3 1 3 2 1 1 1 3 1 1	1.82
Hoey, D-NC	3 3 2 3 2 2 1 1 1 1 1	1.82
Duff, R-PA	0 0 0 1 3 2 1 1 3 0 0	1.83
McClellan, D-AR	3 3 2 3 2 1 2 2 1 1 1	1.91
Langer, R-ND	1 0 2 0 0 1 3 3 3 0 1	2.00
Frear, D-DE	3 3 2 3 2 3 2 2 1 1 1	2.09
Ives, R-NY	3 2 3 1 1 2 2 1 3 2 3	2.09
Saltonstall, R-MA	3 3 2 1 1 3 1 1 3 2 3	2.09
Johnson, D-CO	3 2 2 3 2 0 3 2 1 2 1	2.10
George, D-GA	3 3 2 3 2 0 2 2 0 1 1	2.11
Eastland, D-MS	3 3 2 3 3 0 1 0 0 1 1	2.13
Robertson, D-VA	2 3 3 3 2 2 2 2 1 1 3	2.18
Smith, R-NJ	3 3 3 1 1 3 2 1 3 2 3	2.27
Flanders, R-VT	3 3 0 2 1 2 1 0 3 3 3	2.33
Smith, D-NC	3 3 2 3 2 2 2 0 2 2 0	2.33
Lodge, R-MA	3 3 3 1 3 3 1 1 3 2 3	2.36
Nixon, R-CA	3 3 2 3 1 2 2 2 3 2 3	2.36

LOW SUPPORT

Name	Policy Dimensions	Score
Carlson, R-KS	3 0 3 3 1 2 3 3 3 0 1	2.44
McCarran, D-NV	3 3 2 3 3 0 2 0 3 2 1	2.44

Name	Policy Dimensions	Score
	1 2 3 4 5 6 7 8 9 10 11	

LOW SUPPORT continued

Name	Policy Dimensions	Score
Wiley, R-WI	3 3 2 0 1 2 2 2 0 3 3 3	2.44
Hendrickson, R-NJ	3 3 3 1 1 3 3 2 3 2 3	2.45
Millikin, R-CO	3 3 3 2 1 2 3 3 3 3 1	2.45
O'Conor, D-MD	3 3 3 3 2 2 2 2 0 2 3	2.50
Thye, R-MN	3 3 3 2 1 2 2 0 3 3 3	2.50
Young, R-ND	3 0 3 3 2 1 3 3 3 3 1	2.50
Cordon, R-OR	3 3 2 3 1 1 3 3 3 3 3	2.55
Dworshak, R-ID	3 3 3 3 1 3 3 3 1 3 2	2.55
Ferguson, R-MI	3 3 3 3 1 3 3 2 1 3 3	2.55
Knowland, R-CA	3 3 3 3 2 1 2 2 3 3 3	2.55
Smith, R-ME	3 3 3 3 1 3 2 3 3 2 2	2.55
Watkins, R-UT	3 3 3 3 1 3 3 3 3 2 1	2.55
Byrd, D-VA	3 3 3 3 2 2 3 0 2 2 3	2.60
Bennett, R-UT	3 3 3 3 1 3 3 3 3 3 1	2.64
Schoeppel, R-KS	3 3 3 3 1 3 3 3 3 3 1	2.64
Ecton, R-MT	3 0 3 3 2 3 3 3 3 0 1	2.67
McCarthy, R-WI	3 3 2 3 1 3 3 0 3 3 3	2.70
Dirksen, R-IL	3 3 2 3 1 3 3 3 3 3 3	2.73
Williams, R-DE	3 3 3 3 1 3 3 3 3 2 3	2.73
Martin, R-PA	3 3 0 3 1 3 3 3 3 3 0	2.78
Cain, R-WA	3 3 3 3 1 0 3 3 3 3 3	2.80
Case, R-SD	2 3 3 3 2 3 3 3 3 3 0	2.80
Jenner, R-IN	3 3 2 3 3 0 3 3 3 3 2	2.80
Bricker, R-OH	3 3 3 3 1 3 3 3 3 3 3	2.82
Butler, R-MD	3 3 3 3 1 3 3 3 3 3 3	2.82
Taft, R-OH	3 3 3 3 1 3 3 3 3 3 3	2.82
Bridges, R-NH	0 3 2 3 0 3 3 3 3 3 0	2.88
Welker, R-ID	3 3 3 3 0 3 0 3 3 3 2	2.89
Kem, R-MO	3 3 2 3 0 3 3 3 3 3 3	2.90
Capehart, R-IN	3 3 3 3 3 3 3 3 3 3 2	2.91
Mundt, R-SD	3 3 3 3 3 3 3 3 3 3 2	2.91
Brewster, R-ME	3 3 3 3 0 3 3 - 3 3 3	3.00
Butler, R-NE	3 3 3 3 0 3 3 3 3 3 3	3.00
Hickenlooper, R-IA	3 3 3 3 0 3 3 3 3 3 3	3.00
Malone, R-NV	3 0 3 0 3 3 3 3 3 3 3	3.00

Policy Dimension Key:

    0   denotes that a senator did not scale on the dimension

    1.   Fiscal Policy

    2.   Labor

    3.   Economy in Government Spending

    4.   Displaced Persons

    5.   Extension of Federal Authority

    6.   Social Welfare

    7.   Extension of Executive Power

    8.   Foreign Aid

    9.   National Defense

    10. Business Regulation

    11. Public Power

82ND CONGRESS (N=95)

HIGH SUPPORT (N=28 or 29%)

    Democrats = 27 (96%)
    GOP   = 1 (4%)

MEDIUM SUPPORT (N=30 or 32%)

    Democrats = 20 (67%)
    GOP   = 10 (33%)

LOW SUPPORT (N=37 or 39%)

    Democrats = 3 (8%)
    GOP   = 34 (92%)

ments against the Democrats, only five party members (Morse, Aiken, Tobey, Dworshak, and Ferguson) regardless of their overall scale position, gave anything more than low suppport on National Defense issues. Conversely, only four Democrats (McCarran, Ellender, Byrd, and Willis Smith), regardless of their overall scale position, failed to give anything but high support.

The effect of partisanship on alignments in the 82nd Congress is also apparent in the broad divisions within the GOP. The party's repeated losses in presidential elections had, by 1952, convinced some party members of the need to modernize the party's philosophy. Nine of the ten Republicans who scaled as new conservatives in table 7–1, for example, represented coastal states and embraced a political philosophy then known as "modern Republicanism" or "dynamic conservatism" that helped elect Dwight Eisenhower in 1952. Indeed, prominent early supporters of Eisenhower who scaled as new conservatives included New Jersey's H. Alexander Smith, Pennsylvania's James Duff, Massachusetts's Henry Cabot Lodge, and California's Richard Nixon.

Most of the thirty-four Republicans who scaled as obstructionists in table 7–1, on the other hand, were drawn from interior states. They embraced a political philosophy whose skepticism of the positive state and American internationalism placed them closer to the orbit traveled by Ohio's Robert Taft, the other major contender for the GOP nomination.

Notwithstanding the influence partisan politics exerted on voting alignments in the 82nd Congress, tables 7–3 and 7–4 offer strong evidence of the ideological forces behind the transformation of Senate conservatism. That is, even when domestic and foreign policy alignments were separated, a consistent core of senators, comprising between 25% and 30% of the upper house and drawn mainly from coastal states, scaled in the medium support group. Although these new conservatives, as this study has maintained, generally refused to expand the positive state or American internationalism as far as liberals believed necessary, they simultaneously resisted most of the obstructionists' attempts at retrenchment. By 1952, in other words, the Senate had entered a era of consensus which, in turn, ensured that the political revolution inaugurated by Franklin Roosevelt in 1933 had been consolidated.

Table 7-2

Regional Divisions in Medium and Low Support Groups

MEDIUM SUPPORT (N=30)

Coastal (N=19 or 63%)

Maybank, D-SC	Smathers, D-FL	Russell, D-GA
Holland, D-FL	Tobey, R-NH	Johnston, D-SC
Aiken, R-VT	Hoey, D-NC	Duff, R-PA
Frear, D-DE	Ives, R-NY	George, D-GA
Saltonstall, R-MA	Robertson, D-VA	Smith, R-NJ
Flanders, R-VT	Smith, D-NC	Lodge, R-MA
Nixon, R-CA		

Interior (N=11 or 37%)

Gillette, D-IA	Johnson, D-TX	Long, D-LA
Connally, D-TX	McKellar, D-TN	Stennis, D-MS
Ellender, D-LA	McClellan, D-AR	Langer, R-ND
Johnson, D-CO	Eastland, D-MS	

LOW SUPPORT (N=37)

Coastal (N=12 or 32%)

Hendrickson, R-NJ	O'Conor, D-MD	Cordon, R-OR
Knowland, R-CA	Smith, R-ME	Byrd, D-VA
Williams, R-DE	Martin, R-PA	Cain, R-WA
Butler, R-MD	Bridges, R-NH	Brewster, R-ME

Interior (N=25 or 68%)

Carlson, R-KS	McCarran, D-NV	Wiley, R-WI
Millikin, R-CO	Thye, R-MN	Young, R-ND
Dworshak, R-ID	Ferguson, R-MI	Watkins, R-UT
Bennett, R-UT	Schoeppel, R-KS	Ecton, R-MT
McCarthy, R-WI	Dirksen, R-IL	Case, R-SD
Jenner, R-IN	Bricker, R-OH	Taft, R-OH
Welker, R-ID	Kem, R-MO	Capehart, R-IN
Mundt, R-SD	Butler, R-NE	Malone, R-NV
Hickenlooper, R-IN		

TABLE 7-3

82nd CONGRESS - FOREIGN POLICY DIMENSIONS

HIGH SUPPORT

Benton, D-CT	1.00	Kerr, D-OK	1.00
Green, D-RI	1.00	Pastore, D-RI	1.00
Humphrey, D-MN	1.00	Douglas, D-IL	1.00
Kilgore, D-WV	1.00	Hunt, D-WY	1.00
Lehman, D-NY	1.00	Kefauver, D-TN	1.00
Magnuson, D-WA	1.00	Underwood, D-KY	1.00
Murray, D-MT	1.00	Gillette, D-IA	1.00
Hennings, D-MO	1.00	McMahon, D-CT	1.00
Hill, D-AL	1.00	Clements, D-KY	1.34
Sparkman, D-AL	1.00	Fulbright, D-AR	1.34
Moody, D-MI	1.00	Morse, R-OR	1.34
Anderson, D-NV	1.00	O'Mahoney, D-WY	1.34
Neely, D-WV	1.00	Tobey, R-NH	1.50
Chavez, D-NM	1.00		

N = 27; D = 25; R = 2

MEDIUM SUPPORT

Hayden, D-AZ	1.67	Lodge, R-MA	1.67
McFarland, D-AZ	1.67	Long, D-LA	2.00
Johnson, D-TX	1.67	Johnston, D-SC	2.00
Maybank, D-SC	1.67	McKellar, D-TN	2.00
Connally, D-TX	1.67	Stennis, D-MS	2.00
Smathers, D-FL	1.67	McClellan, D-AR	2.00
Russell, D-GA	1.67	Langer, R-ND	2.00
Holland, D-SC	1.67	Frear, D-DE	2.00
Aiken, R-VT	1.67	Johnson, D-CO	2.00
Hoey, D-NC	1.67	Robertson, D-VA	2.00
Duff, R-PA	1.67	Hendrickson, R-NJ	2.00
Ives, R-NY	1.67	Ferguson, R-MI	2.00
Saltonstall, R-MA	1.67	Ellender, D-LA	2.33
Smith, R-NJ	1.67		

N = 27; D = 18; R = 9
Coastal = 15 (56%); Interior = (44%)

TABLE 7-3

82nd CONGRESS - FOREIGN POLICY DIMENSIONS

LOW SUPPORT

Dworshak, R-ID	2.34	Ecton, R-MT	3.00
George, D-GA	2.50	McCarthy, R-WI	3.00
Flanders, R-VT	2.50	Dirksen, R-IL	3.00
Smith, D-NC	2.50	Williams, R-DE	3.00
Thye, R-MN	2.50	Martin, R-PA	3.00
O'Conor, D-MD	2.50	Cain, R-WA	3.00
Byrd, D-VA	2.50	Case, R-SD	3.00
Nixon, R-CA	2.67	Jenner, R-IN	3.00
Millikin, R-CO	2.67	Bricker, R-OH	3.00
Knowland, R-CA	2.67	Butler, R-NE	3.00
Eastland, D-MS	3.00	Taft, R-OH	3.00
Carlson, R-KS	3.00	Bridges, R-NH	3.00
McCarran, D-NV	3.00	Welker, R-ID	3.00
Wiley, R-WI	3.00	Kem, R-MO	3.00
Young, R-ND	3.00	Capehart, R-IN	3.00
Cordon, R-OR	3.00	Mundt, R-SD	3.00
Smith, R-ME	3.00	Brewster, R-ME	3.00
Watkins, R-UT	3.00	Butler, R-NE	3.00
Bennett, R-UT	3.00	Hickenlooper, R-IA	3.00
Schoeppel, R-KS	3.00	Malone, R-NV	3.00

N = 40; D = 6; R = 34
Coastal = 15 (37%); Interior = 25 (63%)

TABLE 7-4

82nd CONGRESS - DOMESTIC POLICY DIMENSIONS

HIGH SUPPORT

Benton, D-CT	1.00	Hunt, D-WY	1.38
Green, D-RI	1.00	Douglas, D-IL	1.38
Humphrey, D-MN	1.00	Clements, D-KY	1.38
Kilgore, D-WV	1.00	McMahon, D-CT	1.43
Lehman, D-NY	1.00	Fulbright, D-AR	1.43
Magnuson, D-WA	1.00	Long, D-LA	1.43
Murray, D-MT	1.00	Chavez, D-NM	1.43
O'Mahoney, D-WY	1.00	Underwood, D-KY	1.50
Hennings, D-MO	1.13	Monroney, D-OK	1.57
Hill, D-AL	1.13	Morse, R-OR	1.57
Sparkman, D-AL	1.13	Johnson, D-TX	1.57
Moody, D-MI	1.14	Maybank, D-SC	1.57
Anderson, D-NM	1.20	Langer, R-ND	1.60
Neely, D-WV	1.25	Connally, D-TX	1.63
Pastore, D-RI	1.25	Smathers, D-FL	1.63
Hayden, D-AZ	1.25	Ellender, D-LA	1.63
McFarland, D-AZ	1.25		
Kerr, D-OK	1.29		
Kefauver, D-TN	1.38		

N = 35; D = 33; R = 2

MEDIUM SUPPORT

Russell, D-GA	1.71	Eastland, D-MS	2.00
McKellar, D-TN	1.71	Frear, D-DE	2.13
Stennis, D-MS	1.71	Johnson, D-CO	2.14
Gillette, D-IA	1.75	Carlson, R-KS	2.17
Holland, D-FL	1.75	Ives, R-NY	2.25
Johnston, D-SC	1.75	Saltonstall, R-MA	2.25
Tobey, R-NH	1.83	Robertson, D-VA	2.25
Aiken, R-VT	1.88	Nixon, R-CA	2.25
Hoey, D-NC	1.88	Flanders, R-VT	2.29
McClellan, D-AR	1.88	Smith, D-NC	2.29
Duff, R-PA	2.00	McCarran, D-NV	2.29
George, D-GA	2.00	Young, R-ND	2.29

N = 24; D = 15, R = 9
Coastal = 15 (62%); Interior = 9 (38%)

TABLE 7-4

82nd CONGRESS - DOMESTIC POLICY DIMENSIONS

LOW SUPPORT

Wiley, R-WI	2.38	Williams, R-DE	2.63
Millikin, R-CO	2.38	Martin, R-PA	2.67
Cordon, R-OR	2.38	Cain, R-WA	2.71
Smith, R-ME	2.38	Case, R-SD	2.71
Watkins, R-UT	2.38	Jenner, R-IN	2.71
Smith, R-NJ	2.50	Ferguson, R-MI	2.75
O'Conor, D-MD	2.50	Bricker, R-OH	2.75
Thye, R-MN	2.50	Butler, R-MD	2.75
Knowland, R-CA	2.50	Taft, R-OH	2.75
Bennett, R-UT	2.50	Bridges, R-NH	2.80
Schoeppel, R-KS	2.50	Welker, R-ID	2.83
Ecton, R-UT	2.50	Kem, R-MO	2.86
Lodge, R-MA	2.63	Capehart, R-IN	2.88
Hendrickson, R-NJ	2.63	Mundt, R-SD	2.88
Dworshak, R-ID	2.63	Brewster, R-ME	3.00
Byrd, D-VA	2.63	Butler, R-NE	3.00
McCarthy, R-WI	2.63	Hickenlooper, R-IA	3.00
Dirksen, R-IL	2.63	Malone, R-NV	3.00

N = 36; D = 2; R = 34
Coastal = 14 (39%); Interior = 22 (61%)

8

The Two Conservatisms

IN 1952, WHEN DWIGHT EISENHOWER WAS ELECTED AS THE FIRST RE-
publican president in two decades, Senate conservatism, this study
has contended, had undergone a fundamental transformation. Fourteen years earlier, when FDR was midway through his second term
and the nation still grappled with the effects of the Great Depression, conservative opposition to the New Deal was defined largely
by the classic conservative coalition of southern Democrats and Republicans described by James T. Patterson and others. By 1952,
however, Senate conservatism was of two minds on the relative
merits of the positive state. Some conservatives, identified in this
study as "obstructionists," continued to resist adamantly most
expansions of state power as it affected both domestic affairs and
international relations. But others, labeled "new conservatives" in
this study, had generally made peace with the positive state and
with American internationalism. Though most of this new generation of conservatives did not want government's role to grow any
larger, neither were they willing to roll back government's function
to pre-1932 levels, as had often been the goal of conservatives in
the 1930s.

The conservative bloc in the upper house of the late 1930s was
fundamentally an obstructionist force in Senate politics. Composed
mainly of such coastal state Democrats as Harry Byrd, Josiah Bailey, Robert Reynolds, Peter Gerry, Carter Glass, and Royal Copeland, as well as most of the small band of Republicans who
remained after the 1936 elections, Senate conservatism opposed
Roosevelt's revolution out of a combination of sincere philosophical conviction and partisan calculation. When Democratic and Republican conservatives joined forces in the late 1930s they were
able to thwart the expansions of the positive state. But because
Democrats were the main force behind Senate conservatism in this
era, the considerable political clout FDR was still able to wield, especially in election years, was often able to deflect right-wing ef-

forts. Senate conservatism in the late 1930s was, then, essentially an opportunistic and negative force. By throwing occasional obstacles in front of FDR's policy initiatives, it sought to derail the New Deal and thereby restore the conditions that had prevailed prior to 1933.

The other group that opposed the New Deal in the late 1930s, those senators who scaled in the medium support group, was a disparate group with largely unfocused goals. Many of the Democrats who scaled in the group, such as George Radcliffe, James Byrnes, and Pat Harrison were senators who had given strong support to Franklin Roosevelt in the early 1930s. But as the sense of crisis gradually eased toward the end of the decade, these Democrats were often less willing to grant sweeping powers to Washington and/or were more attentive to home-state political needs than they had been previously. The Republican contingent in the medium support group of the late 1930s, including Lynn Frazier, Arthur Capper, and Gerald P. Nye, was drawn predominantly from the last vestiges of midwestern Republican Progressivism. Their moderate support for the domestic initiatives of the New Deal stemmed more from a desire to ameliorate human suffering during the Depression than from an ideological commitment to the positive state. As such, convenience, not conviction, was usually the glue that held together the medium support group of the late 1930s.

The impact of the greatest economic crisis the nation had experienced, along with the recovery spurred by FDR's reforms, this study has argued, initiated the transformation of Senate conservatism. Because the Great Depression convinced many that economic hardship could no longer be attributed to individual failings and that business cycles were not always self-regulating, some conservatives gradually concluded that the rural, agrarian values of limited government and unfettered individualism were no longer able to explain the workings of a modern industrial state. This lesson was underscored strongly by World War II. Not only did that conflict emphasize powerfully the common fate all Americans faced, but through the enormous expansion it required in the role of the federal government, World War II also helped to convince many that government in the modern era could be used for positive, even beneficial purposes. For these reasons, then, this study contends that gradually throughout the 1940s some conservatives modernized their political philosophy to embrace the basic outlines of both the New Deal/Fair Deal domestic agenda and American internationalism.

By 1952 two distinct conservatisms were arrayed against the liberalism of the New Deal and Fair Deal. In that year, to be sure, a small group of obstructionist conservatives continued to offer unrelenting opposition to the positive state and remained deeply suspicious about American internationalism. But in one important sense, the obstructionist conservatives of 1952 were different than their counterparts of 1938. Whereas obstructionist conservatism of the late 1930s and early 1940s drew members from both political parties, that of the late 1940s and early 1950s was almost entirely Republican. The almost complete disappearance of Democrats from the obstructionist group of conservatives by the late 1940s suggest that those senators from Roosevelt's party who had formed the core of the conservative coalition a decade earlier had indeed been replaced by a new, more moderate generation of Democratic conservatives.

That the obstructionist conservatives of the early 1950s were almost exclusively Republicans also indicates that partisan politics continued to play an important role in explaining the unyielding opposition to the positive state. Yet given that a majority of those Republicans consistently was drawn from interior states, it seems reasonable to conclude that partisanship was not the only factor behind obstructionist conservatism. Rather, as this study has maintained, many of the obstructionists were unreconstructed conservatives who remained committed largely to the values of the rural, agrarian past.

The other group that contended with New Deal/Fair Deal liberalism in Senate affairs by 1952 largely constituted a new generation of conservatives. Elected mainly after 1938, these new conservatives, including Democrats Clyde Hoey, Spessard Holland, Burnet Maybank, and Olin Johnston, as well as Republicans Charles Tobey, George Aiken, Irving Ives, Ralph Flanders, H. Alexander Smith, and Leverett Saltonstall had modernized their political views in response to the great upheavals of the 1930s and 1940s. That these new conservatives were fundamentally different than those senators who had scaled in the medium support group in the late 1930s is suggested by a number of factors. The new conservatives of the late 1940s and early 1950s, for example, were drawn in roughly equal numbers from each of the political parties. In contrast to the middle support groups of the late 1930s, whose membership came predominantly from interior states, moreover, the new conservatives of the late 1940s were drawn mainly from coastal states composed of the New England, the Middle Atlantic, the South Atlantic, and the Pacific regions. Because the industrial economies, urban centers, and/or geographical location emphasized the interdependency of both individuals and nations in the mid–twentieth century, this study has contended that the new conservatives had generally come to terms with the positive state and American internationalism. Although partisan political calculations cannot be dismissed as a factor which led to the new conservatives' accommodation, the complete geographic reorientation of the locus of moderation within the medium support group and their tendency to shift their votes between liberals and obstructionists indicates that ideological conviction also defined their politics. After 1945 the new conservatives increasingly used their votes both to protect the advances they believed essential to promote the general welfare of the modern industrial state and to prevent government power or America's international commitments from growing so large as to overwhelm totally individual liberty and the free enterprise system. The new conservatives of the late 1940s, in other words, were thoroughly rooted in the present. Unlike their counterparts of the late 1930s whose political objectives often looked back wistfully to the days of Theodore Roosevelt and Woodrow Wilson, or to the even more distant past of William McKinley and Grover Cleveland, the new conservatives of the late 1940s measured their politics against the standards defined by Franklin Roosevelt and Harry Truman, and anticipated the "dynamic conservatism" of Dwight Eisenhower.

In a broader sense, the transformation of Senate conservatism between 1938 and 1952 appears to be part of the sweeping changes unleashed by the rise of big business and industry in the late nineteenth and early twentieth centuries. The transformation of American political theory that began with the Progressives' efforts to use the power of government to ameliorate some of the problems of industrial capitalism was, perhaps, completed when the new conservatives in the 1940s embraced the general objectives of the New Deal welfare state and of American internationalism. That is, if the Progressives by supporting such reforms as antitrust laws, minimum-wage laws, and even municipal zoning ordinances were among the first groups in American politics to sense that the rise of industrial capitalism had rendered meaningless many of the ideas and institutions upon which the nation had relied to order its existence, the new conservatives of the 1940s, by supporting such measures as federal aid to education, public housing, and other social welfare measures demonstrated that they shared the same fundamental vision of modern America.

The new conservatives' support for American internationalism in the 1940s underscores the accommodation that had occurred in their politics. Though generally less supportive than liberals were of an active U.S. role in the unfolding Cold War, the new conservatives supported such emblems of American internationalism as the United Nations, the International Monetary Fund, the Truman Doctrine, the Marshall Plan, and NATO as necessary components of modern industrial life. Just as the Great Depression had convinced them that America had become a nation of interdependent individuals and regions, so too did World War II demonstrate to them that in both a strategic and economic sense, American security in the mid–twentieth century was inextricably connected to world events. In both the domestic and international realm, then, the new conservatives understood that the changed conditions of life in the mid–twentieth century demanded new solutions, and so accepted that sometimes in the modern era, the security of individuals could only be preserved through the expansion of government power.

The transformation that occurred in Senate conservatism reveals how powerfully the Great Depression and World War II affected the American political system. Both cataclysms and the government's effort to resolve them appear to have nudged many conservatives closer to the center of the American political universe. Policies and ideas about the proper role for the Executive branch within the federal government, the role of the federal government in domestic life, or the role of America in world politics, all of which had been hotly contested in 1932, had become in most cases, the new status quo. That is, debate in American politics after 1945 turned increasingly on the extent to which the positive state should be expanded or the degree of America's international commitments, rather than on the principles themselves. Those individuals who did not adjust their political philosophy to account for this paradigm shift, such as the Senate's obstructionists, were generally regarded as hidebound conservatives by the end of World War II. Indeed, as the statistical analysis in this study has shown, western Progressive senators, who in the late 1930s still accounted for a significant component of the moderate, medium support category, had generally by the mid-1940s shifted into the obstructionist, low support category, or had disappeared entirely from the upper house.[1]

If the transformation of Senate conservatism produced a bipartisan consensus in both domestic and foreign policy after 1945, as this study contends, it also suggests that liberals' fears that the conservative resurgence of the 1940s endangered the foundation of the New Deal were largely groundless. The votes of the new conservatives, when combined with those of liberals, were generally sufficient in the 1940s to ensure that the revolution initiated by FDR would not be reversed. Far from threatening the positive state, the conservative resurgence in the 1940s, by bringing more new conservatives to the upper house, helped consolidate the enduring form of the political revolution begun in 1932. The election of Dwight Eisenhower in 1952, then, did not initiate an era of moderate politics, but rather represented the culmination of a trend toward moderation that began in 1938.[2]

Finally, the findings of this study also suggest that American conservatism underwent a transformation similar to that which produced corporate liberalism in the left wing. In the late 1930s most Senate conservatives still assailed the statist assumptions inherent in both New Deal domestic and foreign policy, seeking to preserve the system of American federalism and strict separation of powers within the federal government that they believed had protected individual liberty prior to 1932. By 1945, the influence of the Great Depression and World War II, combined with pragmatic political considerations, had produced a new conservatism that embraced the positive state, however tentatively, as a means to round off the rough edges of industrial capitalism without endangering that economic system itself. After 1945 the votes of the new conservatives often combined with those of liberals to produce a generation of consensus politics that the historian Godfrey Hodgson has called the "postwar liberal consensus."[3]

A segment of the Senate's right wing, labeled "obstructionists" in this study, remained unreconstructed rebels in the modern America shaped by the industrial revolution. Throughout the 1940s, 1950s, and early 1960s, the obstructionists continued to question the philosophical underpinnings of the positive state. Though they were, in this era of consensus politics, little more than isolated voices crying out in the wilderness, the conservative resurgence that began in the late 1960s and that culminated with Ronald Reagan's 1980 election suggest that the role of the state in modern American political theory has not yet been completely resolved.

Notes

INTRODUCTION

1. James T. Patterson's classic work, *Congressional Conservatism During the New Deal* (Lexington, Ky., University of Kentucky Press, 1967), carefully detailed the formation of the coalition up to 1939. Other studies of the conservative coalition that all stressed the growth in the size and power of the conservative coalition after 1938 are V. O. Key, *Southern Politics in State and Nation* (New York, Alfred Knopf, 1949); Roland F. Young, *Congressional Politics in the Second World War* (New York, Columbia University Press, 1957); Mack C. Shelly II, *The Permanent Majority: The Conservative Coalition in the United States Congress* (University, Ala., University of Alabama Press, 1983); John Robert Moore, "The Conservative Coalition in the United States Senate," *Journal of Southern History* 33 (August 1967): 368–76; John F. Manley, "The Conservative Coalition in Congress," *American Behavioral Scientist* 17 (December 1973): 223–47; Joel P. Margolis, "The Conservative Coalition in the United States Senate, 1933–1968," (Ph.D. diss., University of Wisconsin, 1973). Historical surveys of postwar American politics that emphasize a conservative resurgence include William Leuchtenberg, *In the Shadow of FDR: From Harry Truman to Ronald Reagan* (Ithaca, Cornell University Press, 1983; Alonzo Hamby, *Liberalism and Its Challengers: From F.D.R. to Bush,* 2d ed. (New York, Oxford University Press, 1992); Herbert S. Parmet, *The Democrats: The Years After FDR* (New York, Macmillan Publishing Co., 1976); Eric Goldman, *The Crucial Decade and After: America 1945–1960* (New York, Vintage Books, 1960); Alonzo Hamby, *Beyond the New Deal: Harry S Truman and American Liberalism* (New York, Columbia University Press, 1974); Robert J. Donovan, *Conflict and Crisis: The Presidency of Harry S Truman* (New York, W. W. Norton Co., 1977); Samuel Lubell, *The Future of American Politics* (New York, Harper and Row, 1965); Cabell Phillips, *The Truman Presidency* (New York, Macmillan Publishing Co., 1963); and David L. Porter, *Congress and the Waning of the New Deal* (Port Washington, N.J., Kennikat Press, 1980).

2. In this study, coastal states are those comprised of the New England states (Conn., Mass., Maine, N.H., R.I., Vt.), the Middle Atlantic states (Del., Md., N.J., N.Y., Pa.), the South Atlantic states (Fla., Ga., N.C., S.C., Va., W.Va.), and the Pacific states (Calif., Oreg., Wash.).

Interior states are defined as the remaining twenty-eight: the East North Central (Ill., Ind., Mich., Ohio, Wis.), East South Central (Ala., Ky., Miss., Tenn.), West North Central (Iowa, Kans., Minn., Mo., N.D., Neb., S.D.), West South Central (Ark., La., Okla., Tex.), and Mountain (Ariz., Colo., Idaho, Mont., N.M., Nev., Utah, Wyo.).

3. These ideas are developed in Robert H. Weibe, *The Search for Order 1877–1920* (New York, 1967). On the ideas and values of pre-industrial America, see also Daniel T. Rodgers, *The Work Ethic in Industrial America 1850–1920* (Chi-

270

cago, 1974); John F. Kasson, *Amusing the Million: Coney Island at the Turn of the Century* (New York, 1978); Alan Trachtenberg, *The Incorporation of America: Culture & Society in the Gilded Age* (New York, 1982); and Sidney Fine, *Laissez Faire and the General-Welfare State: A Study of Conflict in American Thought, 1865–1901* 4th ed., (Ann Arbor, 1969).

4. The concept of thrift in pre-industrial America is developed most clearly by Kasson, *Coney Island.*

5. The changed values of the industrial age are discussed in Rodgers, *The Work Ethic;* Kasson, *Coney Island;* and Trachtenberg, *Incorporating America.*

6. William Appleman Williams in *The Tragedy of American Diplomacy* (New York, Dell Publishing Co., 1972) sketched out the general outlines of "corporate liberalism." More recent studies of it include R. Jeffrey Lustig, *Corporate Liberalism: The Origins of Modern American Political Theory, 1890–1920* (Berkeley, University of California Press, 1982); Stephen Skowronek, *Building a New American State: The Expansion of National Administrative Capacities, 1877–1920* (Cambridge, Cambridge University Press, 1982); Martin J. Sklar, *The Corporate Reconstruction of American Capitalism, 1890–1916: The Market, The Law, and Politics* (Cambridge, Cambridge University Press, 1988); Alan Brinkley, "The New Deal and the Idea of the State," in Steve Fraser and Gary Gerstle, eds. *The Rise and Fall of the New Deal Order, 1930–1980,* (Princeton, Princeton University Press, 1989); and Alan Brinkley, "The Problem of American Conservatism," *American Historical Review* 99 (April 1994): 409–29.

7. Patterson, *Congressional Conservatism,* viii.

8. Thomas H. and Doris D. Reed. "The Republican Opposition," *Survey Graphic* 29 (May 1940): 286. Vandenberg's comments are from Arthur H. Vandenberg, "The New Deal Must Be Salvaged," *American Mercury* 49 (January 1940): 2. The moderation of Vandenberg's conservatism is also emphasized by C. David Tompkins, *Senator Arthur H. Vandenberg: The Evolution of a Modern Republican, 1884–1945* (East Lansing, Michigan State University Press, 1971). Other studies whose data suggest a moderation in Senate conservatism in the 1940s are Susan Hartmann, *Truman and the 80th Congress* (Columbia, Mo., University of Missouri Press, 1971); David B. Truman, *The Congressional Party* (New York, John Wiley and Sons, 1959); and Allen Drury, *A Senate Journal* (New York, McGraw-Hill, 1963).

9. Ralph Flanders, "Some Things We Have Learned," speech delivered to the American Society of Mechanical Engineers, New York City, 4 December 1946, p. 6; copy in Box 133, Flanders Papers, George Arents Research Library, Syracuse University. Ives's comments are from "Lincoln Day Speech, 1950," 4, 5; copy in Box 40, Ives Papers, Division of Rare and Manuscripts Collections, Cornell University Library.

10. Aage Clausen, *How Congressmen Decide: A Policy Focus* (New York, St. Martin's Press, 1973), 12–20.

11. The theory behind Guttman scale analysis is discussed in Lee F. Anderson, et al., *Legislative Roll Call Analysis* (Evanston, Ill., Northwestern University Press, 1966). See also H. Douglas Price, "Are Southern Democrats Different? An Application of Scale Analysis to Senate Voting Patterns," in Nelson W. Polsby, et al., *Politics and Social Life* (Boston, Houghton Mifflin, 1963). In this study the Guttman scales for the 75th to 78th Congresses were adapted from James W. Hilty, "Voting Alignments in the United States Senate, 1933–1944," (Ph.D. diss., University of Missouri-Columbia, 1973).

CHAPTER 1. THE ORIGINS OF THE NEW CONSERVATISM

1. Studies which emphasize a conservative resurgence in the late 1930s include James T. Patterson, *Congressional Conservatism During the New Deal* (Lexington, Ky., University of Kentucky Press, 1967); V. O. Key, *Southern Politics in State and Nation* (New York, Alfred Knopf, 1949); Mack C. Shelly II, *The Permanent Majority: The Conservative Coalition in the United States Congress* (University, Ala., University of Alabama Press, 1983); Alonzo Hamby, *Liberalism and Its Challengers: From F.D.R. to Bush,* 2d ed. (New York, Oxford University Press, 1992); Alan Brinkley, *The End of Reform: New Deal Liberalism in Recession and War* (New York, Alfred A. Knopf, 1995); John Robert Moore, "The Conservative Coalition in the United States Senate," *Journal of Southern History* 33 (August 1967): 368–76; John F. Manley, "The Conservative Coalition in Congress," *American Behavioral Scientist* 17 (December 1973): 223–47; and Joel P. Margolis, "The Conservative Coalition in the United States Senate, 1933–1968," (Ph.D. diss., University of Wisconsin, 1973).

2. Radcliffe's comments are from p. 11 of a "Memorandum" dated 31 December 1946, Box 45, George L. Radcliffe Papers, Ms. 2280, Manuscripts Department, Maryland Historical Society, Baltimore, Maryland. Drew Gruenburg, "Inventory of the George L. Radcliffe Papers, Ms. 2280," provides a concise summary of Radcliffe's political career.

The description of Jimmy Byrnes is from Joseph Alsop and Robert Kintner, "Sly and Able: The Real Leader of the Senate, Jimmy Byrnes," *Saturday Evening Post,* 20 July 1940, 41. For Byrnes's disenchantment with the New Deal, see also David Robertson, *Sly and Able: A Political Biography of James F. Byrnes* (New York, W. W. Norton, 1994), 246–87; and Allan A. Michie and Frank Rhylick, *Dixie Demagogues* (New York, Macmillan, 1939), 75–84.

The comments of the *New York Times* on Democratic intra-party divisions are from *NYT,* 3 January 1938, 20.

3. The introduction of the reorganization bill is reported in "Senate Primes Its Guns for Reorganization Bill," *Newsweek,* 7 March 1938, 11.

4. Austin's comments are from "A Republic, If You Can Keep It So," Schenectady *Union Star,* 26 March 1938, 12; clipping in General Correspondence, Carton #2, File 29, Warren R. Austin Papers, Bailey-Howe Memorial Library, University of Vermont. The function of the controller general and the changes proposed by the Reorganization bill are discussed in Henry N. Dorris, "Control of Funds Issue in Congress," *NYT,* 20 March 1938, sec. 4, p. 6; and "Reorganization," *NYT,* 1 March 1938, 20.

5. The roll call vote on the Wheeler amendment is in *Congressional Record,* vol. 83, pt. 4, p. 3645; hereafter cited as *CR* 83:4:3645. Voting alignments on the Byrd amendment and on final passage of the Reorganization bill are from Richard M. Boeckel, "Record of the 75th Congress," *Editorial Research Reports,* 16 June 1938, 407–9.

6. Bailey's concerns were reported in *NYT,* 4 March 1938, 5. The charges made by William King are from *New York Herald Tribune* (hereafter cited as *NYHT*) 4 March 1938, 1. Dorthy Thompson's report is in "The Reorganization Bill," *Washington Evening Star,* 23 March 1938; clipping in Box 25, Austin Papers.

7. *NYHT,* 2 March 1938, 18. Gerry's remarks are in *NYT,* 27 January 1938, 1.

8. Harrison lost the contest by one vote and held FDR responsible for the de-

feat. On Harrison's career, see Martha H. Swain, *Pat Harrison: The New Deal Years* (Jackson, Miss., University Press of Mississippi, 1978).

9. For general summaries of Senate Action, see Roy G. and Gladys C. Blakey, "Revenue Act of 1938," *American Economic Review* 28 (September 1938): 447–58; and Boeckel, "Record of the 75th Congress," 353–58. Pat Harrison's comments are in *NYT,* 13 March 1938, 1.

10. For conference action, see Blakey, "Revenue Act of 1938," 449–54; Boeckel, "Record of 75th Congress, 353–58; and *NYT,* 23 April 1938, 1. Treadway's remarks are reported in *NYHT,* 14 April 1938, 1, 10.

11. The comments of Byrd and Vandenberg are from *NYT,* 15 April 1938, 1; for details of the bill see Boeckel, "Record of the 75th Congress," 364.

12. The minority report is cited in "GOP Initiative Reborn in Drive By 3 Congressmen," *Newsweek,* 23 May 1938, 7–8.

13. On the attempted purge of Gillette, see *NYT,* 2 June 1938, 4; and William E. Leuchtenberg, *Franklin D. Roosevelt and the New Deal* (New York, Harper and Row, 1963), 266–67. Burton Wheeler's idea to "earmark" funds was reported by the *NYT,* 25 April 1938, 2.

14. *NYT,* 2 June 1938, 1.

15. Only six Democrats, Burke, Byrd, Bailey, Copeland, Glass, and Gerry voted against the Administration. For voting alignments, see James T. Patterson, *Congressional Conservatism,* 240; and Boeckel, "Record of the 75th Congress," 408–9.

16. "Congress Adjourns," *New Republic,* 29 June 1938, 200.

17. For the moderation of GOP conservatism, see John W. Malsberger, "The Transformation of Republican Conservatism: The U.S. Senate, 1938–1952," *Congress and the Presidency* 14 (spring 1987): 17–31.

18. Leuchtenberg, *FDR and the New Deal,* 272.

19. The introduction of King's bill is reported in *Time,* 16 January 1939, 13. Barbour's comments are from *NYT,* 4 January 1939, 8.

20. The Jackson Day dinner is reported in the *NYT,* 8 January 1939, 1. For Congressional reaction to the WPA appropriation, see *NYT,* 6 January 1939, 1.

21. Sullivan, *NYHT,* 12 January 1939, 17. For House action on the relief bill, see "National Affairs: The Presidency," *Time,* 30 January 1939, 9.

22. For the vote, see *NYT,* 22 January 1939, 1. Although no record vote was taken in the subcommittee to reject restoration of the $150 million, the *New York Times* reported that the divisions were as follows: voting for the full $875 million—McKellar, Hayden, Overton (Democrats); voting against it—Glass, Byrnes, Tydings, Russell, Adams (Democrats), and Hale, Nye, Townsend (Republicans). See *NYT,* 21 January 1939, 1.

23. Adams's charges are reported in "Garner Victory," *Newsweek,* 6 February 1939; 15. For Byrnes's comments, see *NYT,* 25 January 1939, 1, 11.

24. Johnson to Hiram Johnson Jr., 29 January 1939, quoted in David L. Porter, *Congress and the Waning of the New Deal* (Port Washington, N.Y., Kennikat Press, 1980), 75. For the vote on the McKellar amendment, see *NYT,* 28 January 1939, 1, 2; "National Affairs: The Congress," *Time* 6 February 1939, 8; and Richard M. Boeckel, "Record of the 76th Congress (First Session)," *Editorial Research Reports* 2 (1939): 135–40.

25. Passage of the Logan-Walter bill is reported in *Time,* 14 August 1939, 13. For final approval of the 1939 Spend-Lend bill, see *NYT,* 1 August 1939, 1, 10. For details on the battle over monetary powers, see *Time,* 10 July 1939, 11–12; and Kenneth G. Crawford, "Happy Fiscal New Year!" *The Nation,* 8 July 1939, 35–36.

26. For House action, see David L. Porter, *The Seventy-sixth Congress and World War II, 1939–1940,* Columbia, Mo., University of Missouri Press, 1979, 291–92.

27. *NYT,* 9 July 1939, sec. 1, p. 1; and Porter, *The 76th Congress and World War II,* 46-47.

28. No accurate count was made of those attending the meeting because senators came and went as their duties demanded. But among those attending, according to the *New York Times,* were Lodge, Capper, Bone, Borah, Bennett Clark, Frazier, Holt, LaFollette, Nye, Reed, Shipstead, Vandenberg, White, Danaher, and D. Worth Clark. See "Senate Group Acts to Block Repeal of Arms Embargo," *NYT,* 8 July 1939, 1, 3.

29. On Johnson and the western Republican Progressives, see Ronald L. Feinman, *Twilight of Progressivism: The Western Republican Senators and the New Deal* (Baltimore, Johns Hopkins University Press, 1981). For the change in Progressives' views, see also Otis L. Graham Jr., *An Encore for Reform: The Old Progressives and the New Deal* (New York, Oxford University Press, 1967).

30. Bailey to Judge George Rountree, 14 February 1939; copy in "Political: National Folder," Box 477, Josiah William Bailey Papers, William R. Perkins Library, Duke University, Durham, North Carolina.

31. Justus D. Doenecke, *Not to the Swift: The Old Isolationists in the Cold War Era,* (Lewisburg, Pa., Bucknell University Press, 1979), 24. Ronald Feinman, in *Twilight of Progressivism* makes the same point. See, especially pp. 203–4.

32. Those attending the meeting in Johnson's office on 21 September were Johnson, La Follette, Borah, Vandenberg, Barbour, Capper, Nye, Tobey, Reed, Danaher, Frazier, Gurney, Bridges, and Lodge, Republicans; and McCarran, Downey, Overton, Walsh, Holt, Bulow, Bennett Clark, D. Worth Clark, Democrats; and Lundeen and Shipstead, Farmer-Laborites. For the meeting and FDR's address to the special session, see *NYT,* 22 September 1939, 1, 14.

33. For the drafting of the Pittman bill, see *NYT,* 24 September 1939, sec. 1, p. 1. For the final committee vote, see *NYT,* 29 September 1939, 1, 11.

34. See, for example, Kenneth G. Crawford, "Shadowboxing in Washington," *The Nation,* 14 October 1939, 403–4.

35. For the vote on the amendments, see *NYT* 25 October 1939, 1. For the Administration's willingness to compromise, see *NYT,* 16 October 1939, 1.

36. *CR* 85:2:1024; Porter, *The 76th Congress and World War II,* 74–75; and Thomas Nathan Guinsberg, "Senatorial Isolationism," (Ph.D. diss., Columbia University, 1969), 228.

37. Aiken's comments are from George D. Aiken, as told to Robert R. Mullen, "Pushing the Elephant," *The Christian Science Monitor,* 4 January 1939, 5. Austin's comments are from "Which Way Recovery?," 12 March 1939, typescript copy, Box III, File 215, Speech Files, Austin Papers. For other indications of divisions in the GOP, see William L. White, "The Middle West Drifts to The Right," *The Nation,* 3 June 1939, 635–38. Aiken's characterization of the GOP was cited in "Wanted: A Purge," *Newsweek* 20 December 1937, 16. Aiken made similar remarks in a Lincoln Day address at the Waldorf Astoria in February 1938; see *NYT,* 13 February 1938, 39.

38. Aiken, "Pushing the Elephant."

39. "The New Progressives," *The Nation,* 7 May 1938, 519–20.

CHAPTER 2. THE NATION AT WAR, 1940–1942

1. On the First and Second War Powers Act, see Roland Young, *Congressional Politics in the Second World War* (New York, Columbia University Press, 1956), 29–32.

2. The best overall account of Congress during the war is Roland Young, *Congressional Politics During the Second World War* (New York, 1956). But see also, John Morton Blum, *V was for Victory: Politics and American Culture During World War II* (New York, Harcourt, Brace, Jovanovich, 1976); Richard Polenberg, *War and Society: The United States, 1941–1945* (Philadelphia, Lippincott, 1972); James MacGregor Burns, *Roosevelt: The Soldier of Freedom* (New York, Harcourt, Brace, Jovanovich, 1971); Donald McCoy, "Republican Opposition During Wartime, 1941–1945," *Mid-America* 49 (July 1967): 174–89; and John Robert Moore, "The Conservative Coalition in the United States Senate, 1942–1945," *Journal of Southern History* 33 (August 1967): 368–76.

3. Capper, "Reciprocal Trade Agreements: Markets Depend upon Purchasing Power," *Vital Speeches* 6 (1 February 1940): 232–33.

4. For votes on the Pittman amendment see *NYT,* 30 March 1940, 1; *US News,* 5 April 1940, 15; and "Outstanding Roll Calls," *Editorial Research Reports,* 265–69. The vote on the O'Mahoney amendment was 44 to 36; that on the Adams amendment was 46–34. See *NYT,* 5 April 1940, 1. For the Walsh amendment and the vote on final passage of the Reciprocal Trade bill, see *NYT,* 6 April 1940, 1; "Hull Wins," *Time,* 8 April 1940, 14–15; and "The Shape of Things," *The Nation,* 20 April 1940, 498–99.

5. David Porter, "Senator Pat Harrison of Mississippi and the Reciprocal Trade Act of 1940," *Journal of Mississippi History* 36 (November 1974): 368–69. For similar expressions of the role of the international crisis in the extension of reciprocal trade, see Joseph Alsop and Robert Kintner, "Sly and Able: The Real Leader of the Senate, Jimmy Byrnes," *Saturday Evening Post,* (20 July 1940): 18.

6. The details of the reorganization plan are reported in Arthur Krock, "Is the CAA to Be Drawn Under Executive Control?" *NYT,* 18 April 1940, 22.

7. The voting alignments on the McCarran Resolution are from "Outstanding Roll Calls," *Editorial Research Reports, 1940,* vol. 2, 265–69.

8. The polls are cited in Wayne S. Cole, *Roosevelt and the Isolationists* 1932–1945 (Lincoln, University of Nebraska Press, 1983), 364–65.

9. Wheeler, "Marching Down the Road to War," quoted in Leuchtenberg, *Franklin D. Roosevelt and the New Deal* (New York, 1963), 307.

10. The vote on the Russell-Overton amendment was 69–16. For its adoption, see "President Given Power to Conscript Industry," *Chicago Tribune,* 29 August 1940, 1; and *NYT,* 29 August 1940, 1. Voting alignments on the Russell-Overton Amendment and on final passage of the draft bill are from "Outstanding Roll Calls in the Senate," *Editorial Research Reports,* vol. 2, 265–69. Russell's comments are from Russell to B. W. Cook, 5 September 1940; Copy in Political, General File, Richard B. Russell Jr. Papers, Richard B. Russell Library for Political Research and Studies, University of Georgia, Athens, Georgia.

11. The most important change made by the Senate permitted corporations to compute excess profits on the basis of either the average earnings in the period 1936–1939 or as a percentage of the capital invested, whichever produced the lowest tax. On the bill, see Roy G. and Gladys C. Blakey, "Two Federal Revenue Acts of 1940," *American Economic Review* 30 (December 1940): 724–35; and *NYT,* 12 September 1940, 12.

12. Those voting for final passage of the tax bill included Guy Gillette, George Radcliffe, Harry Byrd, Josiah Bailey, James Byrnes, Walter George, Pat Harrison, Alva Adams, and Joseph O'Mahoney. For the vote, see *NYT,* 20 September 1940, 1, 19; and "Outstanding Roll Call Votes in the Senate," *Editorial Research Reports,* vol. 2, 265–69.

13. Bailey to Mial Dewey, 12 August 1942, in "Political: National" file, Box

477, Bailey Papers, Duke University. Bailey's strong support for the war is also discussed in John Robert Moore, *Senator Josiah William Bailey of North Carolina: A Political Biography* (Durham, Duke University Press, 1968).

14. The Frank Committee's recommendations are reported in *NYHT,* 26 March 1940, 12.

15. For the introduction of Lend-Lease and reaction to it, see "Power to Aid Britain to the Hilt," *U.S. News,* 17 January 1941, 11; "Roosevelt Bill Stirs Nation and Puts Job up to Congress," *Newsweek,* 20 January 1941, 15–17; and *NYT,* 11 January 1941, 1, 3. The best general account of the bill is Warren F. Kimball, *The Most Unsordid Act* (Baltimore, Johns Hopkins University Press, 1969).

16. Austin's position is reported in *NYT,* 12 January 1941, sec. 1, p. 1. Lodge's comments are from *NYT,* 11 February 1941, 1. Johnson's remarks are from *NYT,* 11 January 1941, 1, 5.

17. *NYT,* 24 January 1941, 1.

18. For adoption of the four amendments, see *NYT,* 30 January 1941, 1; and Kimball, *The Most Unsordid Act,* 195–203. That the the liberal community was also behind the limiting amendments is indicated by the repeated advocacy throughout early 1941 of such liberal journals as the *New Republic* and *The Nation.* See, for instance, "The Battle of 1776," *New Republic* 20 January 1941, 69–70; "The President's Plan," *The Nation* 18 January 1941, 59–60; and "Lend-Lease Revisions," *New Republic* 10 February 1941, 166–67.

19. Voting alignments on final passage of Lend-Lease appear in *Congressional Record,* 87, 1, p. 2097; hereafter cited as *CR* 87:1:2097. For the votes on the amendments, see *CR* 87:1:2081–82; *NYT,* 9 March 1941, sec. 1, p. 1; and "Democracy's Arsenal Unlocked as Congress Hands Key to FDR," *Newsweek,* 17 March 1941, 17–18.

20. Sullivan, *NYHT,* 9 March 1941, sec. 2, p. 2.

21. Vandenberg's statement is from Arthur H. Vandenberg Jr., ed., *The Private Papers of Senator Vandenberg* (Boston, Houghton Mifflin, 1952), 10–11. The emphasis is Vandenberg's.

22. Russell's comments are in Russell to Mrs. R. B. Russell Sr., 5 February 1941, Personal File, Family Correspondence (Winder), Russell Papers.

23. The sectional divisions on Lend-Lease were reported by T. R. B. in the *New Republic,* 24 March 1941, 403.

24. The argument that support for an internationalist foreign policy was rooted in the urban, industrial regions is developed in Wayne S. Cole, *Roosevelt and the Isolationists, 1932–1945* (Lincoln, University of Nebraska Press, 1983); and in Joan Lee Bryniarski, "Against the Tide: Senate Opposition to the Internationalist Foreign Policy of Presidents Franklin D. Roosevelt and Harry S. Truman, 1943–1949," (Ph.D. diss., University of Maryland, 1972).

25. *NYT,* 4 July 1941, 1, 5; and "F.D.R. Message on Army Issue Spotlights Peril Facing U.S.," *Newsweek,* 28 July 1941, 11–12.

26. Quoted in *NYT,* 8 July 1941, 1, 2.

27. For criticism of draft extension and Robert Reynolds's announcement that he would oppose his own resolutions, see *NYT,* 13 July 1941, sec. 1, pp. 1, 19.

28. For introduction of the Wheeler and Taft proposals, see *NYT,* 22 July 1941, 1. The same day, a third member of the Military Affairs Committee, Albert "Happy" Chandler of Kentucky, a strong interventionist, proposed that Congress declare that national safety was endangered, which would have automatically empowered the President to extend the draft. For Roosevelt's 14 July meeting with Congressional leaders, see *NYT,* 15 July 1941, 1.

29. Hill's meeting with the press is covered in *NYT*, 27 July 1941, sec. 1, pp. 1, 28. Additional analysis of the debate in the Military Affairs Committee is reported in "Britain and Russia: U.S. Moves to Bolster Both: Senators Debate Service Issue," *Newsweek*, 4 August 1941, 14.

30. The introduction of the Thomas Amendment and the reactions of Wheeler and Taft are reported in *NYT*, 2 August 1941, 1, 13; and in "Draft Compromise," *Newsweek*, 18 August 1941, 15–16.

31. For the vote and Barkley's appeal, see *NYT*, 6 August 1941, 1, 9; and *NYHT*, 7 August 1941, 1. The vote on the Taft amendment is from *CR* 87:6:6741.

32. Votes on the Thomas amendment and final passage of the draft bill are in *NYT*, 8 August 1941, 1, 6; and *CR* 87:6:6853–54 and 87:6:6881, respectively.

33. Tobey to Rev. J. Mace Crandall, 6 August 1941; Copy in Box 80, Charles W. Tobey Papers, Dartmouth College Library, Hanover, New Hampshire.

34. For the Connally Resolution, see *NYT*, 26 October 1941, sec. 1, pp. 1, 25. For FDR's position on neutrality revision, see "Washington Sets a Stiff Pace in Allied Action Against Axis," *Newsweek*, 17 November 1941, 15–16.

35. The AP poll is reported in *NYT*, 5 October 1941, sec. 1, p. 9. Lodge's view is from *NYT*, 5 November 1941, 2.

36. Maloney's comments were reported in the *NYT*, 4 November 1941, 1, 2. George's radio address was reported in the *NYT*, 3 November 1941, 4.

37. For the voting on neutrality revision, see *NYT*, 8 November 1941, 1, 6; "Washington Sets a Stiff Pace in Allied Action Against Axis," *Newsweek*, 17 November 1941, 15–16. The vote on the Thomas amendment appears in *CR* 87:8:8674. The Clark amendment is in *CR* 87:8:8675. Final passage of neutrality revision is in *CR* 87:8:8680.

38. *NYHT*, 29 October 1941, 21.

39. Floyd M. Riddick, "The Second Session of the Seventy-Seventh Congress," *APSR* 37 (April 1943): 290–92. Vandenberg's statement was quoted in Richard E. Darilek, *A Loyal Opposition in Time of War: The Republican Party and the Politics of Foreign Policy from Pearl Harbor to Yalta* (Westport, Conn., Greenwood Press, 1976), 27.

40. The Senate bill is discussed in *NYT*, 4 January 1942, sec. 1, p. 7. For early efforts at price control, see Harvey C. Mansfield, et al., *A Short History of the OPA*, General Publication No. 15, Office of Temporary Controls, Office of Price Administration, n.d.

41. On farm bloc politics during the war, see Alfred D. Stedman, "The Politics of the Farmers in Wartime," in Ray F. Harvey, ed., *The Politics of This War* (New York, Harper and Brothers, 1943), 161–68. Stedman noted that although farm prices in 1942 were 167% higher than the 1909–1914 base period, the hourly wage rates for laborers had risen more than 300% in the same period. See also Walter W. Wilcox, *The Farmer in the Second World War* (Ames, Iowa, State University of Iowa Press, 1947), especially 116–17.

42. Nye voted against the price control bill because of its failure to include wage controls. For Nye's explanation and Senate action on the bill, see *NYT*, 11 January 1942, sec. 1, pp. 1, 34; and "Farm Bloc Triumph," *Newsweek*, 19 January 1942, 48. The vote on the Bankhead amendment is in *NYT*, 10 January 1942, 1. For discussion of the O'Mahoney amendment, see Joseph O'Mahoney, "The Price Control Bill and the Farmer: 'Parity' is Not Equality," *Vital Speeches* 8 (15 February 1942): 286–88.

43. Editorial comments on the Senate bill are in *NYHT*, 14 January 1942, 1; *NYT*, 12 January 1942, 14; and the *Christian Science Monitor*, cited in *U.S. News*, 23 January 1942, 23.

44. "Floor vs. Ceiling," *Newsweek,* 26 January 1942, 44, 47.

45. Clark's remarks and Senate action on the conference report are from *NYT,* 28 January 1942, 13.

46. For Clyde Reed's statement, see *NYT,* 15 January 1942, 10; and Riddick, "Second Session," 303–4.

47. For the letter, and Gillette's outburst, see *NYT,* 26 January 1942, 1, 11; and Riddick, "Second Session," 304–5.

48. Mansfield, *Short History of OPA,* 42–43. For FDR's seven-point inflation plan, see *NYT,* 28 April 1942, 1; and Young, *Congressional Politics,* 92–93.

49. Mansfield, *Short History of OPA,* 444–45.

50. Young, *Congressional Politics,* 94–96; *NYT,* 8 September 1942, 1; "FDR Puts Congress on Spot by Demand for Inflation Action," *Newsweek,* 14 September 1942, 54.

51. LaFollette's statement is from the *NYT,* 8 September 1942, 1; copyright © 1942 by the New York Times Co. Reprinted by permission. Taft's comments are reported in *NYT,* 8 September 1942, 1. The opinion of the *Chicago Tribune* is in "It's Revolution If He Tries It," *Chicago Tribune,* 8 September 1942, 14. For similar reactions, see also Merlo Pusey, "Question of Unity and Power," *Washington Post,* 9 September 1942, 9; and "Inflation Stand of Mr. Roosevelt: Editors' Reaction," *U.S. News,* 18 September 1942, 31.

52. For introduction of the Thomas amendment, see *NYT,* 23 September 1942, 1, 17. Adoption of the substitute is reported in *NYT,* 1 October 1942, 1.

53. For details of the Stabilization Act of 1942 and its adoption by the Senate, see *NYT,* 1 October 1942, 1; Young, *Congressional Politics,* 98–99; Wilcox, *Farmer in the Second World War,* 129; and Wesley McCune, *The Farm Bloc,* (Garden City, N.Y., Doubleday, Doran, 1943), 65–68.

54. Robey, "The Farm Bloc May Be Outrageous, But . . . ," *Newsweek,* 5 October 1942, 64. Mark Sullivan reached the same conclusion in October 1941. See Sullivan, *NYHT,* 26 October 1941, sec. 2, p. 2. The "informed sources" cited by the *New York Times* are from *NYT,* 23 September 1942, 1, 17.

55. On the budget message and the tax hike, see "If You Put It in Figures," *Time,* 19 January 1942, 9; "Record Budget Will Double 1943 Bills of the Taxpayer," *Newsweek,* 19 January 1942, 46. The Treasury Department's goals for wartime financing are succinctly discussed in Roy G. and Gladys C. Blakey, "The Federal Revenue Act of 1942," *APSR* 36 (December 1942): 1070.

56. Blakey, "Federal Revenue Act of 1942," 1072–80; Joseph G. Rayback, "The Strange Story of the Tax Bill," *Current History* 3 (December 1942): 302–11.

57. For Morgenthau's criticism of the House bill, see *NYT,* 24 July 1942, 1. For Senate Finance Committee action, see *NYT,* 13 September 1942, sec. 1, p. 1; and Blakey, "Federal Revenue Act of 1942," 1080. Morgenthau's announcement that he would seek a new revenue bill is reported in *NYT,* 7 October 1942, 1.

58. Tobey to George A. Torsney, 29 April 1942, Box 82, Tobey Papers. O'Mahoney's comments are from "The Declining Power of the States: Bureaucracy is the Road to State Socialism," *Vital Speeches* 9 (1 February 1943): 227.

59. Young, *Congressional Politics in the Second World War,* 31–32.

60. *U.S. News,* 19 January 1940, 26.

Chapter 3. The Senate in Revolt, 1943–1944

1. For the 1942 elections see, "Stiffening Congress Backbone Chief Result of the Election," *Newsweek,* 16 November 1942, 43–51; "Victory and Responsibil-

ity," *Time,* 16 November 1942, 16–17; Harry Palmer Jeffrey Jr., "The Republican Party as a Minority Party in Congress in Wartime, 1943–1944," (Ph.D. diss., Columbia University, 1974), 25–28.

2. For the background to the salary limitation fight, see Roland Young, *Congressional Politics in the Second World War* (New York, Columbia University Press, 1956), 101–3; Harry Palmer Jeffrey Jr., "The Republican Party," 96–99; and David Lawrence, "$600-a-Year Salary for Everybody?," *U.S. News,* 26 February 1943, 24–25.

3. Reed's sentiments were discussed by Mark Sullivan in *NYHT,* 7 April 1943, 23. For a similar analysis of the Bankhead bill, see Luther Huston, "Conflict with Congress Perils New Deal's Aims," *NYT,* 7 March 1943, sec. 4, p. 6. On adoption of the Bankhead bill, see *NYT,* 26 February 1943, 1, 10; and Young, *Congressional Politics,* 103–4.

4. Bankhead's comments and the vote to recommit are from *NYT,* 8 April 1943, 1; copyright © 1943 the New York Times Co. Reprinted by permission.

5. On the development of a withholding tax and the details of the Ruml tax, see Roy G. and Gladys C. Blakey, "Federal Revenue Legislation, 1943–1944," *APSR* 38 (April 1944): 327–28; and Young, *Congressional Politics,* 130–32.

6. For House action on the tax bill, see *NYT,* 5 May 1943, 1; and "The Tax Bill," *Chicago Tribune,* 1 May 1943, 14. Senate action is reported in *NYT,* 8 May 1943, 1, 30; and *NYT,* 15 May 1943, 1, 11.

7. George's comments and the conference committee compromise are from *NYT,* 26 May 1943, 1, 13. But see also *NYHT,* 26 May 1943, 1. The position that the compromise enabled Congress to resist White House requests for higher taxes was echoed by Rep. Harold Knutson (R-Ill), chairman of the Joint Congressional Committee on Internal Revenue. For his comments, see *Chicago Tribune,* 26 May 1943, 14. For FDR's threat of a veto, see *NYT,* 19 May 1943, 1; and *NYHT,* 23 May 1943, sec. 1, pp. 1, 15.

8. Bennett Champ Clark, "The Pay-As-You-Go Tax Plan: Cash Money in Till and No Tax Debt," *Vital Speeches* 9 (1 April 1943): 384.

9. Joseph G. Rayback, *A History of American Labor,* expanded and updated edition (New York, Free Press, 1966), 373–87; Joel I. Seidman, *American Labor from Defense to Reconversion* (Chicago, University of Chicago Press, 1953).

10. For adoption of the Connally bill, see *NYT,* 4 May 1943, 1, 14; and Young, *Congressional Politics,* 63–64.

11. For the override of FDR's veto, see *Chicago Tribune,* 27 June 1943, sec. 1, p. 1; *NYHT,* 26 June 1943, 1; and Young, *Congressional Politics,* 65.

12. George Gallup, "The Gallup Poll," *Washington Post,* 16 June 1943, 17.

13. Robertson's remarks were reported in the *Chicago Tribune,* 25 June 1943, 1, 2.

14. Bailey to H. C. Brett, 22 May 1943, in "Labor and Management, 1943, January–June," Box 360, Bailey Papers. The *Chicago Tribune* regarded the Wagner Act similarly. See "The Second American Revolution," *Chicago Tribune,* 27 June 1943, sec. 1, p. 1.

15. For the origins of the subsidy program see Young, *Congressional Politics,* 109–11; Jeffrey, "The Republican Party," 157–58; and Ralph Robey, "What We Can Expect from the Use of Subsidies," *Newsweek,* 21 June 1943, 76.

16. The Senate vote to ban consumer subsidies is reported in *NYT,* 27 June 1943, sec. 1, pp. 1, 12. FDR's veto message is discussed in *NYT,* 3 July 1943, 1. Clark's comments are from *NYT,* 25 June 1943, 1, 10.

17. Radcliffe, "Radio Speech—W.C.A.O.—7/10/43," 4, 5, in "Speeches—

Politics, Policies" folder, Box 55, George L. Radcliffe Papers, Ms. 2280, Manuscripts Department, Maryland Historical Society, Baltimore, Md.

18. Radcliffe's statement is from "Comments on Security," Speech to the Senate, 12 October 1943, copy in Box 56, Radcliffe papers.

19. For general accounts of the soldier voting controversy, see Young, *Congressional Politics*, 82–89; and Richard Polenberg, *War and Society: The United States, 1941–1945* (Philadelphia, Lippincott, 1972), 195–97.

20. For the vote on the Eastland-McKellar-McClellan bill, see *NYT*, 4 December 1943, 1.

21. FDR's message and Trussell's observations are from *NYT*, 27 January 1944, 1.

22. Quoted in Allen Drury, *A Senate Journal 1943–1945* (New York, McGraw-Hill, 1963), 45.

23. The vote on the Barkley amendment and final passage of the bill are reported in *NYT*, 9 February 1944, 1; and *CR* 90:1:1397–98, 1406.

24. Young, *Congressional Politics*, 84.

25. The Treasury Department's downward revisions of its tax needs are from *NYT*, 18 June 1943, 1; and *NYT*, 5 October 1943, 1. Marshall's announcement is reported in *NYT*, 19 November 1943, 1.

26. The OPA report is cited in *NYT*, 17 May 1943, 14. Arthur Krock's analysis of Morgenthau's message is in *NYT*, 8 October 1943, 18. An excellent analysis of Congressional sentiment on taxes is in Mabel Newcomer, "Congressional Tax Policies in 1943," *American Economic Review* 34 (December 1944): 734–56. For a general discussion of the GOP's attitude, see Jeffrey, "The Republican Party," 111–12.

27. The reduction in budget estimates for the war in fiscal 1944 is reported in "Passing the Spending Peak: The Financing Task Ahead," *U.S. News*, 7 January 1944, 47–48. The return of appropriated funds to the Treasury is from *NYHT*, 26 January 1944, 1. The Treasury report on tax collections is in *NYT*, 14 February 1944, 23.

28. *NYT*, 23 February 1944, 1; copyright © 1944 the New York Times Co. Reprinted by permission. See also Young, *Congressional Politics*, 136–40; "FDR's Contest with Congress: Views of Press," *U.S. News*, 6 March 1944, 40; Drury, *A Senate Journal*, 85–87; Newcomer, "Congressional Tax Policies in 1943," 734–37; and Roy G. and Gladys C. Blakey, "Federal Revenue Legislation, 1943–1944," *APSR* 38 (April 1944): 325–26.

29. Thomas's observations are from Drury, *A Senate Journal*, 93. The most complete account of Barkley's resignation and reelection is contained in Alben W. Barkley, *That Reminds Me* (New York, Doubleday, 1954), 173–82.

30. The comments of the "liberal Democrat" are quoted in Drury, *A Senate Journal*, 91. The veto override is described in Young, *Congressional Politics*, 142–43.

31. See, for example, Krock, *NYT*, 10 August 1944, p. 16. For details of the Kilgore-Murray bill, see *NYT*, 5 August 1944, 1, 7; and Young, *Congressional Politics*, 207–9.

32. Details of the George bill are in *NYT*, 5 August 1944, 1, 7; and Young, *Congressional Politics*, 207–9. The George bill was ultimately approved 55–19 on 11 August. See *NYT*, 12 August 1944, 1, 15.

33. Hatch was quoted in Drury, *A Senate Journal*, 241.

34. Voting alignments on final passage of the George bill are in *CR* 90:5:6917.

35. "Aiken Speech to Senate, 8/10/44," typescript in "Reconversion Bills

1944," Crate 6, Box 1, Aiken Papers. Walter George's Postwar Planning Committee statement was discussed in I. F. Stone, "On Reconversion," *The Nation,* 12 August 1944, 175–76.

36. Dewey's campaign positions were reported in Arthur Krock, "Dewey Tactics in Race Confusing his Backers," *NYT,* 24 September 1944, sec. 4, p. 3; and *Newsweek,* 2 October 1944, 38. His Albany speech is reported in *NYT,* 14 July 1944, 1.

37. Lee spoke to the *NYT,* 7 January 1943, 12.

Chapter 4. The New Conservatism, 1945–1946

1. "Wartime Health and Education: Interim Report"January 1945, 1–22; copy in "Federal Aid to Education," Box 129, H. Alexander Smith Papers, Seely G. Mudd Library, Princeton University. Members of the subcommittee were: H. Alexander Smith, Olin Johnston, J. W. Fulbright, Robert A. Taft, George Aiken, Joseph Ball, Wayne Morse, and Forrest Donnell.

2. The quotation is from "Report to the Special Committee on Postwar Economic Policy and Planning, August 1, 1945," Committee Print in "Housing 1945," Box 649, Robert A. Taft Papers, Library of Congress. The statistical analysis of housing conditions is from U.S. Department of Agriculture, "The Farm Housing Problem," 17 January 1945; and "GOP National Committee News Release, August 1, 1945," both in "Housing 1945," Box 649, Taft Papers. Members of this subcommittee were Robert A. Taft, Robert Wagner, George Radcliffe, C. Douglas Buck, Allen Ellender, Dennis Chavez, and Robert LaFollette.

3. George D. Aiken, "Why Feed Our Chickens Better Than Our Children," *Northeastern Poultryman* (December 1945): 5–6; copy in "Articles, George D. Aiken, 1941–1958," Crate 48, Box 5, Aiken Papers, University of Vermont.

4. Mrs. P. C. Perkins to Aiken, 29 August 1945; in "Education 1945," Crate 6, Box 1, George D. Aiken Papers, University of Vermont.

5. Wayne S. Cole, *Roosevelt and the Isolationists, 1932–1945* (Lincoln, University of Nebraska Press, 1983), 546–47. The list of most conservative Democrats in 1939 is from James T. Patterson, *Congressional Conservatism During the New Deal* (Lexington, Ky., University of Kentucky Press), 348–49.

6. "Speech to Shelby, N.C. Chamber of Commerce, 3/30/45," typescript in "Statements and Speeches, 1945–46," Box 211, Clyde R. Hoey Papers, William R. Perkins Library, Duke University.

7. "Faith, Hope, Confidence, Foundations of Business," *Detroit Free Press,* 24 January 1945, 6; clipping in "Henry A. Wallace File," Box 258, Olin Johnston Papers, South Caroliniana Library, University of South Carolina, Columbia, S.C. Strout's sentiments are in "Is FDR Bent on Managed Jobs? Wallace Maneuver Gives a Clue," *Newsweek,* 5 February 1945, 36–40.

8. "Is FDR Bent on Managed Jobs?" 36–40.

9. Senate action on the Bailey motion and the George bill is discussed in "Senate Delay in Vote on Wallace Puts Off a Right-Left Showdown," *Newsweek,* 12 February 1945, 44; Roland Young, *Congressional Politics in the Second World War* (New York, 1957), 26–27; and Allen Drury, *A Senate Journal* (New York, 1963), 345–55.

10. *U.S. News* maintained, for instance, that the vote was but one symptom of a broad Congressional revolt led by the conservative coalition against FDR's domes-

tic policies. See "A Congress Revolt: Difficulties Facing FDR," *U.S. News,* 23 February 1945, 13–14.

11. For the voting alignments, see *CR* 91:1:679; Arthur Krock, "Halfway Across a Political Whirlpool," *NYT,* 2 February 1945, 18; and "A Congress Revolt: Difficulties Facing FDR," *U.S. News,* 23 February 1945, 13–14.

12. Wallace was confirmed on 1 March by a vote of 56–32. The winning coalition was composed of most New Deal liberals, including Barkley, Pepper, Green, and Guffey, as well as a bipartisan assortment of new conservatives, including Aiken, Ball, Brewster, George, Hoey, Olin Johnston, Maybank, Radcliffe, Russell, Saltonstall, and Tobey. For the vote, see *CR,* 91:2:1616. The vote on the George bill is from *CR,* 91:1:692–93.

13. Bailey to Wheeler, 10 February 1945, in "Political: National," Box 479, Bailey Papers, Duke University.

14. Taft's comments were made on "The American Forum of the Air," 13 December 1942; typescript in "Education—Federal Aid to, 1937–42," Box 536, Taft Papers, LC. The best general history of federal aid to education is Gilbert E. Smith, *The Limits of Reform: Politics and Federal Aid to Education, 1937–1950* (New York, Garland Publishing, Inc., 1982).

15. The NEA's findings were reported in "Education—Why the Federal Government Must Help," National Education Association, March 1945; copy in "Federal Aid to Education," Box 129, H. Alexander Smith Papers, Princeton University. The report on South Carolina was made to one of the state's senators, Burnet Maybank. See S. M. Derrick to Maybank, 23 June 1942, "Legislation—Education, 1942," Burnet R. Maybank Papers, Special Collections Department, Robert Scott Small Library, College of Charleston, Charleston, S.C.

16. Bailey to Miss Selma C. Webb, 12 October 1945, "Education, 1945–1946," Box 287, Bailey Papers.

17. Hoey's testimony was reprinted in "Before the House Committee," *North Carolina Education,* October 1945, 88; clipping in "Statements and Speeches, 1945–46," Box 211, Hoey Papers.

18. Smith to Dr. John Sly, 2 March 1945, "Federal Aid to Education," Box 129, Smith Papers.

19. Smith, *The Limits of Reform,* discusses the liberal view of federal aid.

20. Hoey's statement was reprinted in "Before the House Committee," *North Carolina Education,* October 1945, 88; copy in "Statements and Speeches, 1945–46," Box 211, Hoey Papers. Smith's remarks are in Smith to Beekman R. Terhune, Esquire, 7 June 1945; copy in "S. 717," Box 128, Smith Papers.

21. Quoted in John A. Neuenschwander, "Senator George D. Aiken and Federal Aid to Education 1941–1949," (Master's thesis, University of Vermont, 1965), 55.

22. The most thorough discussion of the Full Employment bill is Stephen K. Bailey, *Congress Makes a Law: The Story Behind the Employment Act of 1946* (New York, Random House, 1964). But see also Robert Lekachman, *The Age of Keynes* (New York, Vintage Books, 1968), 165–75; and Herbert Stein, *The Fiscal Revolution in America* (Chicago, University of Chicago Press, 1969), 197–206.

23. Quoted in Bailey, *Congress Makes a Law,* 145. For similar criticism, see Ralph Robey, "A Clever Trick Designed Just to Fool You," *Newsweek* 23 July 1945, 66.

24. Quoted in Bailey, *Congress Makes a Law,* 193.

25. Smith to Alfred Ely, Esquire, 19 September 1945; copy in "Full Employment," Box 148, Smith Papers.

26. Aiken's comments were from "Speech to U.S. Senate," 1 March 1945; copy in "1945 Speechbook," part 1, crate 48, box 6, Aiken papers.

27. The Taft and Hatch amendments are analyzed in Ralph Robey, "Significant Changes in the Full Employment Bill," *Newsweek* 8 October 1945, 78.

28. I. F. Stone, "The New Reservationists," *The Nation,* 22 September 1945, 274–75. Barkley's comments are in CR 91:7:9130. The final vote is from *NYT,* 29 September 1945, 1, 3. See also Bailey, *Congress Makes a Law,* 125.

29. Tobey to James P. Keenan, 5 November 1945; copy in Box 86, Tobey Papers.

30. This argument has been developed most fully by Wayne S. Cole, *Roosevelt and the Isolationists, 1932–1945* (Lincoln, 1983); and Joan Lee Bryniarski, "Against the Tide: Senate Opposition to the Internationalist Foreign Policy of Presidents Franklin D. Roosevelt and Harry S Truman, 1943–1949," (Ph.D. diss., University of Maryland, 1972).

31. The vote on passage of the extension bill appears in *CR* 91:5:6364. The vote on the O'Mahoney amendment, which was defeated 49–27, is in *CR* 91:5:6359. The vote on the Finance Committee amendment, rejected 47–33, is from *CR* 91:5:6258.

32. Quoted in Harl Adams Dalstrom, "Kenneth S. Wherry," (Ph.D. diss., University of Nebraska, 1965), 495.

33. Quoted in Allen Drury, *A Senate Journal,* 448.

34. The fourteen opponents from interior states were Democrats Wheeler and O'Daniel; and Republicans Taft, Brooks, Capper, Moore, Bushfield, Gurney, Langer, Butler, Millikin, Robertson, Wherry, and Revercomb. The two opponents who represented coastal states were Hawkes and Hart.

35. The diversity of viewpoints in the U.N. vote is discussed by John M. Blum, "Limits of American Internationalism: 1941–1945," in Leonard Krieger and Fritz Stern, eds., *The Responsibility of Power: Historical Essays in Honor of Hajo Holborn* (Garden City, N.Y., Doubleday and Company, 1967), 387–401. Similarly, *a New York Times* correspondent wrote on 1 July 1945 that much of the support for the U.N. charter was based on the belief that it simply committed America to continued postwar cooperation with our allies. "Charter Ratification May Set Senate Record," *NYT,* 1 July 1945, sec. 4, p. 7.

36. "Armistice Day Address Delivered by Senator Olin D. Johnston, Anderson, S.C., November 11, 1946;" copy in "Speeches: 1946," Olin D. Johnston Speeches, Statements 1938–May 1959, Olin D. Johnston Papers.

37. The minority report was discussed in *NYT,* 15 July 1945, sec. 1, pp. 1, 18.

38. For the introduction of the FEPC bill, see *NYT,* 18 January 1946, 1, 4. Good histories of FEPC are Louis C. Kesselman, *The Social Politics of FEPC* (Chapel Hill, N.C., University of North Carolina Press, 1948); and Louis Ruchames, *Race, Jobs, and Politics: The Story of FEPC* (New York, Doubleday, 1953).

39. The end of the filibuster is reported in *NYT,* 10 February 1946, sec. 1, pp. 1, 12. The statement of Burnet Maybank is from Maybank to P. M. Tiller, 6 October 1945; copy in "Legislation—F.E.P.C., 1945," Maybank Papers. Johnston's comments are from "Remarks by Sen. Olin D. Johnston Before the Congress of the United States Directed Against the Passage of the Fair Employment Practice Act, 24 January 1946," 11–12; copy in "Speeches, 1946," Olin D. Johnston Speeches, Statements, 1938–May 1959, Johnston Papers. The opinion of Josiah Bailey is from Bailey to Rev. W. W. Finlator, 29 June 1945; copy in "Labor and Management," box 363, Bailey Papers.

40. Arthur Krock argued during the 1946 FEPC debate, for instance, that southern opposition to the civil rights agency was based in part on their view that it was a symbol of Harry Truman's intention to carry on the social reforms of the New Deal. See Krock, "Democrats' Rift Perils Party's Whole Future," *NYT,* 20 January 1946, sec. 4, p. 3.

41. Hubert R. Fowler, *The Unsolid South: Voting Behavior of Southern Senators, 1947–1960* (University, Ala., University of Alabama Press, 1968).

42. For the growing public dissatisfaction with OPA, see Harvey C. Mansfield, et al., *A Short History of OPA,* (Washington, Office of Price Administration, n.d.), 85–101.

43. Details of Banking and Currency Committee's bill are from *NYT,* 12 June 1946, 1, 10. See also, "Prices: Where Now?" *Newsweek,* 8 July 1946, 21–22.

44. Johnston's comments are from Johnston to Honorable George Warren, 26 April 1946; copy in unfiled letters, Box 295, Johnston papers. Aiken to Mrs. Beth Ferguson, 7 June 1946; copy in "Labor-Strke Legislation, 1946," Crate 6, Box 1, Aiken Papers.

45. For the voting alignments on the Taft amendment, see *CR* 92:5:6729.

46. The OPA extension bill was approved by the Senate on 13 June by a margin of 53–11. The eleven opponents of the bill were an odd coalition of extreme conservatives opposed to any extension of price control, such as O'Daniel, Wherry, and Moore, and extreme liberals such as Mead, Kilgore, and Wagner, who believed the bill was too weak. New conservatives such as George, Hoey, Johnston, Knowland, Maybank, Radcliffe, Saltonstall, Smith, and Tobey, joined with Administration stalwarts like Barkley, Lucas, McMahon, Magnuson, Murdock, and Taylor to ensure passage of the final bill. See *CR* 92:6:6841. The vote on the Pepper amendment is in *CR* 92:6:6817; but see also *NYT,* 14 June 1946, 1, 8.

47. Details of the conference report are in *NYT,* 25 June 1946, 1.

48. The vote on the conference report is from *NYT,* 29 June 1946, 1; and *CR* 92:6:7871. O'Daniel's filibuster is reported in *NYT,* 27 June 1946, 1, 9.

49. Details of the Barkley bill are from *NYT,* 4 July 1946, 1, 10; and 5 July 1946, 1, 8. Truman's veto of the conference report appears in *NYT,* 30 June 1946, sec. 1, pp. 1, 26.

50. The vote on the Eastland amendment was 42–34; see *CR* 92:7:8536. The vote on the Wherry amendment was 51–27; see CR 92:7:8553. The Moore amendment was approved 40–30; see *CR* 92:7:8582. For Senate action, see also *NYT,* 11 July 1946, 1, 12.

51. The final vote on the Barkley bill showed that such new conservatives as Aiken, Brewster, George, Knowland, Morse, O'Mahoney, Smith, and Taft joined Administration forces. The vote appears in *CR* 92:7:8802. The ten sponsors of the Pepper amendment were Pepper, Wagner, Guffey, Murray, Murdock, Mitchell, Taylor, Myers, Kilgore, and Lucas. The vote on the Pepper amendment showed that such new conservatives as Aiken, Ball, George, Johnston, Knowland, and Smith sided with obstructionists who were opposed to continuation of any price control. See *NYT,* 14 July 1946, sec. 1, p. 26; and *CR* 92:7:8798. The vote on the Robertson amendment appears in *CR* 92:7:8782.

52. Undated, untitled statement in "Statements and Speeches, 1945–1946," Box 211, Hoey Papers.

53. Robert J. Donovan in *Conflict and Crisis,* 208–10, provides a good summary of the origins of the Case bill.

54. Lucas's legislation was described in "Senator Lucas's New Role as Leader in Fight for Antistrike Law," *U.S. News,* 24 May 1946, 65–66. The national problems resulting from the coal and railroad strikes are described in *NYT,* 11 May 1946, 1, 5.

55. The alignments on the votes are as follows: Ball, Taft, Smith amendment requiring sixty-day cooling off period, *CR* 92:5:5691–92; Taft amendment requiring fact-finding, *CR* 92:5:5697–98; final passage of Case Bill, *CR* 92:5:5739. For the amendments and final passage, see also *NYT,* 26 May 1946, sec. 1, pp. 1, 26.

56. The veto and the House's action are reported in *NYT,* 12 June 1946, 1, 5.

57. Bailey to Joseph S. Silversteen, 30 June 1945, "Labor and Management," Box 363, Bailey Papers.

58. "Speech to Winston-Salem Jr. Chamber of Commerce, 11/25/46," 2; copy in "Statements and Speeches, 1945–46," Box 211, Hoey Papers.

59. Flanders, "Some Things We Have Learned," 5–6; typescript copy in Box 133, Ralph Flanders Papers, Syracuse University Library, Department of Special Collections.

60. Bryniarski, "Against the Tide," 12–13. Wherry's statement is quoted in Harl S. Dalstrom, "Kenneth S. Wherry," 750.

CHAPTER 5. THE NEW CONSERVATISM AND PARTISAN POLITICS: THE 80TH CONGRESS

1. The results of the 1946 election are discussed in "The GOP Mantle of Power," *Newsweek,* 18 November 1946, 33–34. The GOP majority in the Senate following the election was 51–45 and 246–188 in the House.

2. Leuchtenberg, *In the Shadow of FDR: From Harry Truman to Ronald Reagan* (Ithaca, Cornell University Press, 1983), 23. Similar analyses of the 1946 elections are offered in Herbert S. Parmet, *The Democrats: The Years After FDR* (New York, Macmillan, 1976), 60; Robert Donovan, *Conflict and Crisis* (New York, W. W. Norton, 1977), 236–37; Richard M. Fried, *Men Against McCarthy* (New York, Columbia University Press, 37; and David W. Reinhard, *The Republican Right Since 1945* (Lexington, Ky., University of Kentucky Press, 1983), 15–36. *Newsweek's* view of southern Democrats is from "Democrats: Look Away," 25 November 1946, 33.

3. Lodge is quoted in William J. Miller, *Henry Cabot Lodge: A Biography* (New York, Coward-McCann, 1967), 187. Ives's remarks are from "The Republican Responsibility," 8 February 1947, Box 41, Irving M. Ives Papers, Division of Rare and Manuscript Collections, Cornell University Library. On John Bricker, see Richard O. Davies, *Defender of the Old Guard: John Bricker and American Politics* (Columbus, Ohio, Ohio State University Press, 1993), 115.

4. "The Eightieth Congress," *The Nation,* 4 January 1947, 3–4. For similar contemporary observations on the GOP divisions and their likely impact on legislative affairs, see Cabell Phillips, "Republicans are Cheerful, But Also Anxious," *NYT,* 5 January 1947, sec. 4, p. 3; "Tangles in the New Congress: GOP Division on Basic Issues," *US News,* 10 January 1947, 20–21.

5. Introduction of the budget and the critics' reaction is reported in *NYT,* 11 January 1947, 1, 8; and "Budget Storm," *Newsweek,* 20 January 1947, 23–24.

6. The vote of the Joint Congressional Committee appears in *NYT,* 15 February 1947, 1, 3. For Bridges's position, see *NYT,* 11 January 1947, 1, 8; and Richard Cope, "Bridges of New Hampshire, A Cagey Senator," *The Reporter* 6 (1 April 1952), 6–10.

7. Myers's comments are in *NYT,* 22 February 1947, 1. Magnuson's comments are from *NYT,* 25 February 1947, 1, 19.

8. Aiken's comments are in *CR* 93:1:1164–67. Vandenberg's concerns were reported in *NYT,* 22 February 1947, 1, 2. Republican Charles Tobey had practically the same view as Vandenberg. See, for instance, Tobey to Perkins Bass, 3 March 1947, Box 87, Tobey Papers. A full discussion of the GOP intraparty divisions on

budget reduction is contained in Susan M. Hartmann, *Truman and the 80th Congress* (Columbia, University of Missouri Press, 1971), especially 37–38.

9. The vote on the Taft-Millikin substitute is in *CR* 93:2:1438; and *NYT,* 27 February 1947, 1. "Pappy" O'Daniel represented the conservative extreme. He advocated a reduction of $12 billion. The vote to table the Murray and Pepper resolutions is reported in *NYT,* 25 February 1947, 1, 19.

10. Alsop, "The Divided Republicans," *Washington Post,* 21 February 1947, 19. The journalist Marquis Childs made similar comments during the debate on fiscal policy. See "Scalpel vs. Ax," *Washington Post,* 18 February 1947, 10.

11. Author's emphasis. M. E. Garrison to Johnston, 10 February 1947; in "Bill File for January and February," Box 257, Olin D. Johnston Papers, South Caroliniana Library, University of South Carolina.

12. For the poll see George Gallup, "Many Favor Law to Forbid Strikes, Lockouts for Year," *Washington Post,* 22 November 1946, 6; clipping in "Labor-Management 1946," Box 678, Robert A. Taft Papers, Library of Congress. A good general discussion of the public mood is offered by R. Alton Lee, *Truman and Taft-Hartley: A Question of Mandate* (Lexington, Ky., University of Kentucky Press, 1966), 45–46.

13. Smith to Hon. Vincent Murphy, 4 February 1947; copy in Education and Labor Committee, 1947 General Correspondence, Box 130, Smith Papers. For the introduction of the labor bills, see *NYT,* 5 January 1947, sec. 1, p. 5; 9 January 1947, 10; and 11 January 1947, 1, 7.

14. Joseph Alsop reported on 23 April 1947 that Taft had insisted on an omnibus bill because he expected a presidential veto. In such an event, he reasoned, Truman and the Democratic party would lose much popular support. Alsop also reported that Taft's strategy had been vehemently opposed by Ives, Morse, Lodge, Saltonstall, H. A. Smith, Aiken, and Flanders. See Alsop, "Misery in the GOP," *Washington Post,* 23 April 1947, 15; clipping in "Labor," Box 151, Smith Papers. For a different view of Taft's strategy, see James T. Patterson, *Mr. Republican: A Biography of Robert A. Taft* (Boston, Houghton Mifflin, 1972), 357–58.

15. "Labor: Unclosed Shops," *Newsweek,* 3 March 1947, 19.

16. The committee votes are reported in *NYT,* 15 April 1947, 1, 21; and 16 April 1947, 1, 4. Those voting consistently with Taft for the strengthening amendments were Ellender, Ball, Donnell, and Jenner. On the final vote to report out the bill the only dissenting votes came from liberals Murray and Pepper. See *NYT,* 18 April 1947, 1, 7.

17. Taft's comments are from *CR* 93:3:3834–35.

18. The suggestion to delete "interference" was made by Republican Irving Ives. See *CR* 93:4:4442; and *NYT,* 3 May 1947, 1, 8. Although Taft was widely acknowledged as the moving force behind the amendment, it was officially sponsored by Republicans Joseph Ball and H. Alexander Smith, and by Democrats Walter George and Harry Byrd.

19. Voting alignments on the second Taft amendment are in *CR* 93:4:4676. For Ives's comments and further discussion, see *NYT,* 7 May 1947, 1, 18; and 8 May 1947, 1, 16.

20. Voting against the Ball amendment but for the Taft amendment were such new conservatives as Flanders, Holland, Hoey, Ives, Lodge, Maybank, Saltonstall, Smith, Taft, and Thye. The vote on the Ball amendment is in *CR* 93:4:4847. Alignments on the Taft amendment are from *CR* 93:4:4848. For a fuller discussion of Senate action on the two amendments, see *NYT,* 9 May 1947, 1, 12; and 10 May 1947, 1, 11.

21. The final vote appears in *CR* 93:4:5117. New conservatives voting with obstructionists included Aiken, Baldwin, Ball, Brewster, Cooper, Donnell, Flanders, George, Holland, Hoey, Ives, Knowland, Lodge, Maybank, Russell, Saltonstall, Smith, Taft, and Thye.

22. The changes made in national labor law by the Taft-Hartley bill are discussed succinctly in Lee, *Truman and Taft-Hartley*, 75–77.

23. For the vote on the conference report, see *CR* 93:5:6536; and *NYT*, 7 June 1947, 1, 2. The House voted 320–79 on 4 June to approve the conference report. See *NYT*, 5 June 1947, 24.

24. For the vote on the conference report, see *CR* 93:5:6536; and *NYT*, 7 June 1947, 1, 2. The House voted 320–79 on 4 June to approve the conference report. See *NYT*, 5 June 1947, 24. President Truman's veto message is reported in *NYT*, 21 June 1947, 1, 3. The Senate voted 68–25 on 23 June to override the veto. Alignments on the veto override are in *CR* 93:5:7538. For a fuller discussion of the Senate debate on the veto override, see *NYT*, 24 June 1947, 1.

25. Diary entry for 8 May 1947, in "The Diary of H. Alexander Smith," p. 1947–161, Box 281, Smith Papers.

26. Pepper's views are from a speech he delivered on the Mutual Broadcasting Network in defense of Truman's veto, cited in *Chicago Tribune*, 23 June 1947, 16. The reaction of the Ford employee is in "Idle Pits and Busy Lawyers," *Newsweek*, 7 July 1947, 21–22.

27. Aiken to E. S. Robertson, 24 May 1947; copy in "Labor—1947," Crate 6, Box 1, Aiken Papers. Hoey's analysis is in an undated, untitled typescript in "Statements and Speeches, 1947–1949," Box 211, Hoey Papers.

28. Pre-industrial concepts of labor are discussed in Daniel T. Rodgers, *The Work Ethic in Industrial America 1850–1920* (Chicago, University of Chicago Press, 1974); Alan Trachtenberg, *The Incorporation of America: Culture & Society in the Gilded Age* (New York, Hill and Wang, 1982); and Sidney Fine, *Laissez Faire and the General Welfare State: A Study of Conflict in American Thought, 1865–1901* 4th ed., (Ann Arbor, University of Michigan Press, 1969).

29. Dalstrom, "Kenneth Wherry," 980.

30. For background on the Truman Doctrine see, for instance, Walter LaFeber, *America, Russia, and the Cold War*, 4th ed. John Wiley and Sons, (New York, 1980); Stephen Ambrose, *Rise to Globalism* (Baltimore, Penguin Books, 1971); and John Lewis Gaddis, *Strategies of Containment* (New York, Oxford University Press, 1982). For a contemporary analysis of the uneasiness of Congress over the Truman Doctrine, see James Reston, "Congress is Cautious on Our New World Role," *NYT*, 23 March 1947, sec. 4, p. 3.

31. Vandenberg's comments were recorded in Arthur Krock, "A Very Important Discussion on Semantics," *NYT*, 18 April 1947, 20. Addition of the Vandenberg amendment and additional Foreign Relations Committee action is discussed in *NYT*, 4 April 1947, 1, 8.

32. See "Policy: 6 to 23," *Newsweek*, 5 May 1947, 26–27. Reston's remarks are from "New Course of U.S. Policy Clarified by Senate Vote," *NYT*, 23 April 1947, 2. Voting for the Truman Doctrine were such new conservatives as Aiken, Baldwin, Brewster, Cooper, Flanders, George, Hoey, Holland, Ives, Johnston, Knowland, Lodge, Maybank, Russell, Saltonstall, Smith, Taft, Tobey, Thye, and Vandenberg, and such Administration stalwarts as Chavez, Downey, Green, Hatch, Hayden, Hill, Lucas, McFarland, McMahon, and Elbert Thomas. For alignments on the final vote, see *CR* 93:3:3793.

33. "Radio Address of Senator M. E. Tydings on Sunday, April 13, 1947 Over

Station WBAL," Copy in Foreign Relief, Greece and Turkey, Box 262, Holland Papers. Revercomb's comments were reported in *NYT*, 19 April 1947, 4. The argument that opposition to American internationalism was rooted in a desire to uphold rural, agrarian traditions is also made by Justus D. Doenecke, *Not to the Swift: The Old Isolationists in the Cold War Era* (Lewisburg, Pa., Bucknell University Press, 1979), 86.

34. Quoted in Bryniarski, "Against the Tide," 133. This work also argues that the link between opposition to American internationalism and New Deal domestic reform was the rejection of modern, industrial society.

35. Hoey to Rev. George W. Blount, 1 April 1947; copy in folder #4, Box 148, Hoey Papers. Holland's remarks are in Holland to Hon. E. D. Treadwell Sr., 16 April 1947; copy in "Foreign Relief, Greece, Turkey," Box 261, Holland Papers.

36. For details of the Address and reaction to it, see *NYT*, 8 January 1948, 2; and "The Election Waltz, Opus '48," *Newsweek*, 19 January 1948, 19–20. A more detailed analysis of the Address is in Hartmann, *Truman and the 80th Congress*, 128–32; and Donovan, *Conflict and Crisis*, 347–56.

37. The postwar division within the GOP is discussed in David W. Reinhard, *The Republican Right Since 1945* (Lexington, Ky., 1983); and Hartmann, *Truman and the 80th Congress*, especially 98–99. For contemporary discussion of the GOP's internal divisions, see Ernest K. Lindley, "Party Schisms and the Crisis," *Newsweek*, 22 March 1948, 30.

38. Congressional action of the $4.7 billion tax cut is reported in *Newsweek*, 12 April 1948, 21. For the introduction of the White House proposal for UMT and a new draft, see *NYT*, 5 June 1948, 1, 5. Adoption of the modified training and draft bill is from *NYT*, 20 June 1948, sec. 1, pp. 1, 34.

39. Marshall's testimony was reported in *NYT*, 9 January 1948, 1. The best account of the genesis of the Marshall Plan is John Gimbel, *The Origins of the Marshall Plan* (Palo Alto, Stanford University Press, 1976). See also, Joseph Marion Jones, *The Fifteen Weeks* (New York, Harcourt, Brace and World Inc., 1955); John Lewis Gaddis, *Strategies of Containment* (New York, Oxford University Press, 1982); and Stephen E. Ambrose, *Rise to Globalism* (Baltimore, Penguin Books, 1971).

40. Capehart is quoted in Bryniarski, "Against the Tide," 180. Jenner is quoted in Reinhard, *The Republican Right*, 33. Butler's remarks are from Butler to Earl Dyer Jr. 9 August 1947, quoted in Justus F. Paul, "The Political Career of Senator Hugh Butler, 1941–1954," (Ph.D. diss., University of Nebraska, 1966), 275. Kem's comments are from Kem to Mrs I. J. Haitz, 21 October 1947, quoted in Bryniarski, "Against the Tide," 170.

41. Walter George's criticism was reported in *NYT*, 10 January 1948, 1.

42. "Columbia Speech—Postal Clerks, January 31–48;" copy in "Speeches 1942–1948," Maybank Papers, College of Charleston. Holland's comments are from Holland to John D. Dickin Jr., 13 February 1948; copy in "Marshall Plan (February, 1948)," Box 289, Holland Papers.

43. For the changes made by Vandenberg in committee and Taft's reaction, see *NYT*, 14 February 1948, 1, 2; and Arthur H. Vandenberg Jr., *The Private Papers of Senator Vandenberg* (Boston, Houghton Mifflin, 1952), 382–88.

44. Two weeks before Senate debate opened on the Marshall Plan, a Communist coup toppled the democratic government in Czechoslovakia, and in early March Joseph Stalin demanded that Finland sign a "mutual assistance" pact with the Soviet Union. For Senate introduction of the Marshall Plan, see *NYT*, 2 March 1948, 1, 2.

45. The vote on the Ball-Wherry amendment is reported in *NYT*, 9 March 1948, 1, 13; Bryniarski, "Against the Tide," 173–74; and *CR* 94:2:2703. For the Taft amendment, see *NYT*, 13 March 1948, 1, 6; and *CR* 94:2:2708.

46. Omar C. Mitchell to Spessard Holland, 14 January 1947; copy in "Education, Federal Aid to," Box 261, Holland Papers.

47. Johnston to Truman, 10 November 1947; copy in "Federal Aid to Education 1947–48," Box 242, Johnston Papers. The state expenditures were included in a statement prepared by the NEA, entitled, "Press Comment Concerning Federal Aid to Education, January, 1948;" copy in "Federal Aid to Education 1947–48," Box 242, Johnston Papers. George Aiken described many of the problems facing the nation's schools in an article, "Education—A National Responsibility," which was published in the *New York Times Magazine* on 28 December 1947.

48. Details of the education bill are from *NYT*, 25 March 1948, 36.

49. "Educational Con Game," *Chicago Tribune*, 22 April 1948, 18. Byrd is quoted in Charles J. Williams to Spessard Holland, 16 June 1948; copy in "Education, Federal Aid to, 1948," Box 286, Holland Papers.

50. Smith to Jaspar E. Crane, Esquire, 15 April 1948; copy in "Labor and Public Welfare Committee—Federal Aid to Education," Box 132, Smith Papers. Maybank's comments are from "Statement of Senator Burnet R. Maybank (D.—S.C.) on Behalf of Federal Aid to Education (S. 472), April 1, 1948;" copy in "Speeches and Press Releases 1947–48, January–May," Maybank Papers.

51. The final vote appears in *NYT*, 2 April 1948, 1, 2; and *CR* 94:3:3958. Olin Johnston's views are from Johnston to R. R. Whitlock, 13 May 1948; copy in "Federal Aid to Education 1947–1948," Box 242, Johnston Papers.

52. Aiken's analysis is from Aiken, "The Case for Federal Aid to Our Schools," *New York Times Magazine*, 28 December 1947, 9; copy in "Labor and Public Welfare 1947—Federal Aid to Education," Box 131, Smith Papers.

53. Curtis Hixon to Spessard Holland, 19 May 1948; copy in "Housing Legislation (May–June, 1948)," Box 288, Holland Papers. The best general accounts of public housing legislation and the postwar housing problems are Richard O. Davies, *Housing Reform During the Truman Administration* (Columbia, Mo., University of Missouri Press, 1966).

54. Kem's opinions were reported in *NYT*, 22 April 1948, 28. Wherry's comments are from a 15 July 1948 press release cited in Dalstrom, "Kenneth S. Wherry," 654.

55. Taft's statement is from an undated typescript in "Housing 1948," Box 653, Taft Papers. Flanders's comments are from a speech delivered to the National Public Housing Conference in New York City; see "A Housing Bargain;" copy in Box 134, Ralph Flanders Papers, Syracuse University Library, Department of Special Collections.

56. "Address by U.S. Senator Irving M. Ives before 1948 Oberlin Mock Convention," 8 May 1948," 2; copy in Box 41, Irving M. Ives Papers, Cornell University. Flanders's comments are from "A Housing Bargain." Tobey's analysis is quoted in Dalstrom, "Kenneth S. Wherry," 649.

57. House action on the housing bill and its attempted revival in the special session are discussed in Davies, *Housing Reform During the Truman Administration*, 80–96; and Lee F. Johnson, "How They Licked the TEW Bill," *Survey Graphic*, 37 (November 1948): 448–49. Voting alignments on the Cain amendment are from *CR* 94:4:4683.

58. George Aiken, "Keeping Step With a Changing World," Round Church, Richmond, Vermont, 5 September 1948; copy in "Speechbook, 1948, Part II," Crate 48, Box 7, Aiken Papers.

CHAPTER 6. THE NEW CONSERVATISM AND THE FAIR DEAL

1. The comments of Democratic party leaders were cited in Cabell Phillips, "Truman Plans Face A Series of Hurdles," *NYT*, 20 February 1949, sec. 4, p. 6.

2. Roper's report was in "The Only Hope for the GOP," *The Nation*, 12 March 1949, 297–99. Three other changes occurred in Senate membership in 1948: M. C. Smith in Maine replaced Wallace White, who retired; Hubert H. Humphrey defeated Joseph Ball in Minnesota; and Virgil Chapman of Kentucky replaced Alben Barkley, who was elected Vice President. For a full account of the 1948 Senate elections, see *NYT*, 4 November 1948, 2.

3. The best one-volume account of the 1948 election is Irwin Ross, *The Loneliest Campaign: The Truman Victory of 1948* (New York, The New American Library, 1968). But see also Richard S. Kirkendall, "Election of 1948," in Arthur M. Schlesinger Jr. and Fred L. Israel, eds. *History of American Presidential Elections, 1789–1968,* vol. 4 (New York, Chelsea House, 1971); Norman D. Markowitz, *The Rise and Fall of the People's Century: Henry A. Wallace and American Liberalism* (New York, Free Press, 1973); Robert A. Garson, *The Democratic Party and the Politics of Sectionalism, 1941–1948* (Baton Rouge, Louisiana State University Press, 1974); and Robert Ferrell, "The Last Hurrah," *The Wilson Quarterly* 12 (spring 1988): 66–82.

4. Ferrell, "The Last Hurrah," 72. The "Declaration of Principles" is quoted by Ross, *The Loneliest Campaign,* 131. Dixon's comments are from Dixon to Edward S. Hemphill, 28 July 1948, quoted in J. Barton Starr, "Birmingham and the 'Dixiecrat' Convention of 1948," *The Alabama Historical Quarterly* 32 (spring–summer 1970): 42, n. 67. Luce's description of the Dixiecrats is from Ferrell, "The Last Hurrah," 66.

5. For the decision of southern Democrats, see for example, Gilbert C. Fite, *Richard B. Russell, Jr., Senator From Georgia* (Chapel Hill, N.C., University of North Carolina Press, 1991), esp. 239–42. Johnston's position is analyzed by John E. Borsos, "Support for the National Democratic Party in South Carolina During the Dixiecrat Revolt of 1948," *The Southern Historian* 9 (1988): 11–14. See also Ross, *The Loneliest Campaign,* 230–32.

6. "Strange Combination," *Chicago Tribune,* 2 January 1949, pt. 1, p. 16. Lodge's interview is described in Arthur Krock, " 'Modern' Republicans Seek New Party Line," *NYT,* 2 January 1949, sec. 4, p. 3. Smith's remarks are from Diary entry for 30 December 1948, "The Diary of H. Alexander Smith," 1948–392, Box 282, Smith Papers.

7. The vote is reported in *NYT*, 4 January 1949, 1, 2; and *NYHT*, 4 January 1949, 4. The *Herald Tribune* reported that the fourteenth Republican to vote for Lodge did not want his name revealed, but Taft's most recent biographer suggests it may have been William Langer. See James T. Patterson, *Mr. Republican,* 426–27.

8. Contemporary analyses of the GOP division include Stewart Alsop, "Ring in the Old," *NYHT,* 3 January 1949, 11; and Jack Steele, "Republican Liberals Join to Oppose 'Old Guard,' " *NYHT,* 2 January 1949, sec. 2, p. 1. Taft's most recent biographer, James T. Patterson, argues that the 1949 struggle was a power struggle in which the more recently elected GOP insurgents vied for greater decision-making power within the party hierarchy. See Patterson, *Mr. Republican,* 426–29.

9. Ives's comments are from *NYT*, 4 January 1949, 2. Morse's are from *NYT,* 5 January 1949, 2.

10. The best summary of the 1949 filibuster is in William S. White, *Citadel: The Story of the U.S. Senate* (New York, Harper and Brothers, 1956), 60–64. Details of the State of the Union Address are in "Enter, the Fair Deal," *Newsweek,* 17 January 1949, 17–18.

11. "Brief Summary of the Address by Senator Clyde R. Hoey of N.C., Before the State Building and Loan League at its Annual Convention at Blowing Rock on Monday, June 13, 1949;" copy in "Statements and Speeches, 1947–1949," Box 211, Hoey Papers.

12. "Notes for Speech on Housing Bill in the Senate," 1–3; carbon typescript in "Housing 1949," Box 655, Taft Papers.

13. For the details of the Administration's bill and the introduction of the Taft bill, see *NYT,* 7 January 1949, 1; and Davies, *Housing Reform During the Truman Administration,* 102–5.

14. Tobey to P. F. Merrill, 22 March 1949, Box 89, Tobey Papers. Details of the compromise bill are in *NYT,* 26 February 1949, 9. The sponsors of the bill were Ellender, Maybank, Wagner, Sparkman, Myers, Hill, Pepper, Long, Taylor, Douglas, and Frear, Democrats; and Flanders, Aiken, Tobey, Taft, Lodge, Morse, Young, Baldwin, Ives, Thye, and H. A. Smith, Republicans.

15. Wherry's comments are from a speech prepared for 21 April 1949, but apparently never delivered; quoted in Dalstrom, "Kenneth S. Wherry," 838.

16. Voting alignments are from *CR* 95:4:4903. For details and debate on the two Bricker amendments, see *NYT,* 22 April 1949, 1, 15. Voting alignments on the first Bricker amendment appear in *CR* 95:4:4860. Alignments on the second Bricker amendment, which was defeated 46–32, appear in *CR* 95:4:4861.

17. Tobey to Haven E. Flanders, 24 May 1949; copy in Box 89, Tobey Papers. Lodge's views are from Lodge to James B. Peirce, 12 March 1949; copy in "1949 Legislative File," Lodge Papers, Massachusetts Historical Society. Holland's comments are from Holland to M. M. Rouden 7 May 1949; Copy in "Housing Legislation (March 1949)," Box 316, Holland Papers.

18. "U.S. Schools Found in Need of Ten Billions for Buildings," *NYT,* 4 April 1949; clipping in "Education 1949–53," Box 536, Taft Papers.

19. Details of the bill appear in *NYT,* 6 May 1949, 1, 18. See also Patterson, *Mr. Republican,* 432–33.

20. Byrd's remarks are from *CR* 95:4:5405.

21. The vote on the Lodge amendment appears in *NYT,* 3 May 1949, 18. Voting alignments are in *CR* 95:4:5428. For Lodge's position, see Lodge to Hugh Nixon, 2 May 1949; copy in "1950 Legislative File," Lodge Papers.

22. For adoption of the bill on 5 May, see *NYT,* 6 May 1949, 1, 18 and *CR* 95:5:5687. For alignments on the Bricker amendment, see *CR* 95:5:5679.

23. For details of the Administration's labor bill, see *NYT,* 30 January 1949, sec. 1, p. 1; and "Between the Hill and the White House," *Newsweek,* 14 February 1949, 15–16.

24. Russell's comments are in an undated, untitled transcript of an interview; copy in "Speech Files," Russell Papers. Smith's remarks are contained in " 'Should the Taft-Hartley Act Be Repealed and the Wagner Act Reinstated Without Amendment?' Statement of Senator H. Alexander Smith, Exclusive for 'The New York Daily Compass,' " 30 June 1949; transcript in "Labor and Public Welfare—1949, Management—Labor Relations," Box 133, Smith Papers.

25. "The Taft-Hartley Law and Its Successor," 1–19; copy in "Labor Relations—Miscellaneous 1948–1949," Box 683, Taft Papers. The opinion of the *Atlanta Constitution* is from "Let's Be Specific About It," 4 February 1949, 10;

clipping attached to John H. Cheatam to Richard B. Russell, 4 February 1949; in Legislative file, Labor and Public Welfare Series, Russell Papers. The *Washington Post*'s view is from "Labor Relations Bill," 31 January 1949, 8. The employee's letter to Burnet Maybank is Paul S. Tinsley to Maybank, 1 March 1949; in "Legislation—Labor—Taft-Hartley, 1949," Maybank Papers.

26. Adoption of the three amendments, which were sponsored by Douglas, Humphrey, Hill, Withers, Aiken, Morse, Tobey, and M. C. Smith, is reported in *NYT,* 16 June 1949, 1.

27. For the introduction of the Lucas amendment, see *NYT,* 24 June 1949, 18. The pressures exerted on the Administration by organized labor are detailed in "Between the Hill and the White House," *Newsweek,* 14 February 1949, 15–16.

28. Introduction of the Holland amendment in *NYT,* 24 June 1949, 18.

29. Final action on the bill is reported in *NYT,* 1 July 1949, 1, 2. Alignments on the vote substituting the Taft bill are in *CR* 95:7:8716–17. Alignments on the final vote appear in *CR* 95:7:8717. The vote on the Holland amendment saw such new conservatives as Aiken, Flanders, Gillette, Ives, Lodge, Saltonstall, H. A. Smith, M. C. Smith, and Thye join with Administration forces. But other new conservatives, such as George, Hoey, Holland, and Russell voted with the obstructionists. The vote on the Lucas amendment saw Flanders, Saltonstall, H. A. Smith, and M. C. Smith shift their votes to the obstructionists. See *CR* 95:7:8506–7. For the Holland amendment, see *CR* 95:7:8495.

30. Undated, untitled typescript of Ives's statement, probably before the Committee on Labor and Public Welfare, p. 8; in "S. 249 Hearings," Box 26, Ives Papers. Although Ives ultimately voted against the 1949 Labor bill because he disagreed with its continued use of injunctions, he believed it was far more acceptable than the Administration's bill. See Ives to ?, 16 July 1949; copy in "Labor Legislation—Miscellaneous Material," Box 26, Ives Papers. Holland's remarks are from Holland to Honorable R. H. Rowe, 7 January 1949; copy in "Labor Legislation—Taft-Hartley (January 1949), Box 316, Holland Papers.

31. The votes on the Wherry and Taft-Russell amendments saw such new conservatives as Aiken, Hoey, Ives, Morse, Saltonstall, M. C. Smith, Thye, Tobey, and Vandenberg vote with Administration forces. The defeat of the Wherry and Taft-Russell amendments is reported in *NYT,* 2 April 1949, 1. For voting alignments, see *CR* 95:3:3682 (Wherry); *CR* 95:3:3699 (Taft-Russell). Capehart's remarks were discussed in *NYT,* 21 February 1949, 12. The bill appropriating $5.6 billion for the second year of Marshall Plan aid was approved by the Senate on 8 April by a margin of 70–7. The seven opponents were Ellender, Butler, Capehart, Jenner, Kem, Langer, and Wherry. See *NYT,* 9 April 1949, 1.

32. Watkins's position was reported in *NYT,* 2 June 1949, 15. Details of the NATO pact are provided in *NYT,* 25 February 1949, 1; Timothy P. Ireland, *Creating the Entangling Alliance: The Origins of the North Atlantic Treaty Organization* (Westport, Greenwood Press, Conn., 1981).

33. Holland's comments are from Holland to L. J. Vair, 1 August 1949; copy in "North Atlantic Pact (July 1949)," Box 319, Holland Papers. *NYT,* 22 July 1949, 1, 2. For voting alignments on the Wherry amendment, see *CR* 95:8:9915; on the Watkins amendment, see *CR* 95:8:9916; and on final ratification, see *CR* 95:8:9916. Those new conservatives who voted against the Wherry and Watkins amendments and for final passage of the NATO pact included Aiken, George, Hoey, Holland, Ives, Lodge, Morse, O'Conor, Robertson, Russell, Saltonstall, H. A. and M. C. Smith, Thye, Tobey, and Vandenberg.

34. Only three of the Democrats voting, Ed Johnson, Elmer Thomas, and Joseph

O'Mahoney, deserted the Administration. All Republicans voting supported the peril point amendment. For the vote, see *NYT,* 16 September 1949, 1, 2; and *CR* 95:10:12925.

35. Details of the Malone amendment are from *NYT,* 14 September 1949, 1, 3. For the defeat of the Malone substitute and final passage of the reciprocal trade bill, see *NYT,* 16 September 1949. Voting alignments for the Malone substitute are in *CR* 95:10:12935; and for final passage of the extension bill, see *CR* 95:10:12936. Both votes indicated that such new conservatives as Aiken, Flanders, George, Hoey, Holland, Ives, O'Conor, Robertson, Russell, Saltonstall, M. C. Smith, Thye, Tobey, and Vandenberg had sided with the Administration in support of reciprocal trade. Hugh Butler's remarks are from Justus F. Paul, "The Political Career of Senator Hugh Butler," 279.

36. Lindley, "Tides in the 81st Congress," *Newsweek,* 23 May 1949, 26.

37. William S. White, "Senate's Southern Bloc Still Dominant," *NYT,* 14 May 1950, sec. 4, p. 7.

38. W. H. Lawrence, "GOP 'Rebels' Frame Their Own Platform," *NYT,* 5 March 1950, sec. 4, p. 10, reported on the declarations of the GOP national leadership. For the rise of McCarthyism and its partisan implications, see Richard M. Fried, *Men Against McCarthy* (New York, Columbia University Press, 1976); Robert Griffith, *The Politics of Fear* (Lexington, Ky., The University Press of Kentucky, 1970); David Reinhard, *The Republican Right Since 1945* (Lexington, Ky., The University Press of Kentucky, 1983); and Richard Rovere, *Senator Joe McCarthy* (New York, Harcourt, Brace, 1959).

39. "A Declaration of Republican Principles," 6; copy in "1950 General Correspondence," Leverett Saltonstall Papers, Massachusetts Historical Society. Additional information concerning the Declaration is provided in Henry Cabot Lodge, "Modernize the GOP," *The Atlantic* 185 (March 1950): 23–28.

40. Cabell Phillips, "GOP Progressives Want 'Dynamic Conservatism,' " *NYT,* 11 June 1950, sec. 4, p. 7. So great was the Republican new conservatives' dissatisfaction that leaders from more than twelve states met secretly in Philadelphia on 1 July to form an independent organization, "the Republican Advance," to press for more progressive policies. On the formation of the Republican Advance, see "Rebels in the GOP," *The Nation,* 15 July 1950, 51–52; and *NYT,* 2 July 1950, sec. 4, pp. 1, 27.

41. Details of Title 3 of the housing bill are from *NYT,* 11 March 1950, 6; "Assails Truman Housing Scheme as 'Dangerous,' " *Chicago Tribune,* 11 March 1950, sec. 1, p. 9; and Richard O. Davies, *Housing Reform During the Truman Administration,* (Columbia, Mo., University of Missouri Press, 1966), 117–21.

42. For the introduction of the Bricker-Cain amendment, see *NYT,* 11 March 1950, 6. Bricker's analysis of the bill is from John Bricker to Spessard Holland, 13 March 1950; in "Housing (March 1950)," Box 355, Holland Papers. Cain is quoted in *NYT,* 16 March 1950, 1, 23.

43. Tobey's views are from "Assails Truman Housing Scheme as 'Dangerous,' " *Chicago Tribune,* 11 March 1950, sec. 1, p. 9. For similar criticisms, see "Economy-Riddled Housing," *Newsweek,* 27 March 1950, 23–24. The introduction of the Tobey-Ives substitute is reported in *NYT,* 11 March 1950, 6.

44. Senate action on the housing bill is reported in *NYT,* 16 March 1950, 1, 23; and "Economy-Riddled Housing," *Newsweek,* 27 March 1950, 23–24. Alignments on the Bricker amendment are from *CR* 96:3:3385; and on the Tobey-Ives substitute are in *CR* 96:3:3388. The vote on the Tobey-Ives substitute emphasized the elevated partisanship of an election year. Most GOP new conservatives, including

Aiken, Flanders, Ives, Lodge, Saltonstall, H. A. and M. C. Smith, Thye, and Tobey voted for the amendment, while Democratic new conservatives such as Frear, George, Gillette, Hoey, Holland, Edwin Johnson, Johnston, Maybank, O'Conor, Robertson, and Russell voted no.

45. Taft's views are in "Senate Kills Two Reorganization Plans," *NYT,* 12 May 1950, 1, 18. Alignments on the vote are in *CR* 96:5:6887.

46. Senate action on the six-month extension of rent control approved in March is reported in *NYT,* 10 March 1950, 1, 19. For the alignments on this vote, see *CR* 96:3:3092.

47. Senate action on the bill in June extending rent control for an additional six months is from *NYT,* 13 June 1950, 1, 44. Alignments on the vote rejecting recommittal are in *CR* 96:6:8427. Alignments on final adoption of the bill are from *CR* 96:6:8454–55. On the three votes, new conservatives such as Aiken, Flanders, Holland, Ives, Edwin Johnson, Lodge, Russell, M. C. and H. A. Smith, and Tobey voted with liberals to extend rent controls. Details of the Democratic Congressional conference held on 8 June are reported in *NYT,* 9 June 1950, 1.

48. Connally's views are in *NYT,* 21 April 1950, 1, 7. Hickenlooper's remarks are from *NYT,* 24 April 1950, 11.

49. Senate voting on Marshall Plan extension is reported in *NYT,* 6 May 1950, 1, 2. For voting alignments on the Kem amendment see *CR* 96:5:6442; for the Taft amendment see *CR* 96:5:6445; for the Bridges amendment see *CR* 96:5:6448. New conservatives who voted against the Taft amendment and for the Bridges amendment were Aiken, Hoey, Holland, Saltonstall, and Thye. Other new conservatives voting for the Bridges amendment were Ives, Edwin Johnson, Russell, M. C. Smith, and Tobey.

50. Taft's remarks, as well as those of his opponents are from *NYT,* 12 August 1950, 1, 30. For committee action on the mobilization bill, see *NYT,* 3 August 1950, 1. Details of Truman's special message to Congress are from *NYT,* 20 July 1950, 1, 12, 14; and "Everything He Wants," *Newsweek,* 31 July 1950, 22–25.

51. Wherry's charges are from *CR* 96:9:12591. The attack by four members of the Senate Foreign Relations Committee is described in *NYT,* 14 August 1950, 1. For the breakdown of bipartisanship in foreign policy, see also David R. Kepley, *The Collapse of the Middle Way: Senate Republicans and the Bipartisan Foreign Policy, 1948–1952* (Westport, Conn., Greenwood Press, 1988).

52. Jenner's denunciation of Marshall is in *CR* 96:11:14914.

53. Henry Cabot Lodge Jr., Press Release, 18 January 1949, 3; copy in 1949 Legislative File on Guaranteed Annual Wage, Box 44, Lodge Papers.

54. The assessment of Kenneth Wherry is from William S. White, "Portrait of a 'Fundamentalist,' " *New York Times Magazine,* 15 January 1950, 14.

CHAPTER 7. THE NEW CONSERVATISM IN AN ERA OF CONSENSUS

1. For Hoover's speech see, "What-to-Do Debate," *Newsweek,* 1 January 1951, 10–11; and "Which Way for U.S.—The Choice," *U.S. News,* 19 January 1951, 16–17.

2. Truman's State of the Union Address is reported in *NYT,* 9 January 1951, 1, 12.

3. Taft's speech is reported in *NYT,* 6 January 1951, 1, 4; James T. Patterson,

Mr. Republican: A Biography of Robert A. Taft (Boston, Houghton Mifflin, 1972), 476–84; and in Ernest K. Lindley, "Taft's New Platform," *Newsweek,* 15 January 1951, 27.

4. Lodge's views are discussed in "The Great Debate," *Newsweek,* 22 January 1951, 18–19.

5. For the introduction of the Wherry resolution, see *NYT,* 9 January 1951, 1. General accounts of the Great Debate include Burton I. Kaufman, *The Korean War: Challenges in Crisis, Credibility, and Command* (Philadelphia, Temple University Press, 1986); Ronald J. Caridi, *The Korean War and American Politics: The Republican Party as a Case Study* (Philadelphia, University of Pennsylvania Press, 1968); and David R. Kepley, *The Collapse of the Middle Way: Senate Republicans and the Bipartisan Foreign Policy, 1948–1952* (Westport, Conn., Greenwood Press, 1988).

6. For introduction of the Connally-Russell resolution, see *NYT,* 22 January 1951, 12. Truman's press conference is reported in *NYT,* 12 January 1951, 1, 8; and "Cacophony in Congress," *Newsweek,* 29 January 1951, 19–21.

7. "Radio Script for Senator S. L. Holland's Program for Florida Stations—Weekend April 7, 1951," typescript copy in "Speeches—82nd 1st," Box 391, Holland Papers. Lodge's and Knowland's concerns were reported in *NYT,* 12 January 1951, 1, 10.

8. New conservatives such as George, Flanders, Knowland, Lodge, Saltonstall, H. Alexander Smith, and Tobey voted with obstructionists Byrd, Stennis, Bridges, Cain, Wiley, and Hickenlooper in support of the two amendments. The vote was reported by *NYT,* 9 March 1951, 1, 4. On 13 March the Joint Committee twice voted 13–11 to block efforts to strike the Smith amendment from the resolution, and then voted 24–0 to report the Connally-Russell resolution to the full Senate. See *NYT,* 14 March 1951, 1, 7.

9. In contrast to the Smith stipulation, which required merely that the Administration consult with Congress over future troop movements, the McClellan declaration stated that "it is the sense of the Senate that no ground troops in addition to such four divisions should be sent to Western Europe in implementation of Article 3 of the North Atlantic Treaty without further Congressional approval." Quoted in *NYT,* 3 April 1951, 1, 4. Voting alignments on the McClellan declaration are in *CR* 97:3:3096. The eastern Republicans who voted against the McClellan declaration were Aiken, Flanders, Ives, Lodge, Saltonstall, H. A. Smith, and Tobey.

10. New conservatives who voted with the Administration against the Bricker amendment were Aiken, Duff, Flanders, Frear, George, Gillette, Hoey, Holland, Ives, Johnston, Lodge, Maybank, Nixon, Russell, Saltonstall, and H. A. Smith. Action on the Bricker, Mundt, and Kem amendments is reported in *NYT,* 4 April 1951, 1, 17. Voting alignments on the Bricker amendment are in *CR* 97:3:3190. Alignments on the Mundt amendment, defeated 52–29, is in *CR* 97:3:3194; and on the Kem amendment, defeated 64–24, are in *CR* 97:3:3160. Practically the same group of new conservatives that voted against the Bricker amendment also voted against the Mundt and Kem amendments.

11. Reston, "Issues in the 'Great Debate' are Narrowed," *NYT,* 11 February 1951, sec. 4, p. 3. Similar analysis is offered by Ernest K. Lindley, "Congress and Europe," *Newsweek,* 22 January 1951, 27; and the *NYT,* 5 April 1951, 28. For the alignments on the vote approving the Connally-Russell resolution, see *CR* 97:3:3282. All new conservatives who voted sided with the Administration in favor of the amended resolution.

12. In the 82nd Congress, votes related to the Troops to Europe resolution scaled in the Extension of Executive Power dimension.

13. Bricker's remarks are in *CR* 97:3:2697–98. A good discussion of Bricker's foreign policy views that also emphasizes the Ohioan's concern with the growth of presidential power in foreign affairs is Duane Tananbaum, *The Bricker Amendment Controversy: A Test of Eisenhower's Political Leadership* (Ithaca, Cornell University Press, 1988).

14. For the Administration's request on draft extension, see *NYT*, 6 March 1951, 1, 15; and "Senate Strings on Draft," *Newsweek*, 19 March 1951, 25. The bill reported out by the Armed Services Committee lowered the draft age to eighteen, but required draft boards to induct all available men between nineteen and twenty-six before it began taking those eighteen years old.

15. The vote on the Morse amendment is in *CR* 97:2:1909–10.

16. Senate action approving a ceiling on troops is reported in *NYT*, 8 March 1951, 1, 8. Eleven of the new conservatives who had voted with the Administration to reject the Morse amendment on 5 March switched to the obstructionists to defeat the McMahon substitute. They were Aiken, Frear, George, Hoey, Edwin Johnson, Lodge, Robertson, Saltonstall, H. A. Smith, Willis Smith, and Tobey. For the alignments on the McMahon substitute, see *CR* 97:2:2053. Ten new conservatives who had voted with obstructionists against the McMahon substitute later joined with the Administration to adopt the Robertson amendment. They were Frear, Hoey, Ives, Edwin Johnson, Johnston, Lodge, Robertson, H. A. Smith, Willis Smith, and Tobey. Alignments on the Robertson motion are in *CR* 97:2:2056. Nine new conservatives who voted with the Administration for the Robertson amendment then switched back to the obstructionists to approve the modified Morse amendment. They were Frear, Ives, Edwin Johnson, Johnston, O'Conor, Robertson, H. A. Smith, Willis Smith, and Tobey. See *CR* 97:2:2056–57.

17. The constitutional significance of the troop ceilings was emphasized by Arthur Krock, "Reversing a 'Drift' from the Constitution," *NYT*, 9 March 1951, 24.

18. Truman's request for expansion of the Defense Production Act is reported in "Wanted: Tighter Controls—with Teeth," *Newsweek*, 7 May 1951, 63. His remarks before a nationwide radio and television audience are in *NYT*, 15 June 1951, 1, 12.

19. Details of the bill reported by the Banking and Currency Committee are in *NYT*, 22 June 1951, 1, 13.

20. Senate action on the extension of the Defense Production Act is reported in *NYT*, 28 June 1951, 1, 17; and *NYT*, 29 June 1951, 1, 10. Voting alignments on the first Douglas amendment are from *CR* 97:5:7228. Alignments on the second Douglas amendment allowing rollbacks of up to 10%, which was defeated 58–26, are from *CR* 97:6:7357. The vote on final passage of the bill is in *CR* 97:6:7406. The opponents of extension were mostly all Republican obstructionists from interior states. They were Wallace Bennett, (Utah); Hugh Butler, (Neb.); Everett Dirksen, (Ill.); William Jenner, (Ind.); William Knowland, (Calif.), George Malone, (Nev.); Herman Welker, (Idaho), Kenneth Wherry, (Neb.); John Williams, (Del.); and Milton Young, (N.D.).

21. Maybank's concerns are in Arthur Krock, "A Happy Band of Sworn Brothers," *NYT*, 3 July 1951, 20.

22. George's views are in *NYT*, 19 August 1951, sec. 1, pp. 1, 13. For the House bill, see "Foreign Aid Roaring Through Despite Congressional Qualms," *Newsweek*, 27 August 1951, 19. For the Senate bill reported out of the combined Foreign Relations/Armed Services Committee, see *NYT*, 27 August 1951, 12.

23. The liberals' efforts are reported in *NYT*, 29 August 1951, 13. The ten co-sponsors of the Dirksen amendment were Malone, Wherry, Welker, Dworshak, Case, Schoeppel, Mundt, Williams, Byrd, and McClellan. See *NYT*, 31 August

1951, 6. For Connally's announcement see *NYT*, 27 August 1951, 12. Newsweek linked Connally's about-face on foreign aid to his concerns for re-election. See "Tom Connally's Revolt," *Newsweek*, 13 August 1951, 16, 17.

24. Senate action on the foreign aid bill is reported in *NYT*, 1 September 1951, 1, 4. Voting alignments on the first Dirksen amendment are in *CR* 97:8:10885–86. The only new conservative to vote for the Green-McMahon amendment was Morse. All others voting sided with conservatives in opposition. See *CR* 97:8:10896. Alignments on the second Dirksen amendment are from *CR* 97:8:10928.

25. *NYT*, 9 April 1952, 1, 16. The best account of the incident is Maeva Marcus, *Truman and the Steel Seizure Crisis* (New York, Columbia University Press, 1977).

26. Russell's remarks are from "Speech—Steel Mill Seizure by President—April 21, 1952," copy in Speech file, 1952–53; Richard B. Russell Papers. Hoey's comments are from an undated, untitled statement in "Statements and Speeches, 1950–1952," Box 211, Hoey Papers.

27. *NYT*, 22 April 1952, 1, 18. Truman's appeal was made in a letter to Vice President Alben Barkley. Voting alignments on the amendment, sponsored by conservative Michigan Republican Homer Ferguson, are in *CR* 98:3:4155.

28. Both the Maybank and Monroney amendments were proposed for inclusion in a pending bill to extend the Defense Production Act. New conservatives voting against both amendments included Flanders, Frear, George, Hoey, Nixon, Robertson, Saltonstall, H. A. Smith, and Willis Smith. Ives and Tobey joined the new conservatives in voting against the Monroney amendment. For alignments on the Maybank amendment, see *CR* 98:5:6909. For the Monroney amendment, see *CR* 98:5:6917–18. Since the Maybank amendment permitted seizures after so long a cooling-off period, it raised fears in labor circles, as the 1949 labor debate had, that the Administration, faced with crippling strikes affecting national security, would have to resort to injunctions.

29. Senate action on 10 June is reported in *NYT*, 11 June 1952, 1, 24. New conservatives who voted for the Byrd amendment were Flanders, Frear, George, Hoey, Smathers, Holland, Maybank, Nixon, Robertson, Saltonstall, H. A. Smith, and Willis Smith. Alignments on the Byrd amendment, which was adopted by a vote of 49–30, are in *CR* 98:5:6926.

30. William S. White, "Truman and the Congress: Another 'Cold War,' " *NYT*, 15 June 1952, sec. 4, p. 6.

31. The reasons for Connally's rightward shift are discussed in Albert T. Collins, "Connally of Texas Faces Battle for Senate Seat," *NYT*, 23 March 1952, sec. 4, p. 7. Opposition to foreign aid in 1952 is analyzed by Arthur Krock, "Some Impulses Behind the Appropriations Axe," *NYT*, 27 May 1952, 26. Bridges's views are reported in *NYT*, 7 March 1952, 1, 7.

32. The committee vote was 9–3. Those voting in favor of the reduction were Connally, George, Sparkman, Gillette, Wiley, H. A. Smith, Tobey, Brewster, and Hickenlooper. The three "no" votes came from T. F. Green, McMahon, and Fulbright. See *NYT*, 29 April 1952, 1. During Senate debate, amendments from Republican Herman Welker and Democrats Russell Long and Allen Ellender proposing additional cuts in foreign aid funds were all defeated. New conservatives voting against each of these amendments were Aiken, George, Hoey, Holland, Ives, Lodge, Morse, Nixon, Russell, Saltonstall, H. A. Smith, and Tobey. Alignments on the Welker amendment, defeated 41–33, are in *CR* 98:5:6095; for the Long amendment, defeated 40–37, see *CR* 98:5:6098; and for the Ellender amendment, rejected 43–34, see *CR* 98:5:6107.

33. Connally is quoted in *NYT*, 8 January 1952, 17.

34. Butler radio address, March 1952; quoted in Justus F. Paul, "The Political Career of Senator Hugh Butler, 1941–1954," 343. For the President's request and Congressional reaction, see *NYT*, 12 February 1952, 1, 21.

35. *NYT*, 5 June 1952, 1, 20. New conservatives who voted against the first Dirksen amendment but in favor of the second Dirksen amendment were Aiken, George, Hoey, Holland, Ives, Morse, Nixon, Saltonstall, H. A. Smith, Thye, Tobey. For the vote, see *CR* 98:5:6534–35. On the Capehart amendment, all new conservatives voting sided with the Administration in opposition to the measure. For alignments on the Capehart amendment, rejected 57–22, see *CR* 98:5:6552. Alignments on the first Dirksen amendment, defeated on 29 May, are from *CR* 98:5:6234.

36. Russell's views are from "Quizzing Russell," *U.S. News*, 13 June 1952, 54.

CHAPTER 8. THE TWO CONSERVATISMS

1. The effect of the New Deal and World War II in producing a paradigm shift in American politics is suggested by Alonzo Hamby, *Liberalism and Its Challengers: From F.D.R. to Bush*, 2d ed. (New York, Oxford University Press, 1992); William Leuchtenberg, *In the Shadow of FDR: From Harry Truman to Ronald Reagan* (Ithaca, Cornell University Press, 1983); Alan Brinkley, *Voices of Protest: Huey Long, Father Coughlin and the Great Depression* (New York, Vintage Books, 1982); Wayne S. Cole, *Roosevelt and the Isolationists, 1932–1945* (Lincoln, University of Nebraska Press, 1983); Ronald L. Feinman, *Twilight of Progressivism: The Western Republican Senators and the New Deal* (Baltimore, Johns Hopkins University Press, 1981); J. Joseph Huthmacher, *Senator Robert F. Wagner and the Rise of Urban Liberalism* (New York, Atheneum, 1971); and Otis L. Graham Jr. *An Encore for Reform: The Old Progressives and the New Deal* (New York, Oxford University Press, 1967).

2. Many studies have long argued that the gains of the New Deal were not secured until a moderate Republican president, Dwight Eisenhower, was elected in 1952. See, for example, Hamby, *Liberalism and its Challengers;* William Leuchtenberg, *In the Shadow of FDR;* Herbert S. Parmet, *The Democrats: The Years After FDR* (New York, Macmillan Publishing Company, 1976); Eric Goldman, *The Crucial Decade and After: America 1945–1960* (New York, Vintage Books, 1960); and Samuel Lubell, *The Future of American Politics,* 3d ed. (New York, Harper and Row, 1965).

3. Godfrey Hodgson, *America In Our Time* (New York, Doubleday and Company, 1976).

Bibliography

Manuscript Sources

George D. Aiken Papers. Bailey-Howell Memorial Library, University of Vermont, Burlington, Vermont.

Warren Austin Papers. Bailey-Howell Memorial Library, University of Vermont, Burlington, Vermont.

Josiah William Bailey Papers. William R. Perkins Library, Duke University, Durham, North Carolina.

Ralph Flanders Papers. Syracuse University Library, Department of Special Collections, Syracuse, New York.

Clyde R. Hoey Papers. William R. Perkins Library, Duke University, Durham, North Carolina.

Spessard L. Holland Papers. P. K. Yonge Library of Florida History, Smathers Library, University of Florida, Gainesville, Florida.

Irving M. Ives Papers. Division of Rare and Manuscript Collections, Cornell University Library, Ithaca, New York.

Olin D. Johnston Papers. The South Caroliniana Library, University of South Carolina, Columbia, South Carolina.

Henry Cabot Lodge Jr. Papers. Massachusetts Historical Society, Boston, Massachusetts.

Burnet R. Maybank Papers. Special Collections Department, The Robert Scott Small Library, College of Charleston, Charleston, South Carolina.

George L. Radcliffe Papers, Ms. 2280. Manuscripts Department, Maryland Historical Society, Baltimore, Maryland.

Richard B. Russell Jr. Papers. The Richard B. Russell Library for Political Research and Studies, University of Georgia, Athens, Georgia.

Leverett Saltonstall Papers. Massachusetts Historical Society, Boston, Massachusetts.

H. Alexander Smith Papers. Seeley G. Mudd Manuscript Library, Princeton University, Princeton, New Jersey.

Robert A. Taft Papers. Division of Manuscripts, Library of Congress, Washington, D.C.

Charles W. Tobey Papers. Dartmouth College Library, Hanover, New Hampshire.

Newspapers and Periodicals

Chicago Tribune, 1938–1952
The Nation, 1938–1952

New Republic, 1938–1952
Newsweek, 1938–1952
New York *Herald Tribune,* 1938–1952
New York Times, 1938–1952
St. Louis Post-Dispatch, 1938–1952
Time, 1938–1952
U.S. News and World Report, 1938–1952
Washington Post, 1938–1952

PUBLIC DOCUMENTS

U.S. Congress, *Congressional Record,* 1938–1952

BOOKS

Ambrose, Stephen E. *Rise to Globalism: American Foreign Policy 1938–1970.* Baltimore: Penguin Books, 1971.

Anderson, Lee F., *et al. Legislative Roll Call Analysis.* Evanston, Ill.: Northwestern University Press, 1966.

Bailey, Stephen K. *Congress Makes a Law: The Story Behind the Employment Act of 1946.* New York: Random House, 1964.

Barkley, Alben W. *That Reminds Me.* New York: Doubleday, 1954.

Bass, Jack and Walter DeVries. *The Transformation of Southern Politics: Social Change and Political Consequence Since 1945.* New York: Basic Books, 1976.

Blum, John Morton. *V Was for Victory: Politics and American Culture During World War II.* New York: Harcourt, Brace, Jovanovich, 1976.

Brinkley, Alan. *The End of Reform: New Deal Liberalism in Recession and War.* New York: Alfred A. Knopf, 1995.

———. *Voices of Protest, Huey Long, Father Coughlin and the Great Depression.* New York: Vintage Books, 1982.

Brown, Eugene. *J. William Fulbright: Advice and Dissent.* Iowa City: University of Iowa Press, 1985.

Burns, James MacGregor. *Congress on Trial.* New York: Gordian Press, 1966.

———. *The Deadlock of Democracy: Four-Party Politics in America.* Englewood Cliffs N.J.: Prentice-Hall, 1967.

———. *Roosevelt: The Soldier of Freedom.* New York: Harcourt, Brace, Jovanovich, 1971.

Caridi, Ronald J. *The Korean War and American Politics: The Republican Party as a Case Study.* Philadelphia: University of Pennsylvania Press, 1968.

Catton, Bruce. *The War Lords of Washington.* New York: Doubleday, 1948.

Christenson, Reo M. *The Brannan Plan: Farm Politics and Policies.* Ann Arbor: University of Michigan Press, 1959.

Clausen, Aage R. *How Congressmen Decide: A Policy Focus.* New York: St. Martin's Press, 1973.

Cole, Wayne S. *Roosevelt and the Isolationists, 1932–1945.* Lincoln: University of Nebraska Press, 1983.

———. *Senator Gerald P. Nye and American Foreign Relations.* Minneapolis: University of Minnesota Press, 1962.

Darilek, Richard E. *A Loyal Opposition in Time of War: The Republican Party and the Politics of Foreign Policy from Pearl Harbor to Yalta.* Westport Conn.: Greenwood Press, 1976.

Davies, Richard O. *Defender of the Old Guard: John Bricker and American Politics.* Columbus: Ohio State University Press, 1993.

———. *Housing Reform During the Truman Administration.* Columbia: University of Missouri Press, 1966.

Divine, Robert A. *Second Chance: The Triumph of Internationalism in America During World War II.* New York: Atheneum, 1967.

Doenecke, Justus D. *Not to the Swift: the Old Isolationists in the Cold War Era.* Lewisburg Pa.: Bucknell University Press, 1979.

Donovan, Robert J. *Conflict and Crisis: The Presidency of Harry S Truman, 1945–1948.* New York: W. W. Norton, 1977.

Douglas, Paul. *In the Fullness of Time.* New York: Harcourt, Brace, Jovanovich. 1971.

Drury, Allen. *A Senate Journal, 1943–1945.* New York: McGraw-Hill, 1963.

Fabricant, Solomon. *The Trend in Government Activity Since 1900.* New York: National Bureau of Economic Research, 1952.

Feinman, Ronald L. *Twilight of Progressivism: The Western Republican Senators and the New Deal.* Baltimore: Johns Hopkins University Press, 1981.

Fine, Sidney. *Laissez Faire and the General Welfare State: A Study of Conflict in American Thought.* Ann Arbor: University of Michigan Press, 1969.

Fite, Gilbert C. *Richard B. Russell, Jr.: Senator from Georgia.* Chapel Hill: University of North Carolina Press, 1991.

Flanders, Ralph E. *The American Century.* Cambridge: Harvard University Press, 1949.

———. *Senator from Vermont.* Boston: Little Brown, 1961.

Fowler, Hubert R. *The Unsolid South: Voting Behavior of Southern Senators, 1947–1960.* University: University of Alabama Press, 1968.

Fried, Richard M. *Men Against McCarthy.* New York: Columbia University Press, 1976.

Gaddis, John Lewis. *Strategies of Containment: A Critical Appraisal of Postwar American National Security Policy.* New York: Oxford University Press, 1982.

Garson, Robert A. *The Democratic Party and the Politics of Sectionalism, 1941–1948.* Baton Rouge: Louisiana State University Press, 1974.

Gimbel, John. *The Origins of the Marshall Plan.* Palo Alto: Stanford University Press, 1976.

Glad, Betty. *Key Pittman: Tragedy of a Senate Insider.* New York: Columbia University Press, 1986.

Goldman, Eric. *The Crucial Decade and After: America 1945–1960.* New York: Vintage Books, 1960.

Graham Jr. Otis L. *An Encore for Reform: The Old Progressives and the New Deal.* New York: Oxford University Press, 1967.

Grassmuck, George L. *Sectional Biases in Congress on Foreign Policy.* Baltimore: Johns Hopkins University Press, 1951.

Griffith, Robert. *The Politics of Fear: Joseph R. McCarthy and the Senate.* Lexington: The University Press of Kentucky, 1970.

Hamby, Alonzo. *Beyond the New Deal: Harry S Truman and American Liberalism.* New York: Columbia University Press, 1974.

———. *Liberalism and Its Challengers: From F.D.R. to Bush,* 2d ed., New York: Oxford University Press, 1992.

Harris, Seymour. *The Economics of America at War.* New York: W. W. Norton, 1943.

Hartley, Fred A. *Our New National Labor Policy: The Taft-Hartley Act and the Next Steps.* New York: Funk and Wagnalls, 1948.

Hartmann, Susan M. *Truman and the 80th Congress.* Columbia: University of Missouri Press, 1971.

Harvey, Ray, ed. *The Politics of this War.* New York: Harper and Brothers, 1943.

Hayek, Friedrich A. *The Road to Serfdom.* Chicago: University of Chicago Press, 1944.

Hodgson, Godfrey. *America in Our Time.* New York: Doubleday & Company, 1976.

Huss, John E. *Senator for the South: A Biography of Olin D. Johnston.* Garden City, N.Y.: Doubleday and Company, 1961.

Huthmacher, J. Joseph. *Senator Robert F. Wagner and the Rise of Urban Liberalism.* New York: Atheneum, 1971.

Ireland, Timothy P. *Creating the Entangling Alliance: The Origins of the North Atlantic Treaty Organization.* Westport Conn.: Greenwood Press, 1981.

Israel, Fred L. *Nevada's Key Pittman.* Lincoln: University of Nebraska Press, 1963.

Johnson, Donald B. *The Republican Party and Wendell Willkie.* Urbana: University of Illinois Press, 1960.

Jones, Joseph Marion. *The Fifteen Weeks.* New York: Harcourt, Brace and World, Inc., 1955.

Kasson, John F. *Amusing the Million: Coney Island at the Turn of the Century.* New York: Hill and Wang, 1978.

Kaufman, Burton I. *The Korean War: Challenges in Crisis, Credibility, and Command.* Philadelphia: Temple University Press, 1986.

Kepley, David R. *The Collapse of the Middle Way: Senate Republicans and the Bipartisan Foreign Policy, 1948–1952.* Westport, Conn.: Greenwood Press, 1988.

Kesselman, Louis. *The Social Politics of FEPC.* Chapel Hill: University of North Carolina Press, 1948.

Key, V. O. *Southern Politics in State and Nation.* New York: Alfred Knopf, 1949.

Kimball, Warren. *The Most Unsordid Act.* Baltimore: Johns Hopkins University Press, 1969.

Kirk, Russell. *The Conservative Mind.* Chicago: H. Regnery, 1960.

Kirk, Russell and James McClellan. *The Political Principles of Robert A. Taft.* New York: Macmillan, 1967.

Krieger, Leonard and Fritz Stern, eds. *The Responsibility of Power: Historical Es-*

says in Honor of Hajo Holborn. Garden City, N.Y.: Doubleday and Company, 1967.

LaFeber, Walter. *America, Russia, and the Cold War 1945–1980,* 4th ed. New York: John Wiley and Sons, 1980.

Lee, R. Alton. *Truman and Taft-Hartley: A Question of Mandate.* Lexington: University of Kentucky Press, 1966.

Lekachman, Robert. *The Age of Keynes.* New York: Vintage Books, 1968.

Leuchtenberg, William E. *Franklin D. Roosevelt and the New Deal.* New York: Harper and Row, 1963.

———. *In the Shadow of FDR: From Harry Truman to Ronald Reagan.* Ithaca: Cornell University Press, 1983.

Levine, Erwin L. *Theodore Francis Green: The Washington Years, 1937–1960.* Providence, R.I.: Brown University Press, 1971.

Lodge, Henry Cabot. *The Storm Has Many Eyes: A Personal Narrative.* New York: W. W. Norton, 1973.

Lubell, Samuel. *The Future of American Politics,* 3d ed. New York: Harper and Row, 1965.

———. *The Revolt of the Moderates.* New York: Harper and Brothers, 1956.

Lustig, R. Jeffrey. *Corporate Liberalism: The Origins of Modern American Political Theory, 1890–1920.* Berkeley: University of California Press, 1982.

MacRae, Duncan. *Dimensions of Congressional Voting.* Los Angeles: University of California Press, 1958.

Maddox, Robert. *William E. Borah and American Foreign Policy.* Baton Rouge: Louisiana State University Press, 1969.

Mansfield, Harvey. *A Short History of the OPA.* Washington: Office of Price Administration, n.d.

Marcus, Maeva. *Truman and the Steel Seizure Case.* New York: Columbia University Press, 1977.

Markowitz, Norman D. *The Rise and Fall of the People's Century: Henry A. Wallace and American Liberalism.* New York: Free Press, 1973.

Matthews, Donald R. *U.S. Senators and Their World.* Chapel Hill: University of North Carolina Press, 1960.

Matusow, Allen J. *Farm Policies and Politics in the Truman Years.* Cambridge: Harvard University Press, 1967.

Mayhew, David R. *Party Loyalty Among Congressmen: The Difference Between Democrats and Republicans, 1947–1962.* Cambridge: Harvard University Press, 1966.

McCune, Wesley. *The Farm Bloc.* Garden City, N.Y.: Doubleday, Doran, 1943.

McConnell, Timothy L. *The Wagner Housing Act.* Chicago: Loyola University Press, 1957.

McKenna, Marian C. *Borah.* Ann Arbor: University of Michigan Press, 1961.

Michie, Allan A. and Frank Rhylick. *Dixie Demagogues.* New York: Macmillan, 1939.

Miller, William J. *Henry Cabot Lodge: A Biography.* New York: Coward-McCann, 1967.

Millis, Harry A. and Emily Clark Brown. *From the Wagner Act to Taft-Hartley: A*

Study of National Labor Policy and Labor Relations. Chicago: University of Chicago Press, 1950.

Moore, John Robert. *Senator Josiah William Bailey of North Carolina: A Political Biography*. Durham: Duke University Press, 1968.

Nash, George H. *The Conservative Intellectual Movement in America Since 1945*. New York: Basic Books, 1976.

Nicholas, H. G. *Washington Despatches 1941–1945*. Chicago: University of Chicago Press, 1981.

Parmet, Herbert S. *The Democrats: The Years After FDR*. New York: Macmillan Publishing Company, 1976.

Patterson, James T. *Congressional Conservatism During the New Deal*. Lexington: University of Kentucky Press, 1967.

———. *Mr. Republican: A Biography of Robert A. Taft*. Boston: Houghton Mifflin, 1972.

Peterson, F. Ross. *Prophet Without Honor: Glen H. Taylor and the Fight for American Liberalism*. Lexington: University of Kentucky Press, 1974.

Phillips, Cabell. *The Truman Presidency*. New York: Macmillan Publishing Co., 1966.

Polenberg, Richard. *War and Society: The United States, 1941–1945*. Philadelphia: Lippincott, 1972.

Porter, David L. *Congress and the Waning of the New Deal,* Port Washington, N.Y.: Kennikat Press, 1980.

———. *The Seventy-sixth Congress and World War II, 1939–1940,* Columbia: University of Missouri Press, 1979.

Rayback, Joseph G. *A History of American Labor*. New York: Free Press, 1966.

Reichard, Gary W. *The Reaffirmation of Republicanism: Eisenhower and the 83rd Congress*. Knoxville: University of Tennessee Press, 1975.

Reinhard, David W. *The Republican Right Since 1945*. Lexington: University of Kentucky Press, 1983.

Rieselbach, Leroy N. *The Roots of Isolationism: Congressional Voting and Presidential Leadership in Foreign Policy*. Indianapolis: Bobbs-Merrill, 1966.

Robertson, David. *Sly and Able: A Political Biography of James F. Byrnes*. New York: W. W. Norton, 1994.

Rodgers, Daniel T. The Work Ethic in Industrial America 1850–1920. Chicago: University of Chicago Press, 1974.

Ross, David R. B. *Preparing for Ulysses: Politics and Veterans During World War II*. New York: Columbia University Press, 1969.

Ross, Irwin. *The Loneliest Campaign: The Truman Victory of 1948*. New York: The New American Library, 1968.

Rossiter, Clinton. *Conservatism in America: The Thankless Persuasion*. New York: Alfred A. Knopf, 1964.

Rovere, Richard. *Senator Joe McCarthy*. New York: Harcourt, Brace, 1959.

Ruchames, Louis. *Race, Jobs, and Politics: The Story of FEPC*. New York: Doubleday, 1953.

Salmond, John A. *The Civilian Conservation Corps, 1933–1942*. Durham: North Carolina State University Press, 1967.

Salter, J. T. *Public Men In and Out of Office*. Chapel Hill: University of North Carolina Press, 1946.

Schlesinger Jr., Arthur M. *The Vital Center*. Boston: Houghton, Mifflin, 1949.

Schlesinger Jr., Arthur M. and Fred L. Israel, eds., *History of American Presidential Elections, 1789–1968*. New York: Chelsea House, 1971.

Seidman, Joel I. *American Labor from Defense to Reconversion*. Chicago: University of Chicago Press, 1953.

Shannon, W. Wayne. *Party, Constituency and Congressional Voting*. Baton Rouge: Louisiana State University Press, 1968.

Shelly II, Mack C. *The Permanent Majority: The Conservative Coalition in the United States Congress*. University: University of Alabama Press, 1983.

Sinclair, Barbara. *Congressional Realignment 1925–1978*. Austin: University of Texas Press, 1982.

Sklar, Martin J. *The Corporate Reconstruction of American Capitalism, 1890–1916: The Market, The Law, and Politics*. Cambridge: Cambridge University Press, 1988.

Skowronek, Stephen. *Building a New American State: The Expansion of National Administrative Capacities, 1877–1920*. Cambridge: Cambridge University Press, 1982.

Smith, Gilbert E. *The Limits of Reform: Politics and Federal Aid to Education, 1937–1950*. New York: Garland Publishing, Inc., 1982.

Socolofsky, Homer E. *Arthur Capper: Publisher, Politician, and Philanthropist*. Lawrence: University of Kansas Press, 1962.

Stein, Herbert. *The Fiscal Revolution in America*. Chicago: University of Chicago Press, 1969.

Stromer, Marvin E. *The Making of a Political Leader: Kenneth S. Wherry and the United States Senate*. Lincoln: University of Nebraska Press, 1972.

Swain, Martha H. *Pat Harrison: The New Deal Years*. Jackson: University Press of Mississippi, 1978.

Taft, Robert A. *A Foreign Policy for Americans*. Garden City, N.Y.: Doubleday, 1952.

Tananbaum, Duane. *The Bricker Amendment Controversy: A Test of Eisenhower's Political Leadership*. Ithaca: Cornell University Press, 1988.

Tompkins, C. David. *Senator Arthur H. Vandenberg: The Evolution of a Modern Republican, 1884–1945*. East Lansing: Michigan State University Press, 1971.

Trachtenberg, Alan. *The Incorporation of America: Culture and Society in the Gilded Age*. New York: Hill and Wang, 1982.

Truman, David B. *The Congressional Party: A Case Study*. New York: John Wiley and Sons, 1959.

Turner, Julius. *Party and Constituency: Pressures on Congress*. Baltimore: Johns Hopkins University Press, 1951.

Vandenberg Jr., Arthur H. *The Private Papers of Senator Vandenberg*. Boston: Houghton, Mifflin, 1952.

Viereck, Peter. *Conservatism Revisited*. New York: Scribner's, 1949.

Westerfield, H. Bradford. *Foreign Policy and Party Politics*. New Haven: Yale University Press, 1955.

Wheeler, Burton K. with Paul F. Healy. *Yankee from the West.* Garden City, N.Y.: Doubleday, 1962.

White, William S. *Citadel: The Story of the U.S. Senate.* New York: Harper and Brothers, 1956.

————. *The Taft Story.* New York: Harper and Brothers, 1964.

Wiebe, Robert. *The Search for Order, 1877–1920.* New York: Hill and Wang, 1967.

Wilcox, Walter W. *The Farmer in the Second World War.* Ames: State University of Iowa Press, 1947.

Williams, William Appleman. *The Tragedy of American Diplomacy.* 2d revised and expanded edition. New York: Dell Publishing Company, 1972.

Young, Roland F. *Congressional Politics in the Second World War.* New York: Columbia University Press, 1957.

Articles and Essays

Aaron, Daniel. "Conservatism, Old and New." *American Quarterly* 6 (1954): 99–110.

Aiken, George D. with James C. Derieux. "Why I Am *Not* a Democrat." *Collier's* 1 July 1950, 19.

Alexander, Jack. "Missouri Dark Mule, [Bennett Champ Clark]." *Saturday Evening Post,* 8 October 1938, 5–7.

Alsop, Joseph and Robert Kintner. "Sly and Able: The Real Leader of the Senate, Jimmy Byrnes." *Saturday Evening Post,* 20 July 1940. 18.

Ball, Joseph H. "Liberalism Abroad and At Home: What Is Political Liberalism?." *Vital Speeches* 12 (15 June 1946): 522–28.

Balknap, George M. "A Method for Analyzing Legislative Behavior." *Midwest Journal of Political Science* 2 (November 1958): 377–402.

Blakey, Roy and Gladys. "The Federal Revenue Act of 1942." *American Political Science Review* 36 (December 1942): 1069–82.

————. "Federal Revenue Legislation, 1943–1944," *American Political Science Review* 38 (April 1944): 328–39.

————. "Federal Tax Legislation, 1939." *American Economic Review* 29 (December 1939): 695–707.

————. "Revenue Act of 1937." *American Economic Review* 27 (December 1937): 698–704.

————. "Revenue Act of 1938." *American Economic Review* 28 (September 1938): 447–58.

————. "Revenue Act of 1941." *American Economic Review* 31 (December 1941): 809–22.

————. "Two Federal Revenue Acts of 1940." *American Economic Review* 30 (December 1940): 724–35.

Boeckel, Richard M. "Record of the 75th Congress." *Editorial Research Reports* 1 (16 June 1938): 351–403.

————. "Record of the 76th Congress (First Session)." *Editorial Research Reports* 2 (1939): 73–132.

Borsos, John E. "Support for the National Democratic Party in South Carolina During the Dixiecrat Revolt of 1948." *The Southern Historian* 9 (1988): 11–14.

Brady, David W. and Naomi B. Lynn. "Switched-Seat Congressional Districts: Their Effect on Party Voting and Public Policy." *American Journal of Political Science* 17 (August 1973): 528–43.

Bridges, H. Styles. "Recovery, Morale and Fear: The Cancerous Growths in Our Democracy." *Vital Speeches* 4 (15 April 1938): 400–1.

Brinkley, Alan. "The New Deal and the Idea of the State." In Steve Fraser and Gary Gerstle, eds., *The Rise and Fall of the New Deal Order, 1930–1980.* Princeton: Princeton University Press, 1989.

———. "The Problem of American Conservatism." *American Historical Review* 99 (April 1994): 409–29.

Brogan, D. W. "Recipe for Conservatives." *Virginia Quarterly Review* 13 (fall 1937): 321–36.

Burnham, Walter Dean, Jerome M. Clubb, and William H. Flannigan. "Partisan Realignment: A Systemic Perspective," in Joel H. Silbey, et al., *The History of American Electoral Behavior.* Princeton: Princeton University Press, 1978.

Capper, Arthur. "Reciprocal Trade Agreements: Markets Depend Upon Purchasing Power," *Vital Speeches* 6 (1 February 1940): 232–33.

Cater, Douglas. " 'Mr. Conservative'—Eugene Millikin of Colorado." *The Reporter* 8 (17 March 1953): 26–31.

———. "Senator Cain: Washington Hamlet." *The Reporter* 6 (September 1952): 15–17.

Chapman, Phillip C. "The New Conservatism: Cultural Criticism v. Political Philosophy." *Political Science Quarterly* 75 (March 1960): 17–34.

Clark, Bennett Champ. "The Pay-As-You-Go Tax Plan: Cash Money in Till and No Tax Debt." *Vital Speeches* 9 (1 April 1943): 382–84.

Cohn, David L. "The Gentleman from Alabama: Lister Hill." *Atlantic Monthly,* May 1944, 63–67.

Cope, Richard. "Bridges of New Hampshire: A Cagey Senator." *The Reporter* 6 (1 April 1952): 6–10.

———. "Negativist from Nebraska [Kenneth Wherry]." *The Reporter* 5 (17 April 1951): 10–13.

Cowley, Malcom. "End of the New Deal." *New Republic,* 31 May 1943, 729–32.

Davies, Richard O. " 'Mr. Republican' Turns 'Socialist:' Robert A. Taft and Public Housing." *Ohio History* 73 (summer 1964): 135–43.

Davis, Forrest. "The Fourth Term's Hair Shirt [Harry F. Byrd]." *Saturday Evening Post,* 8 April 1944, 9–11; and 15 April 1944, 20–21.

Dewey, Ralph. "Transportation Act of 1940." *American Economic Review* 31 (December 1941): 15–26.

Ferrell, Robert. "The Last Hurrah." *The Wilson Quarterly* 12 (spring 1988): 66–82.

Ficken, Robert E. "Political Leadership in Wartime: FDR and the Elections of 1942." *Mid-America* 57 (January 1975): 15–29.

Gage, N. L. and Ben Shimberg. "Measuring Senatorial Progressivism." *Journal of Abnormal and Social Psychology* 44 (January 1949): 112–17.

George, Walter F. "New Methods Required to Increase Federal Income: Income Tax Rates At Peak." *Vital Speeches* 10 (15 February 1944): 273–75.

Gervasi, Frank. "Yankee Gad-Fly [Charles Tobey]." *Collier's,* 2 August 1947, 21–24.

Griffith, Robert. "Old Progressives and the Cold War." *Journal of American History* 66 (September 1979): 334–47.

Grimmett, Richard F. "Who Were the Senate Isolationists?" *Pacific Historical Review* 42 (November 1973): 435–59.

Harding, John. "The 1942 Congressional Elections" *American Political Science Review* 38 (February 1944): 41–58.

Huntington, Samuel P. "Conservatism as an Ideology." *American Political Science Review* 51 (November 1957): 455–72.

Jensen, Richard. "Power and Success Scores." *Historical Methods Newsletter* 1 (June 1968): 1–6.

Johnson, Lee F. "How They Licked the TEW Bill." *Survey Graphic* 37 (November 1948): 445–49.

Key, V. O. "A Theory of Critical Elections." *Journal of Politics* 17 (February 1955): 3–18.

Kingdon, John. "Models of Legislative Voting." *Journal of Politics* 39 (August 1977): 563–95.

Laski, Harold J. "Formula for Conservatives." *Harper's* September 1937, 382–90.

Lawrence, David. "$600-a-year Salary for Everybody?" *U.S. News* 14 (26 February 1943): 24–25.

Lodge, Henry Cabot. "Modernize the GOP." *Atlantic Monthly,* March 1950, 13–19.

Lowry, W. McNeil. "Douglas of Illinois: Liberal with a Difference." *The Reporter* 4 (17 April 1951): 6–10.

Malsberger, John W. "The Transformation of Republican Conservatism: The U.S. Senate, 1938–1952." *Congress and the Presidency* 14 (spring 1987): 17–31.

Manley, John F. "The Conservative Coalition in Congress." *American Behavorial Scientist* 17 (December 1973), 223–47.

Mazuzan, George T. "The Failure of Neutrality Revision in Mid-Summer, 1939: Warren R. Austin's Memorandum of the White House Conference of July 18." *Vermont History* 42 (summer 1974): 239–44.

———. "The National War Service Controversy." *Mid-America* 57 (October 1975): 246–58.

———. "Vermont's Traditional Republicanism vs. the New Deal: Warren R. Austin and the Election of 1934." *Vermont History* 34 (spring 1971): 128–41.

McCoy, Donald. "Republican Opposition During Wartime, 1941–1945." *Mid-America* 49 (July 1967): 174–89.

McKitrick, Eric L. " 'Conservatism' Today." *American Scholar* 27 (September 1957): 49–58.

Moore, John Robert. "The Conservative Coalition in the United States Senate, 1942–1945." *Journal of Southern History* 33 (August 1967): 368–76.

Mulder, Ronald A. "The Progressive Insurgents in the U.S. Senate, 1935–1936: Was There a Second New Deal?" *Mid-America* 57 (April 1975): 106–25.

Neustadt, Richard E. "Congress and the Fair Deal: A Legislative Balance Sheet." *Public Policy* 5 (1954): 233–51.

Newcomer, Mabel. "Congressional Tax Policies in 1943." *American Economic Review* 34 (December 1944): 734–56.

O'Mahoney, Joseph C. "The Declining Power of the States: Bureaucracy is the Road to State Socialism" *Vital Speeches* 9 (1 February 1943): 227.

———. "The Price Control Bill and the Farmer: 'Parity' is Not Equality" *Vital Speeches* 8 (15 February 1942): 286–88.

———. "Unemployment and the Preservation of Free, Private Enterprise: Real Jobs at Real Wages." *Vital Speeches* 5 (15 August 1939): 665–67.

Plesur, Milton. "The Republican Congressional Comeback of 1938." *Review of Politics* 24 (October 1962): 525–62.

Porter, David L. "Representative Lindsay Warren, the Water Bloc, and the Transportation Act of 1940." *North Carolina Historical Review* 50 (summer 1973): 273–88.

———. "Senator Pat Harrison of Mississippi and the Reciprocal Trade Act of 1940." *Journal of Mississippi History* 36 (November 1974): 364–79.

———. "Senator Warren Austin and the Neutrality Act of 1939." *Vermont History* 42 (summer 1974): 245–63.

Price, H. Douglas. "Are Southern Democrats Different? An Application of Scale Analysis to Senate Voting Patterns." In Nelson W. Polsby, et al., *Politics and Social Life*. Boston: Houghton Mifflin, 1963.

Rayback, Joseph G. "The Strange Story of the Tax Bill." *Current History* 3 (December 1942): 302–11.

Reed, Thomas H. and Doris D. "The Republican Opposition: Cross-Section of the Party Front." *Survey Graphic* 29 (May 1940): 286–88.

Riddick, Floyd M. "First Session of the Seventy-Seventh Congress, January 3, 1941 to January 2, 1942." *American Political Science Review* 36 (April 1942): 290–301.

———. "The Second Session of the Seventy-Seventh Congress." *American Political Science Review* 37 (April 1943): 290–305.

Rossiter, Clinton. "The Two Conservatisms." *South Atlantic Quarterly* 50 (January 1952): 64–78.

Rothbard, Murray N. "The Transformation of the American Right." *Continuum* 2 (summer 1964): 220–31.

Salmond, John A. "Postscript to the New Deal: The Defeat of the Nomination of Aubrey W. Williams as REA Administrator in 1945." *Journal of American History* 61 (September 1974): 417–36.

Schuman, F. L. "Bill of Attainder in the 78th Congress: Efforts to Drive Three Well-Known Liberals Out of Federal Service." *American Political Science Review* 38 (December 1944): 1153–65.

Shannon, W. Wayne. "Revolt in Washington: The South in Congress." In William C. Havard, ed. *The Changing Politics of the South*. Baton Rouge: Louisiana State University Press, 1972.

Shelton, Willard. "Nine GOP Senate Freshmen." *The Reporter* 6 (1 April 1952): 10–12.

Shister, Joseph. "The Impact of the Taft-Hartley Act on Union Strength and Collective Bargaining." *Industrial and Labor Relations Review* 11 (April 1958): 339–51.

Shoup, Carl S. "The Revenue Act of 1945." *Political Science Quarterly* 60 (December 1945): 481–91.

Starr, J. Barton. "Birmingham and the 'Dixiecrat' Convention of 1948." *The Alabama Historical Quarterly* 32 (spring–summer, 1970): 40–57.

Taft, Robert A. "A 1944 Program for the Republicans." *Saturday Evening Post,* 11 December 1943, 17.

———. "No Substitute for Freedom." *Collier's,* 1 February 1947, 13.

———. "What I Believe." *Collier's,* 12 April 1952, 83.

Vandenberg, Arthur H. "The New Deal Must Be Salvaged." *American Mercury* 49 (January 1940): 1–10.

Viereck, Peter. "The Rootless 'Roots': Defects in the New Conservatism." *Antioch Review* 15 (June 1955): 217–29.

———. "A Theory of Conservatism." *American Political Science Review* 35 (April 1941): 29–45.

Wilson, Francis G. "The Contemporary Right." *Western Political Quarterly* 1 (September 1948): 287–94.

UNPUBLISHED SOURCES

Boskin, Joseph. "Politics of an Opposition Party: The Republican Party in the New Deal, 1936–1940." Ph.D. diss., University of Minnesota, 1959.

Bryniarski, Joan Lee. "Against the Tide: Senate Opposition to the Internationalist Foreign Policy of Presidents Franklin D. Roosevelt and Harry S. Truman, 1943–1949." Ph.D. diss., University of Maryland, 1972.

Curry, Lawrence H. "Southern Senators and Their Roll Call Votes in Congress, 1941–1944." Ph.D. diss., Duke University, 1971.

Dalstrom, Harl Adams. "Kenneth S. Wherry." Ph.D. diss., University of Nebraska, 1965.

Guinsberg, Thomas Nathan. "Senatorial Isolationism in America, 1919–1941." Ph.D. diss., Columbia University, 1969.

Halt, Charles Eugene. "Joseph Guffey, New Deal Politician from Pennsylvania." D.S.S. diss., Syracuse University, 1965.

Hatcher, Susan Arden. "The Senatorial Career of Clyde R. Hoey." Ph.D. diss., Duke University, 1983.

Hilty, James W. "Voting Alignments in the United States Senate, 1933–1944." Ph.D. diss., University of Missouri-Columbia, 1973.

Jeffrey Jr., Harry Palmer. "The Republican Party as a Minority Party in Congress in Wartime, 1943–1944." Ph.D. diss., Columbia University, 1974.

Margolis, Joel P. "The Conservative Coalition in the United States Senate, 1933–1968." Ph.D. diss., University of Wisconsin, 1973.

Neuenschwander, John A. "Senator George D. Aiken and Federal Aid to Education 1941–1949." Master's thesis, University of Vermont, 1965.

Paul, Justus F. "The Political Career of Senator Hugh Butler, 1941–1954." Ph.D. diss., University of Nebraska, 1966.

Philipose, Thomas. "The 'Loyal Opposition': Republican Leaders and Foreign Policy, 1943–1946." Ph.D. diss., University of Denver, 1972.

Pickett, William B. "Homer E. Capehart: The Making of a Hoosier Senator." Ph.D. diss., Indiana University, 1974.

Index